ELWAY

ELWAY

A RELENTLESS LIFE

JASON COLE

BOOKS

New York

Hachette Books
Hachette Book Group
1290 Avenue of the Americas
New York, NY 10104
hachettebookgroup.com
twitter.com/hachettebooks
Instagram.com/hachettebooks

First Edition: September 2020

Hachette Books is a division of Hachette Book Group, Inc.
The Hachette Books name and logo are trademarks of Hachette Book Group, Inc.

The publisher is not responsible for websites (or their content) that are not owned by the publisher.

The Hachette Speakers Bureau provides a wide range of authors for speaking events. To find out more, go to www.hachettespeakersbureau.com or call (866) 376-6591.

Print book interior design by Jeff Stiefel

Library of Congress Cataloging-in-Publication Data

Names: Cole, Jason (Sports writer), author.
Title: Elway: a relentless life / Jason Cole.
Description: First edition. | New York: Hachette Books, 2020. | Includes index.
Identifiers: LCCN 2020013577 | ISBN 9780316455770 (hardcover) | ISBN 9780316455756 (ebook)
Subjects: LCSH: Elway, John, 1960– | Quarterbacks (Football)—United States—Biography. | Denver Broncos (Football team)
Classification: LCC GV939.E48 C65 2020 | DDC 796.332092 [B]—dc23
LC record available at https://lccn.loc.gov/2020013577

ISBNs: 978-0-316-45577-0 (hardcover), 978-0-316-45575-6 (ebook)

Printed in the United States of America

LSC-C

10 9 8 7 6 5 4 3 2 1

CONTENTS

To Henry and Campbell, the two best sons a father could ever imagine. Always chase your passion.

FOREWORD

The Pythagorean theorem and two and a half Chucks.

The equation for measuring the hypotenuse of a right triangle has something in common with the use of a five-foot Hawaiian man as a rudimentary measuring stick.

John Elway was a hell of an inspiration for my buddies and me.

The only notable time I've used the Pythagorean theorem is still vivid in my mind, an electric moment when you see something so ridiculous that it sticks for eternity. Using Chuck Narikiyo to measure a height was joyously comical. Both are touchstones of my youth. Let's start with theorem. On the afternoon of November 22, 1980, I was sitting in the corner of one of the end zones among my fellow Stanford University freshmen at Memorial Stadium on the campus of the University of California at Berkeley. Stanford was in the process of losing to archrival Cal in a steady, cold drizzle, making for a pitifully miserable day.

Then it happened: Elway did what only a transcendent athlete can do.

And he did it on an incomplete pass. It was the most breathtaking, astounding, and monumental incomplete pass I've ever seen, one that defied what humans are supposed to be capable of. On a broken play from the opposite end of the field, Elway ran to his right. He eventually made it within about a yard of the sideline as he looked for an open receiver. Eventually, a receiver got behind the Cal defense on the left sideline. Elway uncoiled his pigeon-toed body, uncorking a throw from approximately his own twenty-yard line.

The receiver ran downfield on the soggy turf, but the ball cut through the moist air as if it were a javelin. The pass sailed over the receiver's head and landed out of bounds at the ten-yard line. Elway had just thrown a ball on an angle across the fifty-three-yard-wide field and sailed it seventy yards in vertical distance down the gridiron. For those who understand even rudimentary geometry, that's way more than seventy yards, which by itself would have been amazing in a live-game situation.

From my angle in the corner of the end zone, I could see the right triangle laid out by Elway's play. I had the theorem still fresh in my head from high school geometry. One side of the triangle was roughly fifty-three yards (the width of the field). The other was seventy yards (the vertical length of the field). If I wanted to figure out Elway's throw (the hypotenuse of this triangle, as it were), all I had to do was add fifty-three squared with seventy squared and then figure out the square root of the resulting sum.

Or, as Pythagoras laid it out himself more than 2,500 years ago, A-squared plus B-squared equals C-squared (yeah, it's pretty easy to remember). It came out to eighty-eight. Elway had just launched a throw eighty-eight yards. I may not have been a great athlete, but I could throw a football. Maybe sixty-five yards. With a good crow hop. On a perfect day. With no one around me to disturb the process, and maybe with a little tail wind. What I just witnessed from Elway stunned me, even if it drew only a few "oohs" and "aahs" from the crowd. Incomplete passes don't wow the masses. But eighty-eight yards? On a wet field? In the rain? With no running start?

I was watching someone who could change the game with his talent. Between his arm and his scrambling ability, Elway redefined the Xs and Os of the game. There are only a handful of athletes at any time who can do that in a given sport. Back then, Magic Johnson and Larry Bird were doing it in the National Basketball Association and Michael Jordan was a few years away. Wayne Gretzky was changing hockey, Martina Navratilova was altering women's tennis, and Lawrence Taylor was redefining what was possible on defense in the National Football League.

Athletes like that change the parameters of sports. With Elway, what you would never imagine in drawing up a play was now completely in the realm of thought. Playbooks could be expanded. The absurd was possible. Conversely, what defensive coaches and players might normally scoff at was now something they had to fear when Elway was under center. Not that they took it on faith. They had to experience it for themselves. Over the rest of Elway's college career and sixteen years in the NFL, defenders facing him for the first time would regularly stop running at a certain point when the receiver ran deep, figuring there was no way he could throw it that far. He'd then make even the best of them look foolish, as Ronnie Lott will explain later.

In the history of the NFL, there have been quarterbacks who have outperformed Elway from a statistical standpoint. Whether it was Dan Marino, Brett Favre, or Peyton Manning, many have compiled great stats, usually aided by better systems and better surrounding talent. Some quarterbacks have won more than Elway, most famously Tom Brady and Joe Montana. And other passers have even had some of Elway's physical ability. Jeff George, JaMarcus Russell, and Drew Henson are among a host with cannon arms. Michael Vick and Steve Young were great scramblers. Cam Newton has the size (relative to his opponents). Bob Griese, Drew Brees, and Troy Aikman were among many who had the intelligence and will.

No one has ever possessed the collection of skills to the degree of Elway.

And now, no other quarterback has ever chased greatness for as long as Elway. Where others have rested on their laurels, he has remained resolute in his chase. These days, Elway is perched high above the fields he once roamed, surveying the game as Denver's president of football operations and general manager.

Because, in addition to his raw skill, Elway possesses passion and an undying love of competition and willingness to chase it, even in the low levels of the game. Few people realize Elway spent his own money in the Arena Football League to get his start in management.

Years later, he put his legacy on the line.

Of course, none of us, Elway included, could know what was to come on that November day in 1980. All I knew as an eighteen-year-old is that I was witness to someone who was startling in his measurable, physical greatness. I felt as if I was watching Zeus toss thunderbolts from his hand. Little did I know I was watching the opening act of a Greek tragedy that would last nearly two decades.

The story of Elway is not about talent easily realized. It is about talent being tested to the point of torture, both on and off the field. He was like Prometheus, who gave fire to humans and then was punished by the gods. Elway was tied to the rocks and made to suffer season after season. This story is about a man so gifted he could have sacrificed working at his craft and still been great; yet he never did, even in the face of epic failure. After Elway finished his career by leading the Denver Broncos to back-to-back Super Bowl championships, he wanted to keep going. Elway is the definition of ceaseless desire.

This story is also about inspiration on a personal level. Elway didn't just enable his coaches to change the parameters of what was possible on the field and help his teammates achieve greatness, he also pushed fans to search their own imaginations. Great artists do that, whether it was Elway on the field, Hendrix with a guitar, or Monet with a canvas and brush. For my friends and me, Elway was our muse. After leaving Big Game that day in 1980, we plotted to steal The Axe (the symbol of the Stanford-Cal rivalry) from Cal. We never did, but we had a plan. It was just too hard to safely acquire and transport that much liquid nitrogen.

In 1981, we executed our first good pre–Big Game prank. Along the northbound side of Highway 280 near San Mateo is a statue of Father Junípero Serra, the priest who wandered the west converting Native Americans to Catholicism. The statue features Serra on one knee with his finger pointing westward. To a bunch of sports-minded college kids, Serra looks like he's a holder for field goals. My buddies and I decided to build a "football" in the form of a collapsible Chinese lantern and paint it red and white with a giant S on the side. The laces read the time-honored phrase "Beat Cal."

There was just one thing we needed to know to get started. What was the height from the ground to the tip of Serra's pointing finger? Being teenage men, we failed to bring a tape measure for our reconnaissance mission. Enter Narikiyo, one of our band of brothers in collective silliness. At five feet tall, he was a walking measuring stick. He stood under the statue and the distance from ground to tip was approximately two and a half Chucks, or twelve and a half feet.

That stunt is also forever embedded in my mind.

Our infatuation with all things Elway turned more serious as time went on. One night, Chuck commanded me to come with him to the Economics Department to help him get his blue books from an exam (do blue books even exist anymore?). Why, I asked, did I have to come along for such a mundane task? "Just do it," Narikiyo said in an unusually serious tone. Upon arrival, he then told me to stand guard at the door. Wait a second. Stand guard? What the hell was going on?

"Elway is in my class; I'm stealing his blue books to get his signature," Narikiyo said. I stood sentry without another word spoken. I admit this years later realizing an honor code violation could still be in the offing.

In 1982, we went bigger and bolder. We pulled back-to-back all-nighters to see Elway play at Arizona State University in a thriller that ended as a bummer. We then drove back bleary-eyed and disappointed after the game, too cheap to pay for an extra day on the rental cars. For Big Game that year, we buried a sprinkler system around the C on the side of Cal's famed Tightwad Hill. The system was built with a timer set to go off at noon on game day and spray red paint on the gold letter. It was beautiful to witness the C go from gold to red in a matter of seconds. That same day, we nearly pulled off our greatest prank by hanging a 120-foot "Go Stanford" banner from the arms of the clock on Cal's Sather Tower.

Sadly, the rope snapped, and the banner floated to the ground. Fortunately, the Cal cops took pity on us. Later that day, our chagrin was overcome by the anguish of witnessing Cal return the final kickoff through the Stanford Band for a game-winning touchdown.

Yeah, that game.

That play not only marked the end of Elway's college career and overshadowed a phenomenal comeback he had led, but it also marked the end of our antics. Though Stanford was never great with Elway, there were some awesome moments, such as beating Oklahoma and smug coach Barry Switzer on their home turf in 1980. In Elway's senior year, Stanford played five teams ranked in the top fifteen, including number two: Washington. Stanford won two of those games (against Washington and Ohio State University) and lost two by four points or fewer (Arizona State and the University of California at Los Angeles).

The roller coaster of Elway's 1982 senior season gave way to the disgust of a 1–10 record in the 1983 season without him. The season was worse than the record looks in type, if that's possible. The energy, interest, and intrigue of watching a singular talent like Elway was gone, and so was any inspiration for our imagination. Instead, my friends and I watched Elway from afar, reveling in his great comebacks and bemoaning the lack of talent the Denver Broncos put around him for most of his career. His first three Super Bowl appearances were a series of double-edged swords. He basically took the Broncos to those games on the strength of his heroics before the inadequacy of the team showed up. The Super Bowl losses gave ammunition to critics who claimed Elway was overrated.

Overrated? Are you freaking kidding me? It didn't matter how any of us argued the case for Elway's greatness; the truth is that quarterbacks are judged by Super Bowl victories. That meant the critics won the early rounds. Terry Bradshaw became a television star at Elway's expense. Bradshaw was able to hide his jealousy of Elway behind his folksy, country accent as the audience conflated conniving with wisdom.

Even when Elway walked away after back-to-back Super Bowl wins, there were claims he was carried there by the performance of running back Terrell Davis. Elway's fierce competitiveness was discounted. When he returned to the game a few years later in the Arena League, few understood how seriously he took the league because they weren't really paying attention.

Again, there was no resting on career achievement. He wasn't satisfied to play golf, sign autographs, and live off simply being John Elway. The man of great talent and accomplishment had morphed into a man driven to compete at the next level of life. That, above all else, is the true genius of Elway. The man who once threw a ball in a way that defied conventional physical boundaries wasn't satisfied with the gifts he had been born with.

He was consumed by reaching a higher level, a level of achievement that can't be measured by any theorem. Or even with the help of a five-foot Chuck.

PROLOGUE:
SWEEP THE GARAGE

Elway studied his reflection in the mirror.

This was a Monday night in early December, the time when the pressure of an NFL season starts to rise, separating the hopeful from the hopeless. On a typically chilly night in Denver, Elway was preparing to get back in the game, enjoying a home field advantage.

As he got dressed, he was more anxious than usual. The numerous fourth-quarter comebacks of his storied career always amped his intensity. Teammates would notice his pupils dilate, making it look as if his eyes were bulging. He would also talk faster and more intently, forcing teammates to focus on every word.

But this wasn't a game in the literal sense. On Monday, December 6, 2010, the fifty-year-old Elway—nearly twelve years removed from his career as a player—had a dinner meeting with Denver Broncos owner Pat Bowlen. At Elway's restaurant in the upscale Cherry Creek section of Denver, the two men planned to discuss his return to the NFL as an executive with the Broncos.

To anyone with common sense and any understanding of the back story, there wasn't much to discuss. Bowlen coming to Elway's home turf was a sure sign that finalizing this deal was just a matter of details. Earlier that day, Bowlen had fired Broncos coach Josh McDaniels after fewer than two full seasons. McDaniels had earned his early dismissal by both losing games and mismanaging the team. That started with trading the perceived franchise quarterback, Jay Cutler, and ended with a cheating scandal. Along the way, McDaniels had done just about everything he could to alienate the fans and media.

The Broncos weren't just among the hopeless; they were humiliated.

To fix that problem, Bowlen turned to a man who was the face of Denver's greatest success and whom Bowlen had grown to love and admire over their twenty-five-year relationship. Bowlen and Elway couldn't have been much closer, and the frequent high-fives they exchanged during dinner were proof Elway's return was simply a matter of dotted i's, not about whether they saw eye to eye.

Yet as much as Elway was in a power position as he prepared for that meeting, he was still a bundle of excitement. He looked at his wife, Paige, and, in the tone of a teenage boy getting ready for a date with the head cheerleader, asked her, "How do I look?" It was a humorous juxtaposition that wasn't lost on Paige. She could hear the anxiety, happiness, and even a little vulnerability in his voice.

For those who love Hallmark movie narratives, Elway's return was the obvious move for Bowlen. When in doubt, call upon the resident hero to save the day. Elway wasn't just the greatest player in Broncos history and a first-ballot Hall of Famer, he was quite possibly the most famous and trusted man in the state of Colorado.

Forget about Adolph Coors or Zebulon Pike—Elway had taken the Broncos and the team's fans to greater heights than anyone could imagine. His daring comebacks were the stuff of legend. His five Super Bowl appearances were a then-record for quarterbacks. The back-to-back titles to finish his career allowed him to walk away after bringing the first major sports championships to the state. With his hiccupped gait, he ambled from the game as if he were John Wayne heading into the sunset after shooting every bad guy.

And now, thirteen years after Elway's retirement as a player, it was time for his return as an executive. The Broncos had been competitive for most of that time under previous coach Mike Shanahan, but never returned to championship greatness. The team cascaded into infamy under McDaniels. Again, that was the easy way to spin the narrative. And again, with that understanding, Elway should have been the picture of confidence. He was the guy with all the leverage, and this wasn't his first dinner with Bowlen. The men had known each other since 1984, when Bowlen bought the team in Elway's second season. The two had broken bread and tossed back more than a few drinks over the years.

So, why the anxiety? Why be so amped that Paige—a woman who was known to operate in her own time zone—made sure she was ready to go at the appointed hour?

The answer was a rhetorical question.

How many times do you get a chance for a second act in life?

This moment was something far deeper than anyone could have imagined for Elway. This dinner, this meeting, and this chance to work in the NFL was what Elway had wanted, practically from the moment he retired. The honeymoon period of Elway's retirement didn't last long.

Getting back in the NFL was something he had spent most of the past decade preparing for, working quietly in the lower echelons of pro sports to prove himself to Bowlen. As he told friends on several occasions over that decade, "My goal in life has always been I wanted to be more than just a football player." He wanted to run a team and compete again at the highest level.

Yet the question of "why?" lingered.

Elway had already done more than most of the men who also happen to wear Super Bowl rings. He had stared down Darryl Strawberry in high school baseball, dipped his toe in the pond of minor league baseball with the New York Yankees under owner George Steinbrenner, and snubbed his nose at the owner of the Baltimore Colts after being drafted number one overall. He had become a scratch golfer, a relentless ping pong player, and a card player who reveled in taking thousands of dollars from his friends in gin.

He had started and sold a car business for tens of millions. He had guided the Colorado Crush from expansion team in the Arena Football League to champion by the team's third season. He combined his fame and his degree in economics to make more money away from the field than on it. Yet there he was, anxiously staring at a mirror on that December night as he got ready for dinner with a man he had known for a quarter century, wondering whether he looked OK.

This was about that burning place in Elway's soul where he couldn't let go of the chase. He couldn't be satisfied. He couldn't just sit back like some general at the top of the hill, watching the soldiers fight, and then march down to bayonet the wounded.

Elway wanted to be in the thick of it. He wanted to go to charming places like Mobile, Alabama, in late January to watch college football players practice for the Senior Bowl. He longed for trips to Indianapolis in February for the NFL's annual scouting combine. He wanted to sit in an office, fidgeting with the controls on a video player as he watched a series of college players move around the field, trying to decipher which was the most able and, more importantly, the most willing. He wanted the challenge of signing free agents and the rush of picking players against the rest of the league during the NFL Draft.

Of course, plenty of people wondered about Elway's resolve before he ultimately accepted the job Bowlen laid out for him that night over dinner. Influential blogger Mike Florio of ProFootballTalk.com presented the naysayer's case two days after news broke of the Bowlen-Elway dinner. *Denver Post* columnist Woody Paige had written a column about the meeting and took extra effort to praise Elway's abilities and preparation.

Florio took issue with that line of thought.

"Paige floats several possible titles for the long-time Broncos quarterback—V.P. of football operations, General Manager, executive V.P. Each implies a level of influence and responsibility that the candidate wouldn't merit if his name didn't rhyme with Smellway," Florio wrote.

> Paige also pumps up Elway's credentials, explaining that he was a "hands-on owner" of the Colorado Crush of the [Arena Football League], and that Elway "sat for hours" with his late father, Jack, as he did the things a scout does. In our view, however, dabbling in scouting is no replacement for the grinding that scouts do as they acquire knowledge of the nuances that

will allow them to make tough decisions once the scout climbs into a position of authority. And that remains our biggest concern. If Elway were suited to serve as an executive with an NFL team, he'd already be one. That's how the industry works. Though the job is less visible than the position of head coach, what Elway hopes to do is no less significant, and the situation should be viewed by Broncos fans as no less alarming.

So this looks to be another case of a star athlete wanting to make a difference with his old team, mistakenly thinking that an ability to throw the football unlike anyone else the organization has employed translates into an ability to run the franchise. It doesn't. And unless Elway has a hidden talent for scouting or untapped high-level business abilities otherwise honed by hard-working men and women during the years that Elway was playing football, it's not going to work.

Other people, including some of Elway's friends and other close associates, wondered why he would take on such a huge challenge. It wasn't just the workload. They wondered why someone who had taken the Broncos to their greatest heights would take a chance on failing.

"This was the low point for the franchise," Denver chief executive officer and president Joe Ellis said.

We were losing and now we had a scandal. Our image with our fans and around the country was bad. I had been talking to John and, frankly, this was a decision we probably should have made a couple of years before. That's my fault. I didn't see that John really wanted to help. I didn't see that he wanted to throw himself into this the way he has.

I just kept thinking: "John has this great life being retired and doing what he wants. Why would he want to do this?" Even though he was telling me he wanted to do the job, I didn't see it. But when Mr. Bowlen made the decision to let go of Josh, we had to do something to reestablish trust in the organization. We had to let our fans know that we were really going to get this fixed. John did that for us.

Elway did that despite having a legacy to protect. Though he returned to the game with a certain cache of respect, it meant little in the ultra-competitive world of the NFL. The only thing respect gets you is a smile and handshake before your opponent tries to beat the crap out of you.

But what Florio and other detractors, even some of Elway's friends, didn't understand was how Elway had been raised to compete. They didn't know how his passion had been nurtured. Most assuredly, they didn't understand how he had been humbled from the time he was a teenager, so his great sense of confidence never became a bloated and satisfied ego.

Those people didn't know Jack.

Jack Elway, that is, John's beloved father and best friend. Jack was many things, from a football lifer, to a raconteur, to a man of ceaseless comedic wit. More than anything, Jack was a devoted father who had a simple yet critical plan for how he wanted to raise his son. In 1983, as John was getting ready to be the number one overall pick in the NFL Draft, Jack explained the goal of his plan to *Sports Illustrated*.

"I just want him to be excited and dollars won't decide that," Jack said. "You can't be great playing on a dollar basis. You've got to have your heart and soul in it. . . . I'd feel real successful if I could just preserve for John the joy of playing ball. Because that's where he'll find his greatness."

At age fifty on that December night, John Elway's heart and soul were still chasing joy. He might not have been playing ball anymore, but he was still searching for his greatness in whatever he tried. Elway didn't just want this job. He *needed* this job. He wasn't doing it for the money or the fame. It certainly wasn't just some nice public relations move to get the fans and media off Bowlen's back. This was about the essence of what made Elway who he is. It was about the sacred moments of youth that become emotional touchstones of adulthood.

It was about pajamas and slippers. It was about sweeping the garage.

The most common misconception about Elway is the assumption that his competitiveness emanated from his physical talent. It's an easy mistake. To anyone who has studied quarterbacks, Elway still stands as the prototype. Decades removed from when he came out of college, his combination of arm strength, scrambling ability, size, and intelligence still rate at the highest ends of the scale. Hall of Fame executive Bill Polian has referred to Elway as the "statue of David" among quarterbacks. Michelangelo's marble representation of David in his youthful state of courage and strength as he prepared to take on Goliath is considered the perfect representation of male human form.

What that observation ignores is how Elway approached the game from a mental and emotional standpoint. Competition was part of everything in Elway's formative years, to the point that it became imprinted on his DNA. Jack made it that way and he was careful to make it joyful. When John, along with his twin sister, Jana, and older sister, Lee Ann, were little, Jack would line them all up and have them race to get their pajamas on. He'd beckon them to start, laugh as they threw on their clothes, and then celebrate the winner.

At other times, Jack would be sitting in the living room watching television. He would ask his son, who was five or six at the time, to get his slippers from the bedroom. Jack would look at his watch and say "Go" to start John on a tear from the living room to the bedroom and back. John would return with the slippers, breathless from his mad dash. Jack would look at his watch and exclaim.

"World record every time," John Elway says with a smile, some five decades later.

Sometimes nurturing John's competitive side would last until the wee hours of the morning. When he was just ten years old, the family was living in Missoula, Montana. Jack was coaching at the University of Montana. John's mother, Jan, would wake up at about 2 a.m. to the sound of ping pong being played in the basement directly below the master bedroom. She'd march downstairs to find her husband and son playing, both shirtless with sweat pouring off their bodies, even in the dead of the Montana winter.

And tears pouring from her son's eyes.

"John was crying because he wanted to beat his dad so bad. They're down there in just their shorts even in the middle of winter because by now they're just going at it. I could see there were marks in the walls from where they had thrown the paddles," Jan says.

"Jack Elway had an innate understanding of how to raise a child," John's longtime agent, Marvin Demoff, says. "In John's case, [Jack] understood how to raise a football player. But if you had given him Michael Phelps, he would have helped him become a great swimmer. Whatever that child's talent was, Jack would have gotten it out of them."

Jack did it without demanding.

For all of Jack's talent as a coach and scout for more than forty years at the high school, college, and professional levels, he never hovered over his son. Except for a meaningless college all-star game after John's senior season, Jack never coached one of his son's teams. He never called or pulled a coach aside to offer advice, even when his son was being recruited by every major franchise in two sports.

The only time Jack ever got seriously involved with what happened between his son and a coach was when a high school coach hit John in practice. Jack said there was going to be either an apology or a fight. The coach apologized. Jack was almost cautious about not coaching his son, as if to protect the father-son relationship from the coach-player relationship. It is one thing to guide. It's another thing to order.

By the time John was graduating from high school, Jack had become the head coach at San Jose State University. John considered playing for his father, but Jack would always defer when his son asked where he should go to school. It was part of a boundary Jack never wanted to cross. He didn't want to control or interfere with his son's life.

Instead, he made it a joke tinged with wisdom.

"I tell people that my offer to John was $2,000 under the table, a new car, and a mortgage on the house," Jack joked to *Sports Illustrated*. "I said I would go so far as to have an affair with his mother. Still, he didn't go for it. I'm not sure *she* would have gone for it."

Then Jack turned slightly serious.

"I know that if I had said, 'John, come with me to San Jose [State],' he would've come, but that wouldn't have been fair to him. Still, there are nights, after I've had about three vodka martinis, when I'll say to myself, 'Jack, old boy, you've got to be the dumbest sumbitch in this whole world. You had the best quarterback in America sitting across the breakfast table from you and you let him get away.'"

Jack resisted the temptation. He didn't want to live vicariously through or in the reflective glory of his son's accomplishments. Rather, he fed his son's desires. He nurtured John's spirit and mind for the game and let his son be on the stage by himself. When John played at Granada Hills High School, Jack would sit in the stands with Jan. If a game was particularly tense, he'd pace while taking drags of a cigarette or two. Or three. Or six.

Jack didn't worry about his son's throwing motion or footwork. He didn't fret over how John threw an out pattern or how often he scrambled. As much as John may have been on his way to becoming the statue of David, Jack wasn't worried about sculpting his son's prodigious physical talents.

He was worried about molding his son's mind and soul.

Above all, Jack could be trusted. He was wise. If he told his son something would happen, invariably it did. Jack also made it a habit to instruct more than simply lecture. He was Socratic in the way he asked questions, prompting his children to think about the answer first. After high school games, Elway's first stop was home. Before he joined his teammates and buddies at Shakey's Pizza in the San Fernando Valley, he and Jack would have a debriefing. Again, it wasn't about plays. It wasn't how John threw a touchdown pass or an interception.

They talked about how John handled situations during the game. What did his body language look like? Did he show the right type of leadership? Did he have a positive attitude when something went wrong? Was he being a team guy first and foremost? Was he encouraging his teammates when they needed a pat on the back? Was he playing the game the right way?

As John got older and turned pro, Jack's lessons morphed. Jack told his son it was important to build team camaraderie away from the facility. One or two nights a week during the season would be spent at bars or restaurants with John making sure everyone felt welcome. These days, John has a picture in his office of his father with one of his most famous quotes inscribed next to the photo: "Above all, when you go out with the offensive lineman, always pick up the tab."

Jack also taught humility, keeping his son's sense of satisfaction in check. If there was a time when John won a particularly big game or had an excessively nice article written about him, Jack had a simple command: sweep the garage.

Jack would send his son to do chores, reminding him that his success didn't excuse him from the hard work that went into those victories and articles and certainly didn't put him on any pedestal. As time went on and John's career grew to greatness, Jack would tell him to "stay off the pedestal," reminding his son to remain one of the guys and not be above doing whatever it takes to be great.

As the years went on, that instruction became an essential part of Elway's personality. When Denver media relations man Jim Saccomano would approach him with a stack of articles about him, he'd ask Elway if he wanted to read them. Invariably, Elway would say no, he had no interest. For most of his career, he rarely revealed much about his deepest thoughts.

"The only thing he'd ask me is, 'Are my quotes accurate?'" Saccomano says. "As long as the quotes were accurate, he didn't care about the rest. I'll say most players weren't like that. By most, I mean just about all. John didn't care about all the attention."

The desire to prove himself again and again was why, well before that December dinner with Bowlen, Elway had worked diligently to prove to the owner he would do whatever it took. In the early 2000s, Shanahan rebuffed Elway for a personnel job with the Broncos. No matter how much Bowlen liked Elway, Bowlen refused to interfere with his coach's decision. Still, he wanted to maintain a strong relationship with Elway.

Bowlen, along with billionaire Stan Kroenke, partnered with Elway to start the Crush. Bowlen and Kroenke gave Elway free rein to run the team as he saw fit. Elway ran the operation for eight years. He checked the books and picked the players. After a terrible first season, Elway realized he had the wrong people in charge and quickly fired the entire coaching staff.

At the same time, Elway's personal life was hell. In 2001, he found out that his beloved twin sister, Jana, had cancer, and then he lost Jack to a heart attack a few months later. Jana died in 2002. Elway's first marriage, to his college sweetheart, was crumbling and ended in divorce in 2003. Friends beseeched him to take time away. Get away from the pressure and decompress. "Just go be John Elway and enjoy life," they told him. Instead, Elway kept telling them that he needed the Crush and the AFL. One day, he was with former Broncos wide receiver Michael Young, who had gone to work for Bowlen and the Broncos in the early 2000s. Elway and Young were sitting in a car in the parking lot of Denver's new stadium.

"John was talking about how serious he wanted to be about [the Crush and the AFL] and he wanted to win the championship," Young says. "I said something like, 'Dude, so I appreciate the fact you want to continue to accomplish things. But you've worked your whole life to get to the top of the mountain. You are at the top of the mountain. You should just enjoy the moment and look down at everybody else who's trying to make the climb.'"

Elway couldn't imagine that. The years of racing to put on pajamas, grab the slippers, or sweep the garage were too ingrained in his soul.

"I'm not wired like that," Elway told Young. "That's not how my father raised me."

So, on that night in December 2010, there was no way Elway would take something for granted. There was no way he would let his chance to compete slip away because of the most minor detail. He needed the Broncos every bit as much as they needed him.

With that in mind, Elway had to know.

How do I look?

CHAPTER 1

JACK

Dee Hawkes was twenty-two when he learned to put the group ahead of himself.

While in the shower.

Hawkes was in his first year of coaching high school football in the fall of 1959 in Port Angeles, Washington. He had recently graduated from Washington State University and was just out of the Marines after deciding not to pursue an officer's career. The six-foot Hawkes was a solid 200 pounds and says, years later, he considered himself "quite a stud."

One night after coaching the Port Angeles High School junior varsity squad against Forks High School, Hawkes was taking a long, hot shower. That was a treat for him. The shower routine in the Marines was ten seconds of water, a quick lather, and then ten seconds to rinse off. Stealing a few minutes of hot water, even in a high school locker room, was one of those simple joys.

Hawkes enjoyed the hot water and solitude behind a vinyl shower curtain when suddenly the curtain got ripped back and three fellow coaches were standing there, looking sternly at him. Hawkes fumbled to cover himself as Port Angeles High head coach Jack Elway delivered a message that couldn't wait. After spraying a few profanities at Hawkes, Elway made his point.

"Stop it with the 'my play' and 'my defense' and the 'my-my-my.' It's our-our-our," Jack said as Hawkes stood there, naked and speechless. "All I could really do was mutter, 'Yes, coach, you're right' as I was trying to cover myself up."

"That was one of the three most important lessons I ever got from Jack Elway. He's probably the biggest reason I went on to be a head coach," says Hawkes, who spent more than thirty years as a high school football coach.

After Jack was done with his lecture, he added an exclamation point.

"He turned on the cold water as I was standing there," Hawkes says. "Even when Jack was angry, he was funny."

And always passionate about coaching.

About nine months after Hawkes got his lesson, twins John and Jana Elway were born on June 28, 1960. Jack was many things: an excellent coach, a wonderful dad, a discerning and wise evaluator of people, a chain smoker of pyromaniac proportions, and a martini-drinking storyteller who could bring down the house with his combination of sarcasm and facial expressions.

In his core, Jack was a man who deeply loved what he did. He loved the art of trying to build and run teams. Right up to his dying day, he was engrossed in how it was done. He loved recruiting players and evaluating talent. He loved teaching the game on a large scale and building camaraderie on a small scale. He loved the overall strategy on game day and, as Hawkes found out, the basic lesson about putting the group ahead of the individual.

Jack also had a knack for recognizing passion. In early 2001, he was working in the personnel department with the Denver Broncos, preparing for the draft. John Elway went to the office. He was trying to learn the scouting business from his dad. Jack was watching a tape of a quarterback and asked John what he thought. John took a quick look and said the young passer looked kind of small for the pro game.

Jack shot back: "Do you see the heart and passion he plays with? Do you see how much he loves the game?"

Jack understood how great Drew Brees was before Brees was drafted. For all of Jack's understanding about measurable qualities and projections, he also knew how to see beyond them. Jack never got to see how right he was about Brees. He passed away of a heart attack in Palm Springs, California, on April 15, 2001, less than a week before the draft and years before Brees became a superstar. Jan found Jack in his chair in front of the television. She joked he must have gone quickly. He didn't have time to switch the station from Home Shopping Network.

Jack had been dealing with heart problems for years resulting from a combination of his smoking, love of a martini, and aversion to exercise. He was old-school when it came to cigarettes and alcohol. But his son believes Jack succumbed to a broken heart as much as a weak one. Two months before Jack died, the family was told Jana had advanced blood cancer.

"He blamed himself," Elway says. "He believed his smoking contributed to her cancer."

Jana's illness was particularly tough on both Jack and his son. Among his three children, Jana was the one most like Jack. She laughed loudly, told a good story, and wasn't afraid to pull out a blender on Friday afternoon at work and mix up margaritas when she was an adult. For Elway, her death cut even deeper. Jack would laugh at the baby twins as they talked to each other in their own language. Jana had a way of knowing her brother's every move. In high school, she was the person who found his mouth guard when he lost it in the middle of the field. More than twenty years later, she was the one who found his Super Bowl ring when it slipped off his hand at a team party.

"I believe in telepathy because I experienced it with Jana," says John, who, years later, would see Jack and Jana in his dreams after they had died. They would always be smiling, which comforted John. Jana was his savior and consiglieri in so many ways. He could cry on her shoulder when the torment of losing got to be too much. When he was balancing football, baseball, and being recruited by half the top college programs in the nation, she would occasionally write a paper for him, taking note of the fact that he'd consistently get better grades than her on the papers she wrote. Jana was an excellent athlete in her own right. Although she never took formal tennis lessons, she became a good enough player that she made the team at San Jose State University.

Jack admired Jana for the way she took care of her brother and managed to achieve on her own. The possibility of losing her crushed his weak heart. A few days after Jack died, a service was held for him in Denver. Roughly fifty coaches who knew or worked with Jack gathered in a hotel bar the night before the service. The group included the likes of Dennis Erickson and Mike Price. Each of them ordered a vodka martini. Then most of them lit up a cigarette, made a toast to Jack, and then spent hours telling stories.

They just scratched the surface.

Jack was born and raised in Hoquiam, Washington, a logging town on the Hoquiam River near Grays Harbor and the Pacific Coast. He was the son of a plumber and the younger brother of two more plumbers. He also had an older sister who worked in the family business for a while. The Elway clan loved to entertain and regularly hosted parties at their home. Almost everyone in the family liked a good story and a better drink.

Jack was an athlete, playing quarterback in football as well as basketball and baseball. His father and brothers said he was sent to Washington State University to play football because "he was too dumb to be a plumber." Jack came by his sense of humor honestly. He could also belt out a tune. When he and his son would go out for drinks on occasion, Jack would often sing a few, including a maudlin classic.

"Almost every time we went out, Jack would end the night singing 'Mr. Bojangles,'" former Broncos backup quarterback, offensive coordinator, head coach, and longtime Elway friend Gary Kubiak says. "If you ever want to get John to cry, play that song."

The other legend, according to tales passed down from Jack's high school coach, Jack Swarthout, is that Jack had a better arm than his son. Jack's football career didn't pan out because his body became a mess. He had surgery on one knee, hurt the other, damaged his throwing shoulder, and suffered an assortment of other injuries. By the time he was a junior in college, he lost his athletic scholarship and worked his way through school by cooking in his fraternity, Sigma Alpha Epsilon. After college, he chased his passion for coaching, starting in Port Angeles.

At twenty-five, he met Jan Jordan back in Hoquiam. They married, had three children in the span of three years, and then the family started hop-scotching around the northwestern US. His first big break came in 1967 after Swarthout got the head coaching job at the University of Montana. Jack joined Swarthout and the program did a 180-degree turn, going from 1–9 the year before they arrived to 7–3 in their first season. Montana went undefeated in the 1969 and 1970 seasons. Jack ran the offense and recruited the players. He could judge talent and, more importantly, convince players to come to Missoula, Montana.

He could also read people, such as the time he helped kick-start the greatest era in Montana basketball and, in a small way, changed the course of college basketball and NBA history.

Yes, basketball.

Swarthout also became the athletic director at Montana by 1971 and was looking to improve the men's basketball program. The team had gone five straight years without winning ten games in a season. It had also gone through three head coaches.

Jack called Jud Heathcote. The two were fraternity brothers and then grad students together in the 1960s at Washington State. At the time, Heathcote was stuck in his eighth year as an assistant coach at Washington State. He had gotten little notice. Heathcote interviewed for the Montana job, going through a labyrinth of six people along the way. He talked to Swarthout, the school president, and the booster club president, among others. Everybody along the way seemed to think the process was going great. Jack approached Heathcote after all the interviews were done and said, "Let's go have a beer." They sidled up to the bar and Jack's first question was, "You're not going to take this job, are you?"

"I told Jack, 'No, the only thing anybody wants to talk about here is how good the football team is. There's no commitment to basketball,'" Heathcote says. "Jack figured it out right away. Then he convinced me to take the job. He said he'd make sure everybody understood. The only reason I took the job was because of Jack Elway. If that doesn't happen, who knows what else happens?"

"What else" is special for Montana and beyond. Montana posted win-ning records in all five of Heathcote's seasons, including an appearance in the National Collegiate Athletic Association Sweet Sixteen in the 1974–1975 season. The Grizzlies lost to eventual champion UCLA by only three points in the tournament, the best tournament performance in Montana history. Even after Heathcote left, the Montana program remained consistent under coaches such as Jim Brandenburg and Mike Montgomery.

Heathcote was hired by Michigan State University in 1976, where he coached for nineteen years. His first recruiting class was his most impressive. He signed a six-foot-eight high school star from nearby Lansing, Michigan. While other programs were telling the prep star he had to switch to forward at the college level, Heathcote went against conventional logic. Heathcote told that big man he could play point guard. By the time Magic Johnson was done with his sophomore season, he and Heathcote had led Michigan State to a national championship. Johnson was on his way to redefining the point guard position during his Hall of Fame career with the Los Angeles Lakers.

Jack was consumed by sports. If he wasn't coaching, he was watching a game at home or in a local bar. He was reading the sports section of the newspaper in the car as Jan drove. That was the deal they struck after she got tired of reading the sports pages to him when he drove. Family vacations came second to sports. One summer when the Elways lived in Montana, the family went to Flathead Lake for some time away. But John made the Little League All-Star team, so Jack would drive him two hours each way for practice every day.

Jack's focus on sports and his job was sometimes to the detriment of being a great husband. On more than one occasion, Jan would have to chase down the groceries from Jack's car when he detoured to a local watering hole to talk with his coaches. She'd fume, he'd make some wisecrack, and they'd find a way to make it work. In the 1980s, Jack joked during public events about how he could dodge anything Jan threw at him.

Candlesticks, saltshakers, kitchen utensils, a vase—it didn't matter. Whatever it was, he still had the quickness to get out of the way. Except for one day. She had him dead to rights. He was about to take one right in the noggin, but this was in the days before cell phones or even cordless phones.

Jack was saved when the phone ran out of cord.

Jack always said work was number one because if he didn't have a job, he couldn't provide for his family. The lesson stuck with his son. For better or worse, work was always central to John's identity. The competitive outlet sports provided became interwoven with work, whether it was playing football or any other business. But Jack made a healthy distinction between prioritizing work and meddling.

"One of the greatest things you can say about Jack Elway is he didn't interfere with John's life the way a lot of fathers might have," says Paul Wiggin, Elway's coach at Stanford. "Just think about college. Jack had the best quarterback in the country living in his house. Jack could have easily made John play for him when he was coaching at San Jose State. He didn't. He let him go to Stanford and let John become his own man and live his own opportunities."

Jack made his way to big-time college football in 1971. He was hired by Washington State coach Jim Sweeney, who was tired of losing in the recruiting wars to Jack and Montana. Over the next four years, they worked together, technically. But Jack and Sweeney couldn't have been more different in approach. Sweeney was an over-the-top workaholic and fitness freak. Sweeney once yelled at a young John Elway in the Washington State locker room. Sweeney and Jack had words over that.

Jack believed in working hard, but also working smart. Sweeney was the kind of guy who would get a second wind around midnight after popping some diet pills. He'd then demand his assistants keep working until 2 or 3 a.m. One night/morning, Washington State was getting ready to play the University of Southern California. Sweeney came into the offensive staff meeting as the coaches were breaking down film of USC's defense. It was already about 2 a.m. and the coaches were wrapping up when Sweeney got some inspiration.

Sweeney noticed that Don Lindsey, the USC defensive coordinator, was signaling the calls to the defense. Sweeney, who had worked with Lindsey in the 1960s, got excited and told the offensive coaches to go over every defensive play to check the signals. It was a laborious task that would take hours, especially in the old days of film and projectors.

As Sweeney finished his request, Jack calmly blurted out, "Yeah, I know Bruce Blevins."

"Who the hell is Bruce Blevins?" Sweeney said.

"Oh, he's the head coach at Port Townsend High School," Jack said.

"What the hell does that have to do with anything?" Sweeney snapped.

"Bruce used to send in the signals, too," Jack said, his voice tinged with sarcasm. "But he'd change the signals every game. I don't know, but I think maybe [legendary USC coach and Lindsey's boss] John McKay is smart enough to do that. What do you think?"

Sweeney angrily left the room.

During one off-season, Sweeney put the coaches on a workout regimen, commanding the staff to run and exercise at lunchtime. Jack's perspective on jogging was different. He told a fellow assistant coach one day, "I see all these people jogging, but they're never smiling." Years later, John got his dad a treadmill. Jack used it as a coat rack.

Jack tried the Sweeney fitness plan. On the first day, he got dressed in his sweats and headed for the track. Limited by his bad knees, he hobbled through about half a lap, slowed to a walk, and then reached into the pocket of his sweats for a pack of cigarettes. He lit one up as he walked through the rest of the lap and then headed for the showers. The next day, he told the other coaches he would meet them after a phone call. They finished the run and headed for the showers. Jack showed up and took a shower, too. They looked at him and wondered what the hell he was doing. He looked, smiled, and said, "I just thought I'd join in on the fun."

One of the things that made Jack smile was a Marlboro Light. A lot of Marlboro Lights. His smoking habit was in full force well before his children were born. The ashtray in his car constantly overflowed. He'd often dump the ashes on the floorboard of the front passenger seat.

"You'd have to shift your shoes around in about an inch and a half of ash and cigarette butts," Hawkes says. After Jack became a head coach in the late 1970s, he'd call off practice on rainy days if he couldn't light up. During position meetings, billows of smoke would come out of the room when the door opened. Occasionally, the smoke wasn't just from cigarettes. As a player was meeting with Jack one time, the player smelled something odd.

The trash can was on fire.

The inability of Sweeney and Jack to turn around the Washington State program contributed to the tension. Sweeney once ordered Jack to return from a recruiting trip and Jack refused, essentially daring Sweeney to fire him. It was no surprise that when Sweeney left Washington State under pressure after the 1975 season, he didn't take Jack with him to Fresno State. The next stop for Jack was California State University at Northridge in the San Fernando Valley in Los Angeles. It was Jack's first shot as a college head coach. Left to his own devices, he did an excellent job there, turning the program into a winner.

Getting Jack to change his habits was another matter. As Jack did on a regular basis, he said he quit smoking. One day, he was leaning back in his chair as he heard his eldest daughter, Lee Ann, coming down the hall. He quickly flicked the cigarette behind him. As she walked in, she asked two things. First, why did it smell like cigarette smoke? Second, why was the trash can on fire?

Jack posted two of the three best records in the forty years Cal State Northridge had a football program. In late 1978, he got the head coaching job at San Jose State. It was midway through John's senior year in high school. From a competitive standpoint, Jack's teams at San Jose State were impressive. They posted winning records in four of five seasons and were part of the best run in San Jose State history. That may not sound like a huge accomplishment, but San Jose State wasn't working with a full tool belt.

Spartan Stadium is, well, quaint. It seats roughly 30,000 people, meaning it could never host a big-time game. San Jose State was mostly a commuter school, so that was about all the student body could support, and school spirit was hard to nurture. The coaching offices at the time were in a converted three-bedroom, 1,600-square-foot house. There would be three or four coaches in each bedroom, somebody in a hall closet, and Jack in one room with his desk. Wherever the coaches could downsize, they did. That started with the secretary. Yoshiko Toyosaki was four-foot-ten and maybe 100 pounds. She could fit into the space of a pocket door.

Jack nicknamed her "Big Girl."

"I'd tell him something needed to get done with expenses or with his courtesy car and he'd say something like, 'Big Girl, I'll get to it,'" Toyosaki says. "He had these big stacks of papers everywhere and I was scared he couldn't find anything. Then he'd reach into a stack and pull out exactly what I needed, smile, and say, 'You didn't think I knew where it was, did you?'

"I'd say, 'You're right, Jack, but the trash can is on fire.'"

Like cigarettes, the courtesy cars coaches received became a running gag for Jack. Big Girl regularly cleaned out his car, which would be filled with coffee cups, newspapers, soda cans, and the obligatory ashes. Then there was the harrowing combination of Jack's smoking and driving. If you sat in the back seat when Jack was driving, you'd better wear flame-proof clothing. He'd flick his cigarette ashes out the window and the wind would blow the ashes into the back seat.

"You'd be putting out fires on your clothes all the time," says Dave Baldwin, an assistant under Jack at San Jose State. "I'd say, 'Jack, come on.' He'd apologize and then do it again without thinking."

The front seat might have been worse.

Jack had to go to downtown San Jose for weekly press conferences during the season to promote the games. The area features a series of one-way streets. Between his declining eyesight and his smoking, riding shotgun was, well...

"It was terrifying," San Jose State quarterback Steve Clarkson says. "He would drive like Mr. Magoo. His face would be practically pressed against the windshield, he'd be smoking with this really long ash burning down until it sometimes fell on him and burned his clothes. As he was brushing away the ash, it was pretty common for him to turn the wrong way down a one-way street and I'd start going, 'Coach, nooooo!'"

In 1984, Jack took over as coach at Stanford. His son was already in the NFL by then and told Jack not to take the job. John didn't believe that Stanford athletic director Andy Geiger was going to support football properly. Jack wanted to do something special there. Jack and Jan were still living in San Jose when Stanford gave him a courtesy car. It was a brand-new Cadillac with all the bells and whistles. Everything was power, the windows, the locks, the radio...you name it, it had a button.

Jack was never much for technology. He was endlessly confused when cars got more complicated. Jack picked up the car one afternoon with Tom Beckett, who was running the football operations at Stanford. Jack headed back to the office and then went home at about 10 p.m. He got distracted by all the buttons and gadgets and ran a stop sign. Then he got pulled over by the police. The first problem was that Jack couldn't figure out how to roll down the power windows. He was shouting to the officer through the window, trying to explain the problem. As that was going on, he proceeded to pop open the trunk, turn on the emergency lights, hit the alarm button, and finally run the wiper fluid, spraying the officer.

After fumbling through a field sobriety test because he couldn't walk a straight line on a perfect day with his bad knees, Jack was brought in on suspicion of driving under the influence. The blood-alcohol test later showed he hadn't been drinking. As the officer turned him around to handcuff him, Jack said, "Marshal Dillon does it in the front."

He couldn't resist.

After being booked into the San Jose jail, Jack needed somebody to pick him up. Fearing Jan might leave him in jail for the night, he called Beckett instead.

"I pick up the phone and it's midnight and he says, 'Hey Tom, it's Jack, I need you to come get me out of jail.' I think it's a prank, so I hang up. Jack calls back and says, 'God damn it, it's really me, I'm in jail!'" Beckett says. "I go pick him up, take him home and get to the front of the house. Then he said, 'Wait here, I might need you to come get me if Jan gets mad.' He said if the lights come on upstairs, he was coming back out. If the lights stayed out, I could leave. I gave it about five minutes. The lights never came on; I left."

From a coaching standpoint, Jack had some amazing moments. In 1980, San Jose State beat number ten Baylor University in Waco, Texas. Baylor featured future Hall of Famer Mike Singletary at middle linebacker. The San Jose State coaches came up with a plan that forced Singletary to run all game covering people. By the fourth quarter, Singletary was regularly taking a knee to catch his breath. Jack made Stanford respectable again. In 1986, Stanford went 8–4 and then went in reverse for a couple of years, and he was fired.

He stayed true to himself the entire time.

"Jack saved me from transferring from Stanford," Dave Wyman wrote in an email. Wyman was teammates with John Elway in college and later at Denver. "Jack was not really your typical Stanford image. I never liked that Stanford image and I said that the first year after Jack got there and it ruffled some people. I said, 'I came here to play football. I know a lot of people came here for academics, but I came here to win football games.'"

One day after practice, Wyman went to a restaurant across from the Stanford campus. He walked past the bar and saw Jack, still dressed in his coaching clothes, sipping a martini.

"I loved that guy," Wyman says.

When future All-Pro safety John Lynch showed up at Stanford as a high school junior, he met with Jack. Lynch was a quarterback at the time. He walked into Jack's office and sat down. He then watched Jack pull a bottle of vodka from his cabinet and pour himself a drink.

"I said to myself, 'This is different,'" Lynch says.

Clarkson adored him. He felt as if Jack treated him like a son. Clarkson has become one of the top youth quarterback gurus in the country in large part because of his experience with Jack.

"Jack taught me to love the game," Clarkson says. "He was unique. You might play Monopoly with him for seven or eight hours on the road the night before a game. He didn't believe in walkthrough practices on Fridays because he wanted his coaches to spend time with their families and the players to be excited about the game the next day. He was very much into the thinking of the group."

Gerald Willhite was an all-purpose star running back at San Jose State under Jack. He also looked at Jack as a father figure. Willhite's own father had died when he was only nine years old. He went on to become Denver's first-round draft pick in 1982, the year before the Broncos took John Elway. They were teammates for six years.

"Jack ruled with cleverness, a sense of humor, and psychology," Willhite says.

He knew who to yell at and when. Even when we were losing, he had optimism and you could see how that rubbed off on John. In Denver, we could be down 21–0 and John would still believe. That came from his dad.

Jack was the biggest single person in my life in terms of how I carried myself and what I have become. He was transparent and he made me transparent....What I could say is who I am today as a person in terms of character, integrity, being genuine and open is because of Jack...when I played with John, we played together and were good teammates, but not necessarily close. But I always wanted to protect him. I went overboard to protect John because of Jack. I wanted Jack to be proud of me. I was never going to let anybody get to John because he was an extension of his dad. I took that seriously.

As with Heathcote, Jack also recognized great coaching talent. At San Jose State, he hired guys like Baldwin and Dennis Erickson. In 1985, he interviewed Sonny Lubick, who went on to help the University of Miami win two national championships as a defensive coordinator and then spent fifteen years at Colorado State University as head coach. Lubick was an offensive coach before joining Jack as a defensive assistant at Stanford. They were talking about defensive schemes when Jack asked how Lubick would play in a certain situation.

"I said, 'Jack, that's a great question and I promise I'll answer you, but your trash can is on fire.' All of a sudden, Jack's secretary, Jan Steele, walked in and said, 'Jack, not again. You need to get out of here before the fire department shows up.' Obviously, this wasn't something new for Jack," Lubick says.

Jack's run at Stanford ended with a 3–6-2 record in 1988. Five of the six losses were by four points or less (including close losses to top-ten-ranked USC and UCLA). Geiger came to Jack after the season and tried to get him to fire some of his coaching staff. Jack refused and was fired. He spent two years out of football, sometimes angry, sometimes depressed, and sometimes both. He returned to the game as head coach of the Frankfurt

Galaxy of the World League of American Football for two years and then got hired by the Broncos to work in personnel.

He spent the rest of his life working with Denver, helping the Broncos eventually win two Super Bowls, and trying hard to prove he wasn't just there because of his son. He was so good he stayed with the organization for three years after Elway retired. Even after he claimed he was going to retire in 2001, he had written letters to Bowlen about plans he had for the personnel department.

"He was a coach to his core," John Elway says. "It never leaves them. They're always thinking about what they're going to do next and how they're going to make the team better."

When Jan called her son with the news of Jack's death in April 2001, John flew to Palm Springs with former Stanford teammate and fraternity brother Dennis Engel, his closest friend outside of Jack and Jana. Elway was at the house for a while, helping take care of details. He eventually took a break and walked down the street with Engel to the neighborhood park. The two sat on a bench, fighting back the tears and not really winning the battle.

Eventually, a young boy walked up to Elway and asked for an autograph. The boy's father stood a few feet away. Elway agreed, with one condition.

The boy had to hug his dad every day.

CHAPTER 2

THE BARRACUDA AND
THE SHERIFF

John Elway has been known to make his point in biting fashion.

Whether he's talking about sports or expressing his deeply held conservative, republican political beliefs, he's not afraid to cut to the chase. He was, after all, also raised by "The Barracuda."

Jan Elway, his mother, picked up the nickname sometime in the late 1960s. She and Jack had been married about ten years, enough time for her to figure out the best way to deal with him and his idiosyncrasies. Such as his smoking habit. He would promise to quit and inevitably start again, always behind Jan's back. The first time she caught him lying, she was incensed.

"That man," Jan says, her face and voice still getting stern more than forty-five years later. A smile then peeked out. "He swore to me he had quit smoking. We're at a party with the rest of the coaches and their families and I was telling everybody about how good he was doing. I was so proud of him. Then, one of the other coaches tells me about how Jack was borrowing matches from him because Jack is still smoking. That man, he lied to me! It was like a punch to the gut."

As she recalled the story, her cadence picked up speed. She was still perturbed. Jack could leave an impression and Jan could hold a grudge, which is another quality her son shares with her. Jan read Jack the riot act right then and there at the party. She then turned and walked out.

Jack followed her as she went out through a screen door. She slammed the door behind her, catching Jack on the nose. He told everyone she had bitten him.

She was officially dubbed The Barracuda.

"That's where he came up with it. That man," she says, smiling with equal parts amusement at Jack and pride that she caught him in the nose. Over the years, The Barracuda became Jan's given name. When the Elways were living in Pullman, Washington, Jack invited Washington State assistant coach Bill Moos for dinner. He told Moos, "The Barracuda is making a pot roast." Jack's contribution to the meal was mixing the martinis. If a couple of buddies asked him to go out for drinks, Jack would have to "check with The Barracuda."

"Jan is a pistol," says Dennis Erickson, a longtime college and NFL head coach who was an assistant under Jack at San Jose State. "She gave Jack everything he could handle. She was perfect for him."

She was, in every way, the backbone of the family. Jan died on March 4, 2020, after a brief bout with pancreatic cancer. In the weeks leading up to her death, her son flew to California seven times to see her even as he dealt with the hectic pace of the NFL offseason. Through her force of will, she was the one who both allowed Jack to chase his career and kept the kids going in the right direction.

Jack may have been the coach. Jan was the quarterback.

Jan was the day-to-day disciplinarian. She worked full-time, got the kids to school, and was the first line of defense in making sure everything operated smoothly. She often led without much more than a look largely developed from dealing with Jack's foibles.

"We were in the middle of an argument one time and Jack said, 'What happened to my little Janny Jordan who used to cry all the time?'" Jan says, discussing how Jack tried to get her to warm up to him one time.

"I had a good teacher," she snapped back, having none of it. Jack and Jan were a derivation of the comedy duo Stiller and Meara, their sense of humor founded in their real-life interplay over forty-four years of marriage. To this day, you can see Jan's glare in her son when he knows something hasn't been done right. Whether it's making a point about the team's style of play or talking with managers of his businesses, John combines his father's wisdom with his mother's style of communication. His friends refer to it as the "stink eye." Chris Sutton, one of John's high school team-mates, saw it firsthand one day when they played golf. Sutton pulled out a couple of footballs for John to sign as they stood in the parking lot.

"I knew I had screwed it up right away; John didn't say a word. He just gives me that look and says, 'Dude, really?' I started to explain it was for some people I know and he just says, 'Dude, you have to learn to say no.' He was totally right," Sutton says. "I was turning our relationship into a transaction."

Jan had an appreciation for direct toughness. When Jack was coaching at the University of Montana from 1967 to 1971, he and Jan would go to the cowboy bars around town and dance the night away. He would sing to her as they strutted the floor.

"He could carry a tune and he knew all the words to every song," she says. The cowboy bars were also just rowdy enough to make it fun. One time, a woman turned over a table full of drinks. Her husband slung her over his shoulder and bid everybody goodnight. His wife was kicking and yelling as they headed out the door. The rest of the country might have been stuck in turmoil in the late 1960s, but Missoula was still the Old West in a lot of ways.

"It was a sight," Jan says, laughing and smiling. In her retirement, Jan spent most of her time at her home in Palm Desert, California, enjoying the heat as she served cold drinks on cocktail napkins that read, "We are the girls our mothers warned us about."

Jan Jordan was nineteen when she first went out with twenty-five-year-old Jack. He was already teaching and coaching at Port Angeles High, and Jan was still living in Hoquiam, where they both grew up. Jan's aunt called her one day to ask whether she was interested in going out with Jack when he came home for a weekend. No, Jan said, Jack was too old. Her aunt talked her into it, saying the event was basically a big party and very casual. Nothing serious. Jack then called Jan again for a second date a couple of weeks later. Jan said she already had a date for the coming weekend.

"No, you don't. Tell him The Sheriff's in town," Jack said.

Three months later, The Sheriff put an engagement ring on Jan's finger. He just had one condition.

"I have to have a son," Jack said, who evidently missed the lecture about X and Y chromosomes. He was a coach, not a doctor.

They were married on June 15, 1957. Daughter Lee Ann was born in early 1959. On June 28, 1960, twins John and Jana arrived.

"We were married and then about seventeen months later had a daughter...and he did like her," Jan says, referring to Lee Ann. "Then, about seventeen months after that, I had the twins, but we didn't know [beforehand] they were twins back then. They didn't x-ray me or anything like that....He took me to the hospital in the middle of the night, then he had to go to work. In those days, the men didn't have anything to do with it, so he went to work. Then he came back and I looked at him and said, 'You had a seven-pound, four-and-a-half-ounce baby girl.' Then I paused and said, 'Oh, and I forgot to tell you there was an eight-pound, two-and-a-half-ounce baby boy.' He just looked at me and said, 'Imagine what we could do if we tried!' Honest, that's what he said to me. That man never missed a chance for a wisecrack."

Jan was one of two daughters born to Harry and Marie Jordan. Harry and Marie also met in convenient fashion. They grew up as neighbors.

"My dad didn't have a car, so he married the girl next door," Jan says.

Harry was a "boom man" in the logging business. When the logging companies would drop off a frame of "sticks" (the term for cut-down trees) on the Hoquiam River, Harry would sort them and then order tugboats to have them hauled to different paper mills. Sorting was more precarious than it sounds. Harry Jordan spent his workdays dancing on the logs as they floated on the water, holding a pole in his hand to help with balance. Walking along floating logs may not be quite as dangerous as his grandson's eventually dodging defensive players in the NFL, but it wasn't far removed, and the pay wasn't nearly as good.

Harry was also quite the outdoorsman. When Jan was growing up, her family owned a small cabin on a lake outside Hoquiam. They'd go there on vacation, mostly in the summer, and Harry would wake up Jan to go fishing early in the morning.

"He didn't have a son, so I was the one he would take fishing with him. I loved it. We'd be out there and then we'd get done and back to the cabin just as my mom and sister were waking up," Jan says. Harry later taught his grandson to hunt and fish. Jack wasn't much of a fisherman. The running joke was that the only time Jack ever caught anything was when his friends tied a fish to his line.

Marie Jordan took care of her daughters until they were grown and then went to work in the furniture business.

Jan was five-foot-nine with a slender but athletic build. She became a golfer later in life and probably would have been a good athlete if women had been pushed more aggressively into sports in her day. She said with mocking pride that she won the top girls athlete award in junior high school based on her outstanding ability to "walk and chew gum at the same time." She had larger hands, longer arms, and longer legs than most women. Physically, Elway picked up his mother's long limbs to go with his father's barrel chest. Jan's build also served as material for Jack.

"When we first got married, he'd tell everybody, 'Look at her hands and arms, I married her for breeding stock,'" Jan says, still incredulous. "He'd tell me to show people my hands and arms all the time at parties. So, after John started playing in the pros, Jack stopped saying that stuff. I don't know if he was embarrassed now or didn't want to give me any credit, but I'd go, 'Hey, what about the breeding stock you used to talk about?' He never said a word. Oh, I got on him about that, turned it right around on him."

In Missoula, she worked as a secretary. In Pullman, she worked for the school board. When Jack was at San Jose State, she worked in the university's development office. She set the example for how the kids were supposed to present themselves. Her hair was always neat and she dressed perfectly, yet with no pretense. She was a coach's wife without caring about the pomp and circumstance that sometimes go with it.

Jan also constantly tried to get Jack to dress better, but it was largely a lost cause. She bought him monogrammed dress shirts when he coached at Stanford, but the sleeves and cuffs inevitably ended up with cigarette burns. Bottom line is she was pretty much no-nonsense. As Elway's daughter Juliana once said about her grandmother, "You could tell she was the head honcho."

Jack managed to warm her heart, even if his technique was questionable. One time during a recruiting trip, Mike Price caught him reading the Lois Bird book *How to Make Your Wife Your Mistress.*

"He was the most unique person I ever met. He could say the funniest things, but then be completely insensitive," Jan says.

Insensitive enough to make The Barracuda walk home on her own one time.

One night when Jack was coaching at San Jose State, he and the rest of the coaching staff and their wives got invited to the house of Alex Stepovich, a dentist and powerful alum. Stepovich liked to have a good time in his day and lived in the hills above San Jose.

As the night was going on, Stepovich was outside with the coaching staff. Most of the wives were in the house with his wife. Eventually, Stepovich's wife politely let people know it was time to adjourn the party. The problem was that the Stepovichs didn't coordinate the message. When Jan went outside to get Jack, Alex Stepovich wanted to keep the party rolling. Jan kept dropping hints that they needed to go home, but Jack was taking the lead from Stepovich. Jack eventually relented and they headed home.

Except now it was an argument.

"I had enough and I told that man, 'Let me out right here and I'll walk home.' It was only about two or three miles and I could handle it," she says.

Jack obliged and pulled over. The saving grace is that Baldwin and his wife were a couple of minutes behind the Elways.

"We're driving by and there's Jan walking down this steep hill from the house. We pulled over and I could tell right away she was mad, so it had to be Jack," Baldwin says. "We take Jan home and the next day Jack comes up to me and says, 'Hey, thanks for bringing Jan home.' And that was it. It was like the whole thing was a totally normal, run-of-the-mill moment."

Then there was the time a few years later that Jack organized a surprise fiftieth birthday party for Jan. By this time, Jack was coaching at Stanford and they were living in a condominium in nearby Menlo Park. On the morning of Jan's birthday, Jack got up and headed to work without saying anything. He was trying to keep the party a surprise but went a little too far with the ruse.

"As he was leaving, I said, 'Oh, maybe we can have dinner.' He said, 'Oh yeah, maybe.' I thought he just forgot, which made sense since he forgot a lot of things. I had some friends in town, including one of my high school girlfriends who flew down from Washington. So, we all went out for lunch. Well, they started serving champagne and they poured way too much champagne and we stayed out all afternoon and into the night. We were having a heck of a time," Jan says.

At home, Jack had the coaching staff, athletic director, wives, and friends waiting to yell "surprise." The appointed time came and went. Another two or three hours went by before Jan and her friends rolled up to the house.

"I drive up and see all these cars and I'm thinking, 'Somebody is having a good time.' I walk into the house and it turns out it's supposed to be me. I was so embarrassed and so mad at Jack for that. He didn't know how to plan it. By the time I'm walking in, everybody was leaving," she says.

Then there were the constant moves, which define the life of just about any coach and his family. Jack never did much in the way of helping with moves. He was the advance man, getting the job and finding a house at the next place. He'd leave the details to Jan. When the family left Pullman, Washington, in the summer of 1976 to head to Southern California, Jan arranged the move. This was before coaches received even simple perks, like having a school or team pay for the move. So, Jan looked for ways to save a few dollars.

She and the kids would go to the stores in town and get boxes. They had so many boxes that John had to lie down on top of them to make sure they didn't fly out of the back of the car. They packed everything, loaded it on the truck, and headed for California, excited about the possibility, a football version of *The Beverly Hillbillies*.

Jack had already started at Cal State Northridge as the kids stayed behind to finish school. As annoying as it was to move again, Jack sold

Jan and the kids on the idea, talking about how great everything was in Southern California. After he bought the house, he described how the backyard had three statues of lions spitting water into the pool. Except when Jan and the kids showed up, the backyard was nothing but dirt. Jack's sole purpose for buying that house was to get his son into the right high school for football and make sure it was close to Cal State Northridge. Jan was having none of Jack's storytelling. The first thing she ordered him to do was put in a pool, complete with three statues of lions spitting water. He complained about the money and then relented when she flashed the stink eye. From that point on, Jan handled the moves and where they lived. Protest became futile for Jack.

After Jack became the head coach at Stanford, the family moved from San Jose to the condo in Menlo Park, about two miles from campus. The condo had an association that ran the whole complex. Jack started to break some rules. He put up a giant satellite dish so he could watch his son's games. That was a no-no. Another time, Jack and a busybody neighbor got into a snit over how early Jack put out his garbage cans. It escalated into an argument that ended with Jack yelling, "Keep your goddamn hands off my garbage cans!"

The upshot is that Jan got tired of the condo commandos. She told Jack it was time to move. Jack resisted, saying they had a three-year agreement they couldn't break. He also claimed that Jan's spending was going to send him to debtor's prison. Now it was a battle of wills. On the day the three-year agreement was up, Jack was on another road trip and Jan had her plan in place. She had purchased a home in nearby Mountain View and set up the move. Jan, Lee Ann, and Jana packed everything and had the new house set up that night.

Then Jan called Jack's secretary and left a message for him.

"'Tell Jack when he comes home tomorrow night, his bed will be at 2165 Woodleaf Way.' That was all I said. The next night, he comes home, walks in the front door, heads down the hall, out into the garage and lit up a cigarette. It was like he had lived there for ten years. He never said a word about it," Jan says.

Jan would find other ways to tweak Jack and make a point. He would get distracted when they were walking around, go into a store or head off somewhere without telling her. That behavior inevitably led her to continue walking for a while before realizing he had meandered off to look at something. One day as they were walking around Fisherman's Wharf in San Francisco, Jack did it again. Jan ducked away and headed to a second-floor bar overlooking the wharf. She drank a glass of wine as she watched Jack look for her for about ten minutes before signaling to him.

"Turnabout is fair play," she says.

Jan was never much to mince words, even with her own children. In January 1998, John had come home from helping the Broncos win the American Football Conference Championship Game in Pittsburgh to qualify for Super Bowl XXXII. It was going to be John's fourth chance to finally win a title, but it also came after three progressively painful losses earlier in his career.

With all the love, compassion, and caring a mother could muster, Jan sat in her son's house that January, looked at him, and said, "Do we really have to go back to the Super Bowl?" The idea of losing again made her wince, but the sharpness of her tone made it sound as if losing was inevitable. The whole idea of competing to the end was a little lost on her. Elway laughed, but also got the point.

Sports was largely a foreign subject to Jan when her husband and son talked. They would be speaking "another language," as she put it. When the 1983 draft came along, she understood very little and cared even less about whether John would play football or baseball. The Baltimore Colts, New York Yankees, or some other team mattered little to her. She only cared that her son was happy.

When John was in high school, the family was playfully talking about how he might become a millionaire someday if he made the pros. John asked his mother what she wanted if the dream ever came true.

A Mercedes convertible, she said, one of those sweet 450 SLs. She's been driving a version of that car for more than thirty years now. She created an environment where Jack could go off, work his way up the coaching ladder, swoop in as a parent when necessary, and do what he thought was important to support the family. Jan even took care of life when Jack went back to school to better himself.

After Jan and Jack got married in 1957, Jack spent two summers taking classes at Washington State to get his master's degree. He would go to Pullman during the week and then come home on weekends.

While in Pullman, he'd hang out with other young coaches who were in the same boat. Among the other coaches were Jud Heathcote and Chuck Solberg. As with most things involving Jack, there were a few drinks to be had along the way, and the trio would often end up at a bar called Rusty's near campus.

"Jack was his usual self, always very relaxed about how he approached life.... We'd have long conversations over a few beers, tell stories, and laugh like crazy," Solberg says. "I remember him saying more than a few times, 'The smartest thing I ever did was marry that woman.'"

CHAPTER 3

FROM A CHEVY

Elway became a quarterback atop Military Hill.

Pullman High School in Pullman, Washington, sits on Military Hill. From that perch, you can see the endless series of undulating hills that make up the Palouse, a vast area of farmland that covers much of Washington, Idaho, and Oregon. The land hasn't changed much from when it was inhabited by Indians, explored by Lewis and Clark, and eventually controlled by gun-toting expansionists.

This is the type of place where facts are subject to interpretation. A reminder is emblazoned on a large metal piece of artwork toward the back of Pullman High. It's a quote from the John Wayne classic western *The Man Who Shot Liberty Valance*.

"This is the West, sir. When the legend becomes fact, print the legend."

The short version of Elway's becoming a quarterback is the stuff of legend. It was life changing and seemed to happen in an instant. At least that's how Elway tells it the many times he has been asked about the moment. Yet the full story is even more interesting, especially if you appreciate the bond between a father and son.

On an August day in 1975, John Elway rode in the passenger seat as his father, Jack, wheeled the family's 1973 Impala (a.k.a. Sheila the Chevy) up the hill. John was on his way to his first high school football practice, fully intending to be a running back.

By the time John got out of the car, after a conversation with Jack, he was on a different path. He was going to be a quarterback. That's the short version of the story and it fits nicely into the perceived legend of John Elway, who grew up akin to some mythic sports figure out of the rural West. He was the embodiment of the fictional Roy Hobbs, the main character from Bernard Malamud's book *The Natural*. He was a blond-haired kid who could turn a football into a rocket with his right arm.

Elway was fifteen and, like any athletic kid, wanted to be in the middle of the action. In football, he wanted to be the running back. His favorite player was running back Calvin Hill of the Dallas Cowboys. Elway even wore Hill's number 35 in honor of the perennial Pro Bowler and Super Bowl champion.

Elway was going to be the next Hill.

That image was in his head even though he was all of five-foot-eight and 130 pounds—if he had eaten a big serving of my mom's pot roast, three baked potatoes, and a side of mac and cheese the night before. Elway was a big growth spurt away from having any real athletic hopes in football.

By contrast, the six-foot-four Hill was regal. He fit Elway's adolescent image of the mighty Cowboys. Dallas was establishing itself as America's team back then. Hill wasn't only a great athlete. He was also tough and smart, an extension of what Dallas coach Tom Landry represented. Landry patrolled the sideline in his trademark suit and hat. He was impervious to the drama of the game. He was a God-fearing, dignified badass.

Hill was cut from that image. He had famously played two games with a broken toe and persevered with a bad knee throughout his career. He had graduated from Yale University. Growing up in towns scattered between Washington and Montana, Elway didn't really understand what Ivy League meant.

All Elway knew was that Hill was the complete package. Not just talented, but tough and smart. That's what Elway hoped to be. He may have been little more than an incoming freshman, but he had the same big dreams as millions of other kids. Nowhere in those many dreams was the idea of being a quarterback. In Elway's young opinion, playing quarterback was, well...

Boring.

Seriously boring. The only thing the quarterback ever seemed to do back then was hand the ball to the running back. Years before his family moved to Pullman, John had played in the Little Grizzly Football program in Missoula, Montana, where Jack was coaching for the University of Montana. John was already a dominant athlete by then, the kind of kid other children would chatter about.

"John was like a legend among all the kids," says Jerry Heathcote, the son of Jud. Jerry and Elway grew up together in Missoula. "It's like if you went up against some kids who had never played against him, you'd say, 'Wait 'til you see Elway.'"

Jack filled out the paperwork for the Little Grizzly program, left on a trip, and had Jan drop John off for the first practice. John tried quarterback. He switched to running back before practice ended. The team might have thrown four passes the whole season. With John running the ball in his brand-new blue Adidas shoes with gold stripes, the team won the championship. He was fast and those shoes made him even faster.

At least in his mind.

Running back was where it was at for the young John as he looked forward to his first high school practice. Even as he looked up to the college guys playing for his father at Washington State—which was only a few blocks from Pullman High—quarterback didn't look like fun. Jack was the offensive coordinator for the Cougars and ran what was called the "veer-option offense." To his son, that was football jargon for veering away from all passing options. At Washington State, Jack's teams regularly ran the ball about 75 percent of the time back then.

The NFL of the 1970s was even worse. Bob Griese of the Miami Dolphins and Terry Bradshaw of the Pittsburgh Steelers had guided the previous two Super Bowl champions. Griese threw seven passes in Miami's win in the 1973 season. The Dolphins ran fifty-three times. Bradshaw, whom Elway would have an interesting relationship with years later, threw fourteen passes and handed off fifty-seven times as the Steelers took the title in the 1974 season.

That's a whopping twenty-one passes between the two biggest games

Elway had ever seen in his life. In today's NFL, twenty-one passes might be an adequate half for a quarterback. In 1975, playing quarterback was like being one of those special guest stars on a Quinn Martin production. You might get in a good line, occasionally.

As he got mentally prepared for his first high school practice, it was running back or bust for John. He would be playing under legendary Pullman High coach Ray Hobbs. Like Jack, Hobbs was a Washington State grad. By 1975, Hobbs had already been the head coach for twenty years and had established his reputation early on. Under Hobbs, Pullman set the state record for consecutive victories with thirty-five in the 1950s and had won four state titles. Hobbs ran the single-wing offense. Like the veer, "single-wing" seemed to be football terminology for the single-minded idea of running the ball. Under Hobbs, you ran the ball first, last, and always. If Elway could be a running back for Hobbs, the possibilities were as vast as the Palouse.

At least that's how John saw it as Jack wheeled Sheila up Hall Drive through the residential neighborhood. The car passed Timothy, Joe, Janet, and Linda Streets before finally turning left at Larry Street on the way to the high school. All the while, Elway's mental road map of how to get to Dallas, take over for Hill, and make a name for himself was laid out in his mind. The varsity team at Pullman High (Elway made the team as a fresh-man) was just going to be one of the pit stops before the Cowboys would come calling. All he had to do was show off his moves, outrun the defense on the way to daylight, and score some touchdowns, and he'd be set.

Jack pulled Sheila up to the school, put his foot on the brake, and kept the car in drive. Sheila was a classic 1970s boat of a car, complete with those bench seats in the front and the vinyl seat covers. The vinyl was always an annoying combo of scalding hot and sticky in summertime. Elway was about to peel himself off the seat and jump out of the car when Jack asked a simple question.

"What position are you going out for?"

"Running back," his son replied.

Like most automatic cars back then, Sheila's gearshift was on the steering column. Jack reached for the shift with his right hand, pulling it slightly in and then up and moving it counterclockwise until it was in park. This was part of Jack's guidance routine. When he was going to make a point, he usually did it while sitting in his car. If John or one of his sisters ever got in the slightest bit of trouble in school, Jack would pick up the offending child and say, "Let's go for a ride." It was time for a serious talk.

Jack was never a big screamer. He had his moments when he'd get upset. A dog must growl once in a while, even just as a reminder. But most of the time—and especially when it came to one of his sessions behind the wheel—he would just ask questions. You could call it the Socratic method. It was more like the Columbo method, as in the 1970s TV detective. That was one of the many nicknames Jack picked up over the years. He earned it mostly because he wore an old, wrinkled trench coat. He also had some of the same mannerisms. He was a little hunched and shuffled a bit, just like actor Peter Falk. More than anything, Jack was deliberate with his questions and observations as he made a point. He accentuated it all with his gravelly voice, turned coarse from years of smoking.

If Jack was recruiting a kid of modest means who was interested in playing for USC or UCLA, he might ask, "You have a nice car, right? You have gas money, right? I hope you do. Getting around L.A., especially if you want to date a girl or two, you're going to need a good car and money. In Pullman, you don't need a car at all." Or if he was recruiting a big, power running back who was interested in archrival Washington, he'd say, "Oh yeah, you like to block, right? You're going to love blocking at Washington. If you do a really good job blocking, you could probably get four or five carries a game in short-yardage situations. That will be great for you. You'll love it."

One time, Jack was on a recruiting trip with Mike Price when they were assistants together at Washington State. Coaches would split rooms on the road when recruiting. Jack and Price got back to their room around midnight and Jack wanted a chocolate sundae. He called room service, but they said they didn't make chocolate sundaes.

"OK, do you make chocolate milkshakes?" Jack asked. "Oh, you do, that's great. I like chocolate milkshakes. I'll take one of those. Could you just do me one favor? Before you put the chocolate syrup and the vanilla ice cream in the mixer, could you pour it all in a bowl and bring it to me that way?"

Jack didn't argue, proclaim, or demand when trying to persuade someone. He made people think. He was about empowering people with wisdom, not overpowering them with rules. On that August day in Pullman, as Sheila's gears shifted to park and the big motor idled, John knew Jack was about to drop a little knowledge on him. John had no idea it was going to change his life and, in some ways, the history of football. What Jack got him to understand was that his future as a running back was going to be brief.

Jack asked his son whether he understood how much more pounding he would take on his body if he played running back instead of quarterback. He asked him whether he understood that other kids were going to catch up in terms of speed. All those kids John used to outrun in youth football were about to get bigger, stronger, and faster. Worse, someday he was going to face even faster kids from other towns and cities.

At fifteen, John had no clue what was ahead. It didn't matter how cool his shoes were. Everybody was going to have cool shoes eventually. Jack knew because it was his job to know. It was his business to project what a seventeen- or eighteen-year-old boy might look like when he became a twenty-one- or twenty-two-year-old man. In Jack's own way, he really was Columbo. Only he was a detective looking for clues about the future, not about the past.

"He's talking about what's going to happen and I just listened because I knew he knew what he was talking about," John says. "I know a lot of kids don't want to listen to their parents. They think they know better. There's no way I knew better than him when it came to football. Certainly not back then."

What Jack was also doing was giving his son a first inkling of the scouting business by scouting his own son. Sure, he was dashing his son's dreams with a serious dose of reality, but he was doing it out of unconditional love. He was talking about John's limitations and pointing him toward the possibilities.

Goodbye Calvin Hill.

Hello Roger Staubach.

In today's quarterback-crazed world, this seems like a no-brainer. Back then, it was buzzkill, even if John would become a huge Staubach fan. By persuading his son instead of compelling him, Jack made the decision belong to John. As John opened Sheila's passenger door and walked toward his first practice at Pullman High, he was going to be the best quarterback he could be, even if he had no idea what it meant.

Elway was also about to walk into his life's passion. This wasn't about a dad's desire to make his son a quarterback. It was something far more meaningful, a lesson that helped build a bond between father and son. That bond became a deep and lasting friendship. Jack was giving his son a hard lesson in the cruel realities of the game. Quarterback was simply a better option, not just a way to chase glory and girls. Jack wasn't trying to create a quarterback as much as he was trying to help his son survive and teach him the ways of the game.

Jack wasn't without some level of strategic manipulation. He held his son (and John's twin sister, Jana) back a year in school for two reasons. First, he knew boys tend to mature physically a little later, so he was giving John a chance to grow. Second, Jack had the personal experience of being a good athlete himself. He had been pushed to play against older kids when he was young. By the time he got to Washington State, he was already banged up from years of playing older kids, and injuries eventually ended his college career.

Though being held back was sensible, it was also annoying for John and Jana. Over the years, other kids constantly asked whether they had flunked a grade. Jack's other big strategic move came later when he had to move the family to Los Angeles. Jack made sure he found a high school where the football team threw the ball. A lot. Still, the goal for Jack was never to create a quarterback as much as it was to create a kid who could enjoy the game and had the best chance for some success.

Sitting there outside Pullman High on that summer day, Jack was explaining football to John in a deeper way than most kids ever learned. Over the years, it was a discussion the father and son would return to regularly. Jack was John's real hero, and the ten-minute conversation inside Sheila the Chevy changed everything for his future. It also helped further fuel John's competitive side. Playing a new position was demanding. It made him work that much harder. Years later when he took over as an executive with the Broncos, he felt the same kind of challenge in the form of doubts and resentment from the fans and the media.

And his response was the same. As his father instructed him to give up being a running back, his advice hit John both logically and emotionally. He was going to listen to his father and he was going to be the best quarterback he could become. He also was going to show his father he really didn't have limitations.

He may not have been on the way to becoming the next Calvin Hill, but he was going to be the best John Elway he could possibly be.

CHAPTER 4

AN ODD WAY TO L.A.

There's a certain alignment of stars that must happen in any success story.

The progression of John Elway from neophyte freshman quarterback to Hall of Famer is no different. In his case, two of the biggest stars to align were a pair of losses in football games he didn't even play in. One loss cost Jack his job at Washington State. The other, which came years earlier, changed the thinking of a man who was vital to Elway's learning to be a quarterback. One of those games happened in November 1975 in Seattle. The other happened in the fall of 1969 in the Los Angeles suburbs John would one day call home.

For now, we'll start in 1975.

John had just finished his freshman season at Pullman High. He was a quarterback, but that didn't mean much in terms of his future as a passer. He might have thrown the ball four times that season thanks to Pullman's run-based offense. To really become a quarterback, John was going to have to change schools. That change wasn't voluntary. It became a necessity.

Jack and the rest of the Washington State staff were fired in the aftermath of the most bizarre Apple Cup game in the history of the annual Washington State–University of Washington rivalry. Washington State traveled to Seattle for a November 22 showdown with archrival Washington. Washington State coach Jim Sweeney was in his eighth season. His tenure had been largely a struggle, posting losing records in seven of his eight seasons, and this season was typical. The Cougars were 3–7 headed into this game, but Sweeney held hope of keeping the job.

He had lasted so long primarily because his good friend Sam Jankovich was the athletic director. Sweeney and Jankovich were both from Butte, Montana, and Jankovich had gotten into the college ranks as an assistant coach under Sweeney. By that season, however, even Sweeney was impatient with himself. He declared to fellow coaches that he would resign if Washington State didn't beat Washington and first-year Huskies head coach Don James. James went on to become the greatest coach in Washington history, but he was just some guy out of Kent State at the time.

"The week of that game, Sweeney stood up in front of the staff and said, 'We're going to show this guy [James] how it's done,'" says Bill Moos, who was a graduate assistant coach at the time.

The pressure going into the game was immense. The conditions that day at Husky Stadium were typically cold and rainy. The rain was so constant that the artificial turf field never drained. When the players hit the ground, the water would slosh up in sheets as if they were headed down a Slip 'N Slide.

Jack was the offensive coordinator for Washington State and had always hoped to be the head coach of his alma mater. As the game played out, Jack's offense was effective as the Cougars ran for more than 200 yards. The Cougars' defense also held Washington and sophomore starting quarterback Warren Moon to fewer than 100 yards. As Washington State dominated the statistics, the team built a 27–14 lead with 3:01 remaining in the game. The Cougars had a fourth-down-and-one situation at the Washington fourteen-yard line. Time-out was called and Washington State quarterback John Hopkins came over to the sideline to talk to Jack and Sweeney.

Before Hopkins walked over, tight end Carl Barschig told Hopkins a certain pass route was open over the middle. Like a lot of young guys, Barschig was thinking about a gratuitous dagger shot against a bitter rival, just to add a little embarrassment. Hopkins felt the same way.

"The one thing we all wanted to do was stick it to the Huskies,"

Hopkins says more than forty years later. Hopkins was known as "Hollywood" because he was from Southern California. After graduation, he returned home and became a successful real estate developer, building more than one hundred shopping centers in his business career, and a volunteer assistant coach at Mater Dei High School. He helped turn the Monarchs into one of the great high school programs in the country.

At this moment, however, emotion was about to get the better part of discretion.

Jack wanted to play the odds. With a field goal looking tough in the conditions, the best plan of action in Jack's mind was to run the ball. If they got the first down, they could almost run the clock out. If they didn't, Washington would still have more than eighty yards to go just to get the first of two touchdowns it would need to win. Based on how the Washington State defense was playing, that appeared to be a strong plan.

"Run it," Jack said, calling for Hopkins to keep the ball himself.

Hopkins then mentioned the pass play to Jack and Sweeney. Jack told Sweeney and Hopkins again, "Run it." Hopkins was getting ready to dash back onto the field. Sweeney yelled to Hopkins to "Run your play." Hopkins interpreted Sweeney's instruction to mean he should call the pass play Barschig had suggested. What Sweeney meant was that he wanted Hopkins to run the keeper play Jack had called.

What ensued was a football disaster. Hopkins faked a handoff and then went to pass. Unfortunately, the running back who was supposed to block in the pass protection failed his assignment, allowing a Washington defender to hit Hopkins as he threw. At the other end of the play, Barschig was nowhere close to open as Washington defensive back Al Burleson stepped in front of the pass.

Burleson intercepted the ball at the seven-yard line and went ninety-three yards untouched for a touchdown with 2:47 remaining in the game. Washington State was stunned, but still had a 27–21 lead. After kicking off, Washington stopped the Cougars from getting a first down and forced a punt.

Washington got the ball at its twenty-two-yard line. Again, Washington had barely moved the ball all game long. Though Moon was just getting started on an amazing career that would end up in the Pro Football Hall of Fame with John Elway, this wasn't a game that indicated future greatness for him. Up to this moment, Moon had completed only three of twenty-one passes for forty-eight yards. The play he was about to make was more about a lucky bounce than brilliant execution.

Moon threw the ball deep down the left side. The pass was intended for wide receiver Scott Phillips, but Washington State defensive back Tony Heath was in a better position to catch it. The ball deflected off Heath twice, ending up behind him and in the arms of Washington wide receiver Spider Gaines. Gaines gathered the ball at the Cougars' forty-yard line and outraced everybody to the end zone. Washington then barely made the conversion kick to take a 28–27 victory in a game that was pure humiliation and frustration for Washington State.

After the game, Sweeney took the blame for the interception by Hopkins.

"The players wanted it and I agreed. I OK'd the pass and it was just a plain stupid decision. We've scored four times on that pass play and with the way we were moving the ball, it just seemed like the right move," Sweeney said.

Likewise, Hopkins felt guilty.

"For me, it was traumatic at the time. I felt so bad at the time for everybody. I was really close to Coach Sweeney, but the person I was probably closest to was Jack and I just felt like I let them down," Hopkins says.

Like so many of Jack's relationships with his players, the connection ran deep. During Hopkins's freshman year, his father had suffered a stroke for the second time. The situation caused havoc on Hopkins's family. His mother had to go back to work and his sisters couldn't go to college. Worse, he was more than a thousand miles from home, unable to help. Jack intuitively understood. He let Hopkins break curfew to spend the night with his family one weekend when the team played in Los Angeles. Another time, Jack sent Hopkins to Southern California under the guise of picking up a car Jack had bought. Hopkins drove it back to Pullman.

"Jack understood what I was dealing with and made sure I got home as much as I could," Hopkins says. "Jack became like a second father to me."

The bus ride from Seattle to Pullman was a funeral procession for the coaches. John himself learned how deeply hurt his father was. As he got on the team bus to sit next to Jack for the five-hour ride, Jack snapped at him.

"Just sit there and shut up," Jack barked. John didn't say a word the whole trip, not even to ask for anything to eat. He was too intimidated by the depth of Jack's anger. This was a different level of pain for Jack. The stinging embarrassment of the loss was about to upend the family's world. Sweeney followed through on his promise to resign, avoiding the ugliness of Jankovich's having to fire him. In Jack's heart, he wanted the Washington State job, and guys like Hopkins even spoke up for him.

"I went in and told [Jankovich] and the administration they should keep Jack, that we'd all play hard for him, but they weren't listening," Hopkins says.

Promoting an assistant coach who had just been part of the most embarrassing loss in rivalry history wasn't going to play well with Washington State fans, even if it would have been a better idea than what happened. The school hired sharp-dressing, smooth-talking Jackie Sherrill, who used the job as a stepping-stone and left after only one year. Sherrill never even moved out of the apartment he was renting, and his family never moved to Pullman.

"The school liked [Sherrill] because he was button-downed and sharp-looking, but he didn't care about the school," says Moos, who years later became the athletic director at Washington State. "Jack cared about the school and loved Pullman."

Jack was out of work and all three Elway children were in high school. Eldest daughter Lee Ann was in the middle of her junior year. Jack proposed a deal to Hobbs, who was the head coach in both football and basketball at Pullman High. One of them would be the head coach in football and the other would take basketball. In return, they would be the assistant coach for each other in the other sport. Hobbs turned him down. Jack then got an assistant coach job at the University of Idaho, which was just ten miles away across the state border. Shortly after getting the Idaho job, Jack heard from Cal State Northridge, an NCAA Division II school that had played football for fifteen years. The program had a winning record in only three seasons and never finished better than 6–4. Still, this was a chance to be a head coach.

For John, it would end up being an even more important opportunity.

"I remember calling Coach Elway after everything that happened and I said, 'I really wanted you as head coach, unfortunately it didn't happen,'" Hopkins says. "'But now you're a head coach and you're down in Southern California. It's the best thing for John. He's going to get with somebody who will throw the ball.'"

John Elway was about to run into the second star of his alignment to greatness.

CHAPTER 5

HAPPY JACK'S FLYING CIRCUS

Jack Neumeier became a radical in 1969.

It had nothing to do with the Summer of Love, which Neumeier could neither understand nor tolerate. It was all about the winter of his discontent.

Neumeier became a *football* radical and a coach who was decades ahead of his time when it came to strategy. He was the head coach of Granada Hills High School in the Los Angeles suburbs of the San Fernando Valley. In 1976, he would become John Elway's coach after Jack took over the program at Cal State Northridge.

For Elway, who showed up as a scrawny sixteen-year-old, it was serendipity. At a time when most high school programs threw maybe a dozen passes a game, Neumeier's teams were throwing thirty to forty a game. For a young man who didn't become a quarterback until he was fifteen, this was the equivalent of an immersion program in passing offense. However, long before Elway ever showed up, it was Neumeier who had to go through a metamorphosis. It was a painful process and nearly cost him the job he loved so dearly. It also was, in a bigger way, stunning to Neumeier's family and friends.

For the first half of Neumeier's coaching life, he was the classic, hard-nosed conservative coach. His teams ran the ball constantly. That style was reflective of his personality, especially from a social standpoint. His friends joked that he made paleo-conservative politician Barry Goldwater look liberal. In today's world, he'd be a flag bearer for the Tea Party.

Truth is, he was a little more complicated than that. In the early 1960s, Neumeier was a Kennedy democrat, identifying with the country's first Catholic president and with Kennedy's emphasis on public service.

"He believed very strongly in the idea of 'Ask not what your country can do for you, but what you can do for your country,'" says his daughter, Jackie Neumeier Cohen, who was Elway's classmate at Granada Hills. "After the Vietnam War started, the anti-war protest and how much the Democratic Party changed, he switched. He hated the social landscape at the time. He hated the long hair and protest of the sixties and what he felt it did to the country."

"We had quite a few post-practice lectures about that stuff," says Dana Potter, who quarterbacked Granada Hills for three seasons from 1968 to 1970. "Granada Hills was a good school, but we had our share of kids who were experimenting with drugs. Somebody told me once we had an average of an overdose a week at the time. Jack didn't like it and he counseled us all the time."

Neumeier was a devout Catholic. He was the brother of a nun and the father of a priest. He grew up in the San Fernando Valley during the 1920s and 1930s, when it was primarily orange groves. It was a long way in time from an area where nearly two million people now live. He was one of twelve children and grew up very poor, much of his formative life spent during the (Great) Depression era. His family attended St. Elizabeth's Catholic Church, where he and his brothers were taught to play football by the priests. By the time Neumeier got to high school, he was a quarterback himself. His bad luck was that he was stuck behind a guy named Bob Waterfield, who went on to play at UCLA and now is enshrined in the Pro Football Hall of Fame.

"What he loved about his childhood was how much love and unity there was to his family. He always put a premium on the family experience and he managed to raise a family and have it so his wife didn't have to work even on his teacher's salary," Neumeier Cohen says. "He was super strict and his whole life was about sports, religion, and family. You could do a great parody of him, actually. When I got in trouble for something, I was never grounded. I was 'benched.' When I got caught forging my mother's signature to get out of class one time, I was 'benched' for two weeks."

She chuckled before turning a combination of somber and serious.

"He was a really good man. He was an extremely honest and ethical man," she says. "He took pride in everything he did and wanted to make sure others around him learned from his example."

Neumeier's players were required to keep their hair cut short so it didn't show from underneath their helmet. In the shaggy days of the 1970s, Neumeier got every player to fall in line. As his daughter explained, "It was almost a badge of honor at Granada Hills to have that haircut. Everybody knew you were an athlete."

At five-foot-eight and roughly 175 pounds, Neumeier was not physically imposing. Yet he had a commanding presence. His dignity and class created an aura around him that was well-established by the time Elway got to Granada Hills. Neumeier also pushed his football players to get involved in school politics, hoping to keep the kind of social order he preferred.

And again, his football philosophy followed his social point of view for much of his life. He was the first coach of Granada Hills when the school opened in 1960. By 1969, he had what many people believed was the school's best team ever. It was loaded with a great defense, a big offensive line, and a power running game. By the standard of the day, this was football perfection. Except for one problem.

The team couldn't score.

"Every team we played would ignore our passing game when we got close to the end zone and just load up to stop our running game," Potter says. "We could run the ball for a lot of yards, but we couldn't score when we got close."

Granada Hills was good. Just not as good as billed. The Highlanders lost to archrival San Fernando, 16–14, then faced off against nearby rival Poly of Sun Valley late in the season with a playoff berth on the line. Granada Hills dominated the game in every way, except the scoreboard. The Highlanders lost 7–5, scoring only a field goal and a safety. Poly finished the game with negative offensive yards, scoring the only touchdown of the game on a kickoff return to open the second half. The rest of the game was a study in frustration. Granada Hills had the ball inside the Poly ten-yard line on four occasions and scored on none of them.

With expectations so high that season, failing to make the playoffs for the tenth straight season had parents calling for Neumeier to be fired. The team had only two starting players set to return in 1970, so the timing seemed right for a change. Potter was one of those two starters. As pressure mounted on Principal Bryce Schurr to fire Neumeier, Potter spoke up.

"I told the principal the reason we didn't win was because I didn't play well. It was true. Yeah, the scheme wasn't great, but there were a lot of things I could have done. I just felt like I owed that to Jack because of the kind of man he was. He always expected the best of you and tried to put you in the best position to succeed," Potter says.

Neumeier took the reprieve as an opportunity for an awakening.

"After that season, everything changed for Jack. He blew up the whole offense and decided to go completely the other way," says Daryl Stroh, the baseball coach at Granada Hills and an assistant coach in football.

In the winter after the 1969 season, Neumeier bought the book *Run-and-Shoot Football: Offense of the Future* by Ohio high school coach Glenn "Tiger" Ellison. Ellison had come up with the concepts for the run-and-shoot in the 1950s when the team he was coaching was severely outmanned and had to find a way to compete. These days, Ellison's concepts are the foundation of the spread offenses seen at all levels of football.

But in the 1970s, Ellison's ideas were still considered outlandish. With the help of men like Neumeier and Darrel "Mouse" Davis in Oregon, the ideas started to gain traction. Neumeier suddenly became Bob Dylan going from acoustic to electric guitar. It didn't take long before the Granada Hills offense became known as "Happy Jack's Flying Circus."

He was also on track to the greatest season of his career. In spring 1970, Neumeier and Potter installed the offense. At the same time, Los Angeles high schools began what is popularly known as the summer passing league. This is only a minor version of what's done today, but it was a vital boost for Granada Hills.

"The timing was perfect. Before then, spring ball was a joke. Even though the coaches couldn't coach the passing league teams, it was a way for everybody to get some work in. Before that, kids wouldn't pick up a football until August 1 for the start of training and that just wasn't working for the coaches," Potter says.

Potter and the receivers went a step further, taking it upon themselves to work extra during Hell Week, the traditional first week of two-a-day practices for the season. Potter would take them out between the morning and afternoon for an extra session to go over the reads and calls that happened at the line of scrimmage. As the season neared, Neumeier's imagination went to places Potter thought were almost psychedelic. Potter would go to Neumeier's house in the Porter Ranch subdivision of the Valley and they'd talk about how to run the offense.

"Jack had this house up in the hills that overlooked the valley," Potter says.

> We'd be up there talking about the season. He was sitting in his den and it was dark so he could see the lights and the view. He was just sitting there, always thinking about what we could do with the offense. Once he read that book, his mind opened up and he got so creative in a short amount of time. He was having so much fun with it and when he found out how much fun we were having playing that style, he just went wild.
>
> At one point he said, "We're going to score like 30 to 40 points a game." I was thinking to myself, "We have nobody coming back and we couldn't score last season." I said to him, "Why are you thinking that?" He just stared out the window and said, "This offense, they can't stop it. No matter what [the defense does], somebody is going to be open."

Neumeier eventually referred to the scheme as being "basketball on grass," a term that exploded decades later as spread offenses caught on. He said Potter would throw for 2,000 or even 3,000 yards. As a sophomore,

Potter had finished second in the league with 996 yards. More than doubling or even tripling his output seemed absurd.

Neumeier's vision quickly became a reality. Granada Hills opened the 1970 season with a game in Las Vegas against Western High School, an extremely rare out-of-state game. After an anxious start, Granada Hills pulled away for an easy win and went on to open the season 7–0. The only loss of the regular season came against archrival San Fernando, a perennial power of Los Angeles County at the time. San Fernando was led by running back Anthony Davis, who went on to play at USC. It was a lopsided 40–15 game, but it set the stage for revenge in the city championship game when the teams played again.

Granada Hills figured out how to attack San Fernando's defensive scheme the second time and won the title 38–28. It was Neumeier's lone city title and helped Potter get a scholarship to Nebraska. Years later, Elway became an even bigger beneficiary.

What also helped John Elway is that Potter returned to be an assistant coach under Neumeier when Elway was there. Elway received some of the most advanced high school teaching imaginable at the time. More importantly, Neumeier's system allowed the quarterback to make all the final decisions on a play at the line of scrimmage. There might be one play called in the huddle, but if the defense lined up a different way, the quarterback had the power to change the call. It gave Elway more responsibility to learn the game. This was a very sophisticated approach, particularly given the era.

"I had more freedom in my high school system than I had the first ten years of my NFL career," Elway says.

"That was something Jack really grew to enjoy because he could see how much fun the players were having in this system," Potter says.

> No one who knew Jack could really believe the transformation, but if you were in the middle of it, it made perfect sense. The more he allowed the players to do, the more fun they had, and the more fun they had, the better the offense would get because they were so happy. It just fed on itself and the further

we would go, the wilder Jack would get. He would have new concepts and formations every week during the season. Every once in a while, he would sit back and laugh about his previous life as a football coach and then what he became.

When Elway arrived, Neumeier was prepared to go even further with football—and it even got a little personal around his house.

"My dad would say when God dropped John in his lap, he had the good fortune to be able to coach the best athlete he had ever seen in his life. He could tell that when John was sixteen. He was just elated with the good fortune to have him and see him throw," Neumeier Cohen says. "My dad thought John was the greatest kid ever. He wanted me to marry him so bad. Both my parents would say, 'Wouldn't it be great if you married John?' We weren't even really friends in high school, but they hoped."

Neumeier lived to be eighty-five, long enough to see Elway enter the Pro Football Hall of Fame on August 8, 2004. He died a little less than a month later following a three-year struggle with cancer.

"He bought this new suit. He was so proud someone he coached had made it that far and accomplished so much," Neumeier Cohen says. "It was all the energy he had left to make the trip. I remember looking at him in that suit and thinking, 'He's probably going to wear this one more time,' and feeling a little sad. He was so frail by that time. But it made him so happy."

CHAPTER 6

HIGH SCHOOL

The first impression of Elway at Granada Hills High didn't match the hype.

"I remember seeing John for the first time because we had heard about this kid, a quarterback who was in town," says Paul Bergman, a classmate of Elway's who ended up being the team's top receiver when they were seniors. Bergman went on to play at UCLA, briefly in the US Football League, and later became a pastor. At the time, Bergman was working with the quarterbacks because Neumeier thought he had a good arm.

"I see John and I'm not trying to be mean, but I was going to feel sorry for him. He was scrawny, knock-kneed, pigeon-toed. Just not a threat. His chest was actually pointed inward. I was like, 'Oh, this poor guy is going to get killed,'" Bergman says.

The sixteen-year-old Elway was an unremarkable five-foot-ten and 150 pounds. But put a ball in his hands and...

"John ends up standing next to me and starts throwing. I swear to you, I think the balls were rockets. You could hear the ball whistle when he threw," Bergman says. "By the end of the practice, I was over working with the receivers. That was it for my quarterback career."

For all of Elway's arm talent, he wasn't exactly Paul Bunyan arriving from the great Northwest to chop down the competition. He made the varsity as a sophomore and didn't start until midway through the season. There was an established starter ahead of him, but the starter moved to

Nevada shortly after Elway arrived. Another quarterback transferred a year later, leaving Elway as the clear number one.

Elway's first game as a sophomore was against El Camino High School. Elway came in as a sub, completed four of ten passes, and had one intercepted on a fourth-and-goal play in a game Granada Hills lost 13–0. Still, the moment was transformative. Neumeier and Potter were giving Elway the freedom to call plays at the line. Elway was quickly falling in love with the art of the game.

"It was fun, I was making decisions, I was learning the game," Elway says. "It was challenging, and I could finally just do something back there. Everything just opened up."

He just needed his body to catch up. As his father predicted, that happened by Elway's junior year. He grew five inches from the end of the 1976 football season to the beginning of the 1977 season. He suffered through Osgood-Schlatter disease in the process. His knees were in constant pain, and he couldn't sit in a car for more than twenty minutes without getting sore. It was a small price to pay in an otherwise glorious time.

Neumeier continued to be demanding as both a coach and a leader of young men. Elway's friend and classmate, Jim Ginnetti, was an example. Ginnetti was a running back and during his senior year had a really bad day of practice. Neumeier made him do something over and over and then yelled at Ginnetti when he couldn't get it right. That evening, Ginnetti was at Elway's house for dinner. He was at the Elway house so much he was like a second son. He and Elway would do stupid things like wrestle in the living room. They'd break the leg on the sofa and then jury-rig it, hoping Jan wouldn't notice. The Barracuda didn't miss anything.

At dinner, Ginnetti started complaining about Neumeier.

Jack Elway lit him up.

"You know what you are? Uncoachable. You think you know better than the coaches. If it took you twenty reps to figure it out, you should have done twenty reps," Jack said as he went on a twenty-minute rant that eventually ended up in the backyard of the house.

"That's one of the most important moments of my life," Ginnetti says.

"Jack tore me up, just laid into me. In our group, you could do that. We'd be over at each other's houses all the time and our parents would watch over us. If you stepped out of line, you didn't have to wait to get back home to get a lecture. You'd get it right then and you'd probably get it again when you got home.

"Jack was right. I wasn't doing what it took to do it right. That lesson stuck with me the rest of my life and I've been pretty darn successful. I always go back to it. Do whatever it takes to do it right. It's simple, but sometimes it takes a lot of people to pound that into the head of a testosterone-filled, teenage kid."

With Neumeier and Stroh riding herd, the athletes and their families became tightly knit. After football and baseball games, the kids and the parents would usually end up at somebody's house, eating through the kitchen, swimming in the backyard, and then listening to Jack tell stories as he embellished every tale with his jokes and facial expressions. The group included a parade of driven, successful people. Potter and Sutton made it big in real estate. Paul Scheper, a teammate, went to Harvard University and became a lawyer.

Elway's role was to be not only the superstar but a valued friend in a group that became a safety net for all involved. Scheper's brother Bobby was a year younger than Elway and dealt with juvenile diabetes. He never played sports, but he was always included. He was the ball boy in football and the bat boy in baseball. More than a few times, Elway would look at him and say, "You're the greatest ball boy, ever."

By 1993, the diabetes got the best of Bobby. He was living in a convalescent hospital. Bobby had lost a leg, some toes, and sight in one eye. At Christmas, Elway sent him a care package, including a signed poster reading, "To Bobby: All of my comebacks pale in comparison to yours. Keep the faith. Be strong. Love, John, No. 7. P.S.: You're still the best ball boy of all time."

"I was thinking John would send something like, 'Best wishes, John Elway,'" Paul Scheper says. "That would have been enough. To remember the little role Bob played on the football team. It was so important to Bob. It was one of the most touching, emotional moments of his life.... He put that poster up on the wall. He had such pride when people came in and said, 'You know John Elway?'"

Elway's high school life was far more than simply finding a school where he could hone his football skills. There were the stupid-yet-telling moments, like the night they got busted for throwing water balloons out of the car. They were driving in the Elways' Datsun B210, which the family dubbed "The Duke." As the boys threw water balloons, the cops were called. They headed back to Elway's house and a police car followed them. The police then turned on the lights and sounded the siren as the boys pulled into the driveway.

It was roughly 11 p.m. and the boys were freaking out inside the car. They quickly hatched a plan to just deny the whole thing, figuring the cops couldn't really prove anything. That's when Jack came out of the house, dressed in his robe and wearing a scowl. As John exited the car, he turned to his buddies and said, "The plan is off, just tell the truth."

On the field, Elway's skills blossomed as his teammates worked hard to adapt to his arm. Sutton and Scott Marshall, the wide receivers, used to practice catching Elway's throws by standing ten yards apart and firing the ball as hard as they could at each other. They all took pride in catching Elway's missiles. A couple of years later, Sutton and Marshall would visit Elway at Stanford and razz the receivers who complained about Elway's velocity.

By 1977, Elway became the full-time starter, and Granada Hills played a formidable schedule that highlighted his talent. The Highlanders opened against powerhouse Banning High School, which had future NFL running back Stanley Wilson and an array of gigantic Samoan and Tongan guys. Banning loved to intimidate. During warm-ups before the game, the Banning players whispered, "Elway, Elway, Elway" in unison. Banning also had dim lights, making it hard for Elway's receivers to see the ball. Banning won in dominating fashion.

Next was another Los Angeles power, Carson High School. Carson was at the height of its greatness, eventually winning nine titles and reaching the city championship game eighteen times in twenty-eight years under coach Gene Vollnogle. Carson also had more than its fair share of Samoan and

Tongan dudes and dominated for three quarters, building a 16–0 lead. In the fourth quarter, Granada Hills mounted a comeback. Elway hit Ginnetti with a fifteen-yard touchdown pass with 1:55 remaining for a 19–16 victory. Elway finished with 256 yards passing and three touchdowns.

Granada Hills then lost to talented Crenshaw High School before starting league play. Now battle-tested from three tough games, Granada Hills went on a roll. In October, the Highlanders faced local rival Kennedy High School. Kennedy was less than three miles away and everybody knew one another. Kennedy also had a talented quarterback in Tom Ramsey, who went on to play at UCLA. Ramsey started from the beginning of his sophomore year. He was cocky and openly told people he was better than Elway. There was a lot of trash talk before the game. Some of the Kennedy players got carried away and decided to graffiti the Granada Hills campus. They spray-painted "Elway sucks" and "Sutton and Marshall die." It backfired when seven of them got caught and couldn't play in the game. Granada Hills won 28–13.

Then came the biggest game of Elway's high school career against San Fernando, the most decorated program in Valley history. San Fernando was a football factory in the 1960s and 1970s, using a bruising wishbone offense to produce running backs like Anthony Davis and Charles White. Both went on to star at the University of Southern California, and San Fernando was a USC pipeline. The school had won the city title in 1974 and 1975, then finished second in the city in 1976.

The 1977 game was played at Granada Hills in front of a packed stadium of more than 9,000 people. The game became a shootout. With 1:45 remaining, Granada Hills was down 35–33 and had the ball at its own thirty-two-yard line. Elway drove the Highlanders to the San Fernando nine-yard line with twenty-five seconds left. Neumeier called for a pass to Sutton, and Elway hit him for the touchdown to win the game.

Not quite.

The touchdown pass was nullified by a holding penalty. A fifteen-yard holding penalty. Brutal situation. Now backed up to the twenty-four-yard line and trying to regroup after the emotion of the negated touchdown, some of the offensive linemen were rattled.

Elway said, "Hey, let's get it together. We can do this." The clock was at twenty seconds remaining. As they were trying to figure it out, Sutton yelled at Neumeier to call the same play. The only problem is the San Fernando defensive back read the play. He covered Sutton and tipped the ball. Sutton maintained his concentration and caught it for a game-winning touchdown with thirteen seconds left.

It was a signature Elway play in a huge game. Elway finished with 454 yards passing and four touchdowns. Granada Hills finished undefeated in league play at 5–0. Everything came together. As Jack walked out of that game with Jan, he said to her, "He might just be as good as I think he can be."

Sutton considers that moment life changing. He grew up in a broken home with no dad and a mom who had issues. He bounced around different homes while growing up. But Sutton has this infectiously positive attitude.

"I'm the luckiest guy in the world and that play is the reason why. . . . I look back at that all the time and just understand that's where it really started for me. I really believe if I would have dropped that pass, my life would have been different," Sutton says. "I really believe getting to be a small part of John's life was a huge factor for me."

In the playoffs, Granada Hills blew out Taft in the first round and then faced Palisades in the quarterfinals. Palisades had Jay Schroeder at quarterback, creating a matchup of two quarterbacks who eventually made it to the Super Bowl. Granada Hills won in overtime under the California tiebreaker format. Now came a rematch with Banning in the semifinals, which didn't turn out any better than the season opener. Elway completed eighteen of thirty-six passes, but for only 170 yards. Granada Hills finished the year 9–3 and felt it had the foundation for a great team in 1978, when Elway was a senior.

The experience at Granada Hills also laid a foundation for Jack Elway. He started adapting a lot of Neumeier's ideas into his offense at Cal State Northridge. Jack eventually adopted the offense because he had so many running backs get injured. Neumeier's offense required only one running back. When Jack left for San Jose State in 1979, he had Neumeier help install the offense.

In the spring of 1978, Granada Hills won the city championship in baseball, and Elway was named the City Player of the Year. Life couldn't have been much better. About the only issue Elway ever had in high school revolved around cars. After the Datsun B210 ran out of steam, Elway inherited a faded pink Buick LeSabre. The car, which the family dubbed Luke LeSabre, was so ugly Jana refused to be seen in it. She demanded she be let out a block away from the school.

That summer, Elway had sixty schools offering him scholarships and visions of a city championship as a senior. Granada Hills lost to Carson early in the season, but that game featured a sixty-four-yard pass from Elway to Steve McLaughlin that traveled seventy yards in the air. After the game, Neumeier told reporter Eric Sondheimer of the *Los Angeles Times*, "Not even in the pros could they do that."

The hope for a title ended while playing at San Fernando. Elway got hit awkwardly and hurt his right knee. Jack came down to check on his son at halftime. The doctor said he had cartilage damage and couldn't make it any worse that day, so they wrapped it and he finished. However, Elway was done for the season. He had surgery to repair the cartilage damage and over the years found out the knee was worse than originally thought. He tore the anterior cruciate ligament (ACL), but the doctors couldn't tell. He got healthy enough to play baseball and helped Granada Hills through a fascinating season. After graduating, his final high school football experience was in the North-South Shrine All-Star game at the Rose Bowl in July 1979. Elway completed twenty-three of thirty-seven for 363 yards and four touchdowns.

As he played, he was back to his old self, running around the pocket and launching throws. At one point, he scrambled hard to his left, planted, looked back to the right, and launched a sixty-yard pass to Bergman, who laid out to make the catch in the end zone. USC coach John Robinson was doing the color commentary for the game. Robinson, whose team had botched the chance to sign Elway, quietly repeated a refrain from the fall.

Elway was the greatest high school quarterback he'd ever seen.

CHAPTER 7

THE RECRUITING TRAIL

At least one University of Missouri cheerleader had plenty of Christmas cheer.

The recruiting process for Elway was constant and overwhelming. He wrote a weekly diary for the *Los Angeles Daily News*, recounting how he traveled around the country and that sixty schools were trying to entice him. More than half of the NCAA Division I college teams at the time were chasing him.

"It was cool and exciting, but it was exhausting," Elway says.

He was the number one player in the country and was getting letters throughout his senior season. Missouri, where Elway family friend Mike Price was coaching the quarterbacks, was particularly aggressive. Price held a special place in Elway's heart because he had helped fix Elway's throwing motion in the backyard of the family's house one day. Price, who spent the rest of his life claiming he taught Elway how to throw, pushed hard to convince Elway to come to Missouri. Elway was getting five letters a day from Missouri alums.

One day in December 1978, he received Christmas cards from sixty-six Missouri cheerleaders, each with a unique message. That included a fairly direct missive from one cheerleader who wrote, "We don't go to bed with teddy bears. We only sleep with Missouri Tigers." Jan saw that one and called Price to give him a piece of her mind. The Barracuda didn't just bite Jack.

As tempting as the young ladies from Missouri made it, John's approach to the recruiting process was decidedly practical. Jack wasn't about to have his kids spend their working careers chasing philosophy or writing poetry. Jack would often walk around the house and exclaim to his children, "We're not going to have any archaeologists in this family!" When it came time to choose a school, John wasn't letting his sports dreams get in the way of securing an education that would prepare him for real life.

The University of Southern California was Elway's hometown favorite. But as Jack noted, USC in the 1960s and 1970s produced quarterbacks who handed the ball to great running backs. When John went to USC for a luncheon, the assistant coach who sat with him and Jan barely knew anything about him. Even though Robinson, the Trojans coach, called John the greatest quarterback prospect he'd ever seen that fall, it was hard to take them seriously as a place to become a quarterback.

Then there was Notre Dame. After battling through a brutal snowstorm to arrive in South Bend, Elway sat in coach Dan Devine's office for an hour as Devine walked past him time after time, not saying a word until Devine was ready to talk. Devine didn't say as much as "hello." He had just led Notre Dame to a national championship in the 1977 season with Montana as quarterback. Elway didn't know what Devine was trying to prove, but he eliminated Notre Dame before Devine said a word.

"The man didn't even introduce himself and he knew I was there the whole time," Elway says. "I don't know what kind of point he was trying to make, but I just kept thinking he was pretty rude not to at least say something the whole time."

The fact that there were no girls at a party he attended that weekend didn't help, either. That's not a mistake Missouri would have made, evidently. Washington was a good option because Elway had family all over the Northwest. Obviously, San Jose State was appealing because his dad had just gotten the head coaching job there.

Stanford had the most complete appeal. It was the best school, and John took the idea of getting a degree seriously because of Jack's combination of pushing for a job-related degree, Jack's series of injuries that ended his college career, and the dose of reality John's knee injury provided. At worst, he'd get a degree in economics and become an accountant. From a football perspective, the school also had a history of producing top quarterbacks, including the likes of John Brodie and Jim Plunkett, the 1970 Heisman Trophy winner and number one overall pick in the 1971 NFL Draft.

Bill Walsh was the coach when the school started recruiting Elway. It was no secret that he was going to be hired by the San Francisco 49ers before Elway officially signed, but that was fine with Elway because Walsh assistant Rod Dowhower was slated to take over. Walsh had taken Stanford to back-to-back bowl games, finished ranked in the top twenty each of those seasons, and was running an advanced passing attack that would later be known as the West Coast Offense. It was another offense that allowed the quarterback to have more control. It eventually propelled Walsh and the 49ers to legendary status. Elway was assured the offense would not change.

The Stanford coaches also encouraged John to play both football and baseball. Most schools would let him do both, but it seemed like grudging support. Finally, the family was in the process of moving to nearby San Jose. John's mother and sisters strongly encouraged him to attend Stanford. Jack stayed out of the process. Still, the idea of navigating an academically rigorous school while trying to play two sports seemed daunting to John. What sealed the deal was a person who sounded a lot like Jeff Spicoli, Sean Penn's famous surfer/burnout character from Cameron Crowe's great book and movie about Southern California high school life, *Fast Times at Ridgemont High*.

Stanford wide receiver Kenny Margerum was five-foot-ten and 170 pounds, including a mop of curly hair that may have weighed fifteen pounds by itself. Margerum was a prototypical Southern California surf rat and now lives in Capitola, California, which is like a retirement community for surfers. He's about three blocks from the beach, still taking in the tasty waves.

In college, if he wasn't headed over the Santa Cruz Mountains to the Pacific Ocean, he was wind surfing on Lake Lagunita in the middle of campus. He drove a beat-up car and talked with the perfect SoCal/Valley Dude accent, honed from his days attending Fountain Valley High. His high school was close enough to the beach that Margerum could ride waves at dawn and still make it to class on time.

He also was a serious football player. He carved out a seven-year career in the NFL despite less-than-imposing size and speed. He helped Chicago win a title in 1985. He was an intuitive football player, both smart and passionate. He coached at the college level after retiring, and Elway tried to convince him to get into scouting after Elway took over the Broncos in 2011.

In the recruiting war for Elway's services, Margerum was Stanford's closer. Dowhower sent Margerum down to the Elway household one day during Elway's senior year. He gave Elway an effective, if somewhat strange, sales pitch. Margerum, who was a sophomore at the time, put Elway at ease. Just as important, his pitch also made Elway feel as if Stanford was taking football seriously.

"Duuuuuude, I know Stanford sounds really egg-headed and intimidating," Margerum recalls years later. "But trust me, bro, if I can make it, you'll be fine."

Righteous.

CHAPTER 8

NUMBER ONE VERSUS NUMBER ONE

Before he was done with high school, Elway had to slay a pterodactyl.

That's one way to describe Darryl Strawberry at age seventeen. In June 1979, as Elway was getting ready to graduate from high school and head to college, Strawberry was a junior at Crenshaw High School in Los Angeles. Strawberry was just a year away from becoming the number one overall pick in the 1980 Major League Baseball draft.

Two future number one picks were about to face off for the L.A. City high school baseball championship.

Crenshaw was fielding perhaps the best team in the nation. Maybe the best ever. At third base was Chris Brown, who would join Strawberry one day as a National League All-Star. Some people thought Brown, Darryl McNealy, and Reggie Dymally were better than Strawberry. All but four players on the team were drafted or played college baseball.

Strawberry was the showpiece, the kind of guy who walked off the team bus and transfixed people. He was a six-foot-five, 185-pound collection of torque-creating pistons and rods otherwise known as arms and legs. His limbs were connected to an inverted triangle of broad shoulders and narrow waist. He ran with the lopping stride of a middle-distance runner. When he stretched out, he looked like a dinosaur that scientists might have unearthed from the La Brea Tar Pits just north of Crenshaw.

The left-handed Strawberry pitched and played outfield. On the mound, his long legs and arms made it look like he was releasing the ball from ten feet away. When he stood at the plate, Strawberry looked like a building crane with his bat waggling back and forth. He was great in any sport. He started at quarterback on the junior varsity team as a sophomore until he found out, as he says with a laugh, "I didn't like to get hit." In basketball, he started for Crenshaw's city championship team as a senior. Baseball was his calling. There were scouts who said he was the best prospect to come along in thirty years. There were others who called him the "Black Ted Williams."

The matchup was about to be the stuff of legends. In 2004, Michael Sokolove researched the terrific book *The Ticket Out*, which examined the vast potential and sad lives of the Crenshaw players. For all their talent, Crenshaw ended up losing to a pitcher from Granada Hills who hadn't set foot on the mound for almost two months because of wildness.

When it mattered, however, Elway was in complete control. Neither Strawberry nor Elway understood the moment at the time. History is lost on teenagers who would rather charge up a hill than think about why. But it's what both intuitively wanted.

"That game led me to understand what that stage was like and made me understand I wanted to be on that stage," Strawberry says.

> I'm sure Elway felt the same way. Having that experience in high school, facing him and even though we got beat, it's what you learn. What do you learn about the stage?
>
> It's the place Elway was pushing toward and I was pushing toward. At the pro level, you get used to the stadium and the crowd and all the stuff around you. But it's the butterflies you deal with, the emotion inside yourself when you have so much on the line. It's a great thing. As you get older, you realize how much you love those moments. You live for them as an athlete.

Though Granada Hills was the defending city champion in baseball, the team wasn't anything close to what it had been in 1978. The 1978 team had eight players who were either drafted or received a college scholarship. In 1979, Elway was the only returning starter. In the early part of the 1979 season, the Highlanders were a mess. They had an entirely new starting infield and only one experienced pitcher, John Stephens. Executing Stroh's demanding, disciplined strategy wasn't easy. They started league play 1–6. Things only changed after Stroh basically challenged the team one day at practice.

"Stroh just drilled the crap out of us one day," says Ginnetti, who played left field. "He was fed up with us and he let us know it. Stroh didn't really yell or curse at us, he just had this look like he expected a certain level of performance and if he didn't get it, he wasn't afraid to change things. I was the leadoff hitter to start the season, but I wasn't getting on base. Stroh wasn't afraid to put me at seven or eight in the lineup if I wasn't performing."

Likewise, Stroh wasn't going to pitch someone just because he had a strong arm. That included Elway. Midway through the season, Elway started a game on the mound and was awful. He hit two batters and walked five before Stroh yanked him and told Elway he was done for the season as a pitcher.

"I told John to go over to third base; he wasn't coming back [to the mound]," Stroh says. "It wasn't really fair to John because we could never work with him. Between football and everything he was doing with the recruiting process and his knee injury from the football season, he just couldn't get on the mound enough. Besides, he was just a thrower. He had a great fastball, but that was all. Jack wouldn't let him throw a curveball."

Elway spent the rest of the season at third base, occasionally played in the outfield, and worked on his hitting. He was great at the plate, hitting over .500 during his junior and senior seasons. Things started to click for Granada Hills. The team won eight in a row to qualify for the playoffs, but the team was a longshot. During the season, the Highlanders had twice lost to league-rival Monroe High School. When the playoffs started, Crenshaw continued to hit like major leaguers playing against high school kids. Crenshaw scored twenty-three runs combined in their first two playoff games. They scored at least ten runs and hit three home runs in a single inning in both games.

Crenshaw feared no one and had scouts drooling.

"That team was loaded," says former Major League Baseball scout George Genovese, who spent thirty-two years scouting Southern California. Genovese knew power hitters. He scouted and signed the likes of Jack Clark, George Foster, Dave Kingman, and Matt Williams.

In Sokolove's book, Genovese said, "Collectively, the 1979 Crenshaw team was the best I ever saw.... No one can say for sure, but I'm going to say they were the greatest high school team ever. Maybe not in wins and losses, but overall talent. My God, everybody all the way up and down that lineup could hit. They just piled on runs. They tore up the opposition."

The greatness of Crenshaw was also a testimony to what the players had to survive to get there. Crenshaw opened in 1968 and quickly rose to athletic prominence. UCLA and NBA star Marques Johnson, Major Leaguer Ellis Valentine, and NFL standout Wendell Tyler had already gone through Crenshaw before Strawberry and Brown played there. Most schools are lucky if they have one guy like that. Crenshaw was just over a decade old and already had five eventual pro athletes roll through. A couple of years later, the school produced basketball star John "Hot Plate" Williams, who played like the next Magic Johnson and was part of Crenshaw's dominant basketball program run. Yet even by Crenshaw's lofty athletic standards, the 1979 baseball team stood out.

"We had like fifty scouts at our games during the season," Strawberry says. "It was crazy how much attention our team got. It wasn't just me; I was just a junior. Our whole team was that good."

And maybe could have been better if not for circumstance. Crenshaw sat in the middle of downtown Los Angeles, a classic inner-city school that dealt with serious inner-city problems. The school and neighborhood became the backdrop for movies such as *Boyz n the Hood* and *Love & Basketball*. Before the baseball season had even started, the team lost talented pitcher Donald Jones, who was kicked out of school. Jones took a baseball bat to the head of a gang member who had been caught trying to beat up his brother Carl, Crenshaw's catcher. The day after Donald Jones got in the fight, there were drive-by gunshots fired at Crenshaw during baseball practice, presumably in retaliation.

By contrast, the biggest problem at Granada Hills was dealing with Stroh's rules, which included short-cropped hair. Sitting at the farthest northern edge of the Los Angeles Unified School District in the San Fernando Valley, Granada Hills was a prototypical "white flight" school of the 1970s. Parents who had enough money moved to places like Northridge, Woodland Hills, and Canoga Park to escape busing and the problems of downtown Los Angeles.

Granada Hills High was only twenty-eight miles from Crenshaw by freeway, but it might as well have been a million miles in terms of reality. Baseball was eventually dominated by schools from the Valley, where organization and constant practice were easier to maintain.

To put it another way, kids at Granada Hills dealt with buzz cuts. At Crenshaw, they dealt with bullets.

The march to the cultural collision continued. In the city semifinals, Crenshaw had to travel to the Valley, facing Monroe at Cal State Northridge. Monroe was no match, losing 10–7. In three playoff games, Crenshaw had now scored thirty-three runs and had drilled a team that beat Granada Hills twice during the season. Granada Hills continued to get by with a combination of good pitching, led by Stephens, and Stroh's bunt-and-run offense. The city finals were held at Dodger Stadium, which was significant for both teams in ways far beyond the fact that it was a Major League ballpark.

For black people in the 1960s and 1970s, Dodger Stadium was something of a shrine. The Dodgers were a symbol of equality, the team of Jackie Robinson. This was the organization that had the courage in 1947 to break the color barrier in baseball, which was America's biggest game at the time. Some black parents from around the country moved to Los Angeles in hopes that their baseball-playing sons would one day play for the team and in that stadium. For many parents and relatives of the Crenshaw baseball players, playing the city championship game there was a sign of hope.

But from a strategic standpoint, Dodger Stadium was the worst place for Crenshaw and the perfect place for Granada Hills. Dodger Stadium was where power hitters went to die. At 330 feet down the lines, 395 to the alleys, and 400 to dead center, the stadium's large expanses combined with the dead air of Los Angeles to make it a pitcher's park. The history of the Dodgers is littered with great hurlers, from Sandy Koufax and Don Drysdale to Don Sutton, Orel Hershiser, and Clayton Kershaw. Their talent was augmented by the pitcher-friendly confines. Crenshaw's power hitters were about to be neutralized and coach Brooks Hurst knew it. To this day, he's still annoyed at the situation.

"It's ridiculous they played a high school championship game in that park. It completely worked against us and the way we played," Hurst says nearly four decades later.

On June 6, 1979, Granada Hills and Crenshaw played in a title game wrapped in great drama: two top athletes facing off with a host of other talented players involved. Predominantly black inner-city school versus a bunch of suburban white kids. Power team versus little ball team. Few people expected it to be much of a matchup. Genovese thought Granada Hills had "no chance." Some people congratulated Hurst before the game, figuring Monroe had been the bigger threat in the semifinals. As the Crenshaw team made the nine-mile trek through downtown traffic to Dodger Stadium, players such as Strawberry shouted to people. The players told the passersby they should come watch the Cougars become L.A. champs. Almost 20,000 people showed up. It was a fantastic atmosphere.

As the sun began to set behind home plate, Strawberry's remarks didn't seem premature. Granada Hills grabbed a 2–0 lead, but Crenshaw responded with three runs in the top of the third to take a lead with one out. Stephens was wild and rattled, but got a second out. Stroh had a relief pitcher warming up when he marched to the mound to pull Stephens. Somewhere between the dugout and the mound, Stroh made a detour in his plan. Whatever it was, by the time Stroh got to the mound, he was pointing at Elway and saying, very simply, "You."

Elway was suddenly a pitcher again.

"As I was walking out there, it just came to me: I have to go to the toughest guy I know," Stroh says. "We're in a fight, we're going to bring a competitor. When you go to war, you take your biggest gun. The attitude John had, the competitiveness, the determination…that was more the deciding factor. In the toughest situation, who was going to give you the best chance to win? That's what I was thinking, and I started looking at him over at third base. John sort of had his back turned to me because I think he knew I was going to call on him. Deep down inside, I bet he loved it."

Elway thought Stroh was nuts, but he loved it.

"That was a pretty typical thing for Stroh to do to shake it up to get everybody's attention," Elway says. "But yeah, I wanted the ball. Who wouldn't?"

In Elway's world, pressure was to be embraced, not shunned. He loved being in control in the biggest moments. He lived for the competition. Preparation be damned, he was going to take his one-pitch arsenal and do whatever he could against Crenshaw's array of studs. In the stands, Jack didn't enjoy the moment quite as much. As Elway took his warm-ups, Jack walked up the stairs in the stands and lit up the first of many Marlboro Lights that night. Jack's usual two-pack habit went to four. Philip Morris stock was on the rise.

"Jack told me after the game when I put John in there, he became a nervous wreck. He said he had never walked that many stairs that many times going back and forth from his seat to the concourse where he could smoke," Stroh says.

On the mound, Elway somehow felt in control. The stage, as Strawberry alluded to, wasn't too big for Elway. Sure, he was in Dodger Stadium with 20,000 people watching and the city title on the line. Yes, Crenshaw had all these great hitters, starting with Strawberry. Yes, Crenshaw had dominated its competition and scored at least ten runs in each of three playoff games going into that night.

Thinking about any of that wasn't going to help Elway. Thinking about anything beyond the next pitch and what he had to do wasn't going to help. People have often asked Elway about how he handled big moments. His answer was that he blocked out as much as he could.

In football, it was easier because there's less time to think. There's a clock running, so you'd better be ready for the next play, no matter what's going on. Baseball has no clock. Baseball can drag until there is a flurry of action when the ball is hit. Your mind can drift to a thousand places other than the game itself. Or you can start to consider every option in the game, fretting too much. Baseball tests you mentally that way. Elway found out even more when he played minor league baseball for the New York Yankees a few years later. Even in only six weeks, he was mentally exhausted from the daily grind of playing baseball.

On that June 1979 night, standing on the mound in Dodger Stadium, the excitement of the moment took over. Elway hadn't pitched in two months, had been told he would never pitch again, and suddenly, on a coach's whim, was hurling fastballs.

And there was no place he'd rather be.

"He looked at me and said, 'We ain't losing this game,'" Ginnetti says.

"I learned to focus on one play at a time in that game," Elway says. "I hadn't pitched in so long, I had to just think about one pitch at a time. I couldn't get ahead of myself…we're playing in Dodger Stadium in front of a big crowd. I had to block it all out. If you start thinking about all that other stuff, you lose focus."

Elway struck out the first batter he faced, Carl Jones, for the final out of the third inning to get out of the jam. He then got through the fourth before things got dicey in the fifth. With Crenshaw still leading, 3–2, the Cougars got a hit and a walk to put two on with nobody out against Elway. That's when Strawberry came to the plate. Strawberry was up and behind him was the heart of the Crenshaw lineup, starting with Brown on deck. The table was set for a Crenshaw feast.

Fortunately for Granada Hills, Hurst had a different view of the situation. In Strawberry's previous at-bat, he had hit a long fly ball that died at the warning track in left field. Other Crenshaw hitters had come up short and Hurst was growing impatient. Hurst signaled to Strawberry to do the last thing anyone would have expected. Strawberry was so surprised he stepped out of the batter's box a second time after getting the sign.

"I thought the signs were wrong, so I stepped out and made sure I saw the signal again," Strawberry says.

Hurst was calling for Strawberry to bunt.

"The infamous bunt," Hurst says, the irritation still obvious years later. "I still hear to this day, 'You're the guy who had Strawberry bunt.' I'd do it again every time. We're playing in this big park, Granada had the infield way back and we had three guys behind Darryl who had hit .400 all season, two of them who hit .400 combined as juniors and seniors."

To this day, Strawberry has never questioned Hurst.

"I've never asked Brooks about that call," Strawberry says. "I love Brooks and everything he did for us, so I've just never wanted to bring it up. A lot of people don't give Brooks a lot of credit for what he did. A white man who came into the inner city and brought all these knuckle-heads, these hard heads, together. The reason we were so good was him. Brooks had taught us to play at such a high level, so I don't want to spoil that over one at-bat...but I was pretty furious at the time. I had never bunted to move the runners over, ever. I mean I bunted for a couple of base hits, but not a sacrifice. I'm pretty sure Granada Hills was over on the other side saying, 'Let him bunt.'"

Strawberry bunted too hard and right back to Elway, who threw to third to force the lead runner. After a runner was caught trying to steal third, Brown struck out. Suddenly, the momentum of the game shifted. Granada Hills was still behind, but Crenshaw wasn't the fearsome hitting force so many expected. The Cougars were a bunch of nervous teenagers, just like Granada Hills, and now they were playing the Highlanders' style.

Or as Brown said in *The Ticket Out*, "[Hurst] hadn't done nothing all year but let us loose like wild horses. And now he is making this man bunt? The Valley kids bunted; we did not bunt."

In the bottom of the fifth inning, Crenshaw unraveled. The Cougars made a second error. Strawberry started walking people and Granada Hills started bunting, running, and slapping the ball around. The Highlanders scored six runs on only three hits. They eventually built a 10–4 lead. From there, Elway was able to pound the strike zone with pitch after pitch. By the time Elway got to face Brown for the final out of the game, he struck him out again. Elway's last pitch was thrown as hard as he could possibly bring it, a high fastball Brown swung through. Elway pitched four and two-thirds innings in relief, giving up three hits along the way. That went along with his going nine for thirteen at the plate during the playoffs.

In the aftermath, Strawberry ran out to center field, disconsolate and in tears.

"It was like a knife got stuck in my gut, I cried so hard. I respect John Elway. He shut us down, so he had to be something special. To think about him at that age, it was so impressive. I've seen him a few times over the years and he's always a gentleman about it. He shakes my hand. I always like to say, 'Man, you broke my heart in high school.' But after seeing what he did to so many teams in the NFL over his career, I don't take it personally. That's what John did his whole career," Strawberry says.

Elway had just helped Granada Hills win back-to-back titles and won his second City Player of the Year Award. The best part is that the school did it with almost completely different teams. It was the first great example to Elway that making big changes on a team didn't mean winning was impossible. How to win might just require a different plan. It also sent Elway to Stanford feeling confident—so confident he told Major League Baseball scouts to pass on him in the draft. Kansas City took a flyer on him in the eighteenth round, but Elway had no desire to sign.

"Elway told me, 'George, don't draft me. Don't waste a draft pick. I have a scholarship to Stanford and I'm going to play football,'" Genovese says. "He said, 'Call me crazy, but I want to play four years of college ball.' I knew the young man and I took him to be honest. He was a man of his word. Now, I know the Yankees drafted him a couple of years later and he signed. But coming out of high school, I appreciated what he had to say."

Elway thought great things were about to happen at the college level and hopefully beyond. Little did he know it was going to take almost two decades to win another championship.

CHAPTER 9

EARLY SIGNS OF TROUBLE

Stanford was perfect with one exception—the football.

And even that wasn't noticeable right away. What was obvious to anyone was Elway's immense talent. When he arrived on campus in July 1979 for football practice, everyone took notice, from players to coaches to reporters.

Within the team, things couldn't have gone much better for Elway. With reporters' constantly asking whether he would displace senior Turk Schonert as the starter, Dowhower did his best to manage the situation. Some problems solved themselves. Shortly after the team began practicing, two other quarterbacks (Babe Laufenberg and Grayson Rogers) transferred.

"I remember seeing John when he was in high school," says Laufenberg, who was also from the San Fernando Valley and later became the Most Valuable Player at Indiana during his senior year. "When he threw the ball, it was like in a video game where the ball moves at light speed."

Despite the affirmation, Elway didn't seem to understand he was doing well.

"He would do something just about every day where we would look at each other and say, 'Did you just see that?'" says offensive tackle Brian Holloway, an eventual first-round draft pick. "Then he'd look at the older guys and ask, 'Am I doing OK?' We would just shake our heads and say, 'Yeah, John, you're doing fine, don't worry.' He was just ridiculous."

The "Elway Cross" quickly became a thing around the team. That was the little red X that would be left on a receiver's chest from where the ball would hit when it wasn't caught cleanly. Elway could split the skin between his receiver's fingers as well.

That wasn't necessarily unique among quarterbacks.

But turning a football into a Cuisinart blade might have been.

Don Lonsinger and Elway were teammates, classmates, roommates, and frat brothers at Stanford. Lonsinger was a wide receiver. On the second day of practice as freshmen in 1979, Lonsinger ran a pattern as Elway dropped to throw. Linebacker Chuck Evans deflected the pass ever so slightly before the ball got to Lonsinger.

"It's a one-hundred-mile-per-hour wounded duck coming at me," Lonsinger says. "I reach back, but I can't catch it. I feel this pain in my pinkie like I jammed it. I looked down and all I see is white with blood starting to drip. I realize that's bone. My pinkie is broken in half and the only thing holding the top part of the finger to my hand is this flap of skin."

Lonsinger didn't scream. None of the players or coaches found out what had happened until after practice. He put his hand behind his back, went over to the trainers, and told them he had a problem.

"There were three trainers. When two of them went behind me to look at it, I heard two gasps and an 'Oh my God.' I was in surgery by that night and my season was over," says Lonsinger, whose pinkie looks like a fishhook to this day. All the tiny tendons basically exploded and couldn't be repaired, so it's stuck in a curved shape.

Stories about Elway's velocity became replete. Even Hall of Fame receivers were reticent to work with Elway. Former Stanford wide receiver James Lofton showed up one off-season to work out on campus and spent a day with Elway. Lofton was the number six overall pick by Green Bay in the 1978 NFL Draft. He played sixteen years and earned just about every accolade imaginable in college and the NFL. He was also a great track athlete, as both a sprinter and a long jumper. In 1978, he won the NCAA long jump championship. As Lofton started running routes for Elway, Elway literally knocked him over with a throw.

"I was done with that in a hurry," Lofton says. "John was tearing up my hands. I walked out and said, 'I'm not doing this again.'"

Elway went back to his buddies and brashly said, "James Lofton sucks." His buddies started ripping Elway. Then there was the time running back Darrin Nelson taught Elway a lesson about how to throw a short pass. Nelson was a great receiving back and eventually a first-round pick in the NFL. He missed Elway's freshman season with a knee injury, but then returned in 1980.

Elway threw a screen pass to Nelson during a practice that season.

"I saw the throw and I didn't even stick my hands out," Nelson says. "I just watched it zoom right past me. That thing would have broken every finger on my hands. I just looked back at John and said, 'You don't expect me to catch that, do you?' Everybody laughed. John was a little mad at me, but that was ridiculous."

There was also Elway's interesting courtship with his first wife, Janet. She was a great athlete in her own right. She was a world-class swimmer until she got hurt. In September 1979, before the two met as freshmen, she won the 400-meter individual medley at the World University Games in Mexico City. The two met that fall. They liked each other immediately, if not somewhat awkwardly. Elway would bring a tennis ball every time he went by Janet's room, tossing it against a wall to cover up how nervous he was talking to her. As their first date ended with a kiss, their teeth collided with a click. Embarrassed, Janet scurried back into her dorm room and shut the door in humiliation. It was a cute and minor faux pas, especially compared to what was about to happen.

One day, the couple decided to play catch. Elway was throwing lightly. Janet said, "Come on, John, throw it!"

Elway threw a little harder.

She egged him on again. He threw a little harder.

Finally, she said something to the effect of, "Oh, come on, John, throw the heat."

Elway put a little more mustard on the throw, still leaving it well short of bone-splitting speed. Janet ended up with a broken pinkie that looks just like Lonsinger's fishhook.

Aside from all of that, Elway did his best to fit in freshman year. That started with his uniform. Elway had worn number eleven in high school, but senior Rick Gervais wore it. Instead of big-timing an older player, Elway switched to number seven and it stuck for the rest of his football career. Dowhower worked Elway in slowly, but it was clear he was going to play. Schonert was a good soldier about the situation because Dowhower was careful not to push the senior aside even when it was clear the coach could have done it.

"This was John Elway we're talking about," Schonert says. "Look, I was pretty confident about my ability, but then you see someone like that and you realize what true greatness looks like. John was good about it. Obviously, he knew he was good and he wanted to play, but he wasn't a jerk."

Stanford went 5–5–1 in Elway's freshman year, and Elway played a big role in an upset of UCLA and Bruins quarterback Tom Ramsey. Stanford also tied then–number one USC in Los Angeles. Elway ended up throwing ninety-six passes that season, and there seemed like a lot of good things to build on.

Then came the first indication that all was not well for the program. Stanford turned down a chance to appear in the Astro-Bluebonnet Bowl because the game wasn't to the school's standard. At least that's what Elway was told. Geiger had become the athletic director at Stanford in 1979 and wasn't part of the group that pushed for Dowhower to succeed Walsh. Geiger started talking to players and built a case to fire Dowhower.

Elway learned an important lesson in the process.

"If you're looking to get rid of a coach, it's not hard. You're going to find plenty of guys who don't like the coaches," he says. "They're not playing, they're not happy, but they're also probably not working hard."

Ultimately, what Geiger did wasn't helping the team. Instead, it allowed the inmates to run the asylum. Geiger was hurting the program by undermining the coaches. At the end of the day, Dowhower was out and Geiger had control. Years later, Geiger pulled the same thing with Elway's dad. Geiger started talking to players again and then ordered Jack to fire two assistant coaches. When Jack refused, Geiger fired him.

During Geiger's twelve-year tenure as athletic director, the Stanford football team went to only one bowl game and had only two winning seasons. It also left the Elway family bitter with Geiger and the school. Elway didn't attend a Stanford event until after Geiger left in 1991. At one point, there was a portrait done of Elway and his father. John was in his Stanford uniform and Jack in a Stanford coaching jacket and hat. The Stanford Quad and Hoover Tower were in the background. After Jack's dismissal, the Elways had the portrait repainted with Jack wearing his San Jose State coaching jacket and hat.

Paul Wiggin succeeded Dowhower beginning in the 1980s season. Wiggin was a fine man and had played in the NFL. He was a Stanford alum, so he fit the image of what everybody thought the school needed. The problem was that Wiggin didn't necessarily fight against the culture of the school.

Beyond Geiger, Stanford had trouble dealing with success in football at the time. Whenever the football program started to become good, the academic side of the school got edgy about it. It was a classic philosophical push and pull over wanting to be good in football but not be known as a football school. The history of the Stanford football program to that point was consistently inconsistent. The team would go to bowl games for a couple of seasons and then quickly return to being bad. The school would then get embarrassed, improve the program, and then continue the cycle.

What Elway thought was a building process under Walsh toward something special was really a cresting wave about to crash. Back-to-back bowl games and then landing the biggest recruit in the country was just a little too much football success for the school at the time. Support for the program dwindled, and Wiggin wasn't going to ruffle feathers in the administration by pushing for players. When some players complained about needing time to study for exams instead of practice, the school would side with the players instead of telling them they also had to make a commitment to the football program.

"It was incredibly frustrating for the coaches," says Jim Fassel, who was an assistant under Dowhower and stayed to become the offensive coordinator under Wiggin. "We're trying to tell the players, 'Hey, you're at Stanford, you're here because you're special and capable of handling the workload.' We're pushing them to be great in both because that's what it takes, but then the administration comes in and tells us to back off."

Stanford ended up with a fair number of players who got into school, realized football really wasn't their future, and needed to concentrate more on their degree. Put it all together and the quality of the football suffered. That showed up in a lot of difficult losses, including against Elway's father, Jack, and San Jose State. It also culminated in one of the most embarrassing losses in college history to finish Elway's career.

Not that Elway realized it at the time. He was in college. He was playing the two sports he loved. He had a girlfriend and his family lived just down the road. In many ways, his life was idyllic. Elway became particularly close with baseball players such as Vince "V-Sak" Sakowski and Mike Aldrete. During Christmas break as freshmen, the three of them went on a road trip in Aldrete's silver 1974 Camaro. The first stop, however, was in San Jose for the trio to get the once-over from Jack.

"You could see right there how important it was for John to see his dad," Aldrete says. "We didn't have an itinerary, no plan, nothing. We're just winging it. But there was one thing we had to do before we went anywhere. We had to drive down to San Jose and see Jack. It was imperative we go see Jack.

"The relationship John had with Jack was the kind I would hope to have with my son.... [Jack] was a mentor, a guy John could trust to get the truth. I remember my dad said to me when I was fourteen, 'You're beyond anything I can do with you baseball-wise, so go and talk to other people.' With John, his dad was the combination of a loving father, football mentor, and friend, all rolled up in one."

After a stop in Fresno, the trio eventually made it to Bakersfield, where V-Sak was from, then continued farther south to see some other friends. The guys would hit and throw in the morning before heading off for whatever the day would allow. After lunch one day, they hit Interstate 5 south with the plan to make it to Orange County. V-Sak dropped in a thick wad of chewing tobacco as they started the quick climb up the Grapevine, a winding, hilly portion of I-5 that connects the southern end of the San Joaquin Valley to the northern end of the San Fernando Valley. It's steep at the beginning, quickly rising almost 1,500 feet.

The combination of the chew, the winding road, and the elevation made V-Sak queasy as he sat in the back seat. He beckoned Elway to pull over.

"Dude, can't pull over. Too dangerous," Elway said.

V-Sak, who uses the F-bomb the way most people blink, threw a stream of invectives at Elway, whose ears were now popping from the elevation gain. As a result, Elway claimed he couldn't make out what V-Sak was saying. The next sound was V-Sak throwing up lunch all over his clothes. Elway finally pulled over. He and Aldrete were doubled over in laughter as V-Sak got out of the car, stripped down on the side of the highway and tossed his vomit-soaked clothes in the scraggly bushes. He got back in the car in just his underwear, dug out some sweats, and MF'd Elway and Aldrete the entire time.

"You got me, dickhead," V-Sak said.

By the end of his freshman year, Elway had fully bought in to the program. He stayed on campus instead of living at home and roomed with Margerum. The pair lived on the second floor of a building known as "The Track House" at the time. It was near all the athletic facilities. The term "house" is generous. It was more like a shack. The place has long since been torn down.

When Elway and Margerum roomed together, buddies would drop by and, at a certain point, there was a tall pile of empty beer cans in a corner of the room. No one is quite sure how the cans got there, but college is loaded with hooligans. One day, Elway and Margerum cleaned up the cans and discovered roughly a half-dozen dead rats.

As they say, alcohol is a killer.

Elway and Margerum determined the rats were "trophy" kills and hatched the genius idea to tack them up to the wall by their tails.

"We obviously weren't doing too well with the ladies," Margerum says.

CHAPTER 10

ELWAY VERSUS ELWAY

In 1981, Jack had to do something he hated: attack his wounded son.

Stanford annually hosted San Jose State in football, and the game became known as the Elway Bowl for the three years Elway started for the Cardinal and Jack coached the Spartans. San Jose State won two of the three games. The family hated everything about it. The Elway women—wife, Jan, and daughters, Lee Ann and Jana—would sit in the stands in cute shirts with both teams' logos emblazoned. They'd smile for the cameras in hopes the photographers would leave quickly. Then they'd count down the minutes until the game was done.

"We just wanted to get it over with," Jan says.

That was particularly the case in 1981.

Stanford was ranked number nineteen going into the season. John was in his second year as the starter, and optimism was high that the team would be a bowl contender. Stanford opened the season with an upset loss at Purdue University and then was set to host San Jose State. Worse, John suffered an ugly ankle sprain against Purdue. He was on crutches for four days. Jack didn't want his son to play. The more times Jack mentioned that maybe John shouldn't play, the more resolute his son became about playing.

The bigger issue for Jack was that he knew how San Jose State's defense was going to have to play. On Monday before the game, San Jose State defensive coordinator Claude Gilbert asked Jack to go for a drink. That wasn't necessarily unusual, but the topic of discussion was. They went to the S&H Keyes Club in San Jose at the corner of Keyes Street and Ninth Street, a hangout where the coaching staff regularly got together for a few laughs between practice and evening meetings. Jack wasn't in a laughing mood pretty much for the entire week. He knew his son was going to ignore his injury and play. He also knew what Gilbert had planned. Gilbert just wanted to make sure Jack was OK with the plan.

"I could tell Jack was nervous about the game," says Gilbert, who was in his first season working for Jack. "Jack got a martini and was sipping on it while he smoked a cigarette. After a minute or two, I said, 'Jack, I know this game is hard on you. But if we're going to have a chance to win, we're going to have to put pressure on John and we're going to have to hit him. A lot.'

"Jack took another sip on his martini and then another drag on his cigarette. Jack was a sipper. He'd really work on those martinis, take a long time to drink 'em. He told stories the same way, really work them. He didn't say anything for a few seconds, just looked straight ahead. Finally, he said, 'Yeah, God damn it, Claude, I know. But I don't want to hear about it.' We didn't talk about it again, ever."

Jack kept nudging John to not play. It was futile. This was the young man who used to cry over ping pong as a child playing against his father. John wasn't backing down from this battle. The worst part was that Stanford's offensive system didn't feature an adjustment for when the defense blitzed. Essentially, the idea was that Elway would make a move to get out of trouble with his superior scrambling ability.

With a bad ankle, it wasn't much of a plan.

"When [Elway] took off, he almost always went left. It just so happened we had a linebacker on that side who was pretty quick, a guy named Bob Overly. He was quick and he played on the edge [mentally]. He's one of those guys every team needs to have to get everybody going. But he was also one of those guys you had to watch so he wouldn't go over the edge," Gilbert says.

Overly crossed the line constantly. In practice, defensive players weren't supposed to hit the quarterback in live drills. One day, Overly nailed scout team quarterback Jack Overstreet, who was all of five-foot-eleven and 190 pounds. The coaches started yelling at Overly, reminding him the quarterback was off-limits in practice. Overly listened carefully, lined up for the next play, and hit Overstreet again, starting a fight and getting kicked out of practice. If you were looking for a guy who didn't think anything was sacred—from his teammates to his coach's son—Overly was your man.

Knowing Elway's tendency to go left, Gilbert set up all the blitzes to attack him from his right side. Gilbert then instructed Overly to wait to rush Elway until after Elway started to scramble left. Overly had a career game, sacking Elway four times. Stanford tried to draw new plays on the sideline to adjust for the blitzes. They didn't work. At one point in the third quarter, Elway looked at teammate and fullback Rob Moore and just yelled, "Block that guy!"

Between Gilbert's plan and Elway's ankle, San Jose State had a recipe for a blowout win. The final score was 28–6. Elway was sacked eight times and completed only six of twenty-four passes for seventy-two yards and five interceptions. It was the worst statistical game of his college career. Jack hated every minute of it. By the end of the third quarter, he was screaming at anybody who would listen to get his son out of the game. He waved a white towel at Stanford coach Paul Wiggin, who didn't get the message. Eventually he got on the headset with the San Jose State defensive coaches and told them to stop blitzing. It was out of fear as much as compassion.

"Jan is going to kill me," he said to his staff.

He also yelled at his son.

"John, will you stop scrambling and just throw the ball," he said.

Elway shot back at his dad, "I'll stop scrambling if you stop blitzing." There might have been a profanity in there somewhere.

The signature moment came in the fourth quarter when Overly sacked Elway for his fourth and final time. As Elway went to the ground, Overly grabbed the little towel Elway kept tucked in his uniform pants to dry his hands. Overly jumped up and started snapping the towel at Elway.

The moment hit a nerve for Jack.

"Jack yelled at me to take Overly out of the game. I waited until the next series to ask him if I could put the kid back in. Jack calmed down by then, but he was really upset. The game got out of hand," Gilbert says.

After the game, Jack came over and wrapped his arm around his son and they walked off the field. To outsiders, it looked loving and tender. Really, it was more Jack looking for cover from his angry wife. Later, Jack found John outside the Stanford locker room.

"Hey, what are you doing tonight?" Jack said.

Elway was planning to lick his wounds with some pizza and beer back at the Delta Tau Delta house, the fraternity he had joined that year. On top of that, Elway had some business to deal with the following day. The New York Yankees had drafted Elway the previous June. Yankees vice president of baseball operations Bill Bergesch had flown to California that weekend to work out the final details of a minor league contract for Elway. The Yankees had until Monday to sign Elway or lose his rights. Elway wanted to take a night to decompress before sitting down with Bergesch. He told Jack no thanks.

"How about just for dinner?" Jack said.

Nah, Elway just wanted to relax.

Jack then became desperate.

"No, John, you have to come home tonight. Otherwise, your mom's not letting me back in the house," Jack said.

John dined at home with his family that night.

That didn't solve the lingering pain for Jack. That had to wait until the next day during San Jose State's film review. All the players gathered in a big room as the film played on a sixteen-millimeter projector, the kind that made a click, click, click sound as the tape went through and the motor hummed. As they got to the play when Overly sacked Elway and grabbed the towel, the players laughed.

Jack went silent, rewound the tape, and played it again. And again. And again. And again. The idea that his players took joy in mocking his son gnawed at Jack's soul.

"Jack must have rewound the tape thirty or forty times over the next fifteen minutes, playing the play over and over and over," Clarkson says.

The first couple of times, the guys kept giggling. Then it got quiet and then it went dead silent except for the sound of the projector. All you could hear was the clicking. He just played it over and over. That was difficult.

Jack finally turned off the projector and told us to go out on the field. We didn't even finish watching the rest of the game. He flushed the whole thing right there and didn't dwell on it. But you knew it hurt him. At that moment, you just understood the pain of competing like that against your own son.

CHAPTER 11

UPS, DOWNS, AND AN AWFUL ENDING

Elway's college career was a roller coaster that ended in chaos.

Literally.

For every glorious moment Stanford had with Elway, there were endless letdowns. That began from the moment he took over as the starter during the 1980 season, when Stanford was ranked number fifteen in the preseason polls. During a 4–1 start, Stanford went to Oklahoma to face the number four–ranked Sooners. Oklahoma had a great team and finished the year ranked number three. But on that rainy September day, Elway was spectacular as Stanford dominated for a 31–14 victory. He threw twenty-five passes in the first half to build a lead before Stanford played keep-away in the second half.

Afterward, Oklahoma coach Barry Switzer was concise with his superlatives.

"Elway put on the best show I've ever seen," Switzer said.

Elway quickly established himself as a leader that season. The lone loss during the 4–1 start was at Boston College. It was a tight game early and offensive lineman Ken Orvick was playing for the first time. Stanford also had senior left tackle Brian Holloway, who ended up being a first-round pick by New England after that season. He played eight years in the NFL and was a three-time Pro Bowler.

Holloway took great pride in understanding how to play with a quarterback like Elway, who wasn't necessarily going to stay in the pocket all the time. Holloway studied Elway's movements and how defensive linemen reacted to Elway so he could figure out what was going on behind him. He protected Elway's blindside in the formations and watched out for him, generally.

Early in the game, Elway ran out of bounds at the Boston College fifteen-yard line. A Boston College defender hit Elway as he went out. Holloway thought it was a late hit and came over to defend Elway. Holloway ended up getting a fifteen-yard penalty for unsportsmanlike conduct. The ball was put back at the Boston College thirty-yard line. Good intentions by Holloway, but bad timing.

Elway screamed at Holloway in the heat of the moment.

"I'm looking at John [scream at Holloway] and his eyes were so wide. You could just see the intensity pouring out of him," Orvick says. "All that backgammon and ping pong and playing cards . . . as intense as that was, it was nothing compared to this. Here's a sophomore quarterback screaming at a senior, and a damn good senior at that. Brian is six-foot-seven and just massive and John didn't have any fear of taking charge of Brian."

Holloway understood.

"Greatness demands that level of intensity," Holloway says. "I understood exactly what John was saying. This was his team and he was taking control. He was taking responsibility. As a football player, you have to be tough and physical. More than that, you have to be smart. John was all of those things and that's the only way you lead. He demanded it of the people around him, but he demanded it of himself first."

That 4–1 start slipped away and Stanford finished 6–5, losing the season finale in the annual Big Game against Cal and losing an invitation to the Peach Bowl. Missing out on bowl games became a theme for Elway and Stanford.

Individually, Elway's talent and performance were recognized. He was named the Pacific-10 Conference Player of the Year twice, broke a host of school and conference passing records, and finished second in the Heisman Trophy voting in 1982. Mostly, however, it was disappointment. Even as Stanford was mired in mediocrity, Elway's talent was undeniable.

In a blowout loss to USC in 1980, Elway stunned one of the most talented teams in the history of the game on one amazing play.

The 1980 USC Trojans finished only 8–2–1, but the roster was loaded. L-O-A-D-E-D.

That USC team included eight eventual first-round picks, including five top-ten picks. Four of the five starting offensive linemen were first-round picks. Three of the four starting defensive backs (Ronnie Lott, Dennis Smith, and Joey Browner) were first-round picks. That team also included three players who were eventually first-ballot Pro Football Hall of Famers (Lott, Bruce Matthews, and Marcus Allen). To put it in perspective, as of 2019, there were fewer than a hundred men who made the Pro Football Hall of Fame on the first ballot. Three of them were playing together for the 1980 USC Trojans.

Suffice to say, it was a tough afternoon for Stanford, losing 34–9. But it was Elway who provided the signature moment of the game. On one play, Elway was able to escape the pass rush of USC defensive lineman George Achica. Elway did a clockwise spin move. The move was commonly called the "Elway Spin." Elway would dip his front shoulder ever so slightly as the defender would run at him from the blind side and then spin, as if he were a matador spinning away from a bull. It was a move reminiscent of Fran Tarkenton from the 1970s. Elway perfected it with his unusual sense of timing and quickness.

Elway escaped to his right and looked for a receiver. As he looked, Achica chased him again. Elway escaped a second time and came back to his left. By the time Elway made the second escape and got back to midfield, the play had lasted more than ten seconds. That's an eternity in football. The crowd of 85,799 was now on its feet. This play had become a spectacle.

Normally, the rule in football when the quarterback breaks the pocket is that the receivers are supposed to come back toward him to make it easier for him to find one of them. Stanford's rule with Elway was the exact opposite. If Elway scrambled, receivers were told to run deep and not stop. There was no outrunning an Elway throw. That sounds simple, but receivers who have been trained for years to come back to the quarterback often had trouble breaking instinct. That's where wide receiver Ken Margerum got involved. Margerum followed the rule perfectly and just kept going and going until he couldn't go any farther. Elway was standing at roughly the Stanford forty-yard line and Margerum was in the back of the end zone, almost seventy yards away.

In between was Lott, standing at roughly the USC ten-yard line, confident he had the play covered.

"I just let Margerum run by because there's no way Elway is going to throw it to him," Lott recalls more than thirty years later. "No way. There are physics involved in throwing a football that far. It has to have a certain arc and I know as a high-level athlete if he throws it there, it will have an arc on it and I'll be able to go knock it down.

"But then you discover that one athlete who can do things no other athlete can do. It's like someone scoring 100 points in a basketball game or somebody running as fast as Renaldo Nehemiah. They are just exceptions. To this day, I still can't believe that throw. Again, there are rules of physics that say you can't throw a pass from Point A to Point B like that. He threw it and I couldn't catch up to it. Everything in my calculations was wrong."

Lott eventually caught up with Margerum, making a vicious hit just after the catch. Years later, people asked Elway to name his favorite throw of his career.

That's it.

There were other times Elway was able to show off his arm. Many of those chances came in baseball. Stanford enjoyed more success in baseball than football with Elway. Stanford baseball coach Mark Marquess had players such as V-Sak, Aldrete, Steve Buechele, Darryl Stephens, Eric Hardgrave, and Mike Dotterer. Along with Elway, that group turned the program around. It wasn't always easy, such as when they were freshmen in spring 1980 and Arizona State coach Jim Brock ran up the score for a 34–2 win. The game was televised by ESPN. Stanford thought Brock wanted to send some type of message. He had his team stealing bases when it was leading by twenty runs. All he did was amp Stanford's talented freshmen.

The next season, Arizona State played at Stanford. The Sun Devils had speedy future major leaguer Ricky Nelson on second base with none out. When the batter hit a fly ball to Elway at the warning track in right field, Nelson tagged up and ran at three-quarter speed to third. Elway threw out Nelson for the second out. Brock was standing at the top of the dugout steps, his mouth agape. With two out, the next hitter singled to right. Elway jogged in slowly, making it appear he was going to lob the ball into second base. When the runner rounded first base a little too far, Elway threw behind him for the third out.

"In all my years in baseball or watching baseball, I've never seen that before or since where an outfielder dominates a single inning like that with his arm," former Stanford assistant baseball coach Dean Stotz says.

Or there was the time in May 1981 when Stanford made it to the NCAA regional title game against the University of Texas. The game was in Austin, Texas, where the fans were rowdy. They talked trash and started early, bringing the noise even in warm-ups. It was an awesome college atmosphere. When Stanford took the field for pregame drills, Elway's arm silenced the crowd.

"John put on a show," Marquess says. "When we got done, the Texas fans gave him a standing ovation. I've never seen anything like that."

Marquess had a long line of great players, from Buechele to Aldrete to Mike Mussina to Jeffrey Hammonds to Jack McDowell to Mark Appel.

"People ask me all the time who was the best player I've coached. I can't answer that. I really can't do it," Marquess says. "But if you ask me who had the best arm—and I've had a lot of kids who can throw—there's no question about it. It's John Elway and it's not even close."

As Elway bounced back and forth between spring football practice and the baseball season in 1981, he hit .361 with nine home runs and fifty runs batted in forty-nine games. In June 1981, he was drafted in the second round of the Major League Baseball draft by the New York Yankees, signing with them the following September.

In 1982, the baseball team rolled on without Elway and continued to rewrite school history. Stanford made it to the College World Series for the first time under Marquess. Over his forty-year career, Marquess led Stanford to the College World Series fourteen times and won two championships. Marquess also put a premium on making sure his players graduated. Over that period, every player who stayed at least three years with Marquess ended up with a degree.

"To me, it's a sin if you don't get a degree from Stanford," Marquess says.

To Elway, that was a symbol of dedication to doing things right. It set a standard by which he operated his athletic and business careers. Elway was also surrounded by people with high expectations like Marquess. From athletes to the son or daughter of world leaders to a twenty-year-old who came up with a treatment regimen for cancer while in high school, Stanford had no shortage of interesting people.

Including Rob Moore.

Moore was a lot of things. First, he was a fullback on the football team who often blocked for Elway. Second, he was a guy Elway's dad refused to let Elway room with in college. At least at first. Moore knew how to push boundaries better than just about any human being. Moore could shotgun a beer in milliseconds, going through a six-pack at a time. He wasn't afraid to pilfer a keg from another dorm's party. He once invited himself and others to a football recruiting dinner at the Sundance Mine Company restaurant. The dinner budget was supposed to be about $400. With Moore ordering drinks, the bill got to about $1,000.

That was the last recruiting dinner done without supervision.

As a freshman, Moore would occasionally walk naked through another dorm. He drove the athletic department so crazy the coaches threatened to kick him out of school halfway through freshman year. At Elway's first wedding, Moore broke out in laughter when the bagpipes started. Elway's first wife, Janet, is Scottish, so the bagpipes were played out of tradition.

"When bagpipes first start, it sounds like flatulence," Moore says, defending his adolescent humor years later.

Another thing Moore did was help his buddies graduate. He then simultaneously got his law degree and master's degree in business administration from the University of Southern California. He graduated near the top of his law class and with a 4.0 in business school. And he probably made more money than all of them. The same guy who intimidated other students with semi-Neanderthal behavior was also a genius. Elway spent many a night before an exam going over material with Moore.

"School just came naturally to me," Moore says. "I'd show up for the first couple of lectures and figure out the goal of the class. I'd spend about ten hours getting ready for the midterm and then another ten for the final and I'd be OK."

There was the time Orvick signed up late for a summer class on European economics. The day before the final, Orvick went to Moore for help.

"He went through the textbook and said, 'OK, this, this, and this are going to be on the final,'" Orvick says. "I spent the night learning that and showed up for the class the next day. The professor didn't even recognize me when I went to get the test. He gave me this look like, 'Who the hell are you?'

"I ended up getting a B-plus."

If only football had been half that easy for Stanford. Stanford's number nineteen preseason ranking in 1981 faded to humiliation with Elway's ankle injury. The team started 0–4 and finished 4–8. But Elway's senior season in 1982 held great hope. He was a Heisman Trophy favorite and Stanford had a senior-laden team. Stanford started 3–1 with wins at Purdue and on national television at Ohio State. The win over the Buckeyes was one of the best games Stanford played in Elway's four years. Down 13–0 entering the second half, Stanford rallied to get within 20–16 when Elway threw an interception that looked like it was going to end the game.

Stanford got the ball back with an interception by Kevin Baird with 1:38 remaining. Stanford drove eighty yards as Emile Harry caught an eighteen-yard touchdown pass in the right side of the end zone after Elway had scrambled almost all the way to the left sideline. Elway completed thirty-five of sixty-three passes for 407 yards. Coincidentally, the NFL happened to be on strike at the time. Denver Broncos public relations man Jim Saccomano was away that weekend with his wife. He was watching the Stanford–Ohio State game, completely unaware about how intertwined his life was about to become with Elway.

"I was watching the game and it was like John Elway against the entire Ohio State team," Saccomano says.

In late October, Stanford looked like it was finally going to have a breakthrough season with Elway. On October 30, Stanford beat number two–ranked Washington, 43–31, in a dominant performance at Stanford Stadium. Stanford was 5–3. Elway, who ended up tied for the NCAA Division I lead in touchdown passes that season with twenty-four, was a slight favorite over Georgia running back Herschel Walker for the Heisman Trophy. The priority was to finally get to a bowl game. Stanford had to win one of its final three games. But the Cardinal suffered a two-touchdown loss to Arizona and a three-point loss to number twelve UCLA.

That left the 1982 Big Game at rival Cal.

That game is somewhat well-known in sports history. Something about the Cal players' running back a kickoff through the Stanford Band for a touchdown to end the game. The return is known simply as "The Play" and might be the most famous finish in college football history.

The game itself was a classic even before the crazy finish. Members of the Hall of Fame Classic bowl game were in attendance to give Stanford a bid if it won. The Hall of Fame Classic desperately wanted to have Elway to sell the game, but 5–5 Stanford had to have a winning record. The game was close throughout and featured its share of questionable calls and mini controversies.

The buildup to The Play featured one of the greatest drives of Elway's life. Stanford was down 19–17 in the final two minutes and faced fourth-and-seventeen from its own thirteen-yard line. In the huddle, emotions were amped. This rivalry predates 1900 and the two schools are at polar ends of the elitist realm. Cal is the bastion of liberal, public-school thought. Stanford is the definition of private-school conservatism.

To put it another way, Stanford creates jobs to keep Cal grads employed. The intense jealousy would play out in the game, such as Cal students' using giant Funnelators to fire oranges and apples at the Stanford Band during halftime. In turn, the band would bring lacrosse players to catch the fruit and occasionally fire it back in the stands.

As Stanford came to the line for the fourth-down play, Memorial Stadium rattled with sound. There was a called play, but coaches don't draw up a lot of fourth-and-seventeen situations. It was pretty much everybody go long and hope the protection was good. As the players broke the huddle, Elway screamed, "Just get open."

Harry did. He ran down the right seam for twenty-nine yards and a first down as Elway fired a tracer bullet Harry caught with a leaping effort. The Stanford sideline erupted in joy and Cal's sideline went quiet. Stanford drove the rest of the way to get in position for a thirty-five-yard field goal. The Cardinal even called a couple of running plays to use the clock to make sure Cal didn't get another possession.

Stanford called time-out one last time, kicker Mark Harmon made the field goal, and Stanford won the game. Yes, Stanford won. The score was 20–19 after Elway led the most dramatic drive of his college career. Elway was finally going to play in a bowl game.

Except for one little detail. Stanford had called time-out to set up the field goal with eight seconds remaining. After the field goal was converted, there were still four seconds left and Stanford had to kick off. That set the stage for the nightmare play and a brutally bitter ending to a college career.

To begin, Stanford was penalized fifteen yards for unsportsmanlike conduct after the field goal when the players rushed the field. Stanford had to kick off from its twenty-five-yard line. Stanford squibbed it and Cal started lateraling. Stanford had Cal down at least once, but the refs missed the call and there was no replay at the time. As that was happening, the Stanford Band and a bunch of fans started running on the field. Cal fans did, too, but the refs missed that.

By the end of the five laterals, Cal's Kevin Moen ran through the band and knocked over Stanford band trombone player Gary Tyrrell, a moment that added insult to Stanford's agony and humiliation. The refs took all of twenty-seven seconds to sort out the play before signaling touchdown. In its own way, the game was a repeat of what happened to Elway's father years before when Washington played Washington State in the Apple Cup. The aftermath has been retold a thousand times. There was an ESPN Classic show done on The Play. Various YouTube videos of it have been viewed more than ten million times.

There was extreme anger in the Stanford locker room. Mike Wyman, Elway's frat brother and a mammoth human being, head-butted the door to the visiting locker room. This was one of those heavy wooden doors that had been there since the beginning of time. Wyman knocked it off the hinges.

Elway was stunned and bitter. He said the event "ruined my last game as a college football player," a comment some critics took to be petulant. The loss meant Elway, who had come to Stanford with dreams of playing in the Rose Bowl and possibly fighting for a national championship, never played in a bowl game during his tenure.

The loss also assured Walker would win the Heisman Trophy.

The Stanford locker room never really calmed down. Some guys were yelling. Some did a slow burn. The players eventually got on the buses to head back to Stanford. As they sat waiting to leave, a Cal fan came up to the bus and started giving them crap. When he started pounding on a window next to where Moore was sitting, Moore took his dip cup of tobacco juice and threw it in the guy's face.

"That one hurt a lot and it took a lot of years to get over it," Elway says. "But the more time goes by and the farther you get away from it, it starts to get funny. I can laugh about it. A little."

In 2007, Elway went to San Francisco to film a special for the twenty-fifth anniversary of the game. Moen was there and they chatted. Tyrrell was there. So was Joe Starkey, the Cal announcer who made the famous emotional call at the end of the game.

"Here we are talking about this game he lost and people are coming up to John the whole time asking for autographs and pictures," Tyrrell says. "I realized pretty quickly how that must have gotten old for him a long time ago. But he was so gracious. We talked a little. It was the first time we ever met."

All those years later, Elway had one question for Tyrrell.

"I just remember he said, 'What if the band had tackled Moen?'"

CHAPTER 12

KILL OR BE KILLED

While football had its disappointment, college life off the field had plenty of humor.

John Belushi–type humor.

During Elway's first two years at Stanford, he lived in a freshman dorm and then spent his sophomore year living in an area of campus known as Manzanita Park. It was a fancy name for a trailer park. Literally, a trailer park. The university brought in the trailers as temporary student housing while it raised money for a new dorm. The trailers were supposed to be there for five years. They lasted roughly thirteen. Each trailer housed four students and featured three bedrooms, a living room, a kitchen, and two bathrooms.

Athletes, particularly football and baseball players, liked Manzanita Park because it was the closest housing to the athletic facilities. Elway was among a group of eight football and baseball players who occupied two neighboring trailers. Aside from Elway, the group was made up of V-Sak, Aldrete, Buechele, Moore, Orvick, Lonsinger, and Hardgrave. It was an over-the-top combination of physical comedy and any type of competition. Elway was the most competitive in whatever game they played. Backgammon boards, playing cards, and Monopoly games would fly whenever he lost. There were more than a few wrestling matches.

Elway was also the stealth prankster of the lot. There was one particularly good prank against running back Mike Dotterer. Elway won Dotterer's car—a hideous AMC Pacer—in a backgammon game. Elway only kept it a week, but the car got around. He lent it to several teammates, including defensive back Ace Eason. Eason was six-foot-four, 190 pounds with a giant Julius Erving-Oscar Gamble-Diana Ross 1970s Afro. Between his hair and his tall, skinny build, he had a faint resemblance to a royal palm tree.

"I'm walking down Escondido Road through campus. I look up and I see Ace Eason with his giant Afro sticking out of the sunroof of my Pacer. I'm like, 'Ace, that's my car!' Elway just gave the keys away," Dotterer says.

As much fun as the Gang of Eight had living in the trailers, the group wanted an upgrade in living conditions. V-Sak hatched an idea. The group would rush a fraternity.

Elway's initial response was succinct: "Ain't gonna happen."

Buechele echoed that.

V-Sak kept selling the idea. Stanford had a housing draw system at the time, so keeping eight guys together was going to be a nightmare. But as a group of eight athletes, including the top quarterback in the country, they had status in the Greek world. The Gang of Eight eventually warmed to the idea. V-Sak quickly narrowed the choice to Delta Tau Delta or Zeta Psi, both of which had big groups of football players and other athletes. He then brokered a deal with one caveat.

"We'll join, but we're not going to do any of the [pledge] crap. Yeah, we'll drink some beers and stuff like that, but nothing else," V-Sak says. Delt House president Samuel "Duker" Dapper accepted the terms. By spring 1981, the eight were Delts.

The Delt House had a sense of history. It's where Jim Plunkett lived for most of his illustrious college career, when he led Stanford to a Rose Bowl victory, won the Heisman Trophy, and then was drafted number one overall in 1971. There was a giant portrait in the house of Plunkett, who was just coming off his first of two Super Bowl championships with the Raiders in January 1981. Plunkett also had an intense love and appreciation for the fraternity and the house.

Likewise, Elway grew to love the atmosphere and formed some of his closest relationships. He and Engel, an offensive lineman, became very close while living there, playing chess, video games, or one-on-one basketball. Anything where there were bragging rights to be had. Engel had a cup of coffee with the Houston Oilers before riding his motorcycle north to hang out with Elway and eventually Janet in Denver. Like Elway, Engel made Denver his home.

When they were still in college, the Delt House was a three-story home on San Juan Street on the far west side of campus. It was a short run up a hill from Mayfield Avenue, the main road of row houses that leads to the heart of campus. About two blocks away was the Lou Henry Hoover house, which had been built by former US president Herbert Hoover and then donated to the university. The president of the school lives in the Hoover House during his or her tenure.

Between the history of the fraternity, a prime location on campus, and the slight elevation that gave the house a romantic view of the San Francisco Bay, the Delt House was . . .

"A shithole," says Dave Wyman, a fellow Delt who played in college and in the NFL with Elway. Notable aside: Elway once referred to Wyman as the "meanest white man alive." Wyman got pissed for limiting him by race.

The Delt House was sadly, but not surprisingly, condemned after the 1989 Loma Prieta earthquake hit the San Francisco Bay area. It later burned down. Elway smiles slyly when talking about the house. Other fraternities had tried time and again to recruit him, but he was never interested. He felt too much like he was being used as an ornament rather than being part of the group. But the Delt House was a place where Elway could be one of the guys and recede from all the attention he was getting everywhere else. The Delt House was a fraternity without all the pomp and circumstance. The Delts were at the top of the fraternity food chain without having to act like it. That was the perfect representation of how Elway was trained to act by his dad. The house also appealed to Elway's rugged side and sense of humor.

"It was the closest thing Stanford had to a true *Animal House*," says Jim

Solberg, a good friend of the group who didn't pledge but would hang out there.

"No question," Dapper says. "The night before we played Oklahoma [in 1978], we all saw *Animal House* for the first time and we were basically watching a movie about us. The part where [Belushi] breaks the guitar could have easily been Jeff Haile."

The makeup of the Delt House was roughly 50 percent football players, most of them offensive linemen. The rest were baseball players, a few wrestlers, and maybe two brave non-athletes.

"There was nothing civilly illegal going on. They couldn't throw us in jail for anything. But within the walls of the house, it was pretty primitive. It was pretty fun. The football players were the dominating force," V-Sak says.

The house had a problem with mice at one point, so the frat got a bunch of traps from the housing office. After being caught, the dead mice were hung over a telephone line. The Delts believed they were making a statement to the other mice. Then there were the neighbors. Down the hill was the Theta Xi fraternity, a more low-key frat. In the late 1960s, a member of the Delts used to shoot arrows at the Theta Xi house (although it was not Plunkett, as has been long rumored).

Next door was Synergy House, a cooperative home where students would plant their own garden, eat from a vegetarian menu, and share coed bathrooms. These were the campus hippies. Occasionally, the Delts would look out from the house and see naked women students working in the garden. It was never quite as entertaining or intriguing as they hoped. The "granolaheads" from Synergy also did little to deter the carnivorous side of the Delts.

"You know on a normal BLT sandwich, you have maybe three or four slices of bacon," V-Sak says. "So Buechele and I would make our sandwiches like that because we're normal-sized guys, about 180 pounds each. Then the football players would come up...they'd put like twenty slices of bacon on their sandwich. When they got done, they'd make another sandwich with twenty more slices. I'm like, 'Dude, you just ate forty slices of bacon!' The food consumption was like nothing I had ever seen."

The Delt House was not a place for anyone with tremendous intro-spection or someone seeking emotional support. Or even just a little peace and quiet.

"You couldn't show any weakness in that house, not for a second. If you did, you were done," Orvick says.

"Pretty much the quickest way to guarantee something would happen is to ask that it not happen," Dapper says. "Nobody got any slack for anything. It was kill or be killed . . . we loved it."

That was true even if you were the quarterback of the football team, a member of the New York Yankees, and about to be the number one overall pick in the NFL.

"It didn't matter. A lot of good players lived there, but there was no pretense. You were just one of the guys. In fact, if you were too good, you might get crap for it and you were probably getting all the tabs from the Dutch Goose or the Oasis," Dapper says, referring to two local dive bars. "That's one of the things I loved most about the house. It was definitely egalitarian."

Orvick and Jim Clymer, a tight end on the football team, went drinking one night and got back around 2 a.m. They were singing one of the verses to "Bargain" by The Who as they passed Elway's room.

In life, one and one don't make two, one and one make one.

They were loud enough to wake Elway. The next day, Elway groused with a rhetorical question, "Hey, could you guys keep it down?" From that point on, every time those guys went drinking, they would serenade Elway with "Bargain" at about 2 a.m. That was benign by Delt standards.

Among Delt traditions at the time were two things. First, each spring the seniors would pick a night to give the cook a break from making dinner. They then took the money that was supposed to go for dinner and headed to San Francisco for a night of eating and drinking. While the seniors drank, the underclassmen stayed back and played out the other part of the tradition: retribution. They filled water balloons to throw at the seniors from the third-floor balcony. This particular year, the under-classmen took special aim at senior linebacker Dave Morze. They took the furniture from Morze's room and arranged it in the parking lot. The only thing they didn't bring down was his television, so the water balloons wouldn't damage it.

Water balloons were the weapon of choice in the Delt house. When Elway bought a Nissan 280Z in 1981 after signing with the New York Yankees, he pulled the car into the house's parking lot. Two of his frat brothers christened the car with a gigantic water balloon they launched from the third floor. The balloon weighed at least forty pounds.

It cracked the front windshield.

With that in mind, Morze's TV was spared. The underclassmen also barricaded the doors and hung furniture from the fire escapes to keep the seniors from coming in the house right away. When the seniors finally returned, Morze didn't seem to appreciate that his furniture had been relocated and didn't notice how considerate his frat brothers were about the TV. He also didn't seem to like the fact that Doug Rogers, a fellow senior who didn't go to San Francisco that night, had joined the underclassmen in battle. The six-foot-four, 280-pound Morze picked up a wooden railroad tie (they were used to mark off parking spots in the house lot) and put it through the front windshield of Rogers's car.

Rogers then pushed the nuclear option. Or at least the television option. He got Morze's TV and tossed it from the balcony into the parking lot. From there, it was all-out war, including the seniors' getting into the kitchen and grabbing bags of beans to pelt the underclassmen with. When the cook came in the next day, he quit immediately upon seeing the mess. It took four days to convince the cook to come back. The Delts had to beg. Nobody else would take the job.

The second Delt House tradition was the annual "Cowboy Party," which featured the frat's signature ice slide. The party coincided with the end of spring football practice and the accepting of pledges to the fraternity. The ice slide, which started in the mid-1960s, was the highlight. The dining area of the house was a hall about fifty feet long. It led to a short staircase down to a recreation room that featured a pool table and a hardwood floor. The pool table would be pushed up against the staircase and a piece of plywood was put on top of the pool table. The plywood would then be covered with plastic bags and ice on top of the bags. Occasionally, alcohol would be poured along the sides of the pool table and lit on fire for a cool visual effect.

The design of the exercise was to run shirtless down the dining hall, leap chest-first onto the pool table/plywood/ice slide, then see how far you could fly off the other end of the table and then land chest-first on the hardwood floor. Invariably, you didn't go very far, but you got plenty of welts on your chest. It was the kind of thing Elway and V-Sak did once and then called it a night. But it was all worth it as the frat brothers raced down the dining hall with screaming, drunken party revelers (most of them women) cheering them on.

Some guys would do it naked. Some guys took it further. One Delt was particularly hirsute. His nickname was "Rug" and will go unnamed because he became a high school teacher. He would spray lighter fluid on his chest and light it on fire before running down the hall. Because he was a mechanical engineering major, this was deemed completely safe.

While the Delts kept themselves legal in the house, they crossed the line at times on the road. In late May 1982, four carloads of Delts, including Elway, went to Fresno State to watch the baseball team play in the NCAA Regional Tournament. Stanford scored at least ten runs in each game and qualified for the College World Series. In the process, Orvick was in the stands and feeling confident as he explained Stanford's dominance to the fans from the other team. His confidence was augmented by a beer or four. Maybe six. Nobody in the stands was supposed to have alcohol, but it was a Saturday night in Fresno. What do you expect?

In the middle of Orvick's celebration, fullback Rob Moore was doing an interview on KZSU, Stanford's student radio station. As Moore answered questions about how spring football had gone, he had to break away from the interview suddenly.

"I have to go, Ken Orvick is being handcuffed, and it's bullshit," Moore remembers saying on air.

The Delts tried to get Orvick out of jail that night, but it was a no go. By late Sunday morning, he was out, but neither well rested nor happy. Not that he was getting any sympathy. The Delts managed to find some more beers and then started the 175-mile journey back to Stanford. This is maybe a three-hour drive on a Sunday. They meandered across the Central Valley and then over the low mountains that lead to the farmlands of Hollister and Gilroy south of San Jose. They were essentially doing the John Steinbeck Tour of California.

Only this was not a research project into *Of Mice and Men* or *The Grapes of Wrath*. This was more of another homage to Belushi.

You have to know which John is in your wheelhouse.

As the Delts drove, they got another idea. Let's go wine tasting! There were a couple of wineries around San Martin, a town south of San Jose. While no one was on a sommelier track, free alcohol is free alcohol. When the wineries finally kicked them out, they played nice and bought a few bottles for the road. Along the way, Orvick passed out and his frat brothers figured it was time to make him pay for getting arrested.

Again, the Hoover House was where the Stanford president lived and was two blocks from the Delt House. The plan was to drive to the lawn of the Hoover House, pull Orvick from the car, and leave him there to sleep it off. By Sunday at roughly 9 p.m., the band of Delts completed the three-hour drive from Fresno in a brisk ten hours and arrived at the Hoover House.

Sadly, they couldn't get Orvick out of the back of his car. It was time to audible. The Delts pushed the car along the side of the Hoover House, where there was a concrete slab patio. They took the keys so Orvick couldn't drive and figured he would just walk back to the Delt House after he woke up. Around 2 a.m. Monday, Orvick awoke, got out of the car, didn't see any of his frat brothers, and started to look around. Orvick thought he was still at a winery in San Martin. It was the last place he remembered.

"I'm walking around, looking for these guys and can't find them. Then I find this exterior staircase that leads to a balcony upstairs, so I climb up. I'm lucky I didn't get shot. Finally, I say, 'Screw these guys' and go back to the car to sleep it off," Orvick says.

By 7 a.m., Orvick woke up again. After one night of sleeping in jail, another night of sleeping in the back of an economy station wagon, taking no shower or shave, all while wearing the same clothes, the six-foot-five,

250-pound Orvick still didn't see any of his buddies and knocked on the door.

Not the front door, mind you. Rather, the side door next to the patio.

Stanford president Donald Kennedy, who was about five-foot-ten and armed with the slight build of a long-distance runner, opened the door and took a step back in mild shock at the sight and smell of Orvick.

"He didn't quite know who I was, but I did inquire about the car and he seemed to get the sense that all was not well," Kennedy wrote in an email years later.

Disoriented from his alcohol-induced lapse in the time-space continuum, Orvick thought he was still at the winery and asked, "Are my friends here?"

Kennedy, a man with a dry sense of humor, said, "I certainly hope not."

Orvick now started to get oriented.

"Are you Donald Kennedy?"

"Yes," said Kennedy, who either listened to KZSU or was informed of its Saturday night content. "And you're Ken Orvick. How did you get out of jail?"

As introductions go, this was not a dream scenario for Orvick. As Kennedy surmised, "It had been a long trip from that baseball game at Fresno State, and I gather not undertaken in a state of complete sobriety."

Orvick pieced the truth together and headed back to the Delt House in a two-block walk of shame. Fortunately, Dapper and other Delt leaders had done a nice job of kissing up to Kennedy and other presidents over the years. Kennedy's daughter also had dated a Delt, so the incident just went by the boards.

"As long as we weren't creating too much havoc or causing bodily harm to other members of the university, [Kennedy] pretty much turned a blind eye to what we were doing," Dapper says.

Kennedy, who died on April 21, 2020, took a photo of Orvick's car sitting on the patio and kept it in his wallet for years. Occasionally, he'd pull it out when talking to administrators from other schools looking for advice. It was sort of a personal case study in student behavior.

CHAPTER 13

GEORGE STEINBRENNER'S DREAM

George Steinbrenner was the greatest football scout Major League Baseball has ever seen.

Before buying the New York Yankees, Steinbrenner spent time as an assistant football coach for the likes of Woody Hayes and Lou Saban. He was a graduate assistant under Hayes in 1954, when the Buckeyes went undefeated and won the national championship. He loved football and, after buying the Yankees in the 1970s, drafted an amazing array of talented multisport athletes who he hoped would one day make for a dream outfield. That vision could have been Elway in right, Deion Sanders in center, and Bo Jackson in left.

Steinbrenner's vision never came close to fruition, but give him credit for finding the greatest cornerback, most gifted quarterback, and perhaps greatest all-around athlete the country has ever seen. That's two first-ballot Pro Football Hall of Famers and a guy who might have made two Hall of Fames had he stayed healthy.

That vision was also something of a nightmare for Steinbrenner's scouts and executives. Starting in 1981, New York used a second-round pick on Elway, then used another second-rounder in 1982 on Jackson and came back in 1988 to use a thirtieth-round pick on Sanders. Though critics have often dismissed those as wasted picks, Steinbrenner had a philosophy that revolved around building greatness. You don't get to that level by playing it safe. It's a philosophy Elway truly appreciated. Steinbrenner gambled on greatness and came up big more times than not. He was looking to take the best, most driven athletes and then let them set the standard for the organization. Though fans think the Yankees were a team fueled by spending on free agents, the reputation overlooks reality.

The foundation of the greatest era of the Yankees under Steinbrenner was laid through the scouting and drafting of players such as Derek Jeter, Bernie Williams, Jorge Posada, Mariano Rivera, Andy Pettitte, and Robinson Cano. Some of the biggest trades the team pulled off in the Steinbrenner era were because of the depth of talent the Yankees assembled. Steinbrenner believed strongly that if you took the best athletes, they would at least have great trade value down the line. The Yankees were able to trade for stars like Ricky Henderson, David Cone, and Paul O'Neill because of their depth.

But you don't get those kinds of players without occasionally losing a few.

Jackson, whom the Yankees failed to sign after drafting him in high school, is the most famous example. He was an all-star in baseball, a Pro Bowler in football, and, by himself, an entire Nike ad campaign because of his highlight-show career. From hitting monstrous home runs to throwing out guys from the warning track to breaking wood bats over his thigh (look it up on YouTube, but don't try it), Jackson was beyond anything even the best athletes could understand.

After seeing Jackson literally run up and down an outfield fence (again, go to YouTube), Kansas City pitcher Mark Gubicza said Jackson was an alien being brought to Earth to redefine athletic achievement. Elway witnessed it personally in the NFL. His evaluation was more succinct.

"The greatest athlete I've ever seen," Elway says more than twenty-five years later.

The six-foot-one, 227-pound Jackson was basically a ball of muscle. He had Marshawn Lynch's love for contact combined with a sprinter's speed. Elway saw Jackson run over Denver safety Mike Harden in 1987 on the way to his first NFL touchdown. Harden played eleven years in the NFL and was a tough run stopper. Jackson literally ran through Harden's attempted tackle. Another time, Jackson ran sixty-three yards for a touchdown against Denver, breaking three tackles along the way before pulling away from defenders over the final twenty yards.

Steinbrenner loved two-sport athletes. He considered them the ultimate in high achievers. When other baseball teams shied away, fearing they couldn't sign serious football players, Steinbrenner chased them even harder. Enter Elway. Steinbrenner wanted Elway even though his scouts discouraged him. That included Gary Hughes, the guy who scouted Elway in college. Hughes and Elway became friends over the years. At the time of the 1981 draft, Hughes was still an area scout for the Yankees, working the Northern California region. Hughes was about as low on the totem pole as you could be, although he'd eventually go on to be a top executive with the Florida Marlins.

As the Yankees prepared for the 1981 draft, Hughes rated Elway as a first-round talent but refused to recommend taking Elway anywhere close to the top of the draft. Hughes always believed Elway was going to play football. Hughes even said as much to Elway personally. Hughes and Elway went fishing around San Francisco Bay shortly after Baltimore drafted Elway in 1983 (but before he was traded to Denver). Elway repeatedly said he would play baseball before playing for the Colts. Hughes laughed each time and said, "You're full of it."

Hughes had never wavered in his belief. The day before the 1981 baseball draft, Hughes and the rest of the staff were in a conference room at Yankee Stadium. Steinbrenner was talking to them over a speakerphone from his home. He kept talking about Elway. Steinbrenner's nickname was "The Boss" and he earned it honestly. He was an intimidating man who could snap at a moment's notice. The son of a shipping magnate, Steinbrenner rebuilt the family business in the late 1960s, made millions, and then seized the opportunity to buy the Yankees.

Steinbrenner already had a well-established history of hiring and firing anybody and everybody in the organization. He was so over the top that some employees, such as public relations man Harvey Greene, would get fired one day and return the next. If Steinbrenner didn't say anything, they were OK. Greene was "fired" four times in the three and a half years he worked for Steinbrenner. Greene was the ninth PR man Steinbrenner had hired in his first fourteen years as owner after buying the Yankees in 1973. He was also the first PR man to reach a fourth season with the team. Greene eventually escaped and took the same job with the Miami Dolphins.

Enduring a meeting with Steinbrenner about the draft was intense. Adding to the pressure in 1981 was the fact that the Yankees didn't have a first-round pick. They had given it up after signing Dave Winfield as a free agent.

The draft was run in a two-day format at the time. The first two rounds were done on the first day and then the rest were done on the second day. Steinbrenner theorized during the meeting that if the Yankees didn't draft Elway in the second round, the rest of the teams would have a night to think about it and then some team would take Elway early in the third round. Scouts and executives continued to throw water on the idea without taking on Steinbrenner directly. Eventually, Hughes was invited to sit at the head of the table to go over his report on Elway with Steinbrenner.

Hughes said he thought Elway would hit for a high average with good power. As a bonus, Elway was a left-handed hitter, which was attractive in old Yankee Stadium with its short distance to the right-field fence. The more Hughes talked, the more Steinbrenner was convinced to draft Elway. Steinbrenner then dropped the hammer. He warned Hughes and the rest of the staff that when the Yankees drafted Elway, he'd better play for them or heads would roll.

"Hey, wait a minute," Hughes remembers loudly blurting out. "I'm telling you not to take him that high. I don't think he's going to play for us. Don't blame me if he doesn't!" The rest of the room went silent as other scouts and executives expected Steinbrenner to fire Hughes on the spot for his insolence. The speakerphone went quiet for several seconds.

"Duly noted," Steinbrenner finally said.

Elway met Steinbrenner only once, but he could immediately sense Steinbrenner's competitiveness. He was the kind of man Elway would want to play for. Steinbrenner's expectations were completely in line with Elway's. In March 1983, when Steinbrenner brought Elway's parents and agent Marvin Demoff to New York, he pulled out every stop possible to get Elway to commit to baseball instead of the NFL. He had Billy Martin entertain Elway's parents. He took Demoff to his office and showed off the projected lineup for the 1985 Yankees, featuring Elway in right field and a first baseman still in the minors at the time. Some guy named Don Mattingly.

Maybe the most important thing Steinbrenner showed Elway is that baseball life isn't easy. During Elway's six-week baseball immersion program in the summer of 1982 at Oneonta of the New York–Penn League, he discovered the drudgery of baseball. Oneonta is a college town nestled amid the Catskill Mountains and Finger Lakes. Bus rides, batting practice, and the inevitable slumps make baseball more about surviving the mental challenge than feeling amped every time you play.

"It was a grind," Elway says. "I wasn't there very long, but I could figure that out in a hurry. I loved baseball, but it's a different thing when it becomes your life and you're trying to make it all the way up from the minors."

Football is like being shot out of a cannon every Sunday. The adrenaline rush is stunning. Stepping on the field to test your talent and your courage every week is the life of a modern-day gladiator. Elway hadn't hit live pitching in more than a year by the time he got to Oneonta. He had done a week of spring training in March 1982, but that was like a vacation compared to this. This was about playing for keeps. Guys were trying to make their dreams a reality. Elway started off with one hit in his first nineteen at-bats. After about a week, Elway called his father.

"Dad, remember when I told you I wanted to hit .300?" Elway says. "I've kind of changed that."

John was hitting about .098 and said he didn't know if he could get to .100.

He figured it out eventually. Of the players who had at least 100 at-bats for Oneonta in the 1982 season, he led them in batting average (.318), on-base percentage (.432), and slugging (.464). That team was also very good by New York–Penn League standards. It included five guys who eventually made the majors (Orestes Destrade, Dan Pasqua, Tim Birtsas, Jim Deshaies, and Jim Corsi). The guys who were full-time baseball players wondered whether Elway took baseball seriously. His locker in the club-house was next to Destrade, who was one of the guys sizing up Elway.

"The first thing you always want to know about a football guy is whether he really has baseball skills or is he just an athlete," says Destrade, who played six seasons in the majors. "Johnny had the goods, you could tell. You could see the athleticism when he hit and when he threw the ball from right. You knew he was special.

"In all my years in baseball, I've seen maybe three or four arms like that. I was the first baseman, so I was lining up to be the cutoff and 99 percent of the time you're cutting it off. If you're not, it's because the outfielder tried to muscle up and sailed it over your head. With John, it was a laser, head high the whole way. It was a thing of beauty."

Not everybody was as accepting as Destrade. There was jealousy because of the deal Elway got from the Yankees. It was $150,000 and the Yankees paid for his last two years of college because Elway lost his football scholarship once he signed his baseball contract. Elway agreed to return part of the money if he didn't go back in 1983.

Steinbrenner also did Elway a favor and never said anything about the details of the agreement. He didn't want to hurt Elway's leverage with NFL teams, even though it might hurt his ability to keep Elway. His reasoning was that by doing everything he could to help Elway, he was endearing himself to Elway and helping his chances of getting him to stay with the Yankees.

In the end, the draw to play football was just what Hughes told Steinbrenner that day in June 1981. And baseball wasn't quite all it was cracked up to be.

CHAPTER 14

PETE ROZELLE'S QUANDARY

NFL commissioner Pete Rozelle was in the winter of his discontent in 1983.

He desperately needed Elway in the NFL, but not so desperately Elway could play for Al Davis and the Los Angeles Raiders. Depending on whom you believe, Elway was very nearly a member of the Raiders until Rozelle and the NFL nixed the deal. That was a bold move by a commissioner who was very much backed into a corner at the time.

By March 1983, Rozelle was dealing with a host of major problems. First, the NFL was still recovering from a player strike that cost the league seven weeks in the middle of the 1982 season, resulting in an abbreviated nine-game schedule for every team. That strike had undercut public confidence in the sport and threatened to impact the league's television contracts.

Second, Baltimore Colts quarterback Art Schlichter had just admitted to gambling on sports, creating a huge black eye for the NFL. Schlichter was supposed to be a rising star. He had been the number four pick in the 1982 draft by the Colts, who hoped he would replace the great Bert Jones. Schlichter racked up more than $700,000 in gambling debts and turned himself in to the Federal Bureau of Investigation rather than fear the wrath of bookies who might force him to throw games.

Schlichter's gambling not only caused Baltimore to pursue Elway with the number one overall pick, but it also added insult to its winless 0–8–1 season in 1982, which was preceded by a 2–14 record in 1981. As much as the Colts were an embarrassment on the field, they were worse off it. Team owner Robert Irsay was warring with Baltimore city officials about wanting a new stadium to replace decrepit Memorial Stadium, a sixty-year-old facility that was so cockroach infested that players would shake their clothes before getting dressed. Irsay had no tact and completely alienated himself from the city. In 1984, he infamously moved the team in the middle of the night, which served as de facto proof of why Elway didn't want to play for him.

Rozelle's third problem was the upstart US Football League. On April 6, 1983, the USFL opened play and was aggressively challenging the NFL. Heisman Trophy winner Herschel Walker, veteran NFL quarterback Doug Williams, and three future Hall of Famers (quarterbacks Steve Young and Jim Kelly and defensive end Reggie White) were among a host of star players who had signed or would soon sign with the USFL. The USFL also eventually had a flamboyant owner who wanted to do nothing more than irk the NFL. Donald Trump was quite the showman in the 1980s and, as it turned out, well beyond.

If that trio of issues wasn't enough, Rozelle was reminded daily about the Elway problem. As Rozelle walked into the NFL office in Manhattan each day, the New York newspapers reported daily about the chance of Elway's playing for the Yankees instead of his league. Rozelle was facing the possibility that the presumptive number one overall pick in his sport not only was going to skip out on playing in the NFL but also might play baseball for the most famous franchise in American sports in the very city where Rozelle worked and lived.

Between the strike, Schlichter, the state of the Colts, the USFL, and the New York Yankees, Rozelle was reminded of how the NFL had let Joe Namath get away to the New York Jets of the AFL in the 1960s. The failure to sign Namath fueled the AFL and put the NFL in a terrible bind. So, as Jan and Jack Elway were visiting the Yankees and being charmed by owner George Steinbrenner and manager Billy Martin (Jan received a necklace with a Yankees pendant on it) that March, Rozelle asked for a face-to-face meeting with Demoff. They had lunch in a downtown Manhattan hotel. Rozelle didn't take long to make his point.

"Pete said he wanted John in the NFL and that was that," Demoff says.

There was, however, one unstated exception to Rozelle's edict: Elway couldn't play for the Raiders and Davis, Rozelle's hated rival and the NFL's resident dissident.

Before that part of the story played out, there was plenty of other action surrounding Elway's draft position. It started after an early-February meeting in which Demoff and Jack Elway told Baltimore coach Frank Kush and general manager Ernie Accorsi that John didn't want to play for the Colts. The meeting at the Los Angeles Airport Marriott was polite, but clear. Jack didn't say it, but he privately despised Kush, who had been the head coach at Arizona State for twenty-two years. Kush was fired in 1979 after being accused of punching his punter in the mouth after a bad punt and then interfering with the investigation of the incident. Kush was everything Jack hated in coaching. That was on top of what Jack and his son thought of Irsay, who they believed had run the Colts into the ground. Despite the direct message, there seemed to be a disconnection between what was explained to Kush and Accorsi and what Irsay was told.

"I've never been sure Irsay was given the right information about John's unwillingness to play for the Colts," Demoff says. "Late into it [after the meeting with Kush and Accorsi], I got a phone call from Irsay's lawyer, Michael Chernoff, about coming to L.A. to talk to me about doing a contract and getting a deal done with Elway. I said, 'You're welcome to come here, but I have nothing to talk to you about. I cannot negotiate a contract with Baltimore, period.' He came to L.A. and we had lunch. The conversation went exactly like that. It was almost like he had never heard this before. This would have been in mid- to late March."

The news that Elway wouldn't play for Baltimore got out before the draft. The Elway camp had to come up with a reason that didn't put the Colts on the spot as they continued to work toward a peaceful resolution. Demoff suggested that Elway say he preferred to stay on the West Coast. Though Demoff was a brilliant agent, he admitted this advice was "ill conceived." Not only did it contradict what Elway was doing with the

Yankees (he explained that away by saying the Yankees played in the summer), but it also gave Terry Bradshaw his first open shot at Elway. Bradshaw, a four-time Super Bowl champion with Pittsburgh, got an early start on his second career as Elway's most vocal critic.

"For a guy like Elway to say, 'I want to be on the West Coast, I want to be on the beach, I'm a California boy,'" Bradshaw said, his sarcasm coated in his Louisiana drawl, "well, who cares what you are? And he said, 'I'll play baseball.' Well, then play baseball. You should play baseball because in my opinion, he's not the kind of guy you win championships with."

Bradshaw, who repeatedly used Elway to catapult himself into a career as a television analyst, was seriously angry. He also was legitimately illogical. Bradshaw said in later years his anger was based on jealousy of the money Elway stood to make as the number one pick. Elway eventually became the highest paid player in the league as a rookie with a five-year, $5 million contract. There was also jealousy over Elway's getting to call the shots over where he played. Bradshaw, the number one overall pick in the 1970 draft, was forced to play for Pittsburgh rather than his home-state New Orleans Saints.

What Bradshaw didn't understand is that Elway's leverage eventually helped all quarterbacks make more money. In a sport where players rarely had leverage, Elway was using every bit he possessed. As the weeks went by, Demoff met with numerous teams. The Raiders, Seattle, Chicago, San Diego, Dallas, Atlanta, New England, and Denver were the most interested. Even San Francisco coach Bill Walsh, who had Super Bowl–winning quarterback Montana as his starter, dabbled with the idea of acquiring Elway in a "fleeting" way, former 49ers owner Eddie DeBartolo says. At the time, the 49ers were intriguing because Walsh's offense was so advanced and because Elway played in Walsh's system in college.

The 49ers had also won the Super Bowl in the 1981 season. They were a good team. What was odd was that Montana was only twenty-six at the time. But Walsh both was fascinated by Elway and, as it turned out, had a wandering eye when it came to quarterbacks. Over the years, Walsh tried numerous times to move on from Montana. Despite that, Elway says the idea of playing for San Francisco "would have been really hard," because of the pressure of following Montana, especially if Montana was traded away.

Seattle, which had the number two overall pick, and Chicago at number six dropped out relatively early. Accorsi's asking price for the number one overall pick was three first-rounders, including at least one among the top six selections in the 1983 draft. Accorsi knew how deep the 1983 draft was with quarterbacks (six were taken in the first round). He also knew the 1984 draft didn't have a lot of quarterback prospects (none were taken in the first round).

The Elways remained so confident a trade would work out before the draft that they set a "sliding scale" of contracts for different teams. For instance, if San Diego, Seattle, or Oakland had taken him, it would have been a deal worth at least $5 million for five years. If it had been an East Coast team such as New England or Atlanta, Elway would have wanted $7 million for five years. As the days went by before the draft, San Diego jumped ahead as the apparent leader in the derby. San Diego had three first-round picks (numbers five, twenty, and twenty-two). The Chargers had coach Don Coryell and personnel executive John Sanders pushing for the deal, and Rozelle was actively encouraging then-owner Gene Klein to do it. Elway, in turn, was intrigued by the chance to play in the "Air Coryell" passing attack. He was even willing to sit a year behind quarterback Dan Fouts.

What didn't make a lot of sense to Klein was getting rid of Fouts, who was thirty-one at the time. Fouts had been named the Associated Press NFL Offensive Player of the Year in 1982, had made the Pro Bowl in four of the previous five seasons, and seemed to have at least a few good years left. The Chargers made it to the AFC Championship Game with Fouts in 1980 and 1981 and made the second round of the playoffs in 1982. Still, Coryell and Sanders wanted Elway because of his prodigious physical gifts.

For a time, the deal was going to happen. Three days before the draft, Coryell called in assistant coaches Al Saunders and Ernie Zampese to give them some news. Says Saunders,

Don said we had an agreement in principle to make the deal for Elway, and Ernie and I were supposed to go to San Jose and meet with John's dad to go over everything. We're jumping up and down, excited about this because we were going to have Elway sit behind Fouts for a year and then make the transition. That would have kept Air Coryell going on for years.

So we go up to San Jose to meet with Jack and discuss the whole thing. We're having dinner at Original Joe's in San Jose and everything is great. Jack was so happy John was going to end up playing in California, close to home, and with a team that was really set to be good for a long time. At the time, we still had Kellen Winslow, Charlie Joiner, Wes Chandler, and Chuck Muncie. We were set. We're hugging and high-fiving. We go back to San Diego and think the whole thing is done and then Don said there was some problem. We never found out what it was, but we all thought we had a lot more to offer than anybody else.

What happened is that Klein used the idea of trading for Elway as leverage to sign Fouts to a long-term contract. Fouts was also a West Coast guy and didn't want to leave San Diego.

Dallas got involved and that was interesting to Elway because he grew up a Cowboys fan. In the 1960s, Dallas president Tex Schramm and vice president Gil Brandt would get the coaching rosters of the top 130 college football programs. They would find out which coaches had sons and send Cowboys jerseys to those youngsters. That's how Elway became a Calvin Hill fan.

"Everybody likes to say they were the first team to uncover a great talent, but I'm pretty sure we were way ahead on Elway," Brandt says with a chuckle. The problem for the Cowboys in 1983 is that they didn't find the right person to talk to in Baltimore.

"We called Baltimore and talked to Kush and asked, 'Who's doing the trade?' Kush says, 'Me, me, I'm doing the trade.' So we're talking to Kush the whole time and come to find out [Accorsi] thought he was doing the trade and then find out Irsay is the one who ended up doing the deal by the time it was all over. We're sitting there with our hat in hand and can't get a deal done," Brandt says. The Cowboys had a legitimate shot because they had veteran quarterback Danny White, who had played for Kush at Arizona State, along with a couple of other prominent starters. On top of that, the Cowboys were willing to give up their first-round pick.

As the process lingered, Irsay became more impatient and impetuous. He took over Accorsi's office, forcing Accorsi to sit at the secretary's desk to make calls in the days leading up to the draft. Accorsi had been on the job for less than a year. With the Chargers out and the Cowboys talking to the wrong guy, the Raiders jumped to the top of the trade sweepstakes. Or at least that's how it appeared.

The Raiders had just moved from Oakland to Los Angeles. They had Jim Plunkett, the former Stanford star, at quarterback. Plunkett was thirty-five and had gone through a history of injuries. He played the early part of his career with a poorly run New England organization after being the number one pick in 1971. Essentially, Plunkett played the career Elway hoped to avoid. Plunkett eventually ended up with the Raiders as a backup, got healthy, and led them to two Super Bowls.

As for Davis, the brilliant and enigmatic owner, he had a deep football background and loved quarterbacks who could throw deep. Davis hadn't personally scouted Elway at all before the draft because he didn't expect to be in position to get him. His interest was based on what his scouts were telling him and what his executives thought they could do now that Elway was on the trading block.

When Demoff first talked to Davis about a possible trade, Davis asked, in all seriousness, whether Elway could throw deep. Demoff says he chuckled and told Davis, "Al, don't ever tell anybody you asked that question." The other interesting thing about the Raiders is that when they talked to Demoff, they didn't seem to acknowledge the existence of any other teams. It was as if the Raiders were their own entity.

"To Al, the Raiders were in a league by themselves," Demoff says.

By contrast, other teams were consumed with the Raiders. During the talks with San Diego, Coryell called the Raiders "evil" and begged Elway not to play for them. It was almost like the negative recruiting at the college level.

The Raiders had the number twenty-six overall pick. That wasn't much ammunition, but that never mattered to Davis, who was one of the most aggressive men in the history of the game.

That history of aggression was what undermined the deal. The foundation for Rozelle's hatred of Davis had been built over the previous two decades. In 1966, Davis became commissioner of the AFL for one year and started a bidding war with the NFL for players. That bidding war and the resulting rise in player salaries ultimately spurred the two leagues to merge. Rozelle, who became NFL commissioner in 1960, pushed his teams to accept the AFL teams. Essentially, Davis was the bad guy who forced Rozelle to the table.

What Davis did in 1980 was a nuclear confrontation compared to the 1966 dustup. It started when Davis declared he was going to move the Raiders from Oakland to Los Angeles, ostensibly taking the spot vacated when the Los Angeles Rams went from downtown Los Angeles to Anaheim. The NFL got a court injunction to bar Davis from moving, claiming the Raiders had violated league rules requiring permission from the other owners. Davis countered by filing an antitrust lawsuit against the NFL in Los Angeles. By winter 1981, the lawsuit was in court in Los Angeles and Rozelle was at his wit's end with Davis. It was a throwdown between the polished PR man Rozelle and the down-and-dirty Davis.

The throwdown played out in public because the Raiders also happened to be great, reaching the Super Bowl against Philadelphia in January 1981. In an interview with NBC's Bryant Gumbel before the Super Bowl, Rozelle called the court proceedings depressing and Davis "an outlaw."

"It is a depressant when you have the play on the field—the excitement of the fans at a level that I haven't seen since I took this job in 1960—and then you get things apart from what's happening on the field intruding and, in certain ways, dominating the proceedings on the field," Rozelle said to Gumbel.

Gumbel then asked Rozelle, very simply, whether he liked Davis.

"I guess the best way to answer that is that I always considered Al kind of a charming rogue. Frankly, I've always liked being in his company. So I'll say charming rogue. This is a much more serious thing where someone comes into a league as one of twenty-eight," Rozelle said, referring to the fact that the NFL had twenty-eight teams at the time. "The Raiders did…and they come in and say, 'OK, I'm going to…abide myself to the rules and the constitution for my admission to the game.' Then they say, a year ago, 'This rule, I don't like, I think it's illegal that twenty-one of the twenty-eight must approve before a team, a franchise, is allowed to move from one city to another.'"

Rozelle then took a deep breath, exhaled, and said, glumly, "And, to me, that's more outlaw than charming rogue."

For Davis, who never responded to Rozelle's remarks, being called an "outlaw" was almost as good as winning the Super Bowl trophy. He was about to get both. Days after the interview, Rozelle had to hand the Super Bowl trophy to Davis when the Raiders handily beat Philadelphia. The photo of the moment is considered one of the great pictures in sports history. Rozelle barely makes eye contact with Davis, who is flashing a deliciously evil grin.

Davis's winning streak continued in court in the off-season, where he eventually won $35 million in damages from the NFL and got the right to move his team. By the 1982 season, the Raiders relocated to Los Angeles. Now, after the first season in Los Angeles, Davis was trying to trade for Elway. And Rozelle was having none of it. For all the pressure on Rozelle to have Elway in the NFL, there was no way Elway was going to the Raiders.

Raiders executive Steve Ortmayer was put in charge of making the deal. The first objective was to get a pick in the top six selections to help satisfy the Baltimore Colts. Ortmayer had the parameters of a deal with Chicago for the number six overall pick. The Raiders were going to give the Bears two players in exchange for the number six overall pick. The Bears got to choose one player from each of two groups. The first group was either cornerback Ted Watts (a 1981 first-rounder) or defensive tackle Howie Long (a second-round pick in 1981 who eventually became a Hall of

Famer). The second group included linebacker Jeff Barnes and defensive backs Vann McElroy, Kenny Hill, and Mike Davis.

In the days leading up to the draft, Ortmayer called Demoff to say the Raiders had a deal with the Bears and, in turn, Baltimore. The Raiders would take the number six pick from Chicago, their own number twenty-six overall pick, and a first-round pick in 1984 and send those three picks to Baltimore for Elway. But on the night before the 1983 draft was set to open on April 26, Chicago general manager Jim Finks called Ortmayer to say there was a problem. Specifically, there was no trade. As the story goes, NFL executive Don Weiss called Finks to put the kibosh on the deal.

Finks, who had announced in late 1982 that he was leaving the Bears and stayed on through the draft because Chicago owner George Halas was ill, had always been considered very loyal to the league. By 1989, he was a leading candidate to replace Rozelle as commissioner until a group of eleven owners refused to vote for him.

"We tried very, very hard to make this happen. We worked the whole week leading up to the draft and it was going at quick speed because I knew [Accorsi] wanted [Dan] Marino," Ortmayer says. "Then, the night before the draft, they pulled the plug. Finks called me on the final communication that this wasn't going to happen. He said, 'It's not going to happen, they're not going to let it happen.'

"This went higher than Don Weiss. [Rozelle] nixed it.... Al was angry, but it was sort of an 'I told you so' kind of angry because he never thought the league would let it happen in the first place."

Fellow Raiders employee Mike Ornstein remembered coming in the morning of the draft and seeing Davis sitting in the room where the Raiders held their meetings.

"He was angry and said, 'The league stopped the deal.' I remember leaving the office the night before thinking the deal was done and coming in the next morning and it was off," Ornstein says.

Days after the trade of Elway to Denver, Davis openly called for an investigation of the matter.

"We think there are enough facts in the Elway–Los Angeles Raiders-

Baltimore Colts-Chicago Bears file to warrant filing an action which would negate the [Elway-Denver] deal," Davis said on May 3, 1983.

No action was ever filed. Finks responded angrily to Davis's charge.

"I think Al Davis has gone over the deep end," Finks said later that same day. "I've heard all the charges and there is not a shred of truth in them. It all started on the Sunday before the draft, but we were never even close to making a deal. I never talked with Al Davis and only Steve Ortmayer. We demanded two players from them and they wouldn't agree and that ended it."

Finks said the Bears wanted both Watts and Long in the deal. Finks also said of Davis, "He is a very difficult man to follow. It is just a typical Al Davis reaction. I'm not going to lose any sleep over it."

Finks died in 1994, Rozelle died in 1996, and Weiss passed away in 2003, taking their sides of the story to the grave. Former NFL vice president Joe Browne strongly denied that the league interfered with the deal.

"Finks told me on several occasions Al Davis backed out," says Browne, adding he knew of at least six people who would corroborate his account. "There was never any deal, but in times like this, there always seemed to be some type of orchestrated paranoia from the Raiders."

For his part, Demoff has always doubted the league's story.

"There was a deal and then suddenly there wasn't," Demoff says, clearly still of the belief that the league interfered. At the time, Demoff said, "Something happened. Someone showed an unusual interest in the deal and it wasn't [the Raiders] or Baltimore....Let's just say I'd have some interesting testimony."

Demoff took copious notes on the whole process because he represented both Elway and Marino, who went number twenty-seven overall to Miami. Those notes became the foundation of a one-hour special by ESPN years later. As great as ESPN's work was, it doesn't do justice to one of the most frenzied trades in NFL history.

When the Raiders deal fell through at the final minute, Irsay became even more impatient. So did the Elways. The Elways had rented space at the San Jose Hyatt on April 26, 1983 (the first day of the draft), to hold a press conference. The family had expected the situation to be resolved. On the morning of the draft, both Atlanta and New England were pressing to get a deal done. By this time, however, the situation was too emotionally charged for any deal to get worked out. Irsay was too angry and Accorsi was steadfast in picking Elway, which he did as soon as the draft started in order to make a statement. Elway then calmly, forcefully, and publicly told the Colts again he wouldn't play for them.

"As I stand here now, it's going to be baseball," Elway said in a press conference at the Hyatt. "I'm really surprised the way things worked out. After three months of telling them I wouldn't play for them, they went ahead and did it anyway. This is the last thing I wanted to see happen."

Elway then explained how his conversation went with Kush. Elway was polite, but direct.

"I said, 'You had a chance to get three number ones and a player, and now you've got nothing.' Then I hung up," said Elway, who also told Kush not to call back. "I don't understand how much power they thought they had. They knew all the time I had a royal flush and yet they still called my bluff."

Jack then piled on with sarcasm.

"I realize Baltimore earned the right to pick first, and I'm sure they're proud of it," said Jack, who also mocked Accorsi. "We never tried to manipulate anybody. We tried to be straightforward and honest. I just hope Coach Kush doesn't mistake good manners for weakness because the bottom line is I think John is saying, 'I won't play for Irsay and I won't play for Kush.'"

That night, Elway went to Los Angeles to appear on a television variety show. Just to make a point, he came on the show wearing a New York Yankees jersey. A picture of him in the jersey appeared in the New York papers the next day, just as Rozelle and the NFL were getting ready for the second day of the draft. It would take another week for Rozelle to get his way.

CHAPTER 15

EDGAR KAISER AND THE PURSUIT OF ELWAY

The man who made the historic trade for Elway is barely a footnote in NFL history.

Hall of Famers and football lifers such as Tex Schramm, Gil Brandt, Don Coryell, and Al Davis all took serious runs at trading for Elway during the 1983 draft. Another half-dozen established NFL teams with longtime owners and veteran football people also took their shots.

So, how is it that Denver Broncos owner Edgar Kaiser made it happen when he had been in the NFL for all of two years? On top of that, his right-hand man was a guy who admitted he knew almost nothing about football, including whether the ball was pumped or stuffed. Adding to the strange tale of how Elway ended up in Denver is that Kaiser and general manager/attorney Hein Poulus were gone from the NFL less than a year after acquiring Elway, disappearing from the football world faster than MySpace left the Internet.

The key to the trade was a combination of vision and savvy from a man raised in one of the great business families in American history. Then there was the clever execution of Poulus, a Dutch lawyer who turned a hotel hallway outside of old Stapleton Airport in Denver into his impromptu office on the day of the trade. Kaiser even envisioned the trade for Elway months before Elway ever said he wouldn't play for Baltimore. Kaiser saw it even as Elway was still licking his wounds from one of the worst moments of his athletic career. Kaiser also made it happen when almost everyone else in the Denver organization thought it was a crazy idea.

On the morning of November 28, 1982, only eight days after Elway's Stanford team had lost to Cal in that chaotic final game, Broncos public relations man Jim Saccomano was summoned to Kaiser's hotel suite. The team was staying at the Town and Country Resort on Hotel Circle in the Mission Valley section of San Diego, getting ready to play the Chargers that afternoon.

The entire NFL was trying to get back to normal after the two-month player strike had cost the league seven games. This was the second week of games after the strike had been resolved, and the Broncos were 1–2 going into the game. They were on their way to a 2–7 finish. But Kaiser was thinking about much bigger, longer-term issues. With more than five months left before the 1983 draft, Kaiser wanted to talk about Elway.

"Mr. Kaiser asked me, 'Jim, what do you think the response would be if we were able to get John Elway?'" Saccomano says, to this day a little stunned by the question. "I said, 'Well, Mr. Kaiser, I don't know how you're going to do that. We're not going to have the number one pick and he's going to be the number one pick.'"

"Never mind that, Jim. What would the value of getting him be?" Kaiser said.

"Well, it would be fantastic, but…" Saccomano recalls saying, once again trying to point out the unlikelihood of obtaining Elway. That's when Kaiser gave Saccomano a lesson in how owners think.

"Jim, anything can be bought or sold," Kaiser said, in a quietly amused tone.

"I look back at that moment and think about what I just heard. It was the first inkling I had gotten into his thinking and it was like the world of imagination just opened up in front of me," Saccomano says. "These are things that most of us don't think about because we don't have the imagination to think it's possible."

Now, it's one thing to have vision. It's another to be a guy who was barely known in NFL circles at the time and still manage to pull off one of the highest profile trades in the history of the league. Kaiser wasn't an ordinary man, as much as he might have looked like one. Though his death in January 2012 barely received much notice in the football world, he was a man of staggering achievement in the real world. The grandson of steel, shipbuilding, and health-care magnate Henry J. Kaiser (the man who built the famed Liberty ships that helped England survive the Nazi blockade of World War II), Kaiser was a businessman and a politician of international prowess who eventually devoted his life to the welfare of others.

Kaiser graduated from Stanford in 1965 and then got his master's in business administration from Harvard. In his heyday, he logged 500,000 flying miles a year, mostly on his private jet. He maintained homes in Vancouver, where he had become a Canadian citizen, San Francisco, and New York, living in a penthouse suite at the Waldorf-Astoria Hotel. Between all the stops, he bought and sold property around the world as if the planet were a giant Monopoly board.

Kaiser was more than simply rich. In critical ways, he was a genius. Before he reached age thirty, he had served under President Lyndon Johnson, a Democrat, as well as President Richard Nixon, a Republican. He was an economist for the US Agency for International Development, specializing in Vietnam as that country dealt with the upheaval of war. In 1969, he was an advance man for Nixon's historic trip to Asia and was later an aide to Interior Secretary Walter J. Hickel.

Kaiser might have stayed in politics and government if not for his father's asking him to return to the family business. It was a bittersweet return because Kaiser had to sell off and reorganize his grandfather's business empire. The steel industry and shipyards Henry Kaiser built were now victims of international competition. When Edgar Kaiser dismantled the companies, he broke down in tears. Later in life, Kaiser raced cars, motorcycles, and boats. He once navigated a yacht up the Amazon River and flew a plane around the world. When he returned home from the plane flight, he took his son to elementary school and held an impromptu geography lesson for the students. In 1998, he wrote and recorded an album, singing his own compositions.

When Kaiser's father, Edgar Sr., died, the family also "retired" his father's champion speedboat, the *Hawaii Kai III.* The boat was towed to the Strait of Juan de Fuca in Washington and then burned to the waterline before being sunk in a ceremony that borrowed on both Polynesian and Viking tradition. Kaiser was a renaissance man. Getting into the sports business was more about joy than pure business, yet business principles still applied. He bought and sold the Vancouver Whitecaps, a soccer team in Canada. Kaiser was thirty-eight when he bought the Broncos in February 1981. He fit neither the cowboy image many Coloradans like to project nor the dashing image of an international businessman. With his owl-lens glasses and stout build, he looked more like an accountant. While he knew the numbers to lend credence to the image, his genius was far less run of the mill.

Paige, the *Denver Post* columnist, wrote in 2012 after Kaiser died,

> Shortly after Kaiser took control [of the Broncos], I repeatedly asked to spend a few days at his home on an island off Vancouver, British Columbia, to write an in-depth story about his life. One day his assistant called and said to be at Stapleton in a half hour. An hour later, we took off on Kaiser's private Gulfstream jet.
>
> "Where we going?" I asked.
>
> "New York City. I have a penthouse apartment at the Waldorf-Astoria, and we have reservations tonight at 21."
>
> Over the next several whirlwind, coast-to-coast days, while listening as Kaiser bought a resort in Maui, made at least a dozen other international business deals, socialized into the early hours and kept up with the Broncos' every move, I learned, as F. Scott Fitzgerald said, the rich are different from you and me.

The way Kaiser hired Dan Reeves as head coach in 1981 was similarly over the top.

"When he first called me to see if I was interested in the job, it was on one of those old ship-to-shore lines because he was on a yacht somewhere," says Reeves, who was a Dallas assistant coach at the time. "Then he's explaining to me I would come meet him on Orcas Island. I was like, 'Where is that?'"

Kaiser had a mansion on Orcas Island, the largest and northernmost of the San Juan Islands, which are north of Seattle above Puget Sound and on the way to Vancouver. To get there, Kaiser explained, Reeves needed to fly to Seattle and then get a seaplane to the island.

"It was the first time I ever landed on water, so that was a little scary. Then, you see his mansion. It's right on the water and I'm expecting Tattoo to come out and meet us," Reeves says with an excellent *Fantasy Island* reference. "We bring the luggage up and Edgar tells one of his people, 'Take this to New Zealand.' I'm thinking, 'Where am I going now?' What it was is his mansion had separate guest houses named after different countries and ours was called New Zealand."

During the interview, Kaiser didn't ask Reeves a single question about football.

"All he said was, 'What do you need for a contract?' I said three years. He said, 'Done.' All of a sudden, I'm thinking I should have asked for five. Then we talked about money and he said, 'What do you need?' I said, 'How's $130,000?' He said, 'OK, fine,'" Reeves says.

With that, Reeves started a twelve-year run as the Broncos head coach.

Kaiser bought the Broncos from popular owner and Denver native Gerald Phipps for $30 million in 1981. The Broncos made it to the Super Bowl once in Phipps's nineteen years as owner, and he was still viewed as a local hero. He had saved the team in 1961 after founder Bob Howsam threatened to move it to Atlanta. Phipps, who made his money in construction, was also the son of Colorado senator Lawrence Phipps. The Phipps family was basically Denver royalty, and he ran the Broncos more as a public service than as a business.

After Kaiser bought the team, Poulus discovered that the Broncos had the highest payroll in the NFL and that payroll was nearly 20 percent higher than the next team in the league (the New York Jets). Despite selling out every game since 1970, Poulus calculated that the Broncos were expected to lose more than $1 million in 1981. That wasn't a small number at the time, particularly when part of the $30 million purchase was being financed.

Compared to Phipps, Kaiser was viewed a rich interloper by the public. He was one of the first corporate types to get into the league, following Eddie DeBartolo of the 49ers and paving the way for men such as Bob Kraft, Jerry Jones, Paul Allen, and Stan Kroenke. More than half the teams in the league have changed hands since Kaiser bought the Broncos. Kaiser stirred fear in the fan base by firing the combination of coach Red Miller and general manager Fred Gehrke less than two weeks after buying the team. Miller and Gehrke were widely credited by fans for getting the Broncos to the Super Bowl in the 1977 season. Kaiser got rid of them after publicly saying he was new to the football business and "had a lot to learn."

Behind the scenes, Miller had put excessive pressure on Kaiser in their first meeting, asking on three occasions whether he still had a job. Gehrke, a man with a long history in football who was credited with inventing the face mask in 1947, didn't fit into Kaiser's plans either. Kaiser then infuriated the fan base by hiring Reeves to replace Miller. The initial PR problem with Reeves was he had spent fifteen years as a player and coach with Dallas. People in Denver had a dim view of anyone from Texas. So many Texans had come to Colorado to buy property, but otherwise invested little in the state. The bottom line is that Kaiser didn't fit the image of what fans were used to. Along with that, the team struggled in his first two seasons, going 8–8 in 1981 and then 2–7 in the strike-shortened 1982 season. Put it all together and you have an owner few people warmed to.

"If you had an opinion poll among the fans about Broncos management and ownership, we *might* have gotten into double digits for approval," Poulus says. When Poulus held a staff party in February 1983 to improve morale around the office, he had Kaiser come speak. Poulus assigned a security team to bring Kaiser from Stapleton to the team offices.

"I was worried," says Poulus, who had become the general manager of the team by then because he was basically the only person who knew how to negotiate a contract. Poulus's tough approach to negotiations in the aftermath of the previous free-spending era earned him the nickname "The Dutch Hatchet" from Paige. But Kaiser wasn't just making a social call when he arrived for that staff party. He had an idea he wanted to spring on the coaching and personnel staff, which were managed by Reeves.

"He came in and said, 'So what if we got Elway?'" says John Beake, who had become the team's director of football operations and eventually became the general manager. Beake spent twenty years with the Broncos, quitting the same year Elway finally retired.

"Mr. Kaiser said that and we all kind of looked at each other out of the side of our faces and said, 'Yeah, sure, that would be great, boss,'" Beake says. The question that lingered was a daunting, one-word response nobody dared ask.

How?

This is where the genius of Kaiser—and some happenstance—took hold. To understand the story, you must rewind it. In October 1980, Kaiser and Poulus were at the suite at the Waldorf-Astoria, preparing to hit the town. Seemingly on a whim, Kaiser said, "How would you like to buy a football team?"

"I looked at him and said, 'The [British Columbia] Lions are publicly owned and not for sale,'" Poulus says, referring to the Canadian Football League team in Vancouver. "Edgar said, 'No, a *real* football team!'"

On an impulse, Kaiser wanted to buy an NFL team. After asking NFL commissioner Pete Rozelle and several other NFL executives, Kaiser and Poulus were told that Baltimore owner Robert Irsay was interested in selling. Kaiser and Poulus were also told that Irsay liked to be wooed. Kaiser, a man who was married three times, knew something about wooing.

"I maintain that in Edgar's heyday, he was the best salesman ever. He knew how to charm people," Poulus says.

Kaiser set up dinners with Irsay at New York's famous 21 Club, a restaurant that dates to the 1920s. The likes of John F. Kennedy, Frank Sinatra, Aristotle Onassis, Elizabeth Taylor, Mae West, and Sophia Loren frequented the place over the years. When Irsay was there, Kaiser would have top financial people such as Charles Allen drop by to say hello.

"Edgar was great at stuff like that. He understood how to impress people," Poulus says. "The problem is, we found out pretty quickly Irsay liked being wooed, but he had no intention of selling."

Kaiser's earnest intentions caught the interest of Rozelle, who then told Kaiser about Phipps's desire to sell. Phipps was in his late sixties and his wife was ill. Phipps was simply tired of owning the Broncos. The deal was closed on February 25, 1981, less than five months after Kaiser's seemingly whimsical statement about buying a team.

Now, fast-forward past the firings of Miller and Gehrke, the hiring of Reeves, and the 8–8 and 2–7 seasons and get to late February 1983. Once again, Kaiser had laid out a seemingly whimsical idea about trading for Elway. At the same time, nearly half the NFL was interested in making this happen, and Elway was doing his best to motivate the Colts to make a deal. Again, Baltimore's Accorsi wanted three first-round picks for Elway, including a top-six pick in order to be in position to take one of the other quarterbacks available in the 1983 draft.

"After Edgar mentioned the idea of trading for John, we talked to Baltimore and asked Ernie what it would take and I felt like the thing was over right then. They were asking for so much there was no way we could do it because we had so many things we needed besides a quarterback," Reeves says.

Unfortunately for Accorsi, Irsay took over the process, eventually changing the asking price. Worse, Irsay didn't have the best relationships around the league. His brusque style and excessive drinking rubbed people the wrong way. As one scenario after another fell apart for Irsay and the Colts, Kaiser and the Broncos were sitting there patiently. Just after the draft, Irsay was dealing with even more pressure because Elway and the Yankees had announced the parameters of an agreement for Elway to play baseball. Reeves had also made a shrewd move along the way. He had talked to Kush when the Broncos initially called about the trade.

"He asked me who we were thinking about taking at number four," Reeves says, referring to when the Broncos were slotted to pick in 1983. "I said we were thinking about [offensive lineman] Chris Hinton. Kush said, 'Would you be interested in trading him if we moved down below you?' At that point, I knew he liked Hinton, but I was also worried he was going to trade Elway to the Raiders or San Diego."

Still, the information on Hinton was valuable. Hinton was from Northwestern and well worth taking at number four. Whether Denver made the trade or not, Hinton would have been a starter at left tackle and was an excellent player (he made seven Pro Bowls at three different positions in his thirteen seasons and was inducted into the Colts Ring of Honor). If the Broncos were able to pull off the trade, Hinton would be a centerpiece of the deal.

The Broncos had one other advantage. Jack Elway and Broncos assistant coach Fran Polsfoot were friends from their days playing together at Washington State. They were also fraternity brothers. As Denver worked through the concept of making the trade, Polsfoot contacted Jack to find out whether John would play for Denver.

"That made us feel a lot more comfortable about proceeding with the idea," Beake says.

Poulus's role was as the analyst. Though he admittedly didn't understand much about football, he did understand the process of evaluating commodities and putting together deals.

"Hein was the precursor of the modern salary cap analysts around the NFL now," Demoff says.

While Reeves technically ran the personnel side of the team and Poulus normally stayed out of Reeves's way, getting this trade completed required layers of expertise. This wasn't just about the trade. Elway was demanding the biggest contract in the history of the NFL and that was Poulus's domain. On the eve of the draft after all the prep work was done, Reeves took his coaches and the personnel staff to dinner at a restaurant called The Colorado Mine Company, a wild place where drunken revelry was not out of the question. Elvis Presley loved the famous Fool's Gold sandwich (it featured peanut butter and bacon) so much he reportedly flew from Memphis to Denver one night just to get it. The place was a steakhouse in the manliest of ways and a favorite of Broncos players, coaches, and staff.

"It served unbelievably huge quantities of red meat," Poulus remembers.

"It was decorated with all sorts of wild animal trophies on the walls and I think they had a deal if you finished a thirty-two-ounce rib eye steak, you got the second one for free. Something like that, and people actually did it a few times."

As dinner went on, Poulus went through the process of gathering information. The group of roughly twenty people was split into two tables, with Reeves and most of the offensive staff at one table. Defensive coordinator Joe Collier and most of his staff were at the other table. Poulus sidled up next to Reeves and asked a simple question. Forget the money, Poulus said to preface the question, but what would you give up in draft picks to get Elway?

"Reeves was a very conservative type of man. He was from the South, pretty religious, and he considered every move he made very carefully before he made it. So when I asked him and he immediately said, 'Whatever it takes,' I was a bit surprised," Poulus says.

Poulus then got up and went over to Collier's table. Collier was a veteran of more than two decades in pro football, starting with the Boston Patriots in 1960. He was also the architect of the great Orange Crush defense that had led the Broncos to the Super Bowl five years earlier. By this time, he had spent more than half his career in Denver.

"Collier was a studious, careful, and also a conservative type of man. Very well-educated and thoughtful. So I asked him the same thing. Just like Reeves, he said right away, 'Whatever it takes,' which surprised me again. But now I had an understanding of what we were dealing with," Poulus says.

Long before any of the talks with Accorsi or the analysis by Poulus, Kaiser had laid the real groundwork for the trade by maintaining his relationship with Irsay. Irsay also happened to have several businesses in Denver. Between Kaiser's newness to the league and Irsay's lack of strong relationships with other owners, they were both outsiders. Kaiser was one of the few people who gave Irsay much respect. Anyone who has ever been in business understands that getting a complicated deal done often comes down to personal relationships and trust. That was Kaiser's wheelhouse.

As the draft unfolded and Elway wasn't traded right away, the situation continued to shift to Kaiser and the Broncos. Three days after the draft, the team held a post-draft event back at The Colorado Mining Company to introduce the rookies, including Hinton—even as the team was privately talking about making the deal.

"I was sitting there after the event with [Poulus] talking about Elway and the ramifications of what would happen. It was three days after the draft and it was still swirling and swirling," Saccomano says. "I didn't know everything that was going on, but what I knew was fascinating."

Between Hinton, a first-round pick in 1984 (which became guard Ron Solt), backup quarterback Mark Herrmann, and the personal bond Kaiser had with Irsay, it was almost enough to entice Irsay. What put it over the top was money. Because of the way NFL teams split gate receipts in the preseason at the time, playing against Denver was a lucrative proposition. The Broncos sold out all their games and half the money in the preseason went to the visiting team.

That meant playing a pair of games in back-to-back years in Denver was worth roughly $400,000 to the Colts and Irsay. Kaiser offered to host the Colts in both the 1984 and 1985 preseasons. Put it all together and there was a deal. In the six days between when the Colts drafted Elway and when Irsay finally agreed to the trade, Kaiser stayed in constant contact with Irsay.

Early on the morning of May 2, 1983, Irsay called Kaiser at his home in Vancouver. Irsay had flown to Denver on May 1 to tend to some of his other businesses. After sleeping on the decision one last time, Irsay agreed to the deal. When Reeves heard the football terms (Herrmann, Hinton, and the first-round pick in 1984), he was floored.

"Edgar called that morning and said, 'We're going to trade them [Hinton], Herrmann, and the first-round pick in 1984.' I'm writing it down and I kept waiting for him to say something else. When he didn't say anything, I asked, 'Is that it?' Edgar said yes, and I said, 'Oh God, I'd do that in a heartbeat.' I didn't think there was any way in the world the Colts would trade him for that," Reeves says.

The verbal agreement was just the start of a whirlwind day. Kaiser had done his part with Irsay. Reeves had done his part by drafting Hinton, doing some reconnaissance on Elway, and telling Poulus what getting Elway was worth. Now it was up to Poulus to put it in writing. He grabbed Beake and they jumped in Poulus's blue Ford Bronco and headed for the Marriott Hotel at Interstate 25 and Hampton Road. That's where Irsay and Michael Chernoff, his attorney, were staying. Once they got there, the four of them sat in the coffee shop of the hotel. As dozens of other people ate their breakfast, the four men hammered out one of the biggest trades in NFL history.

"I was looking around a few times and thinking, 'Nobody realizes what we're doing here,'" says Beake, who had been in pro football for almost twenty years at that point. "You think about it and it's just kinda nuts. Some guy was sitting next to us having pancakes or something while we're finishing the trade for John Elway....I was a young coach with [Kansas City head coach] Hank Stram when we won Super Bowl IV and that was crazy. This went to the top of the list of absurd things. It was unbelievable, but it was a very professional, low-key conversation."

Poulus considered Chernoff's presence a lynchpin to the deal.

"As we were driving there, I was thinking about how this might play out. The league might have stepped in and said, 'Well, Irsay wasn't of sound thinking at the time' or something like that. He did have quite the reputation at the time as a drinker, so it wouldn't have been outlandish to make that argument," Poulus says. "But we got there and he had legal representation. I felt quite relieved at that point."

Not that Irsay was in the best condition.

"He didn't look like he had just come from the spa," Poulus says.

Poulus and Beake also had to play it cool while getting everything done as quickly as possible. There were two issues. First, Poulus and Beake couldn't give the impression they were getting a steal.

"Trust me, we were very calm while we were talking to Irsay, but there were a lot of high-fives in the car on the way back to the offices," Poulus says.

Second, Poulus knew there was another stumbling block: a contract with Elway. Poulus had talked to Demoff on a couple of occasions prior to the draft, including a long, face-to-face discussion at the NFL owners' meeting in March. Demoff made it clear he had the leverage to make Elway the highest paid player in the league. As badly as Elway wanted out of Baltimore, he wasn't going to beg his way out. He had already said he would play baseball rather than play for the Colts or take a bad deal from another football team. At the same time, he wanted to play football. Demoff was the guide and Elway fully trusted him on that front, so Demoff and Poulus had to work it out.

"Poulus called me after the meeting with Irsay and said, 'We can make a deal with Baltimore if we can get a deal done with you,'" Demoff says. "After that, I called Jack and explained the situation to him. In a way only Jack could put it, he said, 'You have an hour to get the deal done.'"

Demoff and the Elways had discussed the "sliding scale" of pay for different teams, but that wasn't as important after spending a week in limbo. Elway was at a point where $5 million for five years would be fine. More than fine. Yes, he had leverage, but this was also his dream. Or as Demoff, who is perhaps the greatest negotiator in football agent history, puts it, "I wasn't in a position to ask for $5.5 million just to satisfy my own desire."

Adding to the frenzy was that Poulus had to get the deal finished before the media seized upon the news. Not that Kaiser helped him on that front. Kaiser called Paige at one point early in the day to tell him the trade was in the works. Fortunately, this was in the days before the Internet, so news still traveled mostly by word of mouth, rather than via Twitter.

Still, word of mouth could be quick.

"By about noon that day I got word from [Beake] the media were asking around about what was going on and I knew I had to get out of the office or I was going to be trapped," Poulus says. "I had a lot of things I had to juggle, including getting the deal done with Demoff and arranging for transportation of [Elway] and Edgar to Denver by that night. We had to get a private jet for them...if I had waited and tried to leave, the reporters would have just followed me around town."

So, Poulus made a move for the airport, which at the time was old Stapleton Airport on the northeast side of Denver. Specifically, he headed for one of the hotels that sat along Quebec Street and created a makeshift office in the hallway. This was in the days before cell phones, so he hijacked a pay phone in the lobby and started making one call after the other.

"It was one of those credit-card phones, so it ended up being a very expensive day, but worth it," Poulus says. "I was talking and talking and sometimes talking in code if people were around. But I thought it was a place where no one would think to find me and where I could come and go as needed."

By 1 p.m. in Denver, Demoff and Poulus had a basic agreement. Jack called Elway at the Delt House and told him to head for the airport. As Elway's frat buddies watched the soap opera *All My Children* (it was a college fad at the time), Elway snuck out and headed for the airport with a suit in tow for a possible press conference.

After Elway was picked up in a private jet, the plane headed to Vancouver to pick up Kaiser and then on to Denver. In the meantime, Demoff had flown to Denver to work out the final contract details. Poulus had gone back to Broncos headquarters to get Beake and returned to Stapleton. The final negotiations took place in the back seat of Poulus's Ford Bronco, waiting for the private jet to arrive at the Ports of Call landing strip on the south side of Stapleton.

"I sat in the car, but the plan was as the jet landed and the door opened, Hein and Marvin would get on the plane," Beake says. "If John agreed to the contract and signed, all four of them would get out of the plane and we'd go to the Broncos facility and get ready for a press conference.

"If Elway didn't agree, only Hein and Marvin would get off the plane, John and Mr. Kaiser would leave, and we'd say John was never actually in Denver and there was never a deal."

Beake waited, nervously.

"I'm watching the future of the team unfold from the car. Finally, they all came out and I was floored. It was an amazing feeling. It was probably 7 or 8 p.m. by then and it was dark outside, but we had just changed the future of the Broncos," Beake says. "In all due respect and fairness, Edgar is the one who planted the seed. He's the one who said, 'How about this?' It wasn't a pipe dream to him. He had a plan. He was extremely smart business-wise. He worked his plan and was serious about it. He wanted to bring something to this team."

That's where the whirlwind started for Elway. The group headed for team headquarters and Elway met with the coaches and staff. Beake had two last assignments. First, he had to call Irsay to officially inform him that the trade had been finalized. Beake found Irsay in Las Vegas and then Kaiser called Irsay as well. Second, Beake had to call Accorsi in Baltimore to let him know about the deal. By this time, Accorsi had heard the news break while watching an NBA playoff game. Irsay didn't have the courtesy to tell Accorsi or Kush the trade had been agreed to. Beake knew Accorsi well and knew this wasn't going to go well.

"I called and said, 'Ernie, I just want you to know the trade for John Elway is official and we've signed him.' Then I told him the terms of the deal and then he said a few things I can't really repeat. Then he went silent and slammed the phone down. I can't really blame him," Beake says.

Accorsi resigned from the Colts after the 1983 season.

By 10:30 p.m., the Broncos were holding a press conference at the team facility. However, because it was so late on the East Coast, they had to do another one the next morning. As Elway walked away from the second press conference, he turned to Saccomano and said, "I can't wait for all of this media stuff to end." Saccomano didn't say a word. He didn't have the heart to let Elway know how little he understood about the business of football at that point.

As crazy, complicated, and visionary as the trade was, Kaiser didn't take the opportunity to enjoy it. By the end of the 1983 season, Pat Bowlen was negotiating with him to buy the team. Once again, Poulus was pushing the deal to its completion.

"Edgar really didn't want to sell, but I looked at this and wondered what it was really worth. Aside from maybe a couple of million dollars in facilities and equipment, there was no asset," Poulus says. "Yes, we sold out all the games, but I remember going to Kansas City one time late in one of the seasons. The Chiefs were a team that had won a Super Bowl, had great fan support, and all that. But it was a cold day in December, and they weren't very good, and they drew about 11,000 people. I kept thinking to myself, 'That could be us.' So I pushed Edgar very hard to sell.

"In hindsight, it wasn't a good decision, of course."

Kaiser more than doubled his money as Bowlen paid roughly $70 million in cash for the team. On top of that, Kaiser had a family crisis in 1984. He never discussed it and his friends have never revealed the details. However, shortly after the crisis unfolded, Kaiser opened a series of drug treatment facilities.

In his own way he left an indelible mark on the NFL.

"The genius wasn't recognizing John Elway was a great talent. It was being able to pull off the deal," Poulus says.

"It was quite a coup and it wouldn't have happened without Edgar," Reeves says. "I thought there was no way going into the draft we could do it. That's one of the reasons we took [quarterback] Gary Kubiak in the eighth round that year. We thought there was no chance to get Elway. But Edgar was a do-er, he got things accomplished. He's the person who built the indoor facility for us so we could practice all year. That helped us win a key game in Seattle because we could prepare for the noise. Edgar was like that. Whatever you needed to get better, he wanted to provide it, and he did it with that trade."

Or as Beake puts it, "No offense to Pat Bowlen, he has been a great owner. But it's too bad Kaiser didn't stick around to get the credit for what he started to build."

CHAPTER 16

ARM OF GOLD, KNEE OF TIN

The videotape of Elway unleashing throw after throw was burned into the young boy's mind.

At eleven years old, Tom Brady couldn't get enough of watching Elway.

In the late 1980s, Tom Martinez was the head coach at the College of San Mateo, just up the road from where the Brady family lived in the San Francisco suburbs. Martinez ran a youth football camp every summer. As part of the camp, he showed instructional videos former Stanford offensive coordinator Jim Fassel had done with Elway when Elway was still in college. Brady, who later hired Martinez as his personal throwing coach, soaked it all up in his typically obsessive way.

"That video is ingrained in my head," Brady says. "[Martinez] believed John was the most mechanically sound quarterback he had ever seen. This is what we were trained on. I can't tell you how many times I watched that video....I watched John go through one drill after another and Tom would just talk about how he was the most gifted thrower. All the drills, all the fundamentals that make a great quarterback, John did them perfectly. So I just watched and watched and watched."

Just as quarterbacks such as Roger Staubach and Fran Tarkenton had influenced Elway when he was young, Elway made a small contribution to Brady's career. It's curious, however, because when Elway was growing up, so many people thought he was physically limited. Between his pigeon-toed gait and knock-kneed legs, there were some people who thought he'd never be an athlete.

Instead, by the time he got to the NFL in 1983, he might have been the most complete quarterback to ever grace a gridiron. What so many people didn't understand is that Elway's perceived "defects" were a massive advantage. His pigeon toes made him spring-loaded to both move in the pocket and unleash throws as if they'd been launched from a cannon. Elway became the standard-bearer. Like Martinez, Steve Clarkson called Elway a "perfect throwing machine" from every imaginable standpoint.

Without getting too deep into anatomy and physiology, being pigeon-toed meant Elway's hips were always locked in the perfect position before he released. It would help drive his torso and shoulder through the throw. And it helped when he scrambled, allowing him to either turn his body quickly to throw to the right if he scrambled left or unleash a throw if he went to the right.

"I've been doing this for thirty years," says Clarkson, who became one of the leading youth quarterback coaches in the country. "John's throwing motion still stands above the rest. John's throwing motion was the most accurate, consistent, efficient motion I have ever seen...it's one of the best throwing motions in the history of sports. He maximized his whole body. The way he could rip his back and hips and tap into every ounce of energy in his body. When he released, his head would even rock in the perfect way. He was always symmetrical and he must have had gorilla hips. You add in he was pigeon-toed, so he was able to just uncoil and snap the ball out."

Hall of Fame former NFL executive Bill Polian was even more effusive:

> What you have in the modern history of the game is Andrew Luck at one end of the spectrum of time and John Elway at the other. They are the prototypes. Both of them are big, strong, can move in the pocket and move fast enough to be a threat, have exceptionally talented arms, are exceptionally athletic, have the intellect and all the intangibles you could want.
>
> Everybody else in between is some version of them. Big Ben

[Roethlisberger] is a version of that. [Jim] Kelly is a version of that. Peyton [Manning] is obviously one of the greatest passers, but he had no running ability and didn't have the big arm. [Dan] Marino had the big arm, but no ability to move. They are all great, but nobody is really complete like Elway or Luck. Those two are the prototypes and everybody else is an offshoot. Does Player X remind you of Elway in some way? We used to ask ourselves that.

Elway held a special place in terms of respect among players. Dave Wyman, Elway's teammate at Stanford and later in Denver, was a rookie with Seattle in 1987. He played on a team including such greats as Hall of Fame safety Kenny Easley, pass rusher Jacob Green, and cornerback Dave Brown. That trio was the nucleus of a defense that forced an eye-popping fifty-four takeaways in 1983. They were men who feared little and respected only the best. During a Monday Night Football party the Seahawks hosted at a local bar in 1987, the Broncos were playing in the game against Minnesota and Wyman learned how much his teammates respected Elway. The players watched as Elway started to put together a drive. Suddenly, the veteran Seahawks players started yelling excitedly.

"'There goes that FREAK!' I wasn't sure what that meant. This was before that term was used to describe every person with any level of athletic talent," Wyman wrote in an email. "'There's that FREAK,' just as it is now, was meant as a term of respect or endearment. And this wasn't from just anyone. It was Jacob Green, Dave Brown, and mostly... Kenny Easley."

When Elway and Kubiak were rookies together with Denver in 1983, their first minicamp was almost their last. Kubiak was an eighth-round pick from Texas A&M University. Smart guy, but he possessed average physical talent by NFL standards.

"My first experience with John was at that minicamp and I thought I was going to have to pay them to play when I saw him throw," Kubiak says. "It was one of the most humbling, humiliating experiences of my life trying to throw with him side by side. Remember, I'm his peer in age and experience and it wasn't even close. I walked away from practice asking myself, 'Can I play pro football?' I called my wife and said, 'You better look for a job because I have no chance.'"

Kubiak played nine years before going into coaching. He served as the offensive coordinator for both of Elway's Super Bowl titles as a player, and eventually coached the Broncos to the championship in the 2015 season. He became one of Elway's closest friends, and minicamp wasn't the only time he had to deal with the strength of Elway's arm.

Or the confidence it produced.

In 1996, Kubiak was the Denver offensive coordinator under Shanahan. The Broncos had drafted quarterback Jeff Lewis in the fourth round that year as a developmental prospect. Lewis had a good attitude and a solid arm. He bounced around the NFL for about five years and even played a year for Elway with the Colorado Crush in the Arena Football League but died tragically at age thirty. One day at practice in 1996, the Broncos were working on a third-and-long drill with Lewis. The offense needed to get fifteen yards, if possible. But Lewis was instructed to throw it to someone running a shorter route if the called route was not open. Shanahan and Kubiak told Lewis, when in doubt, play it safe.

"If we just get a couple of yards and then punt, that's OK, we'll live with it," Kubiak says. "The one thing we tell Jeff is, 'Don't force the ball, don't throw an interception.' We try the play once, Jeff throws the interception. So we tell him again, 'Don't throw that pass, it's OK.' He throws another interception. Then we do it a third time and he throws his third interception and now Mike is ripping his ass, yelling 'What in the hell are you doing?' I'm yelling, too, and we're asking him, 'What the hell are you thinking?'

"Jeff was a little sheepish and said, 'John said I was a pussy if I didn't try.' Mike and I look at John and he's laughing his ass off."

On another occasion, Kubiak was working with one of the backup quarterbacks in a classroom situation. Again, Kubiak was accounting for normal parameters of NFL quarterback arm strength as he instructed the backup where to throw the ball on a certain play.

Elway walked by and looked at Kubiak and the backup.

"Where did you tell him to throw it?" Elway asked Kubiak.

"Here," Kubiak said, pointing at a logical spot in the diagram.

Elway looked at Kubiak with the combination of a sneer and smile of a Greek god viewing a mere mortal.

"You would," Elway said as he walked away.

The other unconventional part of Elway was his right knee. The knee injury he suffered during his senior year of high school was supposedly just cartilage damage. He came back for the baseball season and then played his entire college career. Occasionally, he would tweak the knee in college, either by running the bases in baseball or doing something else, such as intramural basketball. During his sophomore year, Elway, Buechele, V-Sak, Hardgrave, and their other buddies put together an intramural basketball team. They also went to an army surplus store and bought camouflage outfits as uniforms to look more intimidating.

They were total badasses.

During a game, Elway went up for a layup, came down wrong on the floor, and crumpled over in a heap. His teammates came over to show some deep concern.

"We're all yelling, 'Get up, you pussy!'" says Hardgrave, one of Elway's teammates in baseball. "Then we looked at his knee. It was the size of a grapefruit already. We all got scared and scattered like cockroaches."

So much for the badasses.

Elway played well despite the knee problem. He refused to let the NFL examine him before the 1983 draft. He had no desire for the NFL to know how bad the knee was, and teams didn't push the matter at that time. When Elway got to Denver, the Broncos found out he had a torn anterior cruciate ligament in his knee. It had been that way since high school, and his body had essentially adapted to the point that repairing it was no longer feasible or necessary. He was the rare athlete who played without a functioning ACL in one of his knees.

One of the keys for Elway to succeed was the diligent work of Denver trainer Steve Antonopulos, who over his more than forty years with the Broncos was better known as "Greek." Antonopulos designed workout programs to improve Elway's strength and flexibility. Elway wore a brace over the course of his career and, more importantly, followed Antonopulos's advice to the letter.

"If you'd have seen him when he first got here, you'd understand," Antonopulos says, referring to Elway's underdeveloped strength at the time. "From where he started to where he got is all about him working at it.... He did everything and showed up every day. He set the standard. He was the toughest football player we've had."

Over sixteen years, Elway missed thirteen games. Along the way, he went through fifteen surgeries. Other players went through similar situations. Denver offensive lineman Mark Schlereth had twenty-nine surgeries in his twelve-year career, including thirteen on his left knee. Hall of Fame left tackle Gary Zimmerman, who finished his career with the Broncos, played fourteen years until his shoulders gave out after numerous surgeries.

What was most important about Elway is that he didn't complain about the pain, ever. If the quarterback complains, he risks two things. First, he can lose the respect of other players who play through pain. Second, he risks having other players complain and possibly they aren't ready when the team needs them. The other thing Elway made sure to do was get up as fast as possible after he got hit, even if it hurt.

"I never wanted the defense to think I was hurt or have my guys think there was a problem," Elway says. "You can't give the defense that kind of satisfaction and you can't have your guys worry."

And Elway was hit more than anyone by the time he was done. He retired after being sacked a league-record 516 times (Favre eventually surpassed that with 525).

"You could never hit Elway hard enough," says former Carolina head coach Ron Rivera, a former linebacker who played against Elway in college and the NFL. "Every time you hit Elway, he'd smile at you with that big, toothy grin, roll his shoulder pad back into place the way he always did, and then do that John Wayne walk back to the huddle. You thought you had hit him so hard and he'd just pop up and do his whole routine. Man, it drove me crazy."

The "John Wayne walk" was a natural combination of Elway's pigeon toes and damaged knee. Teammates such as Vance Johnson (he was considered the best of the Elway walkers) and even opponents would imitate Elway, mostly out of respect. Seattle coach Chuck Knox would do it to make a point about Elway on the weeks the teams faced off in the old AFC West (the Seahawks played in the same division at the time).

"Elway was the only guy [Knox] ever mentioned in a team meeting that I heard in my five years with Chuck," Wyman wrote. "Only he didn't call him John Elway. He called him John Wayne. The usually stoic Knox could be pretty funny and sometimes even silly in this case. He would say something like this before a week of preparation for the Broncos: 'I don't wanna see freakin' John Wayne over there throwin' the ball deep on us.'"

Knox would stand in front of the team, turn his toes inward, stick his chest out, and throw back his shoulders, Wyman explained. He'd then pretend to line up under center, imitating Elway with a healthy dose of Wayne added in.

"[Knox] would saunter up in that twisted-up manner that was half-quarterback, half-gunfighter. Then he would start shouting out Elway's cadence…and then pantomime a deep throw over a defensive player's head for a TD. The room would burst into laughter because, as I said, it wasn't like Chuck to cut loose like that nor was it customary for him to mention any player at all. You could see the respect he had for Elway," Wyman wrote.

Elway played through an assortment of injuries, including knee problems and high ankle sprains. In August 1997, he snapped the biceps tendon in his right arm. As a result, it forever looks like his biceps muscle is attached to the backside of his arm. Some people thought his career might end with that injury. The Broncos ended up winning their first title that year.

He had rotator-cuff tears, broken ribs, hamstring pulls, and concussions. He rarely discussed them. In his mind, there was no point. If you wanted to play football, injuries were part of the game. By the end of his rookie year, he not only hit the weight room but he also talked to Cowboys legend Roger Staubach about a training regimen and modified it over the years. He worked out with all the linemen and the defensive players and then got competitive about it. In the 1997 season, his fifteenth in the NFL, he set a personal record for weightlifting and set a team conditioning record on the StairMaster.

By the end, his amazing gifts were augmented by his work ethic.

CHAPTER 17

DAN REEVES AND THE QB CULTURE WAR

Neither Elway nor Reeves understood the larger story that would play out in their decade together.

The era of the quarterback was about to overwhelm the era of the coach. Elway's arrival in Denver set off a frenzy in the media. Anything and everything about Elway became news, from what he ate for lunch to when he got a haircut. A section of the *Rocky Mountain News* by reporter T. J. Simers was dubbed "The Elway Watch." In later years, the *Denver Post* wrote about the type of Halloween candy the Elway family gave out. It was absurd, but indicative of the interest the Broncos created by pulling off one of the biggest trades in NFL history.

It was also indicative of the pressure foisted upon both Elway and Reeves. With Elway around, a Super Bowl victory was expected. Elway was being fitted for a bust in the Pro Football Hall of Fame before he had played a down, let alone a full season. That's the absurdist view, but the first look Denver fans got at Elway in a game was like something out of the movie *The Natural*. On August 5, 1983, against Seattle, Elway opened the second half of the preseason game by leading the Broncos on a touchdown drive. Playing with and against mostly backup players, he looked great.

As Elway was playing, a lightning storm was flashing in the distant horizon. He was like Thor, the god of thunder bringing bolts from the sky. That aura also backed Reeves into a corner, essentially forcing him to start Elway in the season opener at Pittsburgh. Before any of it played out, one thing was clear: Reeves and Elway were going to be scrutinized like no coach-quarterback tandem ever before. The Broncos were already easily the biggest sports team in the state and Elway's arrival only amped that. In addition, the *Denver Post* and *Rocky Mountain News* were in the middle of a circulation war. The *Post* had gone from being an afternoon to a morning paper, competing head to head with the *News* and even hiring away key writers.

Any bit of news about Elway or Reeves or their relationship was part of the war. It didn't take long for the pressure to show. During Reeves's first two years with the Broncos before Elway arrived, he had once told the reporters who covered the team, "If I change, let me know." At the time, the media viewed Reeves as an amiable Southern gentleman. Shortly after Elway arrived, Simers wrote a column with the line, "Dan, you've changed." The pressure of having Elway and the expectation that went with coaching a star quarterback made Reeves much more serious.

Privately, the pressure and expectation often morphed into ugliness and frustration between them. Reeves's controlling style was difficult for Elway to understand. Elway's father empowered him to think and act on his own. So had most of his coaches, starting with Jack Neumeier. He had been given incredible freedom as a high school quarterback to call plays and again in college playing in the West Coast offense. Elway chafed at Reeves's style as the two had problems almost from the start. One of the earliest incidents didn't even directly involve Reeves or Elway. Reeves's wife, Pam, was talking to Elway's first wife, Janet, who remembers Pam Reeves said, "How do you live with him? That must be hard."

Elway would come to the sideline in games, look at Reeves, and say, "Why don't you trust me?" Reeves's temper would flare and he'd scream at Elway. Elway would return fire by saying, "Don't ever talk to me that way again." The days between games weren't far removed from that. The headstrong and confident Elway would ask for more say in the game plan. As in the West Coast offense, Elway wanted a script of the first ten or twenty plays going into a game. Reeves wouldn't do it. Elway wanted to at least tell the coaches which plays he liked more than others. Reeves recoiled at that idea.

Elway would ask people around the Broncos facility to explain Reeves to him. He'd even ask reporters. He'd come home on some Fridays so frustrated he'd tell Janet he was going to quit. By Saturday morning, he'd dutifully return to work. All of this was part of a bigger change happening in football, one that Reeves wasn't necessarily prepared for and Elway wasn't cognizant of.

The NFL was in a cultural shift that eventually pitted the way Reeves had grown up in the game against the direction the league was pointing the game. In the mid-1970s, the NFL went through a run of defensive dominance that threatened to turn pro football into something akin to Chinese water torture. By 1977, there were twenty-five shutouts during the regular season, or approximately one out of every eight games. Pittsburgh's Steel Curtain, Minnesota's Purple People Eaters, and Denver's Orange Crush were among a group of teams with historically great defensive units as teams took advantage of the rules. Those defenses were suffocating opponents and the game itself. Men such as innovator and executive Tex Schramm of the Dallas Cowboys fretted that fans would be turned off by the boring style of play.

In response, the NFL changed rules on the placement of the hashmarks, how offensive linemen could block, and how defensive players could guard receivers. All of it was done with the intention of opening the passing game and increasing scoring. That trend in adapting rules to help the offense has continued for more than four decades. In addition to rule changes, coaching strategy changed. Bill Walsh brought his philosophy of short passing to the forefront of the NFL in 1979. The 49ers went 2–14 in Walsh's first season. By Walsh's third season in 1981, he led the 49ers to a Super Bowl title with Joe Montana at quarterback. Walsh's ideas became the rage of the NFL and he was nicknamed "the Genius."

As a result, the quarterback position was about to become bigger than ever. The position was always important. The 1971 NFL Draft featured quarterbacks as the first three picks, and Raiders owner Al Davis preached for decades a defensive philosophy revolved around attacking the quarterback. Or as Davis put it bluntly, "The quarterback must go down and he must go down hard."

Even by those standards of focus and importance, the 1983 draft was a paradigm shift.

With Elway as number one overall, the 1983 draft featured a record six quarterbacks taken in the first round. That's emblematic of a trend that has lasted more than three decades. Starting with Elway in 1983, a quarterback was taken with the number one overall pick in twenty of the next thirty-six drafts through 2018. That's 56 percent. In the forty-seven NFL Drafts prior to 1983, a quarterback was taken number one overall fourteen times. That's only 30 percent.

Essentially, the quarterback doubled in value beginning with Elway's draft. The increased emphasis on the quarterback had an additional impact on the profile of head coaches. Coaches had been the symbol of the NFL to this point. Though there were great quarterbacks such as Johnny Unitas, Joe Namath, Otto Graham, and even Sid Luckman, the biggest names in the game were coaches. Vince Lombardi, George Halas, Paul Brown, Tom Landry, Don Shula, and Chuck Noll were the faces of the game.

Like great generals George Patton, Douglas MacArthur, and Dwight Eisenhower, coaches such as Lombardi were admired for their ability to command men on the field every Sunday. In the post–World War II, Korea, and Vietnam eras, those coaches were admired for their domineering styles and tactical genius. This was life in post-war America. The Super Bowl Trophy was named for Lombardi and the hallowed grounds of Lambeau Field are named after Green Bay's great early coach.

By contrast, Walsh was considered effete and was ridiculed by mainstream football people. He was also considered too emotionally vulnerable to have long-term success. Brown, whom Walsh had worked for in the 1970s, trashed Walsh to other owners and executives for lacking psychological toughness. Brown wasn't altogether wrong. Walsh once broke down in tears on a team flight after a loss. Walsh's assistant coaches surrounded him to keep the players from seeing him in emotional distress.

As time went by, Montana received as much or more credit for San Francisco's success, particularly after the team won a title the season following Walsh's retirement. Between rules that made throwing more prevalent and the success of Montana, Elway, Marino, Kelly, Aikman, and many other quarterbacks, the NFL was quickly tilting toward quarterbacks.

Reeves wasn't ready for the change.

Reeves made the Dallas Cowboys as an undrafted player in 1965. He was an extreme longshot. That was in the days when the draft lasted eighteen rounds and teams carried only forty players. He lasted eight years as a player before immediately becoming an assistant coach under the legendary Landry. Reeves revered Landry and copied much of his style. Reeves brought Landry's offensive system to Denver when he was hired in 1981 and, like Landry, would often dress in suit and tie during games.

Reeves was hired at thirty-seven, making him the youngest head coach in the NFL at the time. He was also a man of great integrity. In high school, he was a star out of Americus, Georgia, and desperately wanted to play for the University of Georgia. He got hurt during his senior year and most colleges stopped recruiting him, except for the University of South Carolina. Reeves committed to South Carolina, healed from his injury, and then played in a high school all-star game at the end of the season.

Georgia was interested now. Reeves was torn. He gave his word to South Carolina, but Georgia was his boyhood team. He and his father talked it through and Reeves told Georgia, "I've got to keep my word." He went to South Carolina. The best summarization of Reeves came from Paul Howard, an offensive lineman who played fourteen years for the Broncos. Howard had already played ten years by the time Elway entered the league.

"If you ever went to Reeves with a personal problem, Reeves would do anything and everything he could to help you. But if you went to Reeves with a football problem...he would cut you," Howard says.

Reeves strongly believed in his ability to solve football problems so much that he considered it an insult to question him. As time went on, that became a central issue between Reeves and Elway. Reeves also blindly believed "winning creates winning." That was his mantra whenever he was questioned, regardless of the situation. If a preseason game wasn't going particularly well in the second half, Reeves would order the first-team offensive linemen back in the game, even after they had taken off their shoulder pads and tape. Reeves pushed and pushed and pushed to create a culture and a mind-set based on winning. Much like Elway, Reeves was competitive to almost maniacal levels. Reeves competed in anything and everything.

Including how to catch a golf ball on the back of his hand.

At every training camp under Reeves, there would be one team meeting in which the coaches and players would do something silly. It would be a bonding activity, such as singing fight songs or doing skits. Reeves would invariably do a series of parlor tricks, such as blowing a dime into a glass. It all looked easy. Then others would try and fail because they didn't know the trick. His best move was bouncing a golf ball off the floor and then catching it on the back of his hand. Again, it looked easy, but others would try and fail. Players would invariably go back to their rooms and you'd hear golf balls bouncing off the dorm room floors.

The backstory was telling. After a round of golf at a country club, the club pro did the trick. The club pro then bet Reeves $5 that Reeves couldn't do it once in five tries. Reeves didn't know the trick and coughed up the five-spot.

"You have to catch the ball on the exact right spot on the back of your hand," Reeves says. Reeves was so annoyed that he went home and practiced the entire night. He returned the next day, betting the pro he could do the trick five consecutive times. He got his money back.

Reeves tended to see the world through the prism of his identity. Aside from Elway, Reeves often picked players who had great heart, yet were somewhat short on pure ability. First-round draft picks were also wasted through a comedy of errors. Reeves hired people he trusted too much. When the team took defensive tackle Ted Gregory with a first-round pick in 1988, Gregory was generously listed at six-foot-one, 260 pounds. He was maybe five-eleven, 240. When he showed up in Denver, it was clear that Reeves had never put eyes on him before the draft, even though Reeves ran the football operation.

"He's so small," Reeves said that day. Gregory was traded before the season began and finished his career playing only three games. Over nine years after drafting Elway, the Broncos had six first-round picks. Only safety Steve Atwater had any long-term impact on the team.

That meant Denver's success during the ten years Elway and Reeves were together rested on two things. First, there was Reeves's ability to design game plans that kept games close. Second, there was Elway's ability to pull out victories in the fourth quarter. During Elway's career, he led the Broncos to forty-seven victories when Denver was either trailing or tied entering the fourth quarter. That was unofficially an NFL record when he retired. More importantly, thirty of those victories came during Elway's ten years with Reeves and earned Elway the nickname "The Comeback Kid."

The reality is that Reeves had almost as much to do with that as Elway. Reeves was an expert at keeping games close by using the running game to protect his defense, which was usually undersized. This was on top of the fact that Reeves was running an offense that was dated, if not archaic. The system featured very little in the way of pre-snap reads or ways of forcing the defense to declare what it was doing. Elway did almost all his reads after the snap of the ball.

Again, Reeves's offense was Landry's offense. It was also numbered backward, making it the only offense in the NFL run that way. In every other offense in the NFL, the odd numbers for holes between the offensive linemen were put on the left and the even were on the right. A running play to the four hole was between the right guard and the right tackle in most normal offenses.

In the Landry/Reeves offense, the four hole was on the left.

Why? Landry started his coaching career in the 1950s as the defensive coordinator of the New York Giants. When it came time for him to draw up an offense, Landry did it by looking at it from the defensive perspective. When you flipped it around to teach it from the offensive perspective, the numbers got transposed.

What's the big deal? When quarterbacks have learned something for years the other way, it's hard to turn it around mentally. It's like learning how to type on a standard typewriter, then having the keyboard changed.

It slows the process. The next issue was that Reeves's offense was maybe the wordiest in the history of the league. What other offensive languages had distilled to a series of numbers or a few words, Reeves would have upwards of fifteen or twenty words to a call. Sometimes there were words in the call that didn't even mean anything.

Denver's quarterback coach in Elway's rookie year was John Hadl, a former quarterback himself who had played sixteen years between the NFL and the AFL. Elway was asking Hadl some questions one day. With a straight face, Hadl said to Elway, "Look kid, I don't understand it myself. Do your best and I'll cover for you."

That's one of the reasons Elway so famously struggled as a rookie. Still, between the trade and the resulting expectations, Reeves had to start Elway. It was ugly in the early going. The Broncos and Elway opened the 1983 season against Pittsburgh and what remained of the Steel Curtain defense. He completed only one of eight passes for fourteen yards, an interception, and was sacked four times. Veteran Steve DeBerg replaced Elway midway through the game. Early in the game, Elway looked across the line and saw veteran Steelers linebacker Jack Lambert. Lambert was snarling and slobbering, his upper front teeth missing.

"I thought to myself, you can have all the money back, I'll go be an accountant," Elway says. Elway not only tripped and fell after one snap, but he also lined up behind the guard instead of the center on another. Elway's first five games of the season were a struggle, and he was eventually replaced by DeBerg as the starter in the sixth game. Elway returned as the starter a month later when DeBerg got hurt. Elway played better in the second half of the season, but the strain was obvious. He lost twenty pounds over the course of the season, getting down to 195, and his father became increasingly concerned.

Beyond the numbering and the verbiage in Reeves's offense, the design didn't make life easy on a quarterback. Reeves believed in deep, downfield throwing set up off the running game. It was very much a 1970s philosophy. The Broncos didn't even have a weakside comeback route, the classic outlet throw. Basically, running backs ran the ball and wide receivers caught it. If a running back or the tight end caught a pass, it was a rarity. From 1983 to 1989, there were two instances in which Elway had a running back or a tight end catch forty passes or more in a season. Sammy Winder had forty-four catches in 1984 and Gerald Willhite had sixty-four in 1986.

Meanwhile, Elway was flanked by offensive systems on each coast that made life much easier on quarterbacks. In San Francisco, the 49ers may have had wide receivers such as Jerry Rice, John Taylor, and Dwight Clark, but they also put a premium on throwing to the running backs and the tight end. From 1983 to 1989 in San Francisco, there were thirteen times a running back or tight end had forty or more catches. Running back Roger Craig alone had seasons of ninety-two, eighty-one, seventy-six, and sixty-six receptions. Fullback Tom Rathman had seventy-three one year. In Miami over the same period, the Dolphins and Marino had eight such performances with running backs and tight ends such as Tony Nathan, Lorenzo Hampton, and Bruce Hardy. The simple throw that was such a big part of progressive offensives such as Walsh's West Coast attack or Don Shula's offense in Miami simply weren't part of the Reeves system.

Beyond the strategic issues the situation created for Elway, it also led to unfair comparisons with Montana and Marino. Fans and media openly wondered why Elway wasn't putting up the same stats as those quarterbacks—and winning championships like Montana.

The Broncos won enough to make those issues minor in the early years. In 1983, they went 9–7 and made the playoffs. Elway threw only seven touchdown passes and fourteen interceptions, but the mistakes could be overlooked if the team was winning. After his rookie season, Elway married Janet in March 1984. He then worked hard to solidify another important relationship by spending the off-season working out with the Broncos offensive linemen. In 1984, the Broncos improved to 13–3 and won the division before losing their first playoff game. The team went 11–5 in 1985 and missed the playoffs.

Still, the offensive scheme and the issues with Reeves would drive Jack to the point of wanting to interfere. Jack would watch the games and then call Demoff to read the letter he was writing to Reeves about the offense.

Demoff would politely tell Jack to send the letters to him, saying he'd hold them until after the season and see what happened. The letters were never mailed to Reeves. About the worst it ever got is Jack mouthed off to reporters about the offense one time.

Even Elway's teammates would tease him about how he didn't put up the same numbers as Marino or Montana. Elway was supposed to be the golden boy. Yet it was Marino who set the then–NFL record for touchdown passes with forty-eight in 1984. In 1986, Marino threw forty-four touchdown passes. It took Elway three full seasons to throw a total of forty-seven touchdown passes. Elway would go out for beers with the offensive linemen, who knew full well what the problems were with the offense. They'd say things like, "Did you see Marino's numbers the other day?"

And Elway would still pick up the bar tab.

As for Reeves, he didn't care about stats. He cared about winning games.

"I respected that part of him. He was fiercely competitive about winning and losing," Elway says. "I disagreed with how he went about it, but I know he wanted to win."

Years later, Elway even channeled some of Reeves's intensity after taking over the Broncos in 2011, but that's a tale for later. When Elway was inducted into the Pro Football Hall of Fame, he talked about his deep appreciation for Reeves's tenacity and desire to win. He also said Reeves deserved a spot in the Hall of Fame for his contributions as a coach. The two men had made their peace by then. But it wasn't easy as the two went through a cultural change in the game they dearly loved.

CHAPTER 18

DRIVING THE BROWNS OUT OF CLEVELAND

The 1986 AFC Championship Game in Cleveland was Elway's coming out party as an NFL quarterback.

The good people of Cleveland were even nice enough to bring treats for the occasion, although their serving skills left something to be desired. Starting in warm-ups and extending throughout the game, Browns fans threw dog biscuits, concessions food, and even the occasional battery.

Elway made them choke on all of it.

"The Drive" was that impressive.

The story of Elway's leading a ninety-eight-yard drive against the Browns at decrepit Cleveland Municipal Stadium on January 11, 1987, is stunning by itself. The drama, the high-wire act, and the resulting first trip to the Super Bowl for the Broncos with Elway constituted a turning point in his career, not to mention the franchise. The victory made it clear to the sports world that Elway was every bit the difference maker expected of a number one overall pick.

Elway had led Denver to an 11–5 record in the regular season and the team's second division title in four years. He then led the Broncos to the first playoff win of his career by beating New England in Denver. Combine that victory with what was about to happen against the Browns, and this was essentially the stamp of approval on Elway as a franchise quarterback.

"It set the tone for the rest of my career," Elway says. He may not have been producing the same stats as Marino and Montana, but he was winning and taking the Broncos to the playoffs consistently. What was about to happen in Cleveland was going to be a transcendent moment. In the backdrop, the Browns featured two individuals who became part of Elway's legacy. They were run by Accorsi, the man who had stubbornly drafted Elway with the number one overall pick for Baltimore in 1983. Accorsi was in his second year as Cleveland's general manager, and Marty Schottenheimer was in his second year as head coach. As the years played out, Elway would go on to be the biggest thorn in Schottenheimer's career.

But this game was about way more than Elway and how Accorsi and Schottenheimer intertwined with his career. This game was supposed to be redemption for Cleveland—not just the team and owner Art Modell but for the entire city.

When the Broncos arrived in Cleveland for the game, they landed in a desperate place. From the late 1960s to the mid-1980s, Cleveland had become a running joke around the country and, in some respects, around the world. The city had thrived with industry from the 1920s to the early 1960s before the local economy tanked. Lake Erie became so polluted that fish washed up dead. The Cuyahoga River was so laced with oil-soaked trash that it caught on fire in 1969, acrid black smoke filling the skies as if a volcano had erupted. The incident became the rallying point for the country's environmental movement of the 1970s. In 1978, the city defaulted on federal loans, essentially declaring bankruptcy.

Cleveland had gone from proud home of the working man to "The Mistake by the Lake." The Browns mirrored the city's rise and fall. In the 1940s and 1950s, the team won seven titles in ten years under the leadership of legendary coach Paul Brown and quarterback Otto Graham. The Browns were considered the first great dynasty of pro football. The glory days continued when running back Jim Brown, arguably the greatest player in NFL history, arrived in 1957 and led the team to another title in 1964.

Modell bought the Browns in 1961 and fired coach Paul Brown in 1963 when the two couldn't get along. The team remained competitive through 1969. In 1970, however, the roof caved in. From 1970 to 1985, the Browns failed to win a playoff game and made the playoffs only five times.

Then came 1986 and what seemed to be a renaissance. Not only did Accorsi and Schottenheimer appear to have the team on the right track, but also quarterback Bernie Kosar had joined the team as a rookie in 1985. Kosar was a Cleveland hero before ever throwing a pass for the Browns. He had been raised in nearby Youngstown and had gone to the University of Miami, where he helped the Hurricanes win a national title. He then cleverly used the NFL Supplemental Draft to achieve his publicly stated goal of playing for the Browns.

Yes, Kosar *wanted* to play in Cleveland at a time when no one wanted anything to do with the city. Kosar helped the Browns make the playoffs in 1985 and then appeared ready to lead the complete rebirth the following season. The team went 12–4 in the regular season and had the number one seed in the AFC playoffs. The Browns survived a dramatic first play-off game by beating the New York Jets in double overtime, ending the sixteen-year drought without a playoff win.

Now, it was time to slay the Broncos and their fair-haired quarterback.

The citizens of Cleveland played their part. The night before the game, Browns fans drove their cars by the hotel where the Broncos were staying, honking their horns to keep the Broncos from getting a good night of sleep. Denver players watched the local news that night. They saw a story about how pet stores were giving out five- and ten-pound bags of dog biscuits to Browns fans who were part of the team's famed "Dawg Pound," a roughneck group of fans who sat in the bleachers just beyond the east end zone. The players thought the pet stores were being generous.

On game day, those Broncos players found out otherwise. They were pelted with dog biscuits during warm-ups and throughout the game. When the fans ran out of biscuits, they threw food, including wrapped sandwiches and fruit. Mixed in was a battery or two. Denver players were told to keep their helmets on all game. Guard Mark Cooper took his helmet off to get a drink one time behind the Broncos bench and had an apple glance off his face. Impressed, he gave the fan a thumbs-up.

On the field, Cooper asked one of the referees why he didn't throw a flag against the Browns for the fan conduct. The ref looked back and said, "Do you think it's going to get any better if I do?"

For Clevelanders, this was way more than just a game. It was a catharsis. It was a chance to erase all the embarrassment and the ill feelings. Fans held up signs reading, "No More Cleveland Jokes!" Others wanted to let their anger pour out. Numerous Broncos players said it was the most hostile crowd they had ever witnessed. As the game played out under a cold, gray sky, the field became a mess. Freezing temperatures from the day before had thawed, leaving the turf a muddy bog. There were divots everywhere and a ring of snow and ice was piled around the rim of the field where it adjoined the seats.

The multipurpose stadium, which had been built in 1931 and made Shawshank Prison look like a spa, was also home to the Indians baseball team. The ground around where the baseball infield normally was located was little more than sandy dirt painted green. The game played out in a slow, slogging style befitting the condition of the turf. Halfway through the fourth quarter, the game was knotted at 13–13.

That's when, by all rights, Denver should have been knocked out. Cleveland was facing a third-and-six situation from the Denver forty-eight-yard line as Kosar came to the line. The six-foot-five Kosar wasn't particularly athletic. When he ran, he looked more like a galloping giraffe. His strength was his intelligence combined with exceptional accuracy and great anticipation.

On the left side of the offensive formation, Kosar saw five-foot-nine, 180-pound wide receiver Brian Brennan matched up against six-foot-three, 200-pound safety Dennis Smith. If this were a decathlon competition or even just normal football conditions, Smith would have dominated the matchup ten times out of ten. But on a crappy field where the footing favored a guy with short, choppy steps, Brennan had an advantage.

Not a big one, but enough of one.

So, as Kosar dropped back with the clock just passing the six-minute mark, he went deep for Brennan. Brennan was running toward the left sideline with Smith in good position. Kosar threw the ball to the inside.

Brennan made a pirouette, cut back to the middle, and got open by a step against Smith. Smith turned and missed deflecting the ball by about eight inches. Brennan caught the ball at the seventeen. Smith stumbled, allowing Brennan to run untouched the rest of the way for a forty-eight-yard touchdown that gave the Browns a 20–13 lead.

"Momentum swings in the playoffs are huge, way bigger than the regular season," Elway says. "That was the biggest shift I had ever felt to that point."

This was an avalanche. Browns fans, who hadn't seen their team win a title in more than a generation, were screaming with joy, and Browns players were dancing on the sideline. Conversely, there was a hush on the Broncos sideline. And the situation was about to get worse. Absurdly worse.

Denver kick returners Ken Bell and Gene Lang set up at the ten-yard line for the ensuing kickoff, anticipating a poor kick from Cleveland's Mark Moseley in the bad conditions. Bell and Lang didn't anticipate just how poor it would be. Moseley's low, line-drive kick hit the ground at the Denver fifteen and skittered past Bell toward the goal line. Instead of letting the ball roll into the end zone, Bell panicked, picked it up at the Denver two-yard line, and fell to the ground to make sure he didn't fumble as Browns defenders converged on him. The Broncos weren't just behind by a touchdown—they were now buried only two yards from their own end zone.

As the Denver offense took the field, the players huddled in the end zone, dog biscuits crunching beneath their feet. There was 5:43 remaining and Browns fans were howling with delight, believing their team was going to the Super Bowl. The idea that the Broncos could go ninety-eight yards to tie the game was far-fetched to begin with. To do it against a defense including linebackers Chip Banks and Clay Matthews Jr. and cornerbacks Hanford Dixon and Frank Minnifield was a joke.

"This was going to take all the concentration we had," Elway says. In the huddle, guard Keith Bishop joked to his teammates that the Broncos had the Browns "right where we want them." Elway then gave his teammates a boost of confidence.

"John comes into the huddle and he was smiling," wide receiver Steve

Watson says. "It was like he loved it. I remember he said, 'If you work hard, good things are going to happen.' Then he smiled again. I think it calmed us all down."

On the first play, Elway faked a handoff, dropped to pass from his own end zone, and completed a short pass to running back Sammy Winder for five yards just to give the Broncos some breathing room. Three straight runs by Winder produced a first down and then put the Broncos in a second-and-eight from its own fifteen.

The last of those three runs changed the whole face of the drive. Winder ran over the left side and was hammered by the Cleveland defense. Veteran NBC play-by-play man Dick Enberg was wowed by the hit.

"Winder didn't get hit by a Brown, he got hit by a brownstone," Enberg said.

From that point on, Denver hitched its hopes on Elway. The final eleven plays of the drive went completely through Elway. He threw eight passes, was sacked once, and scrambled twice. In the moment of truth, Reeves put his trust in Elway. This was the defining moment of what Elway could do if given control.

The first of those two scrambles came on that second-and-eight. Elway lined up in shotgun formation, dodged some pressure from the left, and then took off for eleven yards to get a first down at the Denver twenty-six. Linebacker Chip Banks was supposed to be the "spy" on Elway during the game, but neither Banks nor the Browns defensive staff gauged just how fast Elway could run.

Particularly when he was being chased.

"I knew I could run most of the plays if the situation got bad because of the way they were playing me," Elway says. "I always had a way out of a play."

On the next play, Elway applied the first dagger to the Browns defense. He hit running back Steve Sewell down the right seam of the field for twenty-two yards to the Denver forty-eight. Sewell jumped to make the catch and withstood a nasty hit as he landed. Elway followed that move with a twelve-yard throw to Watson to put the Broncos in first down at the Cleveland forty with 1:59 remaining.

On first down, Elway threw deep for wide receiver Vance Johnson down the right side, but the pass was incomplete. Then came a play that brought Cleveland back to its feet. With 1:52 remaining, Browns nose tackle Dave Puzzuoli sacked Elway for an eight-yard loss. Elway once again tried to escape to his left, but Puzzuoli grabbed him by the ankle and basically lassoed Elway to the ground.

Denver was now facing a third-and-eighteen from the Cleveland forty-eight. The Browns and their fans thought they had Elway and the Broncos cornered.

"It was so loud and you could sense the stands were shaking," Elway says.

Most coaches will tell you they don't have a lot of great plays designed to deal with third-and-eighteen. Defenses generally do one of two things: they either blitz to get to the quarterback before the receivers can get deep enough or they play a zone to take away any easy throws.

On the broadcast, NBC analyst and Hall of Fame defensive tackle Merlin Olsen acknowledged as much with his interpretation of how the strategy should be played.

"Realistically this will take two downs…get some of it [on third down] and go on fourth down," Olsen said. That was logical. The only thing is that Elway didn't do logical. He pulled out his cannon arm and went for it.

But not without Watson's adding a degree of difficulty.

As the Broncos lined up, Elway was in shotgun formation five yards behind the center. Watson had lined up in the backfield on Elway's left and then went in motion from left to right. The motion was designed to tell Elway before the snap if Cleveland was in man or zone defense. The Browns showed zone as Elway stole a glance at the secondary.

As Watson motioned past the center, the ball was snapped and it glanced off his butt. Elway managed to snare the deflection with his left hand while keeping his vision downfield. As Olsen said, the Broncos were "so close to disaster" as the play started. Instead, they pulled off a stunning pass. Rookie wide receiver Mark Jackson dashed downfield along the left side against the soft zone coverage. He faked to the outside and then quickly turned back inside as Elway fired for a twenty-yard completion to the Cleveland twenty-eight. This was the second dagger as the raucous Cleveland crowd was staggered with 1:22 remaining in the game.

Elway threw another incompletion to essentially stop the clock and then hit Sewell on a perfectly executed screen pass for another fourteen yards to the Cleveland fourteen. The Broncos were playing with unbelievable confidence, as if this were practice.

On first down from the fourteen, Elway threw to Watson in the right corner of the end zone. Watson caught the ball but landed out of bounds. On second down, Elway took off again for a nine-yard gain. This time he went right and got out of bounds to stop the clock with forty-two seconds remaining. Elway, the right side of his uniform already caked in mud from his shoulder to his knee, slid out at the Cleveland five. He got up and dried his hands on the back of teammate Clint Sampson's jersey.

That little bit of help for Elway's grip turned out to be crucial.

Now it was third-and-one. At this moment, it wasn't about whether the Broncos would score, but rather, how. Schottenheimer stood on the sideline with his arms draped by his sides, looking almost as hopeless as the Browns fans in the stands. It didn't matter what Cleveland tried to do at this point. It didn't matter that everyone knew the play was going through Elway. The Browns defense was simply no match for Elway.

Elway was again in shotgun formation and this time Jackson was the motion man, starting from the right side and ending up way wide to the left. Vance Johnson was in the slot on the left and ran a clear out toward the middle. Running back Gerald Willhite ran a route from the left side of the backfield toward the left sideline.

That move allowed Jackson to run a slant route from left to right into an open spot in the end zone, essentially splitting the difference between where Johnson and Willhite were going. Elway saw the throwing lane open and fired a fastball that would have made Nolan Ryan proud. Over the years, Elway said it was the hardest he had ever thrown a pass. It hit Jackson in the chest, and he cradled it in his arms as he slid to the ground amid the dog biscuits and soggy turf.

With that third dagger, Elway was like a great bullfighter slaying the beast. "The Drive" was instant legend. The Browns and their fans were in stunned silence. On the fifteen-play drive, Elway completed six of nine passes for seventy-eight yards, ran for twenty, and overcame an eight-yard sack along the way.

In overtime, the Browns had nothing left. They got the ball first but punted after three plays. Elway carved up the Cleveland defense for a fifty-nine-yard drive. He made yet another critical play by getting Denver out of a third-and-twelve situation. He scrambled to his left as if to run and then flicked a twenty-eight-yard throw on the run to Watson along the left sideline to put the Broncos in scoring range. It's the kind of throw only a handful of humans can make.

Three plays later, kicker Rich Karlis ended the game with a field goal, and the Broncos danced all over the muddy field. Rick Telander of *Sports Illustrated* put it best as he discussed how Elway had snatched a bone from a dog's mouth.

"Let's clarify this metaphor," Telander wrote. "Elway didn't just pull victory from the Browns' mouth. He ripped the thing from halfway down their throat."

More than the stats, Elway temporarily felt he had earned Reeves's trust. Surely, the eleven consecutive pass plays called out of shotgun formation were an indication of what brilliance Elway could produce if given the chance. Decades later, Elway still looks bewildered by the fact that Reeves didn't give him more control after that breakout game.

"You would have thought he might have trusted me at that point," Elway says.

While it was a triumphant end of the game for Denver as they qualified for the first Super Bowl with Elway, it was only the beginning of a fascinating run that tortured the Browns over the next four years. Starting in 1986, the Broncos made the Super Bowl in three of four seasons (1986, 1987, and 1989). Each time, they beat Cleveland in the AFC Championship Game.

The AFC Championship Game in the 1987 season may have been even more brutal for the Browns and their fans. Down 38–31 in Denver, the Browns were poised to return the favor by driving the field and looking ready to score. But running back Earnest Byner was stripped as he was about to score and the game went on to be known simply as "The Fumble." The 1989 game was no contest as Denver rolled.

Elway continued to haunt Schottenheimer years later after the coach took over in Kansas City. But nothing ever hurt Schottenheimer as much as The Drive and The Fumble.

"I learned to like John as the years went by," Schottenheimer says with a chuckle. "He was an amazing competitor... [but] he hurt me. He did his job. But he hurt me... deeply."

Cleveland tight end Ozzie Newsome, who made the Pro Football Hall of Fame and later became a great personnel executive with the Baltimore Ravens, was similarly philosophical.

"There are people in your life you have admiration for," says Newsome, who got a small measure of revenge when Baltimore beat Denver in the 2013 playoffs. "Some of that admiration comes from competition. I could never beat John as a player. He got what I wanted three times when he won those AFC Championship games. So my admiration for him is my jealousy of him.... John broke my heart in that game, but I have nothing but respect for him."

There was one other part of this story that was about to play out. One of the lingering images from that run of AFC Championship Games was Modell looking forlorn in his owner's box. At the end of the last one, he had his face buried in the palm of his hand.

Modell badly needed to get to the Super Bowl for the sake of public relations. His relationship with city officials had become problematic as he continually tried to get a new stadium. The sides alienated each other, particularly when the city put its attention on building a new stadium for the Indians instead of the Browns. Modell took the brunt of the criticism because the decline of the team had happened under his watch.

By the end of the 1995 season, the situation bottomed out and Modell did the unthinkable. He moved the Browns to Baltimore, filling the spot vacated when the Colts moved to Indianapolis in 1984. It's the most controversial move in NFL history because it uprooted a historic franchise from a town where the fans were truly devoted. Modell immediately had to leave town for fear of being hurt or killed.

He was burned in effigy around Cleveland and ridiculed around the country. The decision essentially cost Modell any chance of ever being elected to the Pro Football Hall of Fame. He so dearly had hoped to gain entrance to the hall for his contributions to the NFL (Modell was a pioneer on the marketing and television side of the game).

The NFL was so embarrassed by the move that the league allowed Cleveland to keep the Browns name and promised Cleveland an expansion franchise. Both of those moves were unprecedented.

But then, so were ninety-eight-yard drives in the playoffs in hostile environments. When Elway was involved, the unprecedented happened a lot.

And, in a sense, one of Elway's most interesting accomplishments was forcing two teams to move. When the Colts drafted him in 1983 and then traded him, it was the last straw in a deteriorating relationship between owner Bob Irsay and the city of Baltimore. In the case of the Browns, the unraveling took longer, but was nonetheless the same. Elway destroyed Modell's team over a four-year span, starting with The Drive.

In the process, he drove the Browns right out of Cleveland.

CHAPTER 19

SUPER MISERY

Denver's run of three Super Bowl appearances in four years featured one record-breaking performance after another.

Just not the type of records any team would want to be associated with.

After beating Cleveland with The Drive on January 11, 1987, the Broncos faced the New York Giants and their vaunted defense, led by linebackers Lawrence Taylor, Harry Carson, and Carl Banks. The Giants were a nine-and-a-half-point favorite. The game was also at the Rose Bowl in Pasadena, California, so it was something of a homecoming for Elway. He had played the last game of his high school career there, but this was not going to be a day for warm memories. The Super Bowl was competitive in the first half. The Broncos had a 10–9 lead. The game came apart in the second half as Giants quarterback Phil Simms put on a show. Simms set a Super Bowl record by completing twenty-two of twenty-five passes for 268 yards and three touchdowns. New York outscored Denver 24–0 to open the second half, pulling away for a 39–20 victory.

A year later, after the Broncos got past Cleveland because of The Fumble, they faced Washington at Jack Murphy Stadium in San Diego. The Broncos felt they had a reasonable chance because they had beaten Washington in the 1986 regular season. Those thoughts amped on a beautiful day when Denver got off to a 10–0 lead and the Broncos defense forced punts on each of Washington's first three possessions.

No team had ever lost a Super Bowl after building a ten-point lead. In the first quarter, the Broncos had rolled up 142 yards of offense compared to only 64 for Washington. Then the tide changed, as if it were a tsunami. Starting with an eighty-yard touchdown pass from Doug Williams to Ricky Sanders, Washington put together one of the all-time scoring binges of Super Bowl history. Washington scored forty-two unanswered points, including a Super Bowl–record thirty-five in the second quarter alone. Including the bomb to Sanders, Washington scored three touchdowns of fifty yards or longer.

The famed Washington offensive line, which was known as "The Hogs," opened the way for a Super Bowl–record 202 yards rushing by Timmy Smith, who proved to be a one-hit wonder. Smith did that on twenty-two carries for an average of 9.3 yards per carry. During the rest of Smith's three-year NFL career, he rushed for 602 yards in twenty-two games, averaging 3.2 yards per carry. In other words, this was not a magical player putting on a tour-de-force performance. It was the Broncos getting physically hammered, which was a gut shot for the organization.

As humiliating as those back-to-back Super Bowl losses were, the worst was to come. Before they hit bottom, the Broncos dealt with some changes. Before playing Washington in the Super Bowl, the 1987 season featured a significant step of progress in the relationship between Elway and Mike Shanahan, who had officially been named offensive coordinator. Elway finished the season with an 83.4 quarterback rating and led the Broncos to an 8–3–1 record in the games he played (the league featured replacement players for three games during the 1987 strike). Elway was also named the NFL Most Valuable Player. Though his quarterback rating wasn't stunning, it was the only time under Reeves's system that Elway had a rating of 80.0 or better.

Shanahan, who had been a college quarterback, was both demanding and creative. The results showed. The Broncos scored at least twenty points over the final seven games of the 1987 regular season and then two more in the playoffs that season. That may not seem significant by today's standards, but it was torrid by Denver's standards of the time. Prior to 1987, the longest such streak with at least twenty points had been six

Jack and John Elway walk off the field September 19, 1981, at Stanford Stadium after Jack's San Jose State Spartans sacked John eight times and intercepted him five times in a 28–6 victory over the Cardinal. As the two walked off, Jack requested John to come home for dinner as Jack anticipated the wrath of wife, Jan. *(Photo by San Jose State University/ Collegiate Images via Getty Images)*

Elway's college career was filled with amazing highs and lows. That included two upsets of opponents ranked in the top five in the country. That included a 42–31 victory against No. 2 University of Washington on October 30, 1982. That upset win helped propel Elway to the Sammy Baugh Award as the nation's top quarterback, the Pacific-10 Conference Player of the Year Award and finishing second in the Heisman Trophy voting. *(Photo by David Madison/Getty Images)*

Elway, his mother Jan, and father Jack enjoy a light moment prior to the annual Shrine Game college football all-star matchup in 1983. For Jan, the game was a personal highlight. It was the first and only time Jack ever served as John's official coach in a game. That made it the only time she could cheer for her husband and son at the same time after seeing them go against each over for three years at San Jose State and Stanford, respectively. *(AP Photo/Sal Veder)*

In 1981, Elway played his third and final baseball season for Stanford before becoming a second-round pick by the New York Yankees and eventually signing with them that fall. Elway helped kick start the most successful run in the school's baseball history as Stanford finished either first or second in the conference in twenty-two of the next twenty-four seasons. *(Photo by David Madison/Getty Images)*

Only ten days before the NFL Draft in April 1983, Elway met with the New York Yankees and toured Yankee Stadium with legendary manager Billy Martin. Elway's visit to the Yankees, which included his parents, was the subject of front-page news in New York and drove NFL Commissioner Pete Rozelle to distraction. *(Bettmann/Getty Images)*

After telling the Baltimore Colts at least two months earlier he did not want to play for them, Elway was taken with the number one overall pick in the NFL Draft on Tuesday, April 26, 1983. He was, to say the least, not pleased. *(Photo by Bruce Bennett Studios via Getty Images Studios/Getty Images)*

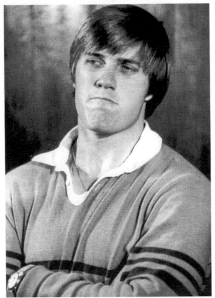

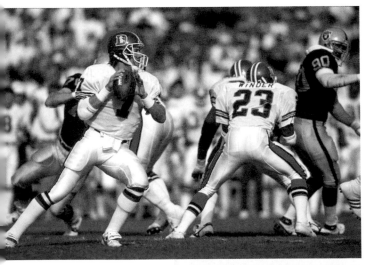

Elway had an up-and-down rookie season in 1983 but helped the Broncos to a 9–7 finish and a playoff berth, the first of ten postseason appearances in his sixteen-year career. The team would go on to make the Super Bowl five times in Elway's career, which was the most appearances by a quarterback in NFL history at the time he retired. *(Photo by Focus on Sport/Getty Images)*

On January 11, 1987, Elway led Denver on one of the most improbable comebacks in NFL history in the AFC Championship Game. The Broncos' ninety-eight-yard drive at the end of regulation forced the game to overtime and is known simply as "The Drive." The victory vaulted Denver to the first of five Super Bowl appearances with Elway at quarterback. *(Photo by George Gojkovich/Getty Images)*

The tension caused by losing three Super Bowls over the previous four seasons started to wear on the relationship between Elway and coach Dan Reeves. In the 1990 season, the Broncos finished 5–11, leading to a blow up between the player and coach. While they worked together for another two seasons after that year, the relationship continued to be difficult. *(Photo by Focus on Sport/Getty Images)*

Elway's pregame study of the Green Bay Packers led to a critical third-down conversion in the Broncos' upset victory in the Super Bowl and the first title of his career. While Elway was best known for his incredible arm strength, it was his run on "The Helicopter" play that helped lead the way to the title. *(Photo by Kevin Reece/Getty Images)*

After fifteen years in the NFL and on his fourth appearance in the Super Bowl, Elway and the Broncos broke through for their first title together. In the process, the thirty-seven-year-old Elway became (and still is) the oldest quarterback to win a title for the first time. To many close to him, that was proof of his overwhelming desire. *(Photo by Mickey Pfleger/Sports Illustrated via Getty Images)*

Elway leaves the field in his final game, a 34–19 victory over Atlanta in the Super Bowl. Elway was named the Most Valuable Player in the game after throwing for 336 yards and one touchdown pass and running for another score. A little more than three months later, Elway formally retired. *(Photo by Bill Frakes/Sports Illustrated/ Getty Images)*

During Elway's sixteen seasons as a player, Mike Shanahan was either an assistant coach or head coach for eleven years, creating a deep bond between them. During its four years with Shanahan as head coach and Elway at quarterback, Denver went 54–18 overall. That included 7–1 in the playoffs with three postseason appearances and two Super Bowl titles. *(RHONA WISE/AFP via Getty Images)*

Elway completed his journey as a football player by entering the Pro Football Hall of Fame as a first-ballot selection. At the time, there were less than 100 first-ballot Hall of Famers in the history of the NFL. Elway was introduced by his oldest daughter, Jessica, on August 8, 2004. *(Photo by David Maxwell/Getty Images)*

In only its third year of existence after being an expansion team, the Colorado Crush won the 2005 Arena Football League title with a 51–48 victory over the Georgia Force in Las Vegas. Elway, who ran the football operations, and Crush owners Pat Bowlen (left) and Stan Kroenke (center) hold the championship trophy. *(Photo by Harry How/Getty Images)*

Elway helped coach his son Jack at Cherry Creek High School during the 2007 season. Jack would end up going to play at Arizona State, one of three of Elway's children who played college sports. Daughter Jessica played basketball for Stanford and daughter Jordan played lacrosse at the University of Denver. *(Photo by Steve Dykes/Getty Images)*

Elway met Paige Green in 2005 during a random moment at a celebrity golf tournament and then didn't call her for almost a year until seeing her on a commercial. By 2009, they married at a private ceremony in Coeur d'Alene, Idaho. *(Photo by Stefanie Keenan/ Getty Images for Celebrity Fight Night)*

Elway and quarterback Peyton Manning celebrate after the AFC Championship Game victory over New England on January 19, 2014, which put Denver back in the Super Bowl for the first time in fifteen years. Elway and Manning spent four years together, during which time the Broncos made the playoffs each year, made the Super Bowl twice and won it once. *(Photo by David E. Klutho/Sports Illustrated via Getty Images)*

On February 7, 2016, Elway became only the second person in NFL history to win a Super Bowl both as a player and as a head coach or top executive. Two of Elway's biggest additions as an executive played vital roles. Quarterback Peyton Manning returned from injury and linebacker Von Miller dominated in the playoffs on the way to being name the Super Bowl MVP. *(Photo by Ezra Shaw/Getty Images)*

games to open 1986. It was rare for the Broncos to have more than two or three consecutive games with twenty points or more. During the 1987 streak, Denver went 8–1 and won four of the games by double digits.

After losing to Washington in the Super Bowl, Shanahan was hired as head coach of the Los Angeles Raiders by Al Davis for the 1988 season. The hire was curious because it was the first time Davis had hired a head coach from outside the organization. Prior to Shanahan, John Rauch, John Madden, and Tom Flores had been elevated from Raiders assistants to the top job. At the same time, the hire made sense. In the four years Shanahan had run the Denver offense, the Broncos were 6–2 against the Raiders and had put up twenty points or more six times. That particularly annoyed Davis, who was also the de facto defensive coordinator of the Raiders.

It also fit the insidious side of Davis, who was known around the league and particularly around the AFC West division for hiring away good assistant coaches from other teams. Davis would then bury them on the Raiders staff before eventually firing them a year or two later. He was ruthless, cunning, and nefarious. What nobody understood is that Davis was now essentially doing that with the head coach position, not a lower-level spot like running back or linebacker coach. From the moment Davis hired Shanahan, they were at war for control of the coaching staff. Davis fired one of Shanahan's top assistants, and Shanahan responded by firing four of Davis's favorite assistants.

In so many ways, the hiring of Shanahan was an indication of how the Raiders were about to decline. Not because of Shanahan but, rather, because of Davis's spiteful nature. The two had no real sense of each other. To Elway and others in Denver, the Davis-Shanahan war was funny to watch as it played out over the next year and a half. It was theatre of the bizarre. After the first four games of the 1989 season, Shanahan was fired and quickly rehired by Reeves in early 1990. In fact, Shanahan versus Davis continued to be a sideshow around the NFL for the next twenty years.

The downside is that losing Shanahan removed the buffer between Reeves and Elway for the 1988 and 1989 seasons. Reeves elevated assistant Chan Gailey to quarterback coach. Reeves didn't hire an offensive coordinator and essentially took back control of the offense. Gailey was nice enough and ended up having a long and relatively successful coaching career. But Gailey's hiring represented the ultimate example of Reeves's hiring his own guys. Gailey and Reeves both grew up in Americus, Georgia. They met when Reeves was an eighteen-year-old high school kid umpiring and coaching Little League baseball. Gailey was a ten-year-old player.

Elway was basically being coached by a direct extension of Reeves. How was Elway supposed to confide in Gailey or expect him to stand up to Reeves? In addition, Reeves and his staff had gone on a run of poor draft picks. In 1988, there was the infamous selection of Ted Gregory in the first round. That move caused Elway to seriously question what was going on. With all of Reeves's Deep South friends around, Elway sometimes felt as if his career were trapped in an episode of *Hee Haw*. Between the two Super Bowl losses, the loss of Shanahan, and the run of draft picks, the Broncos hit a wall in the 1988 season, going 8–8 and missing the playoffs.

While the team got back on track in 1989 by going 11–5 and qualifying for the Super Bowl for the third time, the tension was growing between Elway and Reeves. In fact, there was growing tension between Elway and the entire city of Denver. His habit of taking his teammates, particularly his offensive linemen, out for drinks during the week was becoming a sensitive issue both around town and with Reeves. It was part of Elway's way of following his father's advice and creating camaraderie within the team. Offensive linemen such as Dave Studdard and Keith Bishop protected him on Sunday, and they ran together during the week. Bishop and Elway had a particularly close relationship. In the 1986 off-season, Bishop lost both his father and mother to cancer in a two-month stretch.

"John and his then-wife, Janet, called me and my then-wife every day," Bishop says. "Every single day. We went out with them or we'd go to their house every day. I was really struggling and John saved my life. We'd stop to get something to eat and just talk. It's hard to put into words, but he never left me alone. It was nonstop. It's one of those neat things nobody knows about, the unknown things people do for friends. You realize later in life how fortunate you are to have a friend like that, one who goes that far."

Shortly after Elway took over the football operations in 2011, he brought Bishop back to the team as vice president of security. Bishop had spent nearly twenty years in law enforcement, including a stint with the Drug Enforcement Agency and a final tour in Afghanistan. Elway invited him to his house one night and offered him the job with the Broncos. Bishop said he needed time to think about it. Elway got them each a drink. They took a couple of sips and Elway said, "So what did you decide?"

Bishop took the job.

In 1989, Elway didn't have protection from the public criticism. A Denver gossip columnist noted that Elway was seen drinking a beer while playing backgammon at a public event. From there, people inside and outside the organization started to wonder whether Elway had a drinking problem. It was no secret that he liked to have drinks with his teammates. Again, that was important for team bonding to Elway. He hated when guys would leave early, commanding them to stay. Rick Dennison tried to sneak out once when Elway was in the bathroom. Dennison was in his car and driving out of the lot as Elway tried to stop him from leaving.

If you drank with Elway, you stayed until the "final" round. And then you stayed until the "final, final" round. For Elway, going out to drink with his teammates was a release. Because he was always at center stage on the field or within the confines of the team, Elway felt he had to be incredibly careful about the image he projected in public. To this day, he hates public speaking because he frets over every word and how he sounds. From that perspective, Elway is very much a projection of his mom and her prideful demurred side. In private, after a couple of drinks, he is much like his dad, who would tell a story and be self-deprecating. Or as Jack often liked to say, "The only people who tell the truth are drunks and babies." If Elway wanted to let loose on a night, he was going to have a few along the way.

"If you go out with John, it's going to be a good time," Engel says. "He's a man's man and he wants to get to know you, laugh with you, tell stories. We could be out and run into people we didn't even know and

John would invite them to join in....We didn't go out all the time, but when we went out, there was a purpose."

Elway was also careful to make sure that when he went out, it didn't impact work. First wife Janet remembers how Elway would make sure to be up and out the door the next morning for work no matter how late he got home from a night out with teammates. The son of Jack Elway had been taught that work came first and foremost. John Elway was also never cited for any drinking-related issue. Still, as the 1989 season played out, ESPN reporter Jim Gray questioned Elway about whether he had a drinking problem. Elway denied it, strongly, and was extremely angry about it. It chafed at him.

"[The drinking allegation] bothered me because I look at myself as a role model for young kids, and when they say things like that that are totally untrue, there's going to be people that believe it whether it's true or not," Elway told the *Los Angeles Times* after the Gray interview.

Around the same time, Reeves called Jack and asked for a meeting. Reeves wanted to have one of those coach-to-coach talks.

"Jack, I'd really like you to talk to John about all this stuff," Reeves said to Jack.

"Why?" Jack responded.

"Well, he's hanging out a lot with the other players and I hear he's drinking a lot with them," Reeves said.

"Well, Dan, has he gotten arrested or pulled over for drinking?" Jack asked.

"No," Reeves replied.

"Has he missed any meetings, practices, or workouts?" Jack asked.

"No," Reeves said.

"Has he been late?" Jack said.

"No," Reeves said.

"OK, and isn't him going out with the guys part of the team building you want your quarterback to do?" Jack asked.

"Well, yes," Reeves said.

"So, Dan, what's the problem?" Jack said.

To Elway, it was one thing to be criticized for playing poorly. It

was another for people to make wild guesses based on conjectur_
questions about his drinking were only the beginning of the invasio_
his life that year. On Halloween, the *Rocky Mountain News* reported wh_
type of candy the Elway family gave out (along with other celebrities
around town). When Elway was late to a charity dinner he hosted, it
was also reported. It all led to Elway's feeling overwhelmed. He did an
interview with Rick Reilly of *Sports Illustrated* and said, "I'm about to
suffocate. They talk about my hair, they talk about my teeth, they talk
about how much I tip, how much I drink, how I'm playing, when I'll talk
to the media. I'm sick of it."

He continued in another article with complaints about how the media
dealt with him.

"I wanted to be a quarterback here, but it came down to if they painted
the building, the media wanted to know what I thought about it," Elway
told the *Los Angeles Times*. "I was avoiding questions instead of saying no.
I just didn't want to answer them. I held a lot of animosity toward [the
media] and I didn't want to give them any time. I had been very open
with them."

In reaction to those comments, *Rocky Mountain News* columnist Jay
Mariotti wrote that Elway was a "greedy and scared punk" and offered if
Elway didn't like it, "Go ahead John, leave. Get out of Denver, baby. Go.
You'll be crawling back here after a week."

Mariotti, a noted hit-and-run artist among journalists and a guy who
rarely talked directly to his targets, went on to explain: "My contention
in my column was that he's smothering himself. He does so much on the
side that the media isn't smothering him, he's smothering himself with
his profit-making ventures."

Mariotti ultimately took more criticism than Elway. Still, 1989 was a
tough year for Elway even as he and the Broncos were on their way to
their third Super Bowl appearance in four years.

An appearance that would make Terry Bradshaw a media star.

CHAPTER 20

BRADSHAW POURS IT ON, 49ERS REIGN

Jack Elway saw Terry Bradshaw in the French Quarter.

When Elway's greatest advocate and greatest critic collided, Bradshaw got an earful. Not that Bradshaw much cared then. His career as a broadcaster was just taking off, largely because of his willingness to rip Elway. In late January 1990, Denver was preparing to play in its third Super Bowl in four years. They were facing the defending Super Bowl champion San Francisco 49ers. The 49ers had gone 14–2 yet somehow still had a chip on their shoulders.

Yes, one of the greatest teams in the history of the league still felt that it had something to prove. The 49ers were in their first year without coach Bill Walsh, who had retired after the previous Super Bowl victory. Players such as Montana and wide receiver Jerry Rice felt as if Walsh, "The Genius," received (and took) too much credit for the success of the 49ers.

To seemingly prove a point, Montana had the best statistical season of his Hall of Fame career and won the first of back-to-back Most Valuable Player awards in his first year without Walsh. Rice led the league in receiving yards and touchdowns. The 49ers led the league in scoring, were third in the league in points allowed defensively, and won their two playoff games leading up to the Super Bowl by a combined score of 71–16. The 49ers weren't a buzz saw. They were a laser cutter. The Broncos were again a massive underdog, making them likely to lose the title game for the third time in four years. Ever the opportunist, Bradshaw seized the chance to unload on Elway again. Bradshaw made his criticism from 1983 look tame.

"The first thing I think of is, [Montana's] got three Super Bowl rings. John Elway is more concerned about promoting himself than winning a Super Bowl. He's been babied. He hasn't won any championships and that's the bottom line," Bradshaw said during a promotional gig for a beer company during the middle of the week leading up to the game. Bradshaw was then asked about Elway's effort on The Drive in Cleveland three years before.

"A lot of guys with great arms have played this game. To be great, you've got to play well over the long haul. One great game doesn't cut it for me," said Bradshaw, who was just getting warmed up. "I think things bother John more than they bother [Montana]. He's got to get a little tougher emotionally, a little tougher mentally.... He's making $2 million a year. Hell, things don't bother you when you're making $2 million a year. Wait until you get out and have to get a job. It will bother you then. You have to get tougher. John's problem is he's been babied—you know, babied by the city until this year and babied by the coach a little bit. It's just too easy. And you know what I went through in Pittsburgh. There's nothing worse than just getting hammered. You fight that stuff. I think John's got to get tougher."

Finally, Bradshaw was asked for a prediction on the score of the game. He picked 55–3.

Reeves defended Elway with a good one-liner. When told that Bradshaw made the remarks at a beer promotion, Reeves responded, "I think he may have had a few too many." Elway's reaction was that Bradshaw could "stick it in his ear." Elway's reaction and the media attention made for drama in the lead-up to the game. Bradshaw's prediction not only proved prescient but it also got him a platform. In the lead-up to the 49ers-Broncos Super Bowl, Bradshaw's comments about Elway and his prediction were huge news. He was working for CBS, but he wasn't supposed to be part of the Super Bowl coverage for the whole week. After the comments at the beer promotion, Bradshaw headed home to Texas. When he landed, as he said years later, "All hell had broken loose."

CBS had Bradshaw return to New Orleans, and he spent the rest of the week pouring it on. Bradshaw then really cashed in during the off-season. He was elevated to the top studio analyst for CBS after the network went through a shakeup. A few years later, Bradshaw moved to FOX for its NFL coverage and has been a fixture on football coverage for nearly thirty years.

Not surprisingly, Jack was none too pleased at the time. That week, as Jack and Jan were walking down Bourbon Street in the French Quarter, Jack spied Bradshaw working on a second-floor balcony set for CBS. Jack decided to lead a chorus of Denver fans and anybody else in a two-word serenade.

"Bradshaw, bullshit. Bradshaw, bullshit. Bradshaw, bullshit," the crowd chanted as Jack served as lead singer and maestro. Years later, Bradshaw admitted his rivalry with John was based on jealousy. In a lot of ways, Bradshaw's rivalry with John was like Brian Bosworth's rivalry with John. "The Boz" picked on Elway as an act of self-promotion. Bosworth's mouth was unrelenting. In his 1988 biography (he was all of twenty-three at the time), he called John "Horseface" and a "human Ken doll." In a 1988 game, Bosworth kept jabbering and called John "Mr. Ed" at one point. John responded by flipping him off after the two went out of bounds on a play.

Other than that brief episode with Bosworth, John Elway didn't develop many direct rivalries during his career. Even his quarterback cohorts from the class of 1983 were rivals in name only. Unlike Tom Brady and Peyton Manning, who played each other seventeen times, Elway faced Marino only three times in their careers. Elway played Kelly only six times and got hurt during their lone playoff game. In some ways, Elway, Marino, and Kelly were more kindred spirits than competitors. The fact that Elway had to wait until the end of his career to win a title while Marino and Kelly never won one became an ironic twist to the men who defined the class of 1983.

Likewise, Elway's five Super Bowls didn't provide him with a true rival. He never faced the same quarterback more than once. Elway may have been coach Marty Schottenheimer's kryptonite, but player-coach rivalries don't really rate, and their rivalry was pretty one-sided. The closest thing Elway ever had to a real rival was Bradshaw. Again, it was primarily one-sided. Elway was essentially a prop for Bradshaw to bash, and Bradshaw carved out a good television career by slicing up Elway.

And he never even sent as much as a thank-you note to Elway. The closest Elway got was an apology years later... after Bradshaw had cashed plenty of checks.

"[It was] an emotional outburst on my part. I wanted to be thought of the same way as Elway, the same way as [Roger] Staubach. It was a huge mistake," Bradshaw said in January 1998 before Elway helped Denver beat Green Bay. Bradshaw even said he was cheering for Elway by then. "John said I was jealous. He was right. I still am. I wish I had all that money and hair. I wish I could ski and play golf like he can."

The other chip on Bradshaw's shoulder is that he didn't get much credit for leading the Steelers. Even though he was twice the MVP of the Super Bowl, the Pittsburgh defense received more credit and Bradshaw was mocked as being stupid.

"I was a quarterback constantly ridiculed, constantly questioned," Bradshaw said. "Even when we won, it was because of everybody else. I had a chip on my shoulder."

All of it bubbled to the surface in January 1990. Bradshaw took no prisoners when it came to Elway. He piled on to his critique with his stunning prediction and continued to pour it on during the pregame show. On January 28, 1990, Elway saw it for himself. There were televisions in the Broncos locker room of the Superdome. The TVs were tuned to the pregame show and Elway let himself get caught up in the moment, transfixed as Bradshaw ripped him.

Denver wide receiver Michael Young started screaming at the equipment people and the coaches to turn off the TVs. No one could find the remotes and the TVs were hung from the ceiling, too high to reach. Young tried to distract Elway. Elway just kept looking and then proceeded to look bad on the field. He completed ten of twenty-six passes for 108 yards and two interceptions. That was a problem by itself.

"By the time I got on the field, it was like we had no chance," Elway says. "The truth is we didn't. The 49ers were loaded. That might be the best team ever."

It was nowhere near as big a problem as the Denver defense. Some Denver fans held out hope that the Broncos could keep the game close based on previous games against the 49ers. The teams had faced off twice in the 1980s during the regular season. Denver won both games and held San Francisco to fewer than twenty points in each game. Montana had combined to complete fewer than half his passes in those games and had thrown only one touchdown pass. The most recent matchup had been during the 1988 season when the Broncos took a 16–13 victory. What people didn't understand is that Reeves had made a change on the coaching staff that was about to backfire on him.

After the 1988 season, Reeves fired defensive coordinator Joe Collier, who had been with the Broncos for twenty years. Collier was the architect of the defense for the first three Denver teams that made the Super Bowl. While his defenses weren't good in the Super Bowl, they had been effective against the 49ers. Collier played mostly zone defense against the 49ers and usually rushed only three defenders. His scheme forced Montana to throw either safe passes underneath that did little damage or deep, low-percentage passes. Collier would also rotate his defensive linemen.

"The starting defensive linemen would play the first two series and then I'd put in the second group for a series because playing only three guys puts a strain on them," Collier says. "It used to make Dan nervous when I put in the backups. He'd come over and say, 'Why aren't the starters out there?' But I knew how hard those guys wanted to play to prove they were better than the starters and because they knew they weren't going to play much."

The problem between Reeves and Collier started after the 1987 season. Reeves wanted Collier to change some of the defensive staff after Washington hammered the Broncos in the Super Bowl. Collier refused, and Reeves backed down. In 1988, after the Broncos went 8–8 and the defense gave up a lot of points in the second half of the season, Reeves decided it was time for Collier to go. Reeves brought in Wade Phillips for the 1989 season. Phillips's attacking, blitz-oriented defense was excellent, limiting opponents to twenty points or less in thirteen regular season games as the Broncos improved to 11–5 and won the division.

Phillips went on to have a great career as a defensive coordinator. Denver even brought him back in 2015 when Kubiak was hired as head coach and Phillips ran a defense that spurred the Broncos to a title. But as the son of legendary coach Bum Phillips, Wade Phillips was weaned on an aggressive style. When it came to playing San Francisco, his approach was problematic. In San Francisco's West Coast offense, the post pattern was the default throw against coverages the Broncos tended to play, especially when Phillips called for blitzes. Elway knew because he had played in the West Coast offense in college. In practice that week, Elway and Kubiak ran the scout team against the Denver defense and hit the post route time after time for one big play after another.

"We kept trying to tell them this is what the 49ers would do if we showed them that defense," Elway says. Phillips's staff didn't listen. Broncos defensive backs coach Charlie Waters told Elway and Kubiak to stop throwing the post route because the 49ers never threw the post. Elway again tried to explain to Waters that he was wrong, but Waters wouldn't hear it.

During the game, Montana threw three touchdown passes on post routes. Years later, Denver wide receiver Michael Young ran into Montana and some other 49ers at an event. Montana explained how stunned he was when Denver played that coverage. San Francisco had spent the week practicing against different coverages, figuring the Broncos would change what they did all season and borrow the concepts Collier had used. When Montana came to the line for the first series of the game, he was happily shocked to see Denver in its usual coverages. He finished the game completing twenty-two of twenty-nine passes for 297 yards and five touchdowns. Rice ended up with seven catches for 148 yards and three touchdowns.

But then, there's probably not much Denver could have done.

"That was probably the greatest team of all time," Elway says.

This was a great and driven 49ers team that had destroyed Minnesota and the Los Angeles Rams on the way to the Super Bowl. The 49ers weren't just trying to win. They were trying to make a point. They did, 55–10. To this day, that's the biggest rout in Super Bowl history. In three Super Bowl appearances with Elway, Denver opponents had set three offensive or scoring records. The 49ers also made Bradshaw look like a genius and increased the pressure on Elway. Not that there's much a quarterback can do when his defense gives up thirty-nine, forty-two, and fifty-five points in successive Super Bowls.

Still, in the immediate aftermath, Elway was shaken. He showered long after the game had ended and got dressed to join his family for a small dinner, skipping the team party that didn't figure to be much of an event. As Elway was brushing his teeth, he paused for a moment and stared straight ahead. Young saw him and asked, "Dude, are you all right?"

Elway looked up and said, "They're never going to forgive me." He was devastated, knowing fan reaction would be brutal. He felt he had let his teammates, the organization, and the entire city down. The Super Bowl losses were starting to weigh on him. That night at dinner, Elway could barely speak to his parents and wife, eventually wandering away from the table in the middle of the meal to be alone in his thoughts.

"We all tried to talk to him and cheer him up somehow, but he wasn't hearing any of it," Jan says. "He didn't want to eat. He didn't want to talk. He was just miserable."

That was the short-term impact. In the long term, the strain would weigh heavily on the relationship between Reeves and Elway over the next three years.

CHAPTER 21

PAT BOWLEN, RED TEETH, AND REEVES

Once upon time, Elway and Bowlen would laugh so hard they'd cry. On the opening day of Broncos training camp in 2014, all Elway could manage were tears.

Elway had to announce that Bowlen was officially no longer able to operate the franchise. Bowlen had turned seventy earlier in the year, was in his thirtieth year as owner, and the effects of Alzheimer's disease had overtaken him. The specifics of who was responsible for running the team were irrelevant at that point. It was about what the moment signified, particularly to Elway. As he spoke to the media, the cracks in his voice were telling.

"[The organization] will never be the same," Elway said as he dabbed away the tears. "I can say that, at least from the inside out, it will never be the same. Having worked for him for thirty years . . . it's going to be very hard to not see him walk through the front doors every day.

"He has . . . he has given me so much. As a player, to be able to play for him, and as I said when I retired, as a player all you want is an opportunity to be the best and be able to compete for world championships . . . he has given us every opportunity."

Bowlen was a quiet yet driven man. Like Elway, he didn't necessarily like being at center stage. He understood it was a consequence of wanting to compete at the highest level. He had started his career by following his father into the oil and gas business and then became a real estate developer in Canada. Along with his sister and two brothers, Bowlen bought the Broncos from Edgar Kaiser in March 1984 for $70 million. With Elway at quarterback and Bowlen at the helm, it was no coincidence the Broncos started a run of five Super Bowl appearances and two titles over the next fifteen years. It wasn't necessarily easy, but the foundation of that success was largely based on Elway and Bowlen's combination of desire.

Bowlen, who was inducted into the Pro Football Hall of Fame in 2019, was an extraordinarily competitive man as an athlete. He ran marathons, competed in Iron Man triathlons, and raced outrigger canoes off the shores of Hawaii. His workouts on the StairMaster at the Broncos facility were legendary, the sweat covering every inch of his clothes by the time he was finished. When the Broncos held training camp in Greeley, Colorado, Bowlen would ride his bicycle fifty-five miles from his home in Denver for the opening day of camp in the hot July sun.

Bowlen was more than just a rich man who owned a team. He was a man's man and the team loved it. At the end of games, he would stand on the sideline in his dark blue suit, orange tie, and cowboy boots. In winter, he'd often wear a fur coat on the sideline. He had a quiet swag. He always preferred to talk to the players, usually in the privacy of the locker room, the training facility, or even his home. As years went on, Elway became his favorite and most trusted player.

Elway had the red teeth to prove it.

In the late 1980s and early 1990s, Bowlen and his wife, Annabel, started inviting Elway and his first wife, Janet, to Bowlen's home for dinner. Bowlen eventually started inviting Shanahan and his wife, Peggy, to join the dinners. Conspicuously absent were Reeves and his wife. The dinners were old-fashioned. Annabel rang a bell for each course and the couples would sit around a long table in an ornate, old-world-style dining room. They would also drink red wine. As the wine flowed, things would get loose. Bowlen, Elway, and Shanahan would tell stories, getting louder as the night wore on. The wives would inevitably go upstairs and play with makeup. Janet was the Barbie doll for Annabel and Peggy. They'd all end up laughing, their teeth stained red from the wine. It was both a moment of bonding and Bowlen's way of finding out what was going on with his team.

All of that led to a more sobering dinner in the 1991 off-season.

The lead-up to that dinner started with the 55–10 demolition the Broncos suffered to San Francisco in the Super Bowl in January 1990. The game was deeply humiliating for the organization and, particularly, Elway. The blowout loss had a long-lasting hangover. Though Shanahan had returned after his brief tenure with the Raiders, that didn't do anything to stem the tide from Denver's lost confidence in the 1990 season, and the roof caved in.

That fallout started with the increasingly frayed relationship between Elway and Reeves. The pair had now combined to lose three Super Bowls in four years. Though getting to the Super Bowl was a mighty accomplishment, the progressively ugly results grated heavily on everyone, particularly those two. After a 2–1 start in 1990, Denver lost nine of its next ten games on the way to a 5–11 season. It was the first time the Broncos had finished with a losing record with Elway. The season was beyond miserable. As bad as Elway's rookie season had been, this was far worse. By early November, the Broncos had fallen to 3–6 when Elway did an interview with *Denver Post* columnist Dick Connor. At this point, the idea of tension between Elway and Reeves was nothing more than a rumor.

Elway made it fact.

"I think I'm going to have to express my opinions from the player level," Elway told Connor. "I'm going to have to go to Dan. And I'm going to have to go . . . they may not like what I have to say. But I'm going to give it to them and they can take it for what it is worth. I think, for what I want to do and where I want us to go, we've got to make some things happen . . . we've got to get the attitude changed. Dan's got to hear it from the players' level."

Finally, Elway ripped off the scab on all the lingering pain from the Super Bowl losses and related problems. Connor asked him about his relationship with Reeves.

"This year has been the worst. We hardly talk to each other unless it's game time," Elway said.

Elway went on to criticize Reeves for personnel decisions, such as moves to let go of veteran players at a time when teams like the 49ers were bringing in veterans to stay competitive. Elway tried to fall on the sword, but it came up short of the criticism.

"I know I'm not easy. It's not his fault. I'm a competitor. I feel like I've been in the league long enough to know what I feel comfortable with," Elway said.

Though this wasn't Elway's shining hour in public relations, he wasn't about to apologize. He was about to do quite the opposite. After the column ran, Reeves called Shanahan to his office. Reeves threw a copy of the *Denver Post* at Shanahan and read him the riot act. Shanahan says he told Reeves, "Why are you talking to me? John is the one who said it."

Shanahan then got the bright idea to get Elway and have the three of them talk it out. Elway was in the weight room when Shanahan found him. They made their way to Reeves's office, and Shanahan acted like the counselor, telling Elway and Reeves they should talk through the issues. Shanahan thought Elway and Reeves were going to hash out all their problems from all the years together. The era of the quarterback was going to have a meeting of the minds with the era of the coach.

Or maybe not.

Elway looked directly at Reeves and said, "I hate you more than any person on this planet."

"That's when I realized maybe this wasn't such a good idea," Shanahan says. "I spent seven years in Denver doing everything I could to keep that relationship intact, but it finally blew up right then and there."

Years later, Elway regretted having said it.

"It's one of those things you immediately wished you could take back," Elway says. "But I was angry. Dan was angry. We didn't know how to talk to each other...in some ways, it was actually a good thing. It got everything out in the open and we didn't have to dance around it anymore."

At that moment, however, the discussion got more heated. Elway screamed at Reeves about how Reeves wasn't paying attention to the offense and he didn't understand what they were trying to do. Reeves yelled back, saying he didn't care what Elway thought and he was taking over the offense. It also taught Elway a very important lesson he valued years later. Again, the tension between Elway and Reeves subsided after they had it out. It may have been ugly, but it was honest. Perhaps if they had talked out all their issues years before, they might have been more productive. The situation couldn't be fixed now, but Elway told himself he wasn't going to hold back his thoughts in the future.

Still, the relationship hadn't quite hit its lowest point. That happened during the following off-season. In early July 1991, Elway ran into running back Earnest Byner, who had been with Cleveland during the two dramatic back-to-back Broncos playoff victories over the Browns. Byner had moved on from Cleveland to Washington, where he helped the Redskins win a Super Bowl. The two men were in Lake Tahoe at a celebrity golf tournament. Eventually, Byner said, "Man, we thought we had a trade for you."

Trade? Elway was caught off guard. What trade was Byner talking about? Reeves ran the football operations and had never mentioned anything to Elway about a trade. Byner said the word around the Washington locker room was that the Redskins had almost pulled off a deal for Elway. Rod Dowhower, a Washington assistant coach who had been Elway's head coach at Stanford in his freshman year, had been one of the intermediaries in the deal and confirmed how close the deal was to happening.

"We really thought we had it done," Dowhower says.

A week or so after Elway met with Byner and as training camp for the 1991 season neared, Elway was at dinner at Bowlen's house. Then-wife, Janet, and dad, Jack, were there as well. There wasn't any wine flowing this time. Bowlen said the story about the trade was true. Reeves had come to him with a proposed trade. Washington had made a play for Elway and Reeves was ready to make the deal, Bowlen told Elway. He just needed permission from Bowlen. To this day, Reeves says Washington pushed for the deal. He says all he did was listen and relay the information to Bowlen.

"I would have been run out of Denver if I tried to trade John," Reeves says.

Regardless of what's the exact truth, Elway felt blindsided. Bowlen said he wrestled with the trade before ultimately calling it off. Elway was shocked and felt further undercut by Reeves. All the ugliness from the previous season came bubbling up again. The last thing Elway wanted was to play for another team.

"I wasn't going to let somebody else control my family's life at that point," says Elway, who by then had lived in Denver longer than any place in his life. He and Janet already had three children and a fourth was on the way. Elway didn't want to uproot his children the way he moved around as a child. The information about the trade fueled Elway's desire to have a plan about how to run his life. He had dabbled in the car business for a few years and now was intent on buying his first dealership. He was going to build a business that allowed him to walk away from football, if necessary.

Just as Elway had worked to control his career so he didn't have to play for an organization like Baltimore, he wasn't going to let anyone dictate his life. Bowlen understood the bigger picture as well. He knew finding a quarterback was a lot harder than finding a coach. Bowlen knew Reeves and Elway had reached the end. Though it was too late to change coaches before the 1991 season, Bowlen kept saying to Elway that he knew there was no way they could continue to work together past the 1991 season. Bowlen made Elway a promise.

"This is Dan's last season," Bowlen said. "After this year, he's done. I don't care if he wins the Super Bowl or doesn't make the playoffs."

"What happens if we make the AFC Championship Game?" Elway recalls saying.

Without hesitation, Bowlen said, "He's done."

It sounded almost convincing at the time. Elway knew better. The Broncos made the AFC Championship Game in 1991 and Bowlen kept Reeves for another year. It was a prolonged and painful end, which was a story unto itself and included one last major problem between the coach and the quarterback.

What impressed Elway years later is how Bowlen managed to juggle all the egos and desires. Bowlen intuitively understood how to play the PR game as he kept just enough peace between Elway and Reeves. Keeping

Reeves around helped spread the blame in the public eye. When Bowlen finally got rid of Reeves after the 1992 season, he and Elway became the main targets for blame from fans and the media.

"I remember there was one time some reporter wrote something really vicious about Pat," says Michael Young, the former Broncos wide receiver who worked in the team's front office after he retired. "I said to him, 'Mr. Bowlen, you should really say something.' He just looked at me and said, 'Michael, it's OK. You have to understand two things. First, it would be a real problem if they *weren't* talking about us. Second, if we win, that will take care of everything.'"

What Elway came to appreciate about Bowlen is that he was completely focused on achieving something unique, not just making money. On the multiple occasions when Elway renegotiated his contract to give the team salary cap relief or money to hire a coach, the team spent the money. Bowlen never pocketed any of it. Bowlen's vision not only led the Broncos to two titles, but eventually he and Elway inspired the people of Denver to approve a new stadium. Elway spent his entire career playing in the original Mile High Stadium, which had been built in 1948. The stadium would shake when the fans got excited. There were times people thought the place was about to crumble.

And when Bowlen famously said, "This one is for John!" after the Broncos beat Green Bay in the Super Bowl in January 1998, people couldn't have known the bond that had developed between the two men by then. Elway had restructured his contract so many times that Bowlen felt obliged to defend Elway during an important negotiation. Bowlen, Beake, and Demoff had worked on the final details of Elway's last contract with the Broncos when they called up Shanahan to let him know. As they reviewed the contract, Shanahan said, "That's too much money."

Demoff fired back with, "OK, Mike, who's going to play quarterback for you then?" The situation got testy in a hurry, threatening to divide the team. Bowlen stepped in and calmed the situation, telling Shanahan they would go back to the table and work it out. What ended up happening was pretty much the exact same contract they had agreed to.

Bowlen always wanted Elway to be part of the inner workings of the team, which is why he offered him an ownership stake. That offer became a soap opera when Edgar Kaiser filed a lawsuit in 2000 saying he had the right to buy a portion of the team first. People around the NFL believe Al Davis of the Raiders encouraged Kaiser to file the lawsuit.

Davis, who still held a grudge against Shanahan from their time together and against the league over the failed Elway trade in 1983, accused Denver of cheating because of salary cap violations. In 2004, the league eventually fined Denver $950,000 and took away a third-round pick for the transgressions from 1996 to 1998.

Through all the drama involving Shanahan, Kaiser, Davis, and the NFL that could have undermined the relationship between Bowlen and Elway, Bowlen never lost sight of what Elway meant to him and the Broncos. The two men developed a special bond. After Jack died in April 2001, the family had a service for him in Denver. People spoke, including a touchingly funny moment when John's nephew Pat Walsh, who was about twelve, described Jack's perfect drink.

Ice and Skyy vodka.

Bowlen followed by stepping in front of the crowd. He pulled a flask from his suit pocket, said, "This one's for Jack!" and took a healthy swig. And on February 7, 2016, after Denver won Super Bowl 50, Elway finally got the chance to repay his disabled boss. Elway stood on the podium, held the Lombardi Trophy aloft, and yelled, "This one's for Pat!" Over the years, Elway worked hard to help get Bowlen elected to the Pro Football Hall of Fame. It finally happened in February 2019. Only four months later, Bowlen died at age seventy-five.

CHAPTER 22

THE END WITH REEVES

Between trading barbs in 1990 and trade rumors in 1991, Reeves and Elway were headed for a divorce.

It was just going to take two seasons and more controversies between them to make it official. Shortly after Elway had dinner with Bowlen and was assured Reeves would be gone after the 1991 season, the Broncos started training camp. As camp progressed, Reeves tried to make peace with Elway by offering him the play-calling responsibilities and allowing Elway and Shanahan to design the game plans. The problem was that Reeves's olive branch was laced with thorns.

"I wasn't going to let him do it unless I knew he had the capability," Reeves said at the time. "That was a given. We were in training camp coming off a 5–11 year and I had a conversation with him. He wasn't having any fun in football. He was dreading every day. I had to find something to get him motivated, so I suggested calling his own plays."

Elway and people around him took that as a backhanded compliment. Elway was entering his ninth season. He had already been calling and executing plays in one furious comeback after another for Reeves. He had grown up the son of a coach, been taught to call his own plays at the line of scrimmage in high school, and played in Bill Walsh's West Coast offense in college. But only now had Reeves deemed him ready to call plays?

It seemed to be further proof of the long-held rumor that Reeves didn't think Elway was very smart. People around the organization said Reeves would say that from time to time. At least that's what got back to Elway. Again, Elway's string of comeback victories, background in football, burgeoning success in the car business, and Stanford degree weren't enough to convince Reeves. Instead, Reeves had to dole out control with the most grudging remarks.

All things considered, Elway was happy with the decision. It gave him the freedom he wanted and felt he deserved. He and Shanahan could do some slightly advanced things, such as script the first fifteen plays, which Walsh had been doing in San Francisco for years. Kubiak, Elway's backup and one of his closest friends on the team, was also helping with the game plans. Denver started the season 4–1 and Elway completed at least 59 percent of his passes in three of the first four games. That wasn't some amazing mark by modern standards, but it was only the second time Elway had ever done it. Again, the usual design of the Reeves offense was to throw deeper, lower-percentage passes. With Elway, Shanahan, and Kubiak planning things, the Broncos incorporated shorter, higher-percentage throws to increase efficiency.

In the fifth game, the Broncos squeaked out a win at Minnesota, 13–6, when Elway didn't play well. In the sixth game, Denver got hammered in Houston, 42–14, by an extremely talented Oilers team. Houston had three Hall of Famers in quarterback Warren Moon and offensive linemen Bruce Matthews and Mike Munchak. The Oilers also had one of the nastiest defenses in the league and were at the tail end of a run of seven straight years in which they made the playoffs.

Regardless, the Broncos were 4–2. That's when everything blew up again. Reeves decided he was going to take back control of the play calling. He also strongly implied Elway and Shanahan were scheming behind his back to run "scripted" plays and Shanahan was trying to undermine him to become the head coach. Elway and Shanahan were dumbfounded, wondering how Reeves could logically think that after he voluntarily gave up control of play calling. Beyond that, the scripted plays were exactly what Elway had been requesting for years.

"In hindsight, I didn't have any proof, but that's how I felt at the time," Reeves says.

As unpleasant as it was for the rest of the season, the Broncos went 8–2 with Reeves calling the plays. They finished 12–4 overall. That was critical because Houston stumbled in the second half of the season and finished 11–5. Denver met Houston again in the playoffs, this time at Mile High Stadium. Houston threatened to make the game another blowout by jumping to a 14–0 lead in the first quarter. Elway led another comeback, and the Broncos were down 24–23 with 2:07 remaining in the game. Just as in Cleveland four years earlier, Denver started on its own two-yard line.

That move set up what is known as The Drive II. Elway converted a fourth-and-six and then a fourth-and-ten. It was a hair-raising series in front of jubilant Broncos fans. The drive ended in a twenty-eight-yard field goal by Denver kicker David Treadwell as the Broncos advanced to the AFC Championship Game for the fourth time in five years.

In the AFC Championship against Buffalo, Elway was knocked out of the game early with an injury and the Broncos lost 10–7. Despite all the hard feelings between Elway and Reeves, it was clear Elway wasn't going to let his personal feelings get in the way of trying to win.

"I know people used to ask me all the time about how Reeves and Elway didn't like each other, but I truly never noticed it like people were talking about," says running back Steve Sewell, who played with Denver from 1985 through 1991. "To me, it was always business. Those guys were about winning and that was it. I know what they've said since then, but I know John never brought that in the locker room."

As Elway predicted, getting within one game of the Super Bowl meant Reeves was coming back for the 1992 season despite what Bowlen had promised. Two people weren't coming back, however. The first was Shanahan. Reeves blamed Shanahan for the problems he was having with Elway, still believing at the end of the season that Shanahan was insubordinate. That created a rift between the two coaches that lasted for years. The second departure was Kubiak, who retired after nine seasons and headed back to coach at his alma mater, Texas A&M. Elway had lost two of his closest friends and confidants on the team.

Shanahan ended up getting job offers from Pittsburgh and San Francisco. Mike Holmgren had just left the 49ers to coach Green Bay. San Francisco was obviously still loaded with talent, but Shanahan really liked the idea of going to Pittsburgh, a stable organization and a city where he could afford to buy a home and raise his family. Instead, Elway and others talked him into going to the 49ers to learn the West Coast system and how the 49ers ran their organization.

"John was adamant I should go to the 49ers," Shanahan says. "I was really committed to the idea of Pittsburgh, but John and a couple of other people really talked me into going to San Francisco and it ended up being the best decision I could have made."

Shanahan spent three years with the 49ers, eventually helping them win a Super Bowl in the 1994 season with Steve Young at quarterback. More importantly, Shanahan learned about the complete and total commitment San Francisco had to winning. Shanahan returned to Denver as head coach in 1995 and was better prepared than ever. In a lot of ways, the situation worked out for the best. However, the Reeves-Elway relationship continued to deteriorate. The 1992 NFL Draft was going to prove that again. As the draft approached, the word from inside the organization was that Denver would take wide receiver Carl Pickens of Tennessee in the first round with the number twenty-five overall pick. Pickens was considered a can't-miss prospect and ended up having a strong career at Cincinnati. He was vastly more talented than any receiver Reeves had ever drafted for Elway.

People in Denver often bring up the "Three Amigos," the receiving trio of Vance Johnson, Mark Jackson, and Ricky Nattiel, who joined the Broncos in the mid-1980s. The nickname was cute. The production was mediocre. Those three receivers combined to play twenty-three seasons with the Broncos and finished with a total of sixty-nine touchdown catches and only one 1,000-yard season. Pickens played nine seasons, finished with sixty-three touchdowns, and had four 1,000-yard seasons. Pickens would have been a great addition. Elway was at Stapleton Airport as the draft was unfolding when a fan came up to him and said, "Did you hear who the Broncos drafted?"

The thirty-one-year-old Elway was under the belief it was going to be Pickens.

"I told him they took Pickens," Elway says. "The fan looks at me and says, 'No, they took Tommy Maddox.' That caught me by surprise."

Tommy Maddox, a quarterback from UCLA. Pickens went number thirty-one overall.

Reeves—the man who had spent years warring with Elway, entertained trade offers for him, gave him the play calling, yanked it back, and then fired his most-trusted coach—had just invested a first-round pick in a man who played the same position. Instead of giving Elway a weapon to help him, Reeves took a guy to replace him. NFL teams don't take quarterbacks in the first round unless they expect them to play. Reeves could say anything he wanted about needing another quarterback to develop in case something happened to Elway, but all the words rang hollow to anyone who understood the game.

Somehow, some way, Reeves had just created even more tension between him and Elway. At that point, Elway didn't say anything to Bowlen about the situation. What else was there to say? Elway also made sure he never took it out on Maddox. It wasn't Maddox's fault he was thrown into the middle of all the discord.

Reeves also replaced Shanahan with George Henshaw, who had only been in the NFL as a coach for four years and had never been an offensive coordinator at the pro level. Henshaw was one of Reeves's guys and did what Reeves wanted. As 1992 began, the long-term effects of a strained relationship were about to take hold on the team. Elway had the second-worst season of his career and the worst since his rookie season, finishing with ten touchdown passes and seventeen interceptions. His quarterback rating was an abysmal 65.7. There were plenty of times he was ready to quit. Denver finished the season 8–8 and Elway got hurt along the way. Despite Elway's poor stats, the Broncos were 8–4 with him starting and 0–4 with Maddox starting.

Ultimately, taking Maddox only made things worse for Reeves. It was further proof to Bowlen that Elway was harder to replace than Reeves. In a sense, the era of the quarterback had truly displaced the era of the coach. At the end of the 1992 season, Bowlen fired Reeves, ending the ten-year run with Elway and the twelve-year run in Denver. After Bowlen made the decision, Reeves took several days to clean out his office. In today's NFL, coaches are gone in a few hours. The NFL was different then. Teams were run more like family businesses than corporations. By the third day, Reeves said his goodbyes to the staff members and finished up at Saccomano's office.

As Reeves stood at the door, he broke down crying at what he probably viewed as inadequacy for the first time in his professional life. The man coached the Broncos to three Super Bowls in ten years and somehow considered that failure. That's how the NFL affects people's perspectives. Just like Elway, Reeves poured his soul into chasing greatness.

With Reeves fired, the first call Bowlen made was to Shanahan. As fate would have it, it was another connection that didn't happen. At least not right away. Shanahan ended up resisting the offer and stayed in San Francisco. Again, that ultimately turned out to be a good thing, even if it didn't feel great at the time. From a public relations perspective, Shanahan didn't want it to seem as if Reeves's claims of insubordination in 1991 were true. Shanahan didn't want the football community to think he was really undermining Reeves to get the Broncos job.

The bigger issue Elway didn't understand at the time was that Shanahan wanted more control over the roster than Bowlen was willing to give him. Elway was playing negotiator between Bowlen and Shanahan during much of the talks. Each would call Elway to find out what the other was thinking. After days of doing that, Elway finally asked Shanahan, "What's the problem?" Shanahan said it was about money. Elway said, "OK, how much? I'll give Pat the money out of my contract." Shanahan didn't have a good answer.

"I got caught there because I never expected John would make that offer," Shanahan says. "What I couldn't tell him is Pat wouldn't give me permission to spend to the salary cap if I wanted. I wasn't going to have final say over the roster and I felt I needed that to make it work. I couldn't tell John because I didn't want him to think Pat was the problem. So I just said we couldn't agree on the salary and then he tells me he's going to give up part of his contract to make it work."

Bowlen and Shanahan couldn't work it out, and the Broncos had to go a different direction. They promoted Wade Phillips from defensive coordinator to head coach, starting a two-year run that got Elway back in the right frame of mind toward playing. At that moment, however, the failure of Reeves and Elway to get the job done led to their undoing and the animosity wasn't going away anytime soon.

The New York Giants hired Reeves shortly after he was fired by Denver. By the time training camp rolled around for the 1993 season, Elway was ecstatic to start over without Reeves around and made that clear in comments to Adam Schefter of the *Rocky Mountain News*. That created a big stir, the quotes from Elway turning into a *Sports Illustrated* cover story. The magazine put alternating photos of Elway and Reeves with a superimposed tear between them. On Elway's side was the headline, "Good Riddance." On Reeves's side it read, "Grow Up."

CHAPTER 23

THE WADE YEARS

A big part of Elway just wanted to have some fun.

After three Super Bowl losses, a championship was still what Elway craved. His competitive fire was further stoked by the fact that younger quarterbacks were passing him by. Troy Aikman had just won a title in Dallas in only his fourth season and was surrounded by a talented roster assembled by coach Jimmy Johnson. Steve Young had taken over in San Francisco and was being coached by Elway's good friend Shanahan. Brett Favre was starting to emerge in Green Bay and had been joined by transcendent defensive lineman Reggie White during the 1992 season.

Yet at the most basic level, Elway just needed to exhale and enjoy the game again. His ten years working with Reeves had grated on both men, and the emotional wounds were still fresh, as Elway's flare-up at the beginning of training camp in 1993 showed. Enter Phillips, a man who understood a few things about enjoying the game for what it is. Phillips's famous father, Bum Phillips, was equal parts defensive genius, cattle rancher, and football philosopher. Bum was born, raised, and eventually died in Texas. On the sideline, he wore a trademark cowboy hat and possessed a quick wit that matched the depth of his Southern drawl.

Phillips was cut from his father's cloth, the type of man who could outsmart most people with his defensive schemes and then cut the rug with his wife at the team Christmas party. Maybe he had run the wrong defense against San Francisco in the Super Bowl, but that was because he believed in being aggressive. In the heat of a tense game or a meeting, Phillips was the type of man who could come up with a one-liner to remind everyone this was, after all, just a game.

Elway loved it because it suited his sense of humor. In college, the first time wide receiver Don Lonsinger got into a game, Elway saw the anxiety on his buddy's face. Lonsinger had almost lost a finger to a wobbling Elway pass, so his first game action was filled with personal meaning. As Lonsinger entered the huddle, Elway smiled and said, "Man, look who's here. Isn't this great. Welcome, big guy!" Lonsinger started mumbling under his breath, "Shut up, Elway. Shut the hell up."

When Wyman made his NFL debut with Seattle in 1987 at Denver, Elway was ready to tweak his old college buddy.

"I was standing there across the line from Elway, my knees knocking together. He surveys the defense and then rests his eyes on me, and then smiles and winks. I could've killed him," Wyman says. "I was scared out of my mind and he was having a casual moment of recognition. Sort of, 'OK, it's second-and-ten, they're in three-deep with an odd front, looks like that outside backer is gonna buzz the flat...hey I know that guy. What's up Dave? How you doing?' Inside my mind I was thinking, 'Don't screw up, don't screw up. Oh God, please don't let Elway recognize me and notice how scared I must look.'"

Elway pulled the same stunt on Tampa Bay safety John Lynch in a 1993 preseason game. Elway came to the line, saw Lynch, and went into the cadence.

"Red 98," Elway yelled. "Red 98, Johnny Lynch." After the snap, Elway threw the ball into the flat and Lynch made a quick tackle.

"I go back to the huddle and I've got all these veteran guys like Hardy Nickerson and Martin Mayhew in there. They don't say, 'Nice play, rook.' All they say is, 'You know Elway?' It was embarrassing, but also kind of cool, like I belonged a little," Lynch says.

There were fun moments off the field as well in 1993. The Broncos were staying at the Paper Valley Inn in Appleton, Wisconsin. It was the night before a game at Green Bay. Elway was in the TV production meeting when a woman approached Saccomano. The woman was a bridesmaid in a wedding party at the hotel that evening. She asked nicely if Elway could come to the wedding to take a picture or two with the bride and groom. They were big fans, she said.

Saccomano, as he always did, smiled and said he'd ask. He also made sure she understood Elway was busy and had a game to prepare for. As Elway walked out of the meeting, Saccomano made the request. Elway wasn't paying close attention. All he heard was "wedding" and "pictures" at a time when he was more concerned about Reggie White and LeRoy Butler. Elway walked into the elevator. As the doors closed, Saccomano looked at the woman and said, "I'm sorry." Then, just as she was about to walk away, the doors opened. Elway stepped out and said, "What is this thing you want me to do?" Some couple in Wisconsin ended up with Elway pictures in their wedding album.

"It took him about twenty minutes, but you could see how happy he made those people," Saccomano says. Moments like that broke up the monotony of the game. Under Reeves, moments like that were overwhelmed by tension. That made Phillips a welcome change in 1993 even if he wasn't Shanahan. Phillips brought in Jim Fassel as offensive coordinator. Fassel had been Elway's offensive coordinator at Stanford. The two had a strong bond. In college, Elway would seek out Fassel for advice on how to manage his hectic life and budding relationship with girlfriend (and later wife) Janet.

In Denver, Fassel used his relationship with Elway to solve problems, such as Elway's love of riding motorcycles. Over the years, Reeves, Bowlen, and even Elway's father had asked Elway to stop riding to no avail. Fassel put a stop to it with a couple of questions one day.

"John, do you like my kids?" Fassel asked Elway.

"Yeah, Jim, I love your kids. They're like family to me," Elway said.

"OK, if you loved my kids that much, why are you putting my job at risk by riding that motorcycle?" Fassel said.

Elway was done riding.

What Fassel mostly understood is that Elway needed to return to the basics. Elway's throwing mechanics and fundamentals had fallen into disrepair. On top of that, Fassel gave Elway input into how the offense would be run. If Elway didn't like something, the Broncos' didn't do it. The things he liked to do became staples. Fassel brought in the West Coast offense.

The results were immediate. Elway posted career bests in passing yards (4,030), completion percentage (63.2), touchdowns (25), and quarterback rating (92.8). It also started a remarkable statistical turnaround for the thirty-three-year-old quarterback. After ten years of playing statistically ugly football, Elway began a run many athletes and sports experts would consider strange. Elway's final six seasons are, statistically, his best. From age thirty-three on, he peaked. That's not supposed to happen. At age thirty-three, most athletes are preparing to slow down.

"I was finally allowed to run an offense that made sense and have some say over what I liked," Elway says. "It wasn't really hard to figure out."

Elway seemed to just be getting started. Denver went 9–7 in the loaded AFC West in 1993 (four of the five teams in the division were 8–8 or better). The Broncos lost to the Raiders in the first round of the playoffs, 42–24. The important development from that game was tight end Shannon Sharpe. Sharpe caught thirteen passes for 156 yards and a touchdown, putting an exclamation mark on his breakout season (eighty-one receptions, 995 yards, and nine touchdowns). Sharpe was a seventh-round pick in 1990 out of Savannah State University and was the greatest late-round find by Reeves.

Sharpe was gifted but not trained in football. He had played basketball and football and run track in college. It took him two years to get a handle on how to be a receiver in the NFL, particularly when having to line up to block against linebackers. At six-foot-two, Sharpe was often listed at 240 pounds on the roster, but he was lucky to hit 230 on most days. Having him block regularly wasn't only questionable, it was a bad idea. It was like trying to turn a thoroughbred into a plow horse. In 1992, he had a solid season with fifty-three catches and made the Pro Bowl, but there was room to grow still. The 1993 season was the beginning of a special run for Sharpe.

Starting that year, Sharpe had sixty catches or more in ten of the next

eleven seasons and basically didn't stop until he got to the Pro Football
Hall of Fame. The only exception in that eleven-year run was an injury-
shortened 1999 season. Sharpe was a fitness freak who liked to play with
people's minds. He was smart but wanted people to think he wasn't. His
favorite line was, "I didn't graduate magna cum laude. I graduated 'Thank
you, Lawdy.'"

One time, Elway and Sharpe were playing a *Jeopardy!* board game.
Sharpe knew the answer to the question. Elway didn't. Elway demanded
the answer.

"I'm not telling you," Sharpe recalls saying.

"Tell me or you're not getting the ball," Elway said.

"I looked in Elway's eyes and I knew he wasn't kidding," Sharpe says.

The Broncos' switch from Reeves's offense to the West Coast offense
was important for Sharpe because it put an emphasis on throwing to the
tight end. As the years went on, Sharpe became an increasingly important player for Elway. The other important thing for Elway in 1993 was
that Jack became a scout with the Broncos and later worked his way up
to director of pro personnel. Jack had coached the previous two years for
the Frankfurt Galaxy of the World League of American Football. Jack
and Jan loved living in Europe, but he longed to be part of something
more serious.

Jack also made life amusing along the way. He and fellow Broncos scout
Jerry Frei—another football lifer—would room together during training
camp and watch practice together. They became the Broncos version of
Statler and Waldorf, the grumpy old men from the Muppets who sat in
the balcony and mocked the show. Jack and Frei would sit back and heckle
the team under their breath with one-liner after one-liner. Jack would
occasionally let an insult get out from under his breath. The next morning,
he would ask Frei, "OK, who do I have to apologize to today?"

In 1994, Denver's offense continued to develop, but Elway missed
two games with injuries. The Broncos lost both games, finished 7–9, and
missed the playoffs. The problem for Phillips was that the team seemed
sloppy in other ways. The Broncos started the season 0–4, losing two
games by less than a touchdown. They then won seven of eight games to

put themselves in contention before losing the final three games. Overall, Denver went 4–5 in games decided by less than a touchdown.

At the same time, Phillips was pretty much a goner because Shanahan was now ready to return. Behind the scenes, Shanahan and Bowlen were talking on a regular basis. Elway was aware of it, but not in the middle of it the way he had been in 1993. This time, Shanahan had the leverage to get complete control of the football operations. Shanahan created leverage by continuing to improve his resume as one of the top offensive minds in the game. In his third season with San Francisco as offensive coordinator, the 49ers were number one in the league in offense, went 13–3, and won the Super Bowl. They scored thirty points or more in eleven of their final thirteen games, including all three play-off games. In fact, they *averaged* more than forty-three points in their three playoff games. Between Shanahan's success and Denver's middling results under Phillips, the stage was set for Shanahan to return.

CHAPTER 24

DON'T BE AFRAID TO MANAGE

Elway's desperation met Shanahan's discipline.

The results were sometimes rocky, but ultimately magical. Such is life between driven people.

After twelve years in the NFL, Elway was increasingly conscious of his legacy. By the start of the 1995 season, his last Super Bowl appearance had been six years earlier. His last AFC Championship Game had been four years earlier. With other young quarterbacks rising to the top, Elway was wondering about his place in the game. More specifically, how would he be perceived if he never won a title?

"A lot of thoughts go through your head," says Elway, who turned thirty-five prior to that season, his first with Shanahan as head coach. "You try to justify it's going to be OK if you don't win one, that you did everything you could. That's a hard one to swallow. I said to myself at one point it was going to be OK. Then I won the first one. I realized I was lying to myself."

Elway also wondered about the bigger question of where he stood next to the greats of the game. He went to Woody Paige, the *Denver Post* columnist and, at the time, the local selector for the Pro Football Hall of Fame. He asked Paige about his chances of making the Hall at that point. The answer wasn't necessarily what Elway wanted to hear.

"Win a Super Bowl and don't retire the same year as Dan Marino,"

Paige recalls saying. In other words, Elway's resume for immortality in the game he loved so much wasn't complete. He didn't have a title. He also didn't have the outrageous numbers of his fellow quarterback from the class of 1983. Something was going to have to happen and it was going to have to happen soon. Shanahan was that something. More specifically, Shanahan's approach to chasing greatness was that something. Shanahan officially returned to the Broncos on January 31, 1995, getting his second chance to be a head coach. Between his ill-fated stop with the Raiders and his three-year stint as offensive coordinator with the 49ers, he was a perfect combination of motivated and educated. He also had perfected a critical characteristic of being a great manager.

Don't be afraid to be disliked.

"If you're going to manage people, you have to be willing to tell them the complete truth about where they are or what they are not doing in their career," Shanahan says. "That's hard to do initially because people don't really want to hear the truth. Not the hard truth. But when you tell them, eventually they come back to you, sometimes years later, and tell you, 'I appreciate what you said because you were really honest with me.'"

Shanahan's experience in San Francisco was multileveled. He learned immediately what the demands of greatness looked like. Coaching with the 49ers was akin to getting an MBA in the football business. This wasn't simply an advanced degree in football. It was organizational and management theory. Shanahan's eyes were opened to a whole different way of thinking. San Francisco put an emphasis on well-executed football and on perfection throughout the entire organization. In the first organizational meeting after Shanahan arrived in San Francisco in 1992, the team spent eight hours meeting with everyone from players to office staff to groundskeepers to discuss the expectations about how to help the team win. It wasn't about football or practice times or where to get equipment. It was about standards.

"I said to myself right then wherever I ended up as a head coach, this is what I was going to bring to the organization, this type of expectation and attention to detail," Shanahan says. "When I came back, one of the first things John asked me is, what's going to be different?"

The short answer was everything. There were going to be demands on the organization from top to bottom. No one was going to be immune. Of course, the football lessons were paramount. Shanahan studied Bill Walsh's West Coast attack in greater detail and now his mind was racing with ideas on how to improve it. He learned the stories of Walsh's demanding style, such as repeating plays in practice. It wasn't enough for Joe Montana to complete a pass to Jerry Rice in practice. Walsh wanted the ball in the exact spot for Rice to catch the ball at full speed. Walsh would order another rep if it wasn't done perfectly. Walsh also made sure his offense had balance. As much as it was pass-based, a key to the operation was making sure the running game was effective.

For Shanahan, that was paramount to bring to Denver to help Elway.

"The first thing I said is we were going to have to get a better running game to help John out. He was getting hit way too much and I said, 'There's no way your body can take the punishment after all these years,'" Shanahan says. "Next, we were going to set the tempo for practice and he was going to be the one who led us in practice."

As the son of a coach, Elway understood that implicitly. Shanahan returned to Denver not only for the money and the control, but also because he knew he had a quarterback who was, in his view, "The greatest locker-room quarterback, ever."

"There can't be days off for the quarterback when everybody else is working. The rest of the team has to see that guy and has to see him working harder than everybody else, whether it's on the field, in the weight room, or in the classroom," Shanahan says. Years after Elway had retired, Shanahan faced the opposite end of the spectrum when veteran quarterback Jake Plummer didn't want to show up for all off-season work. Shanahan quickly made the move to get a replacement for Plummer. In 1995, however, Shanahan knew exactly what kind of quarterback he was getting with Elway. There was no need to convince Elway to work hard. The man had swept plenty of floors over the years.

Elway loved Shanahan's demanding style. More to the point, he knew the Broncos needed it. The previous three seasons had produced a 24–24 record in the regular season and a single one-and-done playoff appearance.

Elway wasn't going to let anything get in the way of Shanahan's push for success, even if that made him juggle life with his friends. In the 1995 off-season, V-Sak asked Elway to help with a charity golf tournament for his high school in Bakersfield, California. Elway committed, then backed out because the tournament was on the first day of Shanahan's first off-season camp. It was a voluntary camp, but voluntary doesn't exist in the NFL when you have a first-year coach and an aging veteran quarterback trying to win a title. Ten days before the tournament, Elway gave V-Sak the bad news. It bugged Elway to no end. Five days before the tournament, he came up with a solution. He'd jump on a private jet right after practice, fly to the tournament after everyone was done golfing, tell some stories, sign some autographs, and shake some hands. Then he'd jump back on the plane and return to Denver for the second day of the camp.

"The whole thing turned out amazing," V-Sak says. "He comes in, speaks for twenty minutes, tells the story about me and the Grapevine, talks about my brothers and my mom. It's awesome. He signs autographs, has dinner, sits at the bar with everybody until 11:30, and then jumps back on the plane at the last minute.... I know when he had to let me down, it bothered him. I'm not a Hall of Famer, but he put himself out there like that for me."

That was the type of commitment Shanahan needed as well. The quarterback isn't just another player. He is an extension of management. A franchise quarterback such as Elway is even more important because he's also the highest paid player on the team. Whatever Elway did, other players fell in line behind him. The NFL had also changed structurally over the previous three years. In 1993, free agency began, meaning veteran players would be moving around the league at a greater rate than ever. It meant personnel analysis was going to be more critical than ever.

It meant, in Shanahan's view, the head coach needed to have more influence than ever on which players were going to be on the roster. Shanahan was ready. Only two days after leading the 49ers to a dominating victory over San Diego in the Super Bowl in Miami, on January 29, 1995, Shanahan and Bowlen finalized the agreement that was essentially a *fait accompli.*

"This is a long-term commitment on both Mike's part and my part, a seven-year deal," Bowlen said at a news conference. "Mike will have full control of the football operation, which is the way I want it to be."

The deal had been more than a month in the making. In truth, there was no doubt Shanahan was taking the job. He wanted to be in a place where he trusted the owner and had a franchise quarterback in place. Most of all, after the meltdown with the Raiders and Davis, he wanted a place where he could be in control and be himself. Shanahan the head coach was cold, exacting, tough, and demanding. His standards didn't allow for deviation. If that meant Shanahan got crosswise with someone, so be it.

From Bowlen's perspective, he needed Shanahan and Elway together for another reason. By 1995, Mile High Stadium had long outlived its usefulness. It had been built in 1948 and creaked with age. More than that, it was simply outdated. Around the NFL, one team after another was either building a new stadium or moving somewhere in hopes of getting one. Atlanta opened the Georgia Dome in 1992. St. Louis fueled the frenzy by building a stadium before it had a team, eventually attracting the Rams away from Southern California in 1995. The Cleveland Browns moved to Baltimore to get a new stadium. The Houston Oilers moved to Tennessee. Then both Cleveland and Houston eventually built stadiums to lure expansion teams. Washington opened FedEx Field in 1997. New England, Tampa Bay, Philadelphia, Pittsburgh, Seattle, and Detroit weren't far behind, and eventually Jerry Jones started pushing for his palace of a stadium in Dallas.

The Broncos had to keep pace. For Bowlen, it wasn't about keeping up with the Joneses. It was about keeping up with the Dow Joneses of football. The impact of a stadium on a team's ability to compete can't be overstated. In an entertainment business like the NFL, the venue became critical to revenue. From high-end suites to bigger concourses for selling merchandise, modern stadiums include all sorts of amenities. To get a new stadium, Bowlen needed a championship team to help melt public resistance.

That is why Bowlen, Shanahan, and Elway were, in so many ways, the perfect combination of owner, coach, and quarterback. All three were incredibly motivated simultaneously. From the outside, that didn't necessarily show up in the results in 1995. The Broncos finished 8–8. What was clear to anyone inside the Broncos facility is that Shanahan was demanding more. Much more. If players didn't make weight, they were fined. If they were late, they were fined. Shanahan was meticulous.

Even with his stars.

During training camp that season, tight end Shannon Sharpe missed a lot of practice time with an ankle injury. Sharpe worked diligently to be ready for the regular season and proved it by catching ten passes for 180 yards in a 22–7 win over Buffalo in the opener. The next day, Sharpe was called in to see Shanahan for what he thought would be a very positive meeting.

"Mike puts in the tape of the game and we're watching one example after another about how I didn't play well," Sharpe says. "There's one of me dropping a pass, then there's a missed block. He's pointing out everything and I'm thinking, 'What's going on? I just had ten catches for 180 yards.' That's when Mike said, 'I won't accept anything in a win I wouldn't accept in a loss.' He just went on and on and said, 'Yeah, we won, but if we had lost, these are reasons we could have lost and that's not acceptable.' Mike was not an easy guy to play for. He was a coach with a very high expectation level. He was very demanding."

Shanahan was developing a culture of expectation and Elway loved it. He could see the focus, direction, and determination. That wasn't all just about Shanahan. It was also about people Shanahan brought in. Denver didn't have any picks in the first three rounds of the 1995 draft because of a string of earlier trades. Shanahan made the most of what he had. Wide receiver Rod Smith, who had been undrafted out of college and signed by Denver in 1994, was developed. Shanahan also signed free agent wide receiver Ed McCaffrey, whom he had coached in San Francisco. Smith and McCaffrey combined to be mainstays of the passing game. Shanahan also brought in defensive linemen Mike Lodish and Michael Dean Perry for depth and guard Mark Schlereth to solidify the offensive line.

Perhaps the two biggest moves Shanahan made were what led to the creation of one of the greatest running games in the history of the league and an offense that took so much pressure off Elway. First, Shanahan hired offensive line coach Alex Gibbs, a former Broncos assistant who had gone with Shanahan to the Raiders and then worked for several other teams. If Shanahan was one of the best offensive minds in the NFL, Gibbs was his cerebellum. Gibbs created the physical foundation up front to allow Shanahan to come up with his schemes.

Second, Shanahan drafted Terrell Davis, a little-known running back from Georgia, in the sixth round. What the Broncos ended up with was the perfect running back to match with the scheme Shanahan and Gibbs were devising. Gibbs was renowned for his ability to teach the zone-blocking scheme. Though that scheme was incredibly effective, there was something much deeper to what Gibbs was able to do with those linemen. He created a unity that overcame the perceived lack of physical talent. By the time Denver got to the Super Bowl in the 1997 and 1998 seasons, the offensive line featured mostly guys who were not considered physically gifted when they came in the league. Schlereth is the symbol of those lines. He was a tenth-round draft pick in 1989 by Washington and made himself into a two-time Pro Bowler with a combination of toughness, guile, and self-sacrifice. Brian Habib was also a tenth-round pick when he came into the league. The NFL Draft doesn't even last ten rounds anymore.

Tony Jones was undrafted. Tom Nalen and Harry Swayne were seventh-round picks. Gary Zimmerman, who was a first-round pick in 1984 and came to the Broncos in trade in 1993, was around for the first championship and then retired because of shoulder injuries. Dan Neil came into the league in 1997 as a third-round pick. Those seven guys combined to start the back-to-back Super Bowl victories in the 1997 and 1998 seasons. Gibbs molded them into a group that played with a sense of unity. The sum of the parts was a lot better than the individual values. Gibbs did that by commanding their respect with his attention to detail. He was a master technician at the position.

Elway thought so highly of Gibbs he brought Gibbs back to the Broncos as an advisor after taking over the football operations in 2011 (Gibbs refused to be a full-time coach again). Gibbs created unity that extended beyond the field. He encouraged the offensive linemen to resist individual attention. The linemen spent years not talking to the media, not because they didn't trust the media, but because they didn't want one guy to appear above the group. The linemen took it a step further with their own kangaroo court. One time, backup David Diaz-Infante, who had played for Jack Elway in college and was friends with Elway, was fined for having a drink with Elway.

"They were all accusing me of kissing up to the quarterback," Diaz-Infante says with a laugh. "I'm like, 'I've known this guy for ten years.' They knew. They just wanted to set some example." Elway took his share of punishment. There were occasional games when Elway would take a couple of early hits. He'd get in the huddle, look at the offensive linemen, and say, "OK, what did I do wrong this week?" They would smirk and then block their asses off for him the rest of the game.

Beyond creating that culture, Gibbs was the biggest advocate for the running game and wasn't afraid to get on Shanahan. He would be in Shanahan's ear throughout games, reminding Shanahan the running game had to come first and had to be developed. Shanahan agreed with that principle, but even the most disciplined play callers occasionally get pass-happy. Put it all together and there was a breakthrough in 1995. During the 1994 season, Denver had run 431 times for 1,470 yards, an average of 3.4 yards per carry. In 1995, the Broncos ran 440 times for 1,995 yards, averaging 4.5 yards per carry.

That improvement was staggering—4.5 yards per carry was the highest average Denver had posted during Elway's entire career. In his first twelve seasons, the Broncos cracked the 4.0 per carry only three times and topped out at 4.1. Most importantly, this was the beginning of a trend. Over the next three seasons, Denver averaged 4.5 yards a carry, then 4.6 yards, and finally 4.7. Elway could feel the impact. Over the first twelve years of his career, he had been sacked an average of thirty-four times a season. Over the final four years of his career, that figure dropped to an average of twenty-five times.

As much as Gibbs and the offensive linemen were important, Davis was critical. Davis's road to the NFL was odd. He had suffered through an injury-marred senior season at Georgia after transferring there when Long Beach State University shut down its program. Davis was roughly sixth on the depth chart as a rookie and worked his way up. He caught the attention of coaches on special teams with a big hit during an exhibition game in Japan. He was the starter by the season opener, by which time Elway had started to give him some attention. After twelve years, Elway had learned not to get too attached to rookies until they proved something.

"I remember the first time John talked to me, it was at the end of camp and we were back [in Denver]," Davis says. "He comes up to me and says, 'Hi, I'm John.' I'm like trying not to get all giddy and say something stupid, but in my head I'm thinking: 'John knows who I am! This is great! I have to call my friends!' It's like the first time the pretty girl at school notices you and you're like, 'I've arrived.'"

It was hard to ignore just how good Davis was after he got some chances. Davis had the innate vision to see the cutback runs built into the offense and then see how the defense was trying to play the run all the way through the secondary. In addition, he could get to top speed after his cuts in a step or two. Put it together and Davis had amazing breakaway ability even if he wasn't the fastest back in the NFL. He had at least one run of fifty yards or longer in each of his first four seasons before getting hurt. During those four healthy years, Davis rushed for 6,313 yards and fifty-six touchdowns. In 1998, alone, he rushed for 2,008 yards and twenty-one scores. He also caught 152 passes for 1,181 yards and five touchdowns over those four years.

The only running backs to ever have a better four-year run in the history of the NFL were Eric Dickerson and Earl Campbell, a pair of first-ballot Hall of Famers. It took Davis more than a decade to get into the Hall of Fame because of his injury-shortened career. Where Davis really blew the field away was in the playoffs. He was better in the playoffs than in the regular season. In eight playoff games, he rushed for 1,140 yards and scored another twelve touchdowns.

Not only did Davis *average* 142.5 yards per game (the highest average in NFL playoff history), but he was also on pace for 2,280 yards rushing if you project that over sixteen games. That would be an NFL record in the regular season. Davis was doing that against the best of the best in the most intense situations. He also did that while battling recurring migraine headaches throughout his career.

This was a perfect setup. But the key was still Shanahan's intensity. Shanahan came back to Denver with a vengeance. The firing by Reeves was still a fresh wound. As for the Raiders experience, not only did Al Davis fire Shanahan after just over a season, but also Davis stiffed him out of $250,000. When Shanahan was still an assistant with San Francisco, he had Steve Young throw a pass at Davis during pregame warm-ups as Davis stood on the field. That move sent Davis sprawling to the ground, furious with anger.

Upon returning to Denver, Shanahan and Elway proceeded to go 7–1 against the Raiders in the four seasons they were together. Shanahan extended the gamesmanship to press conferences. At the beginning of the 1995 season, the Raiders coaching staff had gotten away from playing man-to-man coverage in the secondary even though Davis was a staunch believer in it. The Raiders were playing mostly zone coverage and were 5–1 in the process, so Davis didn't interfere.

The Raiders came to Denver in week seven. Early in the week, Shanahan told the coaching staff and some of the players, including Elway, to expect the Raiders to switch back to man coverage. The coaches and players thought Shanahan was joking around.

"Just watch and you'll see," Shanahan recalls saying to the team. In the Wednesday press conference before the game, Shanahan came out and praised the Raiders coaching staff for what a great job they were doing playing zone coverage. He went on and on about it, effusively talking about how the Raiders had made the switch so effectively. That week, the Raiders played man coverage and the Broncos won 27–0. After the game, one of the Raiders defensive coaches came up to Shanahan.

"He said, 'We all know what you did, Mike,'" Shanahan says.

One thing that began to change between Shanahan and Elway was their relationship. They had been very close, socialized together, golfed together, and had very open communication when Shanahan was an assistant coach. By the end of 1995, the relationship grew more professional and, therefore, more distant. The communication was done through Kubiak, Elway's former backup who had been brought back as the offensive coordinator by Shanahan. None of that was by accident. Just like Walsh, who had built walls between himself and even great players such as Montana, Shanahan was building walls. It was all part of the job in Shanahan's view. If he was going to be completely honest with people, he had to take the emotional connection out of the equation.

There was, in Shanahan's view, only one way to manage.

CHAPTER 25

SUNFLOWER SEEDS

There were times when games became easy beginning in 1996.

Shanahan's improved running game and defense meant Elway didn't have to constantly save games in the fourth quarter. The Broncos not only built big leads but they also protected them. The stress was reduced to the point that Elway got caught snacking during a game one time. The Broncos went 6–0 against division-rival Seattle from 1996 to 1998. It got so bad future Hall of Fame defensive tackle Cortez Kennedy complained to Elway on the field.

"I was looking up and I said, 'John, come on, man, you spittin' sunflower seeds?' I mean, we weren't any good and he was just gonna hand it to [Terrell Davis], but man, don't be chewing sunflower seeds on the field," says Kennedy, who died in 2017. "He looked back and kinda said, 'Sorry, Tez.'"

With Davis running the ball, the games were sometimes that simple. Davis emerged as one of the top runners in the NFL in 1996. He rushed for 1,538 yards, finishing second in the league to Barry Sanders by only fifteen yards. He also scored thirteen touchdowns and would have led the league in rushing if the Broncos hadn't rested him for most of the final three weeks of the regular season.

Ultimately, there was a harsh lesson to be learned from resting Davis in 1996.

With Davis piling up big numbers as the focal point of the offense, the Broncos had the most dominant season of Elway's career to that point. Denver started off 3–1 and then won nine straight. By the time they got to 12–1, the Broncos had clinched the top seed in the AFC. The Broncos turned the final three weeks of the regular season into one bye week after another. Elway didn't play in a 41–6 loss in the bitter cold at Green Bay. The Broncos beat the Raiders the following week and then lost to San Diego to end the season at 13–3. The Broncos then had a playoff bye week as they watched Jacksonville qualify to come to Denver.

To most people in and around the Broncos, this matchup seemed like a joke. First, the Jaguars were in only their second year of existence after being an expansion team in 1995. There were some people who said they didn't even know what state Jacksonville was in. Woody Paige wrote a column in the *Denver Post* referring to the Jaguars as the "Jagwads" and asked if they were a team from a minor league. That was pretty good fuel for Jacksonville.

This was a Jacksonville team that had two starting wide receivers who had been cut earlier in their careers and a head coach who seemed more prepared to run the Marine Corps. Years later, everybody in the NFL realized Keenan McCardell and Jimmy Smith were a talented duo, and coach Tom Coughlin went on to win two Super Bowls. Still, this game seemed like a walkover with Denver being a two-touchdown favorite after going 8–0 at home during the season. The Broncos had beaten visiting opponents by an average of fourteen points a game. The game shouldn't have been close in any way, shape, or form.

Except that it was.

On January 4, 1997, at Mile High Stadium, Denver took a 12–0 lead in the first quarter. The rout seemed to be on. Then Jacksonville scored. Then it scored again. And again. And again. After scoring on six consecutive possessions, Jacksonville built a 30–20 lead. Their final scoring drive featured a great fade pass to the left corner of the end zone from quarterback Mark Brunell to Smith on third-and-five for a sixteen-yard touchdown with 3:44 remaining. It was an extremely gutsy call. Denver scored, but then botched the onside kick to secure the win for the Jaguars. Jacksonville had also run for 203 yards and passed efficiently. Years later, that game became known as the "Ambush at Mile High." It's considered one of the four or five biggest upsets in NFL playoff history.

The loss was just the beginning of some huge problems.

This was the most painful loss of Elway's career. He was thirty-six years old and the greatest regular season of his career had just been wasted. Shanahan was so concerned that he called players after the game to try to console them. Later that night, Shanahan, Elway, and their families ended up having drinks together at the bar at Cherry Hills Country Club. Elway's anger erupted. He yelled at Shanahan for getting too cute with the game plan. Nothing could console Elway that night. His wife, kids, mom, and dad all tried to no avail. He eventually called his twin sister, Jana, and just cried. He thought his best hope of winning a Super Bowl and everything that went with that had slipped away.

Everyone seemed to think that. Sharpe said the loss could take years to overcome. Elway didn't have a lot of years left. It was the type of loss that can split a team as players and coaches blame one another. That's what had happened between Elway and Reeves after three Super Bowl losses. As the off-season went on, tempers calmed and the team got back on track for a 1997 season that was a lot more difficult, yet a lot more satisfying in the end.

The off-season featured numerous changes. The Broncos signed free agents such as defensive end Neil Smith and offensive tackle Harry Swayne. There were subtle changes to the coaching staff, such as hiring John Teerlinck as a pass-rush specialist. One thing didn't change: Elway's resolve. Despite the brutal loss, the outburst at Shanahan, and the tears, he was back during the off-season program, running, lifting, and doing whatever was necessary. That left an impression on people such as Smith.

"I showed up for my free agent visit after Kansas City let me go and John's first words to me were, 'Welcome to the good side,'" Smith says. "But what I thought was a bit strange was how hard this man was working. The one reason I went to Denver was John Elway. I looked out on their practice field and it's Ed McCaffrey, Rod Smith, Terrell Davis, and John Elway all out there running sprints. It's March and they're preparing for the next season after losing that game [to Jacksonville].

"What John was doing told me something. Quarterbacks don't run, they don't show up for off-season camp, especially when they're thirty-five or thirty-six or whatever John was back then. Quarterbacks don't do that. But John did. Whatever he had to do to get that bitter taste out of his mouth, he was going to do it."

Swayne also took note.

> It's like the kid who just knows if he doesn't do something he's supposed to do—clean up his room, clean the bathroom, whatever—he knows he's going to be in trouble. You've been doing it day after day after day, but you keep doing it. The Broncos got a whooping [against Jacksonville] in that game and he came back the next time and said, "I'll deal with it, I'll be back the next day."
>
> It's like the way he played. One of the offensive linemen might make a mistake and he'd get hit. He'd just get up and not say anything to that guy. We all knew what happened, but he never got angry on the field. If you're a lineman and your quarterback is that kind of guy, when he asks for another second or two at some point in the game, you're going to give him an extra hour. That's the mentality. That's the kind of quarterback you want to play with and win for.

Elway continued to build bonds with teammates in other ways. That included a visit or two to Club Shay Shay every training camp. Club Shay Shay was a highly exclusive, invitation-only, private club in Greeley, Colorado. It was open only during training camp and was hosted by Sharpe, Smith, and cornerback Ray Crockett.

In their dorm room.

Still, it had standards.

"We had a big, old defensive lineman come in wearing just his underwear and a T-shirt. No sir, he was out. No underwear or tighty-whities allowed in Club Shay Shay," Sharpe says.

Elway would show up and shoot dice with the rest of the crowd—and, inevitably, take everybody's money. Though he would eventually spend far more money on his guys than he took from them in dice or cards, there's nothing he enjoyed quite as much as winning a wager.

"Elway would come in and he'd win at dice, too," Smith says. "Here he is the quarterback, with all the glory, all the money, and he's got to beat us in dice, too? That wasn't right."

As the 1997 season unfolded, the Broncos got back on track after one weird physical hiccup for Elway. They were playing the Miami Dolphins in Mexico City in a preseason game on August 4. During the off-season, Elway had had surgery to clean up some right shoulder damage, and the doctors noticed some fraying of the biceps tendon that kept the muscle attached to his shoulder. In the early part of training camp, the shoulder was still sore. Not significant, but sore. So, as the Broncos were playing the Dolphins on a hot night, Elway went to make a throw and the biceps tendon snapped.

The result was disturbing to look at. Elway's right biceps basically relocated to the back of his arm. To this day, it's still there. While there was some initial pain, the injury also seemed to relieve the pain in his shoulder. Still, the sight of his biceps muscle on the back of his right arm was concerning. Elway thought he might have to have major surgery and miss part of the season. Within a few days, doctors told him he didn't need surgery. His arm would be sore for a while and he should take some time off. However, he'd be able to play the rest of the season, even with the relocated biceps.

As the 1997 season opened, Denver won its first six games and got off to a 9–1 start. Six victories came by more than ten points, and the Broncos were on the way to leading the NFL in scoring with 472 points. The Broncos then lost to Kansas City before winning the next two to get to 11–2. The two losses were by a total of five points, so the Broncos were roughly two plays from being undefeated with three games to play.

However, Kansas City was 10–3 and Pittsburgh was 9–4 in the race for the top seed in the AFC. The Broncos had back-to-back road games at Pittsburgh and then San Francisco before finishing the season against San Diego. In the next two games, the Broncos played like anything but a playoff team. Pittsburgh overcame an early deficit to take a 35–24 win over Denver as the Broncos defense gave up 186 yards rushing and 303 yards passing.

Then came a truly ugly performance against the 49ers. Denver squandered a 10–0 lead on the way to a 34–17 loss. The Denver offense grounded to a halt in those two games. The Broncos were now behind both Kansas City and Pittsburgh for the top seed in the AFC. Worse, the loss to San Francisco created a national distraction. Denver linebacker Bill Romanowski was caught on camera spitting in the face of San Francisco wide receiver J. J. Stokes. It was clear on camera and it was ugly. The moment was accentuated by the fact that the game was played on a Monday night, making it the only game being played at the time.

It also had all sorts of racial overtones because Romanowski is white and Stokes is black. Combine the still-lingering memory of the Jacksonville playoff, the back-to-back losses, and the spitting incident and you had the making of serious tension in the Denver locker room. After having Tuesday off, the Denver players gathered for a players-only meeting Wednesday to hash it out. Romanowski apologized. Most of the players understood Romanowski was a guy who pushed the limits as hard and as far as possible to get any kind of edge. He would dangle his foot over the line all the time, even if just to get inside an opponent's head. In the process, he was fined at least a half-dozen times in his sixteen-year career, including for the Stokes incident.

Most players didn't think Romanowski was racist. They thought he hated everyone equally. Still, not all the players were buying it. An apology and a few words weren't going to heal it. That's when Elway got up and put it in the best perspective he could manage. He knew not everybody was going to be satisfied.

"Guys, if you have something to say, we have to say it now. After this, we have to move on. We still have a season left to play," Elway said. The meeting ended shortly after that. Not happily, but at least everyone believed they had been heard. Then Shanahan pulled a move that got everybody refocused on the objective at hand. That day, with the team still reeling, Shanahan cut defensive tackle Michael Dean Perry, a guy who had been a Pro Bowler the year before.

Perry had come to the Broncos in 1995 when Shanahan was hired. He had been signed after playing the first seven years of his career with Cleveland, where he made five Pro Bowls. He had developed a reputation as one of the best interior pass rushers in the NFL during his heyday, averaging more than seven sacks a season with the Browns. His first two years in Denver were very productive. He had six sacks and stabilized the interior defensive line in 1995. In 1996, he had 3.5 sacks and made the Pro Bowl. In 1997, he didn't get a sack in his first nine games and then missed time with a leg injury. By the middle of December, he was practicing, but Shanahan had seen enough.

"I pulled him in and watched the tape with him. I asked him directly, 'Do you really think that's good enough?' His teammates couldn't see it yet because they believed he was going to get it back. But he wasn't playing hard and that wasn't going to be acceptable," says Shanahan, who was also making a statement to the team. He made it clear he wasn't waiting around for anyone, even someone he had brought in himself. Nobody was safe.

The move paid off in both the long and short terms. Over the long term, the Broncos won twenty-two of their next twenty-four games and put on one of the most dominating runs in the history of the league, winning two Super Bowls. In the short term, the Broncos found incredible focus. They beat San Diego 38–3 in the season finale. Kansas City and Pittsburgh also won their final games to clinch the top two seeds in the AFC. In the first round of the playoffs, the Broncos hosted Jacksonville again. This time, the game was a rout. Denver ran for 310 yards as both Davis and backup running back Derek Loville topped the 100-yard mark in a 42–17 victory.

In the backdrop, Elway's family and friends came out in force, not knowing if one of these games might be his last. Elway's buddy Dennis Engel watched from the sideline. Elway made him go to every game after that as a good luck charm.

Then came the playoff game against division-rival and top-seeded Kansas City at Arrowhead Stadium. More than that, it was the latest battle between Elway and Chiefs coach Marty Schottenheimer.

After the trio of disappointing playoff losses with Cleveland against Denver in the 1980s, Schottenheimer resigned when Browns owner Art Modell ordered him to make changes to the coaching staff. Schottenheimer quickly joined the Chiefs and built the Chiefs into a consistent contender with the likes of Hall of Fame linebacker Derrick Thomas. Over the four seasons leading up to this game with Schottenheimer coaching the Chiefs, Kansas City had won five of the eight games against Denver. That included winning the previous three games in Kansas City and four of five games decided by a field goal or less. None of that seemed to ease Schottenheimer's fear of Elway.

This was a classic matchup in another sense. Denver had led the league in scoring that season, and Kansas City had led the league in fewest points allowed. In most playoff situations like this, defenses rule. But as the game played out, the defensive player who ruled most was Neil Smith, the former Chief who had joined Denver as a free agent. In his playoff return to his old stomping grounds, Smith finished with two of Denver's four sacks and was a force all game. He had spent nine years with the Chiefs before being cast aside and wanted his former team to pay.

"The fans in Kansas City have forgiven me, but it took a while," says Smith, who retired in Kansas City. By the most simplistic analysis, Denver won the game 14–10 when its defense came up with a game-saving stop at the end. Denver cornerback Darrien Gordon knocked away Kansas City quarterback Elvis Grbac's fourth-down throw to the end zone with twelve seconds remaining to seal the win.

But Elway created the situation. Even though he threw only nineteen passes as an ice storm blew through Kansas City on a 30-degree day, Elway was still in Schottenheimer's head. The many fourth-quarter comebacks and ego-crushing losses had a Pavlovian impact on the longtime coach. When the game came down to the final moments, Elway was as much a part of the Broncos defense as anything else.

Before the game even started, Schottenheimer made a seemingly odd decision. Instead of going with Rich Gannon as the starting quarterback, Schottenheimer went with Grbac. Grbac had helped the Chiefs to a 7–2 start before getting hurt. Gannon came in and Kansas City went 6–1 with him, including six straight wins to close the season. People wondered why Schottenheimer would change quarterbacks with the team on a roll. With the possibility of having to get in a scoring duel with Elway, Schottenheimer thought Grbac was the better option. Grbac's rust showed, even though he had a decent statistical game.

With all of that in the backdrop, Schottenheimer and the Chiefs began their attempt to win the game with four minutes remaining. Kansas City took over at its own seventeen-yard line after Denver punted. The Chiefs had plenty of time, but obviously needed to score a touchdown to overcome the four-point deficit. They got to midfield quickly after a twenty-three-yard pass interference call. Their drive then fluctuated. They faced a fourth-and-nine before Grbac hit Lake Dawson on a nice pass along the right side for a first down. On the next play, the Broncos sacked Grbac for a ten-yard loss, putting the Chiefs in second-and-twenty. Then Grbac hit wide receiver Andre Rison for a twenty-two-yard gain to give them another first down with two minutes remaining. In its own way, this was shaping up as Schottenheimer's payback for The Drive.

That's when the Chiefs started to do some very odd things. On three consecutive plays, Grbac threw short to set up a fourth-and-two situation at the Denver twenty-yard line. On each of the three plays, the Kansas City receiver stayed in bounds to keep the clock running. The Chiefs got to the line of scrimmage with about forty-four seconds remaining for the fourth-down play. The natural thought was they would complete a short pass for a first down, either getting out of bounds or then spiking the ball to stop the clock.

As the Chiefs lined up for the play, the seconds continued to tick away. The clock whittled past forty seconds, then thirty, then twenty. From the fans in the stands to the Broncos on their sideline, people were wondering what was going on. That's when everyone realized the Chiefs were going for a touchdown. What Schottenheimer wanted was to score right then and not leave Elway enough time for another drive. Instead of playing the obvious strategy, Schottenheimer was playing for the perfect ending.

Shanahan was screaming for the Broncos defenders to get back. Denver defensive coordinator Greg Robinson had the situation covered. Robinson made a brilliant decision to play the cornerbacks in off coverage in the short-yardage situation. Robinson was essentially conceding the first down to prevent the touchdown. It was a perfect decision.

"Great call by Greg Robinson. Absolutely great call," Gordon says.

What made it odd is how the Broncos defense had played most of the season. The hyperaggressive Robinson usually had the cornerbacks playing up close to the line and near the receivers. Robinson liked to put pressure on people rather than sit back. Grbac and the Chiefs refused to audible out of the play and take the first down. Schottenheimer was hell-bent on his strategy.

"John Elway was definitely in my thinking," Schottenheimer says.

"I worked with Marty for a lot of years and he was a pretty conservative processor," says Al Saunders, who was Kansas City's assistant head coach at the time. "That was his philosophy and he won a lot of games along the way. But John Elway was different. There was The Drive in Cleveland and all those other games. John Elway was the thorn in Marty's side for a lot of years and he articulated that before the game. He didn't want the ghost of all those comebacks…he didn't want to see John Elway on that field again if he could help it. I'm sure everybody thought we'd go for the first down, but Marty was prepared to take the chance in the right situation to get out of there and get off the field without John Elway having a chance to beat us."

After Gordon knocked the ball away, the Broncos jumped around the field like a bunch of bank robbers who had gotten away with the money. Shanahan, a man who normally kept a dour, calm look on his face, smiled broadly. Now, the Broncos had to reproduce the same feat of beating a team it had recently lost to on the road. Denver had to return to Pittsburgh for the AFC Championship Game.

Once again, Denver got off to a good start. With an improved running game (the Broncos finished with 150 yards on the ground) and better balance (they ended up calling thirty rushes and thirty-one passes), they were able to build a 24–14 lead by halftime. Davis rushed for 139 yards and a touchdown. It was the first time all season the Steelers defense, which was ranked number one against the rush, allowed someone to run for 100 yards or more. As effective as Davis was, the Steelers defense stifled Denver in the second half just like in the first game. Fortunately for the Broncos, their defense did the same to Pittsburgh's offense.

Denver's defensive guys were a little pumped for this game. In the regular season game, Broncos defensive end Alfred Williams got into a shouting match with Steelers coach Bill Cowher when Cowher started celebrating a little too much. In the playoff game, Denver intercepted Pittsburgh quarterback Kordell Stewart three times, including twice in the end zone. Neil Smith also forced a fumble by Stewart that Denver recovered. After the second interception by Stewart, Romanowski mocked Stewart right to his face by indicating Stewart was not very bright.

Romanowski could never help himself.

Finally, Pittsburgh broke through for a touchdown when Stewart hit Charles Johnson to cut Denver's lead to 24–21 with fewer than three minutes remaining. After the kickoff, Denver ended up with the ball at its eleven-yard line with 2:45 to play. The Broncos quickly faced a third-and-six situation from their own fifteen with two minutes to go in the game. Denver desperately needed this first down to run the clock down even more. Otherwise, the Steelers were getting the ball back, likely around midfield with plenty of time remaining. The home crowd at Three Rivers Stadium was going nuts with anticipation.

That's when Shanahan called for a pass play to Sharpe. It's a play Denver had run numerous times in which Sharpe ran an outside curl to the left. Problem was, the Broncos hadn't practiced it all week. In fact, they hadn't practiced it in several weeks. Sharpe pitched a bit of a fit. Sharpe hated it when the team would run a play it hadn't practiced or even discussed during the week of preparation. He was big on visualizing plays. He wanted to go over it in his head, not just in practice.

"We got 120 pass plays and seventy run plays every week in the game plan and so let's go and call a play we haven't even run or practiced or put in the game plan," Sharpe says, still annoyed by the moment. "So when John called it, I said, 'It's not in the game plan.'"

Elway barked at Sharpe, "It is now!"

Sharpe was still uncomfortable.

"I still don't know what's going on, so I throw my hands up and say, 'What do you want me to do?'" Sharpe says. That's when Elway reached back to his famous fourth-and-seventeen moment against Cal in 1982. He looked at Sharpe and said, "Just get open."

The interesting part of this play is that Pittsburgh didn't cover Sharpe the way Elway expected. That's likely because he had completed eleven passes to Rod Smith and McCaffrey already and the Steelers cornerbacks were susceptible. The Steelers sent help to the outside to cover the receivers and left Sharpe one-on-one with linebacker Jason Gildon, a guy who usually blitzed. Gildon was stiff in coverage, so when Sharpe made a quick turn to the outside, Elway knew Sharpe was going to be open.

"John threw it so hard it stuck to my shoulder pads," Sharpe says. "I didn't catch that ball. It caught me."

The eighteen-yard gain gave Denver the critical third down and better field position. The Broncos got another first down on a run by Davis and then ran out the clock, celebrating its latest bit of redemption. In that run of three playoff wins, the Broncos had beaten the Jacksonville team that had upset them the previous season and two teams that had beaten them during the regular season.

Most of all for Elway, he was getting his fourth shot at the Super Bowl. As usual, the prospects seemed slim by the oddsmakers' estimations. Denver was facing the defending Super Bowl champion Green Bay Packers with Favre, defensive end Reggie White, and coach Mike Holmgren. The Broncos were an eleven-point underdog, and the AFC was riding a string of fourteen consecutive losses in the Super Bowl. To top it all off, Elway's mother wasn't exactly pleased. That week, Jan came by Elway's house and famously said with doom in her voice, "Do we really have to go back to the Super Bowl?"

The pressure was truly on.

CHAPTER 26

BEATING THE PACKERS

Elway talks to himself when he plays gin.

It's usually after his opponent makes his first discard. Elway surveys the card and his hand. Then he mutters to himself as he pictures what his opponent is holding. In a similar way, Elway is a gadget freak. He hooks up a golf swing monitor when he's on the driving range. It assesses all the details, from his swing angle to how the clubface hit the ball to the distance the ball traveled. His house is littered with cell phone and computer accessories.

Even when Elway is just relaxing, he is a sponge for information. His children marvel at how he'll simultaneously watch the History Channel, play solitaire on his computer, and be engaged in a conversation. He loves intellectual stimulation. He'll dive into a political discussion at a moment's notice, usually taking a strong conservative position. He campaigned for Republican presidential candidate Mitt Romney, wrote a letter in support of conservative judge Neil Gorsuch for the US Supreme Court, and attended the inauguration of President Donald Trump. Like almost every great quarterback, Elway is exceedingly curious about how things operate and what's going to happen. Elway tells people he likes to "go by my gut" in making decisions, but that gut is filled with information. He consumes it constantly, forming a picture in his mind of what is going to happen and why.

And, most importantly, what he should do in reaction to those circumstances.

When it came to the defining play of Elway's career, that curiosity and consumption of information were essential to making it happen. If not for his habit of asking questions and seeking more information, the most important play of Elway's career never happens.

"The Helicopter" probably crashes before it ever takes off.

The Helicopter play is Elway's mad dash for a critical first down in the Super Bowl against Green Bay on January 25, 1998, in San Diego. It was the play that strategically and emotionally ignited one of the greatest upsets in the history of the game and vaulted Elway to his first title. It is also further proof that natural ability is a wonderful asset, but knowledge takes you the final distance. As the thirty-seven-year-old Elway prepared for his fourth Super Bowl appearance, he and the Broncos were again massive, eleven-and-a-half-point underdogs. To pull off the upset, the Broncos were going to need every available bit of information. After beating Pittsburgh in the AFC Championship, the Broncos spent a week in Denver getting ready. Shanahan put together the game plan with the rest of the staff and gave it to the players after they arrived in San Diego.

There was a lot of talk that week, most of it coming from the Packers. Green Bay was defending its title, and the Packers players were a cocky bunch, led by quarterback Brett Favre and his swaggering style. The Packers not only were the favorite, but the national media largely said they had already won the Super Bowl. Beating San Francisco in the National Football Conference Championship Game was the real title game, most of the media believed, and the Super Bowl would be a formality.

A headline in *Sports Illustrated* read, "As the 49ers Found Out in the NFC Title Game, the NFL's Best Team and Quarterback Reside in Green Bay." A preview article of the Super Bowl matchup by famed *SI* football writer Paul "Dr. Z" Zimmerman was titled "Pack It In: Crafty Coordinator Fritz Shurmur and His Green Bay Defense Figure to Make Life Miserable for Denver." The Packer defense featured future Hall of Fame defensive end Reggie White and star safety LeRoy Butler. At the end of the article, Zimmerman picked the Packers to win, 24–10.

On Monday and Tuesday night of Super Bowl week, Broncos players ran into the Packers players around San Diego. The constant theme was about how little respect the Broncos received from the Green Bay players. That was perfect as far as Elway was concerned. Being an underdog was good. Getting disrespected was even better. It kept everyone on the Denver team as focused as possible.

Beyond being the defending champs and heavy favorites, the Packers had buried Denver in their previous meeting. That was a 41–6 drubbing late in the 1996 season, shortly before the Broncos were upset by Jacksonville in the playoffs. Elway didn't play and Davis barely played, but the Packers still talked about how lopsided the game had been. By January 1998, the sports media and the Packers figured this game was going to be a rollover. Elway didn't concern himself with the bravado of the Packers. He was more concerned with their defense and how the Denver offense was going to attack it. The Packers defense had held opponents to seventeen points or fewer in ten of the previous thirteen games, including both of Green Bay's playoff victories.

On offense, the Packers had Favre and a deep receiving corps led by Robert Brooks and Antonio Freeman. Denver's plan, as it had been all season, was to lean on Davis. Shanahan found a flaw in Green Bay's defensive scheme allowing the Broncos to manipulate Butler into bad positions against the run depending on the formation. It paid off in a big way as the game began. Davis had a monster performance with thirty carries for 157 yards and three touchdowns. He did that while battling a migraine that was so painful that he basically couldn't see at times. Davis, who was establishing himself as the greatest postseason running back in NFL history, was named the Most Valuable Player of the game.

Though Elway produced mediocre stats, completing twelve of twenty-two passes for 123 yards, he came up with the biggest play of the game and a couple of key throws. That critical play was based on Elway's inquisitive nature that led to a gut reaction. Midway through the third quarter, the game was tied 17–17. The Broncos were pinned at their own eight-yard line, needing to go ninety-two yards for a touchdown. The Packers defense was looking for a quick stop so they could get the ball back in good field position and take the lead.

Denver got out to its thirty-one-yard line. Then Elway completed his longest pass of the game, a thirty-six-yarder to McCaffrey. That put the ball at the Green Bay thirty-three. The Broncos eventually drove to the Green Bay twelve, where they faced a critical third-and-six situation, just as they had against Pittsburgh in the AFC Championship Game. Get a touchdown and the Broncos would put Green Bay on the ropes, shaking the Packers' defensive confidence with a ninety-two-yard drive. No team that season had driven ninety-two yards on the Packers vaunted defense. Settle for a field goal and the Packers would have a chance to counterpunch for control of the game.

Earlier in the week, Elway was going over the game plan while sitting in his hotel room with backup quarterback Bubby Brister. Just as in the Steelers game, the throw to Sharpe was going to be the call in a critical third-and-six situation (and this time it was actually in the game plan to placate Sharpe). It was pretty much the same concept as the play against Pittsburgh with a slight alteration for the Packers defense. As Elway looked over the game plan, there was something he didn't like about that play in this potential situation.

"All I remember is John sitting there talking about that play and saying how he didn't like the look," Brister says. "He just kept talking about it and talking about it and asking, 'Well, what if they don't play this coverage?'"

Elway kept thinking because the Broncos had just used that play on such a critical down in the win over Pittsburgh in the AFC Championship Game, there was a good chance Green Bay would come up with something to deal with it. When Elway talked to Shanahan and Kubiak during the week, they told him repeatedly Green Bay had never played any other coverage in that situation. One day in practice, Elway again asked Shanahan, "Mike, what if they don't play that defense?"

"It's 100 percent, they've played that defense the whole year exactly that way," Shanahan said. Something in Elway's gut told him to beware. Based on his studying, it was in his head all week the Packers would have a change of pace on defense in this situation.

"John just says, 'If they take away Sharpe in this situation, I'm going to run,'" Brister says. "He just knew the best option right there was to take off. If you go back and look at that play, that's the most important thing John did. He didn't wait. He didn't look around to see if something else might develop. With a guy like me, I probably would have looked around and just hesitated enough. John didn't think twice. As soon as his back foot hit the ground, he took off."

Elway's attitude throughout his career was that third down was completely on the quarterback. He would often say to Shanahan and Kubiak, "You guys have first and second down, but third down belongs to me." If not for that planning and approach, the world might never have witnessed the glory of what Elway laughingly calls "my three-inch vertical leap." Just as Elway suspected, Green Bay had no intention of letting him throw to Sharpe. Elway came out of the huddle, lined up in shotgun formation, and looked over the defense, only to see something completely different from the Packers.

So much for 100 percent.

The Packers double-teamed Sharpe to the left and came at Elway with a three-man pass rush and a linebacker hanging out around the line of scrimmage in case Elway stepped up to throw. If Elway had hesitated and looked for another receiver, he would never have been able to escape. His aging knees gave him just enough speed so he could get close to the first down. But close wasn't enough. He tucked the ball away and leaped headfirst. He also went high, anticipating that the Packers would think he'd go low to avoid contact and protect himself.

No one would have begrudged Elway for going low at age thirty-seven, but this wasn't the time to play safe. All his years of working out to lead his teammates and get ready for this chance added up to going big at the biggest moment. As he leaped to get over the defenders, Elway was triangulated by the combination of Butler, linebacker Brian Williams, and safety Mike Prior. They lunged at him, sending him spinning parallel to the ground. He looked like the blade of a helicopter rotating. By the time he landed, Elway's legs were stretched out toward the end zone as he finished a 180-degree turn.

Suddenly, a man who had been defined by the ability of his right arm had just made the biggest play of his career with his aging legs and declining leaping ability. This eight-yard gain was now Elway's signature play and it sent his teammates into a frenzy. Elway got up quickly, appearing discombobulated after his Flying Wallenda move. He looked at the sideline and saw his teammates exploding with joy. Rod Smith immediately came over and hugged Elway. Linemen Brian Habib and Tom Nalen high-fived him. Sharpe was howling in Elway's ear when they got back to the huddle.

"I looked around. Everybody was going crazy on the sideline and I feel the hair on the back of my neck just stand up," Elway says, the moment forever etched in his mind as if it had happened yesterday. "My teammates are screaming. The whole stadium was screaming. That's as intense a moment as you could imagine. It was pretty cool."

Denver scored two plays later for a 24–17 lead, and the emotional swing of that drive—and particularly The Helicopter—was huge.

"In that split second, you knew John wanted it and wanted it more than any person on the football field," fullback Howard Griffith says.

"At that moment, we just knew we were going to win. That play changed the whole game," Sharpe says. "You see a thirty-seven-year-old quarterback giving up his body like that. That doesn't happen. You see that, you're pumped. That was an adrenaline injection."

Green Bay tied the game early in the fourth quarter, but then Denver's defense stopped the Packers without a first down on the next two possessions. That gave the Broncos the ball in great field position at the Packers' forty-nine. The Packers defense was wearing down. The Broncos finished the game with 179 yards rushing. The Green Bay defense was drained from having to contain Davis.

After a penalty against the Packers, a twenty-three-yard pass from Elway to Griffith, and a seventeen-yard run by Davis, Denver was in a second-and-goal situation at the Green Bay one-yard line with 1:47 remaining. That's when Packers coach Mike Holmgren made an interesting call. He let the Broncos score to take a 31–24 lead. Davis practically walked into the end zone on second and goal, scoring with 1:45 remaining in the game. What Holmgren figured is if the Packers had stopped Denver on second and third down to force a field goal attempt, he would have had to stop the clock, burning his last two time-outs and leaving the Packers with roughly 1:40 remaining to drive and score. Holmgren liked his chances of a Favre touchdown drive with two time-outs more than his chances of advancing far enough with no time-outs for at least a field goal attempt. And, of course, the Packers might not have been able to stop Davis even if they'd tried.

On the ensuing drive, Green Bay drove to the Denver thirty-one before the Broncos defense stopped the Packers on a fourth-and-six. As Elway knelt on the final play to let the final twenty-eight seconds tick off the clock, all he could feel was the burden coming off his shoulders and the rush of joy flowing through his body. In the aftermath of the game, Bowlen said, "This one's for John!" Elway felt it was for everybody, and not just the current Broncos players. It was for all the former Broncos players who had been part of the previous four Super Bowl losses. In the locker room, former Denver players such as Billy Thompson and Tom Jackson stood there taking it in, some of them with tears in their eyes. Elway's personal journey to finally winning a Super Bowl at age thirty-seven—and becoming the oldest starting quarterback to ever win for the first time—was the obvious narrative.

The journey of an entire organization to finally get to this point was a better one. It was a lot more satisfying to Elway. It was also incredibly nerve-racking. On the field, the Broncos had to get through Davis's migraines and Green Bay's talented team. In the stands, Elway's wife, Janet, was so nervous she literally couldn't watch the game. It turned out she was on the way to getting seriously ill. By August 1998, she had to have surgery on her intestines, and there were times her family worried whether she would survive. That was a harrowing time for the Elway family in the aftermath of this great victory.

But that night was all about relief. Jack had a joyous smile as he celebrated with his son and the rest of the family. All the seasons of frustration melted away. It had been nineteen years since he tasted championship success and he was going to savor this moment. His journey as a real-life

Prometheus having to relive his pain again and again was finally over. What Elway loved most about everything was that it wasn't just about him. The burden of his early career had been removed. He had played his role when necessary. In Kansas City, he'd gotten into Chiefs coach Marty Schottenheimer's head. In Pittsburgh, he had come up with the key throw at the end of the game. Against Green Bay, it was his mind and legs working in unison on the most emotionally packed play of the game.

Elway's pure euphoria lasted about a month. He went from San Diego to Hawaii to play in the Pro Bowl. Then he discovered he was too "injured" to play in the game. His elbow was worn out from sipping mai tais all week on Waikiki Beach. Shanahan and Elway hung out there celebrating the moment. Elway milked the celebration for all it was worth. All the years of working out and setting an example had paid off. He was fifteen years into his career and felt completely accomplished.

Of course, that eventually led to the question of whether Elway was going to play again. Shanahan left him alone for a few weeks, but he eventually needed to know Elway's plan. What Elway didn't understand was that this was the beginning of a further decline in his relationship with Shanahan.

CHAPTER 27

1998

Elway had one question for his father in early March 1998.

Can I still play?

After fifteen seasons, all sorts of injuries, and now, finally, a Super Bowl title, John Elway needed to hear the answer from the man he trusted the most. Jack had a couple of questions before he gave his answer. He asked his son how he felt. Could he handle the rigors of another off-season? The tone of the conversation wasn't much different from so many years before, sitting inside Sheila the Chevy atop Military Hill. Just like all those years before, John knew Jack would be brutally honest.

Jack had no problem being brutal. About six months later during the season, he cut his own son to the quick. John threw three interceptions in the first half of a game. As John ran to the locker room for halftime, Jack was standing outside the door. John asked his dad for a little guidance.

"What do you think?" John said.

"I think you better work on your tackling if you're going to keep throwing it to the other team," Jack said. John smiled and laughed.

Given that level of communication between them, John knew that when Jack told him he had enough left to play again, a legitimate encore was worth pursuing. John didn't tell Shanahan right away, and later that March, Shanahan instructed Kubiak to go get the answer from him. Kubiak and John Elway met at Bennett's Barbeque on Arapahoe Road near the Broncos facility in Englewood. It was a hangout for the players. Elway quickly said he was coming back for the 1998 season. Then he said, "Gary, you don't have to be in any hurry. Let's enjoy a couple."

There was another reason Elway returned, although it was hardly the deciding factor. In November 1998, Denver voters were scheduled to go to the polls to vote on a measure to build a new stadium to replace Mile High Stadium. Though Elway never played there, he knew how important the stadium would be for Bowlen and to the long-term survival of the Broncos. Elway felt indebted to Bowlen to play another season if he felt good enough.

At the same time, Shanahan was making his preparations for the future. In April 1998, Shanahan drafted quarterback Brian Griese from Michigan in the third round. That didn't bother Elway. What did bother Elway was that it was clear Shanahan wanted less and less interaction. Again, this was Shanahan's way of creating distance to keep emotion from clouding his judgment about Elway.

"I would just think to myself, 'Mike, I get I'm close to the end, just tell me what you think.' He didn't have to be that way," Elway says. The tension was unnecessary in Elway's view. It was an unavoidable issue from Shanahan's perspective. Shanahan had always viewed Elway as his best friend. But Shanahan had a method and he was going to stick to it. The relationship had hit a low at one point during the final contract negotiation of Elway's career. Elway once again agreed to take a reduction in salary, but it also meant the Broncos had to guarantee part of his contract. That was the infamous moment when Shanahan complained that the contract was too much and Bowlen had to play peacemaker.

Where Elway felt Shanahan got it wrong was if he had just talked to Elway about the end, they could have worked it out easily. Regard-less, the decline in the relationship had no impact on the team. Just as Elway had handled his issues with Reeves over the years, he handled his disagreements with Shanahan outside the realm of the locker room, the field, or any other team-related spot. That showed as the 1998 Broncos had a dream season. The team started 13–0 and probably could have gone undefeated if it had been really focused on that goal. The season involved very little stress for Elway, who only had to lead one game-winning drive in the fourth quarter.

Elway also didn't have to push himself through undue situations. He missed three games completely and most of a fourth because of injuries. Prior to that point, Elway had missed only nine starts because of injury. Before a game against San Diego, he took ten pain-killing injections in his ribs and still had to bow out after one series. Elway's supporting cast was amazing that season. The offensive line was great even though Zimmerman retired. Elway tried to get Zimmerman to come back by making a special trip to a biker event in the Black Hills of South Dakota during training camp. Zimmerman still passed. His shoulders simply couldn't take the punishment.

Tony Jones switched from right to left tackle and played awesome while Swayne took over on the right side. Rod Smith followed up on his breakout 1997 season with eighty-six catches for 1,222 yards and six touchdowns. The other receivers also had great years. McCaffrey had 1,053 yards and ten touchdowns. Sharpe had sixty-four catches and ten touchdowns. Backup quarterback Bubby Brister was also excellent.

As good as all of them were, Davis was on another level. He rushed for 2,008 yards on 392 carries. He averaged 5.1 yards per carry and scored twenty-three touchdowns. He was both durable and explosive. If not for one off game against Miami late in the season, he might have set the NFL rushing record. Denver finished the regular season at 14–2. The Broncos were second in the league in scoring and topped 500 points for the first time in Elway's career. Elway even finished the season with a flourish. He threw four touchdown passes in the season finale at home against Seattle. That gave him exactly 300 touchdown passes for his career.

After getting a bye week in the first round of the playoffs, the Dolphins and Dan Marino came to Denver on January 9, 1999, for a rematch. Davis, who had only twenty-nine yards rushing against them in the regular season, had 199 yards this time and the Broncos won 38–3. The Broncos struggled against the New York Jets in the AFC Championship Game. With the winds whipping at twenty miles per hour in Denver, the Broncos couldn't get in synch on offense until the third quarter. They were down 10–0 and then scored the last twenty-three points. That included a thirty-one-yard touchdown run by Davis, who finished the game with 167 yards on thirty-one carries.

After the game, Elway took a victory lap around Mile High Stadium. Though he hadn't made a final decision about retirement, it was clear to everyone including himself that this was likely the last home appearance of his career. The Broncos were back in the Super Bowl. Elway became the first quarterback to get to five Super Bowls. The coup de grace was the opponent the Broncos and Elway were about to face. Just before the Broncos defeated the Jets, the 14–2 Atlanta Falcons upset the 15–1 Minnesota Vikings. It was a stunning overtime victory for the Falcons, who were led by quarterback Chris Chandler.

But the irony was who coached the Falcons. Dan Reeves was leading the Falcons and now in his fourth Super Bowl. This game was about to become a very strange reunion in Miami. Going into the Super Bowl, Shanahan and Elway thought all the history with Reeves had been put to rest. During the 1998 off-season, the three men had played a round of golf at Augusta National. More recently, Elway and Shanahan had sent their best wishes to Reeves when he went through a quadruple bypass surgery in December.

The fact that Reeves was coaching at all after the surgery was a minor miracle. But that's how driven he was to compete. During the off week before the teams arrived in Miami, Reeves let all the sting of the past get to him. He talked about the "wounds" that would never heal and how he felt he had to fire Shanahan because he thought Shanahan and Elway were conspiring against him. By the time the Falcons got to Miami, Reeves was apologizing for the remark, but he had already set Shanahan on fire emotionally.

"For Dan to bring it all up again, I didn't understand," Shanahan says. "I thought we were past that. It brought it all up again and made me look like I was the bad guy."

During the week, Reeves got Elway going by saying the Falcons were going to have to stop the run to beat the Broncos. It may have been completely logical, but it still worked as motivation for Elway and

Shanahan. Some people in the media also argued that Chandler was now a better quarterback than Elway. Among all the story lines, Elway faded into the background.

"To me, this was perfect," Elway says. "I told Mike, 'Dan is mad at you. They think Chris Chandler is a better quarterback. I'm just going to sit in the corner and hide out.' It was absolutely perfect. I said, 'We're going to get a chance because they're going to try to stop Terrell.' This was the opportunity I'd always been waiting for. It was right there."

There was, however, one final detail that put the whole thing over the top. The game was telecast by FOX with its team of analysts.

That included none other than Terry Bradshaw. Part of Bradshaw's job was to be on the field after the game to hand out the Most Valuable Player award and the Vince Lombardi Trophy to the winning team. Bradshaw spent the week publicly apologizing to Elway to anyone who would listen. He admitted to all the jealousy and anger for all the years. Elway heard about it and said little. He was waiting for it to all play out on Sunday. It was a perfect script for what was likely to be Elway's walk-off moment. In fact, it was too perfect.

"You don't write that script in Hollywood because they wouldn't believe it," Demoff says. For Elway, it was all coming together in one triumphant send-off. All his former adversaries were going to have to watch him.

Now, he just had to win.

That week, Shanahan and Elway put together a game plan centered on Elway's throwing the ball early. Shanahan pulled out every stop, including putting Davis split out as a wide receiver and Rod Smith in the backfield as a running back. It was all designed to create havoc in the Atlanta defense. Little did anyone know how much havoc one Falcons player would create before the game started.

As much as Elway wanted to be great in this moment, Shanahan's intensity was boiling through his skin. Shanahan hated the story about his undermining Reeves because it was patently wrong in his mind. He was the one who tried to keep the peace between Reeves and Elway. He ranted to members of the team and even members of the media about what Reeves said. The week featured some other distractions, such as Atlanta's Ray Buchanan and Denver's Shannon Sharpe trading barbs about who was the ugliest of them. But no one was quite ready for what was going to happen the night before the game.

Teams are usually sequestered the day before the Super Bowl. They have a walk-through practice, some time with the family, and then hang around the hotel waiting for the final prep meetings the night before the game. As the Falcons got ready, safety Eugene Robinson had some other, uh, thoughts on his mind. Robinson got a rental car to drive around downtown Miami and solicited a prostitute for oral sex. Unfortunately for Robinson, the prostitute was an undercover cop. This is the same Robinson who earlier that day had received the Bart Starr Award for his "high moral character."

The news was all over the place by the morning of the Super Bowl. Robinson and the rest of the Atlanta team were humiliated and distracted. Denver was already planning to go after Robinson at some point in the game, but this situation raised the stakes. Football is ruthless that way.

Elway slept well the night before the game, fully confident in the game plan. Unlike the year before, there wasn't any defensive situation or formation he questioned. His only significant concern was the weather.

"It's kind of funny...my greatest nightmare was having a Super Bowl in the rain because I can't throw a wet ball. I couldn't grip it. My nightmare was having 800 million people watching the Super Bowl and me throwing it straight up in the air because I couldn't grip it," he said. In keeping with his voracious appetite for information, Elway is a weather junkie. To this day, he buys and compares weather apps on his phone. That week, he checked the forecast constantly, sometimes several times a day. There was a strong chance of rain that Sunday in Miami. As luck would have it, the rain didn't start until after the game.

Elway knew he was going to be the centerpiece early on. Likewise, Davis was completely comfortable with the game plan. Even though he was the NFL MVP that season and had dominated the league with more than 2,000 yards rushing, Davis was content to play decoy. Shanahan continued to be a ball of fury on game day. He went to Elway's room at one point to go over the game plan one more time. He was amped long before the Broncos started to make their way to the stadium.

Atlanta got off to a solid start with a field goal for a 3–0 lead, and Denver responded with a touchdown to go up 7–3. The Broncos got the ball again and the drive ended with an interception of Elway off a deflected pass. However, that turnover gave Denver some vital information. Elway and the coaches saw Robinson was taking a chance in coverage. Each time Rod Smith ran a certain route, Robinson jumped the route and completely disregarded the idea that Smith might run deep. Eventually, Denver built its lead to 10–3 and then took possession on its own twenty-yard line in the second quarter.

The situation was set up perfectly.

The Broncos called for a play-action fake with what looked like a short pass to Smith. As he had done all game, Robinson jumped the short route. Part of Robinson's willingness to take a chance was his history against Elway. Robinson had played in Seattle for eleven years when the Seahawks were in the same division as Denver. He had also played in the Super Bowl the year before with Green Bay. Between those games, Robinson had intercepted Elway four times. His confidence against Elway was also now fed by his desperation to erase the humiliation he'd suffered the day before. He needed an interception or some type of big play to ease the pain.

Instead, the humiliation was about to get worse. Robinson was going to have to swallow his pride with a bitter pill. Smith took off deep and Robinson was left in no man's land, sort of naked on the street as it were. Smith, who wasn't exactly a speed demon, was wide open, caught the pass, and ran all the way for an eighty-yard touchdown to make it 17–3.

The rout was on. Armed with a two-score lead, Broncos defensive coordinator Greg Robinson put heavy pressure on Chandler, hammering him with hits until he threw three interceptions and had four turnovers in total. Denver scored seventeen more points in the fourth quarter, capped by Elway's running in from three yards out. As he scored, Schlereth fell on top of him. Elway looked up to see Schlereth's big face looking down at him. Schlereth laughed and said, "Hey, buddy, how ya doing?" Elway looked back with a smile and said, "Dude, you're an idiot." It was as if Elway was twelve years old again, playing on some field in Montana or Eastern Washington.

Elway had completed eighteen of twenty-nine passes for 336 yards, thrown for one touchdown, and run for one. He had also beaten Reeves with a game plan Reeves neither expected nor, ironically, would have ever designed for Elway. After the game, Reeves was classy about it, coming up to Elway during a postgame interview to shake hands and congratulate him. Underneath all of Reeves's fire, he was an incredibly well-meaning man. But the most ironic moment of the night played out on the podium after the game. After sixteen years of mocking and ripping Elway, Bradshaw had to hand the Super Bowl MVP award to his object of scorn.

Elway didn't say a word. He just smiled, took the trophy, and acted graciously. He says he just thought, "You can't say anything bad about me ever again." Shortly after the game ended, the rain started to fall. Elway took a picture with Janet on the field. He already knew he was likely retiring, but his mind wasn't completely made up. Elway thought about coming back for a moment, but it was for all the wrong reasons. He was back in Hawaii for the Pro Bowl and Demoff was with him. Elway told Demoff he wanted to play another season.

"Why?" Demoff remembers saying in his usually measured way.

"Because I don't want Mike to win one without me," Elway said. It was an impulsive reaction to the deteriorating relationship between the two men. As much as the two men needed each other to get to the top, the coach-quarterback relationship had put a strain on their friendship. Elway and Shanahan were hardly unique that way. The history of pro football is littered with coach-quarterback relationships that go sideways, whether it was Paul Brown and Otto Graham in the 1950s, Chuck Noll and Bradshaw in the 1970s, or Walsh and Montana in the 1980s. Highly driven and prideful people don't always see eye to eye. Graham once recounted how Brown had pulled him from a game because Graham had scrambled too much. Brown then ripped Graham on the sideline.

"If I had a gun, I would have shot him right there," Graham said years later with no hint of a joke in his voice.

As fate would have it, Shanahan would coach fourteen more years and never make it back to the Super Bowl. But at that moment on the serene island of Oahu with back-to-back Super Bowl titles to his name, Elway's angst over retirement had him in a slightly bitter state. Demoff listened closely to his client, paused for a moment, and recalls saying, "That's not a good enough reason, John."

Elway didn't have a deadline for making his decision but felt obliged to tell the team before the start of the NFL Draft on April 17, 1999. For all intents and purposes, the decision was made. By the end of 1998, Elway's body had taken enough shots over the years. The more than 500 sacks in the NFL and countless injuries from high school on through the pros had left him limping more than ever.

This time, Elway didn't have to talk to Jack about the decision. Instead, he let Jack be the first to know. On the night of April 13, 1999, they were sitting in the bar of John's house when John looked at Jack and said, "Well, this is it." He then told his wife and called Bowlen, who was in Australia. John and Jack then drank several "final finals." The next day, he and Kubiak returned to Bennett's Barbeque. Kubiak already knew the decision, but wanted to hear it from Elway, who had a beer in hand as they spoke.

"Kubs, I'm done and don't bother trying to change my mind, but we're going to sit here and have a few," Elway said. The formal announcement of Elway's retirement was supposed to be at a press conference on April 21, 1999. The tragic mass shooting at Columbine High School on April 20 made Elway push it back to May 2. The news began to trickle out a few days before the press conference. Elway thought he was ready for the final moment. His teammates teased him by betting on how quickly he would start crying.

Elway lost inside the first minute. After saying, "I can't do it physically anymore and that's really hard to say," his emotions got the better of him. Finally, the man who finished with 300 career touchdown passes, was sacked an NFL-record 516 times while rushing for the fourth most yards

(3,407) by a quarterback in league history summed up how he wanted to be remembered.

"As a competitor," Elway said before referring to himself in the third person. "He may not look good every time he throws the ball, but you better be ready. You better be buckled up for sixty minutes because you know I'm not going to quit until it's over. No matter what it looks like, I'm going to stay after it and I'm going to compete."

CHAPTER 28

RETIREMENT

Elway walked away from football at the top after more than two decades of climbing.

His fall to the lowest point of his personal life took only four years.

Elway's first problem was that his retirement plan was bought out before it ever started. In October 1997, he completed a transaction with billionaire Wayne Huizenga to sell his series of auto dealerships in Denver to Huizenga for $82.5 million. Huizenga was in the process of building his AutoNation business. As part of the deal, Elway became a spokesman for the company and agreed to a ten-year non-compete clause.

In the short run, it was a magical time for Elway. He cashed in on his business interests and less than four months later won the first of back-to-back Super Bowls. In the long run, it was part of what made him miserable in retirement. Less than two years after making the deal with Huizenga, Elway retired. He was thirty-eight years old, wealthy, and married with four beautiful children.

But there were no floors to sweep.

There was no real competition to be had. There was no place for Elway to channel his passion. While his physical ability had declined to the point that he couldn't play football at the level he expected, his desire never faded. There was golf and he was good at it. He was so good he competed regularly in Pro-Am events around the country and even won the Cherry

Hills Country Club championship in 2008. During his first year of retirement, he competed so much in golf that his kids complained they had seen him more when he was still playing football. His friends tried to talk him into playing professionally and perhaps one day going out for the PGA Senior Tour. Ultimately, golf wasn't fulfilling enough to chase.

"You can only play so much golf," Elway says.

Golf was an individual sport for a man weaned on being part of a team. Likewise, golf didn't provide the intellectual challenge Elway found in business. He was offered chances to work in television, but the idea left him cold.

"What's interesting about talking about how the quarterback threw an interception?" Elway says. "Everybody can see what happened. You're just sitting there talking about what everybody already knows. That just never appealed to me."

What Elway loved was running a business. He loved going to the office on Tuesday to read through reports and meet with managers. He would scan the profit and loss ledgers, looking for mistakes and getting joy out of showing he was more than a football player lending his name to a company. His love of numbers and accounting was real, not simply a pragmatic way to get his college degree. Elway also enjoyed the process of building a sales team. After getting back into the car business and opening a steakhouse years later, he would strategize with his managers on goals. He would compel them to build a business that wasn't just financially successful, but also representative of the brand he was trying to build. Restaurateur Tim Schmidt partnered with Elway to start the casual-yet-upscale Elway's Steakhouse. As they planned the endeavor, Elway told Schmidt to be careful of one thing.

"Don't ruin my brand," Elway said.

In those first two years of retirement, all of that was missing. Worse, he and Janet weren't on the same page. Elway and Janet had been together for twenty years by the time he retired. Those two decades were more about dealing with the life of a star athlete and raising a family. Like his father, Elway was married to his job during the season. When he added the car businesses, it only fed his obsession. He followed his father's credo that his job was the top priority. He'd go to the dealerships on off days during the season and multiple days during the weeks of the off-season. He was hell-bent on being great in business. As his dad had always said, there would be no food on the table or roof over their head if he didn't have a job. In many ways, Elway expected Janet to be like his mother, Jan, had been with Jack. Just work it out at home and he'd provide.

That wasn't what Janet expected. After Elway quit, Janet wanted to buy a home in a remote part of Colorado and get away from the hustle and bustle of their previous life.

"She wanted something completely different from what I was thinking," Elway says. "I had all these things going on in Denver and businesses I wanted to pursue. She wanted none of that."

Both John and Janet would complain to Engel, their mutual friend, about what was going on. In turn, he would tell each of them they needed to talk about expectations. They never would. Janet had been fiercely loyal and loving toward Elway and his family for much of their relationship. In college, she and Elway's twin sister, Jana, became incredibly close. Jana would come up on weekends for parties and would stay with Janet. The two of them might just hang out and not even see John. Or the two of them might head off to Lake Tahoe for a weekend of skiing.

After Elway and Janet got married in March 1984, they quickly started a family, beginning with daughter Jessie in October 1985. Two months after Jessie was born, Janet was at a home game against Kansas City, sitting in the stands with a bunch of friends, including Engel. The Broncos were on the way to winning the game 14–13, but Elway had a rough day. He threw five interceptions, a career high. After the fifth pick, a guy who was sitting behind Janet screamed, "You can get your [bleeping] wife pregnant, but you can't do anything else."

Janet turned around and slapped the guy in the face. The friends interceded and the guy apologized. Over the next six years, daughter Jordan (1987), son Jack (1989), and daughter Juliana (1991) followed. Jessie was an excellent high school basketball player who played one year at Stanford. Jordan was a standout lacrosse player who played at the University of Denver. Jack was a quarterback and played at Arizona State.

Juliana never was much for sports, but was incredibly driven to become an educator, eventually graduating from the University of Arizona and becoming a teacher.

The Elways tried to raise their children as normally as possible. They attended public schools and were expected to show toughness and leadership when they played sports. Jessie learned by playing basketball in the driveway with her dad. He would never let her win when she was young, using his strength to back her down to the basket when they played.

"I hated it at the time, but I understood later what he was doing," Jessie says.

In high school, Jessie once played the entire second half of a basketball game after breaking a finger in her right (shooting) hand. It was so bad she had to shoot a free throw left-handed. Jessie also understood how to handle coaches and the game. Once during a club game, her coach lost his cool and started yelling at the ref to the point where it became distracting. Jessie was the one to ask the coach to calm down.

Jordan dealt with much the same. She got hurt playing lacrosse one time and her dad told her to tough it out. Days later, when her ankle still hurt, Janet took her to the doctor and found out it was broken. Jordan gave her dad an earful. Jordan was nicknamed "Hurricane Jordan" for her willingness to tell people exactly what she thinks. She once gave one of her teachers an earful. When the Broncos hosted the Jets in the AFC Championship Game in January 1999, the teacher teased her all week about how the Jets were going to beat her father. When the Broncos won, she spared no words on the teacher.

Jack and Juliana were both quieter kids in high school and college. Jack had a big arm as a high school quarterback but quit a couple of years after he got to college. Elway lamented later that Jack should have probably played linebacker, a position he enjoyed more at the time. Being Elway's son came with expectations from others. Juliana may have become the hardest worker of the family. She was driven to succeed academically and loved the idea of teaching. As all of that was going on for the family, Elway and Janet never learned how to communicate. Elway just kept expecting it to work out. Conversely, Janet wasn't good at telling Elway what she expected.

"We just sort of drifted apart," Elway says. The couple tried counseling, but the resentment over what each one wanted continued to grow. That was only the beginning of Elway's problems. As this was going on, he was trying to convince Shanahan to give him a job working in the personnel department with the Broncos. Elway would have been happy to work his way up as a scout. Shanahan was resistant, concerned that having Elway working for the organization would create a distraction. Additionally, Elway's problems with Janet put a strain on the friendship with Shanahan and his wife, Peggy.

Elway tried hard to convince Shanahan. The two would go to Del Frisco's restaurant until the wee hours discussing the subject. Shanahan wouldn't relent. As difficult as post-career boredom and a strained marriage were for Elway, life was about to take a far more serious and dark turn.

In March 2001, less than two years removed from retirement, Elway received a call from his older sister, Lee Ann. Jana was diagnosed with a rare and advanced form of blood cancer. Lee Ann started to take care of Jana. Lee Ann was so dedicated that she became a nurse after Jana passed away. Jana was also going through marital problems at the time. Elway helped to get her set up on her own and get her treatment at Stanford Medical Center.

Jana was, in many ways, the glue of the family. She was the one who set up family reunions and was the most like Jack. She was the life of the party and possessed his hearty laugh. She eventually became a celebrated elementary school teacher after being a physical therapist. Jack died in April 2001, a little more than a month after getting the news that Jana was sick. As for Elway, his father's death accentuated his own sense of denial about Jana's illness. He had just lost his best friend. Accepting the idea that his sister and closest confidant was dying was simply too much for him to consider. She was an intense fighter in the face of cancer. She survived much longer than most doctors expected. That fed Elway's denial.

"I just never thought she was going to die," Elway says. "Yeah, they told me it was serious and she was in trouble, but I just kept thinking things would be OK. She was going to get better. I never wanted to believe anything would go wrong."

Jana's recovery was made worse by her own marital problems. Like Elway, Jana never wanted to get divorced. Jack had always told his children they should find a way to make it work. In contrast, Lee Ann was pushing Jana to get divorced. She believed it would help Jana recover. Lee Ann's first marriage ended in a divorce that was upsetting for the family. She had married one of Jack's assistant coaches, a guy Jack really liked and wanted to keep on his staff, let alone keep employed to make sure his grandchildren were cared for.

By July 2002, Jana's health took a turn for the worse. John got a call from Lee Ann telling him to get to California as soon as possible. He still couldn't fathom that Jana could possibly die. She was having serious trouble breathing when he arrived. The cancer was cutting off her ability to get oxygen to her blood, so she had to wear an oxygen mask. On that day, Jana's divorce papers had arrived, but the doctors were busy trying to get some tests done. The doctors were taking her for an MRI, but Jana was trying to talk to her mother, brother, and Lee Ann. She had to stop talking every step, alternating between walking, taking off the mask to speak, and then putting it on to breathe. Her mother kept telling her to just go take the test and they would talk afterward. Jana ignored the instruction. She was, after all, a decidedly hardheaded Elway.

Finally, Elway looked at his sister and said, "Jana, put the damn mask on."

Jana looked up at her brother with a smile as if to say, "Really, you're going to tell me what to do, huh?" As she slowly put the mask on, she had her middle finger sticking up from the rest of her hand with a devilish grin on her face. They all laughed.

Then Jana walked to her death. She died on the MRI table on July 23, 2002, the cancer choking off her body. She never signed the divorce papers. It took her brother more than ten years before he could accept that she was really gone and visit her grave site. Jack's and Jana's deaths also fed his fear of dying and his desire to accomplish as much as possible in the face of mortality.

Three years removed from the fantasy end of his career, Elway's personal life was crushed. The family held the funeral for her. Afterward, he and Janet flew to Cambria, California, to visit friend and former teammate Michael Young. Elway simply wanted to get away from the sadness, so he headed for his buddy's beachside home. Young was also helping Elway as he got involved with the Colorado Crush. But Elway wasn't going to Young's house to talk business. He just wanted a quiet place to get away from the sadness of his sister's death.

Young and his wife did everything to make Elway and Janet feel comfortable, but their problems were obvious. Over the previous couple of years, Elway had been sending Young occasional jokes about how tough it was to get along with a woman. It seemed like normal, married-guy cracks.

"You think it's just something to blow off steam, but then you look back and you realize there were weeds in paradise," Young says.

That night, as Young and Elway talked, Janet was in the kitchen chatting with Young's wife. Eventually, Janet said, "What I would do to change lives with you." Less than a year later, Janet and Elway were officially divorced. They had separated for a time, got back together, but were unable to reconcile. Their split ran deep. At one Broncos game, Janet entered Elway's luxury box and yelled at the other guests before leaving in tears. For Elway's part, he would sometimes return to the family home when the two were separated and pick weeds out of the garden while pondering what went wrong.

There was no way to recreate paradise. After the divorce, Janet stopped talking to Engel, which was disappointing to him because they had all been so close for so long. Less than four years after Elway had retired from the pressure of an NFL career, he had lost his business goals, his father, his twin sister, and his marriage. After the divorce, Elway split a two-bedroom condo with close friend Craig Andrisen, who owned Andrisen Morton, a high-end clothing store in Denver. Andrisen was also going through a divorce at the time. Elway eventually moved back into his longtime home after Janet built her own place.

This was the first time Elway lived outside of some tight-knit family circumstance.

"You should have seen John living at this place. Here he is a guy who had been living in this giant house for years and years and now we've got this tiny bachelor place. But we did have one hell of a TV," Andrisen says. "John was pretty damn proud of that TV. It was something to be happy about."

Elway did find one task to keep him busy and keep his mind off the issues. Bowlen and Stan Kroenke approached him in 2001 to help start the Colorado Crush of the Arena Football League. The team was scheduled to begin playing in winter 2003, and Elway was put in charge of the entire front office and football operation.

That didn't quell Elway's bitterness about the divorce. In January 2004, Elway was voted into the Pro Football Hall of Fame. Woody Paige gave the presentation to the selectors for the Hall of Fame. Normally, presentations take roughly ten minutes and are followed by about twenty minutes of discussion. Paige said simply, "Ladies and gentlemen, I present John Elway," and then sat down. There was no further discussion, Elway became one of fewer than a hundred men at the time who made the Hall of Fame on the first ballot.

On Sunday, August 8, 2004, Elway was officially inducted into the Hall along with running back Barry Sanders, defensive lineman Carl Eller, and offensive lineman Bob Brown. In his speech, Elway thanked just about everyone. He cried when talking about his father and came close again when he talked about Jana. He paid great respect to Reeves, praising his "competitive fire" and saying Reeves also deserved enshrinement in the Hall of Fame. Reeves sat next to Elway's mother during the ceremony. Elway thanked his mother, his sister Lee Ann, Shanahan, Jack Neumeier, Steve Antonopulos, Demoff, and so many others. Good friend Jim Armstrong of the *Denver Post* helped Elway organize the speech and even came up with the idea for Elway to give the fans the Mile High Salute at the end.

But there was one person Elway didn't mention.

Janet.

When Elway got back to Denver, Armstrong says he called Elway and said, "John, you forgot to mention Janet." Elway said simply, "I know." He was too hurt and too angry at the time. Elway took heat for the omission, particularly from women fans. Years later, the two patched up their differences enough to work together as parents and help each other in the community. At the time, however, Elway's life in retirement was complete unrest.

CHAPTER 29

THE ARENA CHALLENGE

Rashad Floyd had one question in 2004.

Was Elway committed?

Such a question might sound like heresy to those who know Elway in even a passing fashion. It's like asking whether lions like red meat or if fish like to swim. Floyd wasn't ready to accept anything on face value. This was about his passion and his craft. Floyd was one of the top free agent players in the Arena Football League that off-season. While some players in the lower echelons of pro football were just happy to meet Elway, Floyd wanted serious answers.

Floyd wanted to know if this was as important to Elway as it was to him. Based on the first season of the Colorado Crush, Floyd wasn't necessarily wrong for asking. The 2003 Crush was an expansion team. It was, in so many ways, Elway's distraction and salvation in the face of his personal problems.

Kroenke had beaten out Bowlen and Elway in 2000 to buy the NBA Denver Nuggets, National Hockey League Colorado Avalanche, and the Pepsi Center in Denver where those teams played. Kroenke, Bowlen, and Elway eventually went in together for the rights to the Crush, to provide the Pepsi Center with another tenant. With Elway as part of the brand, the team was a commercial success right from the start.

On the field, however, the team went 2–14 in a season that quite possibly was worse than it looked. The Crush weren't just bad because they were an expansion team. They were bad because Elway and the coaches he hired didn't understand how different the arena game was from the game he had played from high school to the pros. The AFL wasn't just played indoors; it was on a fifty-yard-long field that was less than thirty yards wide. The end zones were smaller. Missed field goals would carom off screens at the back of the end zone and be live balls. Each team played with only eight men per side. The scores were regularly in the fifties or even sixties for both teams and played at video game speed, making it more like college basketball than football. The small rosters required guys who played both offense and defense on a regular basis. The first season was eye opening.

"We didn't know what we were doing, from top to bottom," Elway says. But Elway was hell-bent on learning. He talked to AFL commissioner David Baker about how to run the organization. He visited with Cowboys owner Jerry Jones in Dallas to see how Jones ran his arena team.

"John worked his butt off at it, that's really true," Baker says. "We were talking one day about it and I said, 'Why are you doing this?' Running a team is like any business. It's hard. He just said, 'You know, playing golf is not enough.' He was a great golfer. He holds the course record at a bunch of places, but he would say it just wasn't the same. When you play football, every Monday was a report card on how you did. You were judged on your play and that scoreboard. He talked about how he was testing himself every week. He missed the ultimate competition and he wanted that again."

When faced with the results of the first season, Elway had to put emotion aside and do what was best for the organization. That was easier said than done. The first coach of the Crush was Bob Beers, a man Elway had known since he was a child. Beers got his start in college football playing for Jack at Montana in the late 1960s. Beers was a linebacker and was twice named All-America. He coached and scouted from the high school to the NFL level, eventually rejoining Jack in the Broncos personnel department in the late 1990s.

That's when John, Jack, and Beers started to discuss their plans for running a team if they ever were put in charge. John would run the business operations. His father would pick the players. Beers would do the coaching. When John started running the Crush, he was bent on making that dream a reality. He just didn't have his dad by his side. When other people advised him to hire an experienced AFL coach, he said Beers was the man for the job, along with assistant coaches such as former teammate Keith Kartz.

Sadly, not only did the plan not work, but also Elway felt taken advantage of by some people he'd hired. One assistant coach regularly showed up to work with the smell of alcohol on his breath. The staff was overmatched against coaches and players who understood the nuances of the arena game, complete with the low walls that lined the sides of the fields. Elway felt he had to act quickly and decisively to change the direction of the team. He made the gut-wrenching decision to fire the staff, starting with Beers.

In only his first year of running a team, John Elway had already done something his father would never have done. Jack was loyal to a fault. He kept assistant coaches for years, even when they weren't always up to par or when they cost him his job at Stanford. To Jack, loyalty to his staff was paramount. For John, getting the right people was too important to let his judgment be clouded. He had wasted too much of his own career working with head coaches and assistants he didn't believe in. He wasn't going to repeat anything close to that type of mistake as an executive.

Beers took the decision in stride. It hurt the relationship between the two men. But when asked about Elway's decision, Beers didn't hesitate with his response.

"I was in favor of it," Beers says.

The situation got testy when Elway fired the assistant coaches. He and Kartz nearly came to blows during the meeting. Others yelled about not getting a fair shake. For Elway, it was the first test of whether he could handle being a football executive. There were plenty of other moments that proved vital to the learning process. Negotiating contracts and dealing with practice facilities were part of the job. It may not sound like the multimillion-dollar deals of the NFL, but when you ask a player who is making $50,000 to take a cut to $40,000, it's still not easy. When it's in the living room of the player's apartment with his wife and two kids by his side, it's even more delicate.

Still, the act of firing people, including a family friend of forty years and a former teammate, was one of Elway's first lessons in the unpleasant side of running a team. But Elway was going to do what he felt was necessary to win. This time, he found coach Mike Dailey, who had spent seven years as head coach of the Albany Firebirds and eventually finished his career having spent nineteen years in the league. Dailey had led Albany to the title in 1999. That team was later voted the greatest team in AFL history.

Dailey immediately impressed Elway with his plan. He had a list of free agents he wanted, starting with Rashad Floyd. He knew the trades he wanted to make. He knew how he wanted to manage the team under the league's strict salary cap and twenty-four-man roster. He was sharp and took the AFL very seriously. When people would refer to the AFL as minor league, Dailey would shoot back with, "Once you take that first dollar to play, you're a professional." That resonated with Elway. Like Floyd, Dailey wanted to hear Elway's side. Dailey was looking for Elway to be the engine of the organization, not just a hood ornament.

"I didn't know where John stood before I got there," Dailey says. "I went into it with high hopes it was something he was involved in on a day-to-day basis and was sincere about it, that he wanted it to be one of the top franchises. I had the feeling going in and then he proved it."

The Crush eventually worked out a trade to deal three players for Dailey. Then came the next test for Elway. He had to impress Floyd, the top player on Dailey's list of acquisitions.

"I had five teams looking at me and Denver was the best one because it was the closest to the West Coast," says Floyd, a defensive specialist who had grown up in the San Francisco Bay area and who was perfectly suited for the arena game because of his quickness.

"But they also hadn't been very good. I knew they had a new coach and they were making a lot of changes. What mattered to me is whether John Elway was really into this. Was he just putting his name on it or was this

his franchise he was running because he really wanted to be good at this?" Floyd says.

When the Crush arranged for the free agent visit with Floyd, he made it clear he wanted to meet with Elway. Floyd wasn't trying to get an autograph. He wanted to know Elway's plan.

"I was actually really impressed," Elway says. "He wanted to know what I was about. This was serious business to him."

Elway showed his dedication in all sorts of ways. He and rocker Jon Bon Jovi, who owned the Philadelphia Soul, did a pair of over-the-top commercials to promote the league on NBC. The first featured Elway suiting up to play. The second ended with Bon Jovi as a lounge singer in a leisure suit and Elway dressed in a white, Elvis-style jumpsuit to promote the arena title game in Las Vegas. Elway didn't know how or when, but he knew this was the beginning of his way back to the NFL. He knew this was his equivalent of a master's in business administration in football. It was an incredibly expensive equivalent, but an equivalent nonetheless. A lot of the learning involved hands-on experience, including going over the books: even the smallest detail of the books.

"The first thing that caught me off guard is how much he loves numbers," says Young, who helped run the front office.

> He loves poring over spreadsheets and numbers and looking at all that. One of the things I remember the most is when he was debating our [chief financial officer] about some details. We were going over ticket sales, merchandise, everything and I'm not even paying attention. I hate that part of it. I like to sell, I like to create, all that. I figured I'd just let our CFO do this.
>
> Well, John is going through these numbers. Sure enough, he's debating them and he was right. I didn't even think he was paying attention. I just figured he would take for granted what our CFO says and what I say and that would be enough. But he literally was poring over every single number and found two errors that were somewhat significant.

Elway was intent on proving he was more than just the face of the organization. The Crush was his personal redemption. It put him back to work and got him out of the horrible routine his life had become in retirement. He needed a distraction, even the most mundane distraction. He needed to sweep the garage.

Or, in this case, fold T-shirts.

Like all AFL teams, the Crush was not exactly loaded with staff people. Everybody does a little bit of everything, especially when a shipment of 600 specialty-order, souvenir T-shirts shows up late the day before a game. Over four hours that night, Elway, Young, and two other Crush staffers folded the T-shirts onto cardboard cutouts.

"You get to a point where you're actually kind of quick at it," Elway says, smiling at the memory. It was around this time Young and Elway were discussing the importance of the Arena League for Elway and why he was pushing so hard to be great at it. As Elway broke down crying about his father, a family of Broncos fans happened upon them and started waving at Elway. Instead of waving them off, Elway got out, composed himself, and signed autographs for them.

"It was easier than telling them to go away. It doesn't take much effort to make people happy and they didn't know what was going on. If I tell them to go away, they're just going to think I'm a jerk," Elway says.

Elway's aspirations to be great in the AFL began to come together. With Dailey there to run the team, Floyd as a leader, and quarterback John Dutton as the emerging starter, the Crush were on track for a quick improvement. Elway learned to trust Dailey and, in the process, understand the healthy distance an executive must maintain from the team and the coaching process. Elway would show up occasionally at practice and mostly just listen. He was not giving input unless he was asked. There was one day when one of the players started mouthing off to Elway, asking whether the former quarterback had any juice left in his right arm. Elway tossed a few passes at about 75 percent force and the player kept talking smack.

Finally, Elway proved his point with a full-force throw. The player ended up on his back after getting hit by the ball.

"The rest of us all fell down laughing," Floyd says.

In 2004, the Crush finished at 11–5 and tied for the best record in the league before losing in the playoffs. It was an excellent one-year turnaround. In 2005, the team went 10–6 and beat San Jose in the first round of the playoffs and then beat Chicago in overtime during the semifinals. That set up a showdown with the Georgia Force for the AFL Championship on June 12, 2005, at the Thomas & Mack Center in Las Vegas. The atmosphere of the game was electric. Elway, dressed in a suit and tie, spent much of the second half on the sideline with Kroenke, who wore a blazer, and Bowlen, who was in a Hawaiian shirt.

Colorado twice built eleven-point leads in the first three quarters. Georgia would never fold. The Crush had a 31–27 lead going into the fourth quarter and then the game went wild. The teams combined for forty-one points in the final quarter. Georgia came back to tie the game three times, including the final time with eighteen seconds remaining in the game. Dutton then turned eighteen seconds into a drive Elway could appreciate. He hit Kevin McKenzie for a thirty-seven-yard gain and Georgia was called for a penalty. That put kicker Clay Rush in position for a twenty-yard field goal as time expired for the win. After the ball went through the uprights, Baker was standing next to Elway.

Baker, who later became the president of the Pro Football Hall of Fame, asked in jest, "So John, how does this compare to winning a Super Bowl?"

With a straight face and complete sincerity, Elway said, "It's better."

"Come on, John, you don't mean that," Baker says.

"Yeah, I do," Elway said.

It was a different sense of pride. After all Elway had been through personally and all the challenges he faced trying to create a team that could win, this was a different accomplishment. This wasn't just about playing quarterback or selling cars. This was the mental challenge of building a team from the bottom up.

It was about making a lot of hard choices and putting in a lot of time. It was about competing, and the other people in this league were serious. Aside from Bowlen and Kroenke, fellow NFL owners Jones and Tom

Benson owned teams in the AFL. Arthur Blank, the owner of the Atlanta Falcons, owned the Georgia Force. These were not people who were just joking around.

More than anything, however, this was personal accomplishment. It was the very thing Elway's dad had taught him to do.

So, yes, in some ways, it was better than winning a Super Bowl.

CHAPTER 30

PAIGE

First, Elway won a title. Then he met a woman. Sort of.

June 2005 turned out to be a hell of a month for Elway in his professional and personal comeback. Shortly after helping the Colorado Crush win the Arena Bowl, Elway went to Los Angeles to participate in Marcus Allen's annual charity golf tournament. It was there he met Paige Green.

It may be better to say Elway crossed paths with Green, a former Los Angeles Raiders cheerleader who was helping host the tournament. The term "host" should be defined loosely in this context. Mostly, Green was goofing off with her good friend Rhonda. Paige and Rhonda were passing out beers at one of the tees and trying to be entertaining. The pair had put out a table of relationship and self-help books to serve as oddball conversation starters. That included titles such as *Men Are from Mars, Women Are from Venus* and *Why Men Love Bitches: From Doormat to Dreamgirl.* That had most of the guys wondering just what these women were all about. Elway didn't even try to find out. He just observed and didn't say anything to Paige when he saw her. He thought she was good-looking and funny. When Rhonda blurted out Paige's phone number, Elway saved it to his phone.

Then he forgot about her for the next seven months.

One night back in Denver in early 2006, Elway was watching the

Golf Channel and talking on the phone. The program ended and he left the channel on as he talked. An infomercial for the Orbitrek elliptical machine flashed across the screen. Working out on the elliptical during the infomercial was Paige, whose name popped up on the screen. Elway remembered, stopped his phone call, and dialed Paige. There was no answer, so he left a decidedly low-key message.

"Hi, this is John Elway," Elway remembers saying. "I'm sorry, I don't know if you're married, I don't know if you're seeing somebody. I don't know anything about you. I just know we met last year at Marcus's tournament and I get out to L.A. every once in a while, and I'd like to take you to dinner if you're not with somebody. If you are, I'm sorry, don't take offense. Just thought I'd give you a call."

It wasn't exactly, "The Sheriff's in town."

Elway was taking his approach to single life somewhat slowly. He'd been divorced for two years and had gone through a rebound relationship with former *Playboy* playmate Carrie Stevens. His friends wondered why he was with her. He'd shrug and say he just felt like being a bad boy after more than twenty years of playing his personal life so close to the vest. He was trying to have fun and had no plans to get married, let alone have a serious relationship. His divorce hit him deeply because it's not how he had pictured his life. When he was in high school, he often told his parents he wanted to get married while he was still in college. Find a good woman and settle down. That's almost exactly what he did. He dated Janet from the time he was a freshman and got married after his rookie year.

Just two years after signing the divorce papers, Elway wasn't ready to plant the seeds of another serious relationship. Neither was Paige. For everything Elway had been through during his marriage, he was about to date a woman who had experienced far worse. When it came to marriage, Paige had been through an emotional grinder.

Paige grew up in the same part of the San Fernando Valley as Elway, and her brother had attended Granada Hills High, the same as Elway. Adding to the coincidences, her first husband also had attended Granada Hills, roughly six years before Elway. Long before she and Elway met, Paige had been married to Randy Green, who also played football at

Granada Hills High with Dana Potter. That's the same Potter who helped
Jack Neumeier change the Granada Hills program and then returned
years later to help Neumeier coach Elway. Potter, Green, and two other
men eventually partnered to start a real estate company. The four of them
were highly successful, driven in large part by Green's exceptional sales
ability. Until drug addiction got the best of Green.

"When I started working with him, it was about eight or nine years
after high school," Potter says. "He had already had a problem once
and cleaned up. I didn't even know he'd had a problem. He had been
married once and got divorced, but he was this amazing guy. He was so
charismatic, so charming, handsome, just the life of the party. People were
just drawn to him. At the same time, when he was using, it was exactly
the opposite."

Paige was twenty-two and Randy was thirty-five when they met and
eventually got married. Shortly after, he started using again and spiraled
out of control. The situation got to the point where his father, mother,
Paige, and business partners held an intervention. He went to rehabili-
tation, cleaned up for a while, and then started using again. He repeated
the routine time and again. Green was in and out of rehab so much even
close friends lost count. Maybe it was four or five. It could have been six
or even seven. Paige stayed with him each time, standing by him as he
faltered. They didn't have children together, so she could have moved on
easily. Most people who know the story are shocked she didn't. Instead,
she stayed with him for fifteen years of incredible joy and crushing
weakness.

"It was amazing to me because it was like one of those older couples
you see that have been together for years and years and one of them
stands by the other through a disease," Potter says. "They loved each other
so deeply because they have been together so long. But the truth is they
hadn't been together that long. She stayed through some very difficult,
sometimes embarrassing moments. But she held her head high and acted
with dignity the whole time.... I think other women, other people, in the
same situation, would have left long before it got that bad and nobody
would have blamed them."

Paige's devotion was based on a simple premise.

"You didn't know him," she says. "He was such an important part of my life. I guess I always saw the good in him. Addicts are typically very good people with a horrible disease they can't control...it had gotten to the point we were talking about divorce. We were in the process of filing, but we were still talking because I had never been through something like that. I never in my mind ever thought it would actually happen because we were totally codependent on each other. Everybody in my life around me told me they could understand why he stayed with me, but they couldn't understand why I could stay with him."

Adding to Paige's vulnerability with Green, her father had died when she was only thirteen.

"You've got to remember he was thirteen years older than me....I think that had a huge part in me marrying him because he was like a father figure to me. He took care of me just like I was a kid. He was that father figure, husband, lover, best friend...all of that to me," she says.

Paige eventually demanded Green go into rehab and do the entire process. She wanted him to live in a Sober Living house instead of simply returning home after the first part of rehab. Green thought he was strong enough to handle rehab on his own. He constantly convinced family and friends he could do rehab his way. As Paige was putting her foot down, so were Green's business partners. They forced him to sell his share of the company. Between family relationships and friendships, it was a difficult, emotional split.

The dissolution of the company revolved around disability insurance policies the company had taken out on each of the partners. Although the drug addiction left Green unable to function in a business sense, he wasn't disabled in the classic sense. When his partners told him to stop being active—water skiing or training, or even engaging in foot races up the stairs of high-rise buildings—he refused. Inevitably, the insurance company got photos of him in action and fought the disability claim. On the day of the final talks, all the parties met in a downtown Los Angeles office. There were about eight attorneys on hand to represent everyone, and everybody showed up.

Everyone except Green. Paige sat there alone. Amid the emotion, anger, tension, and negotiation, she kept her calm.

"I thought to myself, 'This woman is remarkable.' She understands situations and people on a different level. Think about how difficult it is to be confronted by a bunch of top-notch attorneys when your husband is supposed to be doing this, but he's not capable," Potter says. "She was in uncharted waters. I was in uncharted waters. I was just amazed at her patience, compassion, and her desire to help. She was a rock when everything was crumbling, completely steadfast."

After the settlement, Green finished rehab, but a car accident led him to start taking Vicodin. That led to yet another relapse. After rehab, he was supposed to go to the Sober Living facility again in May 2003 (at roughly the same time Elway was finalizing his divorce). Instead, he checked himself out and went to a furnished apartment. After a rare stretch of days in which they didn't talk, Paige checked his credit card statements. She called the apartment building and he was found dead from an accidental overdose.

"I had even asked him, 'You don't ever want to kill yourself, do you?' He would always say, 'No, I don't,'" Paige says. "I never thought he killed himself. Through everything, he was a very, very hands-on dad and his kids are remarkably healthy throughout this devastating thing. So I never got the feeling he wanted to kill himself. I always thought he was trying to do everything he could to solve his problem."

Elway was dating a woman who could share in the depth of his pain and, more importantly, was deeply loyal. Dating a former superstar athlete didn't intimidate her, nor did it define how she viewed herself. Not wanting to put himself out there, he proceeded carefully. He was in Los Angeles one time to see her and do some business, but he didn't want to let her know he had his own private jet. He didn't want her to know just how much money he really had. The plane was parked at the Van Nuys airport, near where she lived. They had gone on a date and now it was roughly midnight. Elway had to be back in Denver the next morning for a meeting. Finally, he said, "I have to go catch a flight." Paige looked at him quizzically and said, "Where are you catching a flight at this hour?"

Not that she pressed him for answers. Paige was more than happy to take things slowly. Instead of pushing the relationship, she showed in many small ways how much she cared. In May 2006, the couple went to the Kentucky Derby. It was supposed to be a frivolous weekend of sports, mint julips, and the race-day fashion show that is the derby. As they departed, Elway left his phone charger behind in the hotel room. A couple of days later, he was at home in Denver and high school buddy Chris Sutton was visiting. A package from Paige arrived. It had three items.

A photo album of their weekend at the derby.

A package of gummy bears, Elway's favorite candy.

A phone charger.

Sutton looked at Elway and recalls saying, "Dude, she's a keeper." By 2007, Paige moved to Denver. She still played it cool about how serious the relationship had become when she was interviewed by *Denver Magazine*.

"Well, we've all been on first dates," she said. "It either gets better or worse from there. In this case, it got good enough that I moved to Denver a year later."

Then she was asked about what she envisioned of her future with Elway.

"We pretty much live one day at a time," she said. Paige wanted to be a partner first and worry about the rest at whatever time that happened. As she did that, it melted Elway's frosty thoughts toward getting remarried. As their relationship blossomed, Elway's business life changed again. The Crush were disbanded after the 2008 season, and Elway returned to the car business, buying one of the largest Toyota dealerships in the country in Ontario, California.

Elway immediately set out to transform the dealership to make it more profitable and then buy other dealerships in California and Colorado. Even in that business, Elway set higher goals than simply making money. At a Toyota corporate meeting, the company described its highest honor. It was a simple lapel pin a dealer could receive as the President's Cabinet award. It's like the Lombardi Trophy for Toyota dealers. As the award was described, Elway leaned over to whisper in the ear of his top executive, Pierce Gagnet.

"I want that," Elway said, simply.

By September 2008, Elway wanted something more with Paige. The couple went on a trip to Europe and ended up in Venice, Italy. Elway had a couple of Scotches to get up the courage as they took a late-night walk through Piazza San Marco. It was about 11 p.m. and there was no one in sight as the rain came down. They were in the middle of the square when Elway dropped to one knee and proposed.

Just as he asked, a man walked by. Elway had the man take a picture and the photo now hangs in the guest room of their home. By August 2009, they were married at Elway's vacation home in Coeur d'Alene, Idaho. Less than eighteen months later, Elway would be asking Paige how he looked as he made his return to the NFL.

CHAPTER 31

TEBOWMANIA

Elway's first year as an executive had more than the usual challenges. After his December 2010 meeting with Bowlen, he was officially put in charge of the team's football operations on January 5, 2011.

In the days leading up to the official announcement, Elway was already in work mode. On January 3, 2011, he attended the Orange Bowl to see Stanford take on Virginia Tech. Elway was there for more than just a chance to see his alma mater play. First, he was making a final check on the availability of Stanford coach Jim Harbaugh, who had become the hot name in NFL coaching circles after turning around the Stanford program. Harbaugh took the San Francisco 49ers job four days after the Orange Bowl game and then Elway hired John Fox on January 13.

The second reason Elway went to Miami for the bowl game was to take a long look at Stanford quarterback Andrew Luck. The Broncos had the number two pick in the 2011 NFL Draft and Elway already knew one thing: he needed a quarterback. Cam Newton of Auburn was considered the likely number one overall pick in the 2011 draft, but Elway loved everything about Luck, a junior who was establishing himself as a top prospect as well. After Stanford and Luck overwhelmed Virginia Tech, Elway hoped Luck would come out early.

Luck didn't and that set the stage for Elway to draft Texas A&M linebacker Von Miller with the second pick. The Broncos also spent a tremendous amount of time scouting quarterback Colin Kaepernick as a possible second-round pick, but eventually opted not to take him. Luck's decision to stay in college and for the Broncos to pass on Kaepernick led to one of the strangest seasons in the history of NFL quarterback play.

In April 2010, former Denver coach Josh McDaniels made the controversial decision to select Tim Tebow in the first round of the NFL Draft. McDaniels even traded up to the number twenty-five pick to get Tebow when most teams in the league didn't think Tebow was anything close to a first-round-caliber pick. Most teams viewed him as a third-round pick, at best, and a complete project as a passer. Tebow's erratic throwing style and penchant for running meant he was going to need a lot of work if he was ever going to make it as an NFL quarterback. Some teams believed he had a better future as a fullback or halfback.

On top of all that, Tebow had a devout group of fans. Extremely devout. His strong faith, great story from birth, and feats on the field in high school and college made him a hero and role model in the Christian community. Aside from his helping the University of Florida to two national championships and winning the Heisman Trophy, Tebow's mother said doctors advised her to abort her pregnancy with Tim due to medical concerns.

She persisted.

Elway and the rest of the Broncos intellectually understood the story. What they weren't ready for was the full depth of devotion by the "Tebowites." There were steps leading up to the whole Tebow experience. It started with the hiring of Fox. Fox was the counter to McDaniels's high-strung style. Fox was "Good Time Charlie," a guy who smiled and joked throughout the day. The thinking in hiring Fox was that he would be a positive influence on the locker room as Elway and his staff rebuilt the roster. Fox was not only good in the locker room but he was also great with the media, which had quickly grown tired of McDaniels's disregard for them. The thinking from a football standpoint was that Fox, who had a strong defensive background, would emphasize Denver's best strength and keep the players happy as the team struggled on offense.

Finally, Fox was an experienced head coach with more than twenty years in the NFL. That tenure was critical as the entire NFL dealt with the 2011 lockout in the off-season. Owners and players clashed for five months over the Collective Bargaining Agreement and didn't resolve it until late July. Even with the selection of Miller at number two overall, the Broncos weren't a good team. Denver got off to a 1–4 start. The team simply wasn't deep with offensive talent and the quarterback situation was a mess. Veteran quarterback Kyle Orton opened the season as the starter and proved to be his mediocre self. Three of Denver's first four losses were by less than a touchdown, largely because of Orton's inability to convert key situations on third down or in the red zone.

As that played out, the Tebowites grew louder and louder. During a season-opening loss to Oakland on September 12, 2011, some fans chanted for Tebow to be put in. After the game, a group of fans took to Internet message boards to discuss buying billboards to urge the team to start Tebow. On September 29, after the team fell to 1–2, the idea became a reality. Just outside downtown Denver, a billboard with a rotating electronic image read, "Broncos fans to John Fox: Play Tebow!!" After the Broncos fell to 1–3 with a loss at Green Bay, Fox met with Elway to talk about making a switch at quarterback. Despite Orton's struggles, it wasn't an easy call. Tebow had been inconsistent in practice, at best. During training camp, longtime NFL reporter Mike Silver of Yahoo! Sports quoted a Broncos source about Tebow's performance.

"If everything was totally equal, and this were a competition based only on performance at this camp, Tebow would probably be the fourth-string guy," the source said. "[Orton] is far and away the best, and Tebow's way behind [Brady] Quinn too. And I'm telling you, Adam Weber is flat-out better right now."

In meetings, Tebow struggled to understand and explain concepts in reading defenses and executing the offense. As one teammate put it bluntly that season, "He has no idea what's going on out there. If the first read doesn't work, he's just making it up." Numerous Broncos coaches would simply shake their head when asked about Tebow's classroom understanding of professional concepts. Still, it's not like the Broncos had many better options. Quinn was a first-round bust in Cleveland and didn't perform any better than Orton in practices. Orton, who started in the fifth game as Denver fell to 1–4, clearly wasn't the solution. Both Elway and Fox felt that the organization had to find out the answer to one obvious question.

Could Tebow play quarterback in the NFL? The strange part is that in going on a 7–4 run for the rest of the season, making the playoffs, and coming up with a dramatic win over Pittsburgh in the postseason with Tebow starting, the Broncos' conclusion ran counter to the results.

Tebow couldn't play.

It's the same conclusion three other teams (the New York Jets, New England, and Philadelphia) came to later. Still, that conclusion was part of a season-long debate that swallowed up the sports world, particularly the sports media. Tebow Time or "Tebowmania"—whatever you called it—became a daily obsession on every sports outlet in America. Skip Bayless made Tebow a cottage industry on ESPN. The debate became a confluence of sports and religion. No matter how ugly Tebow played, he and the Broncos found a way to win. That justified his continuing to start. Football purists who pointed out that the Broncos were overcoming Tebow's foibles rather than succeeding because of his talent weren't just critics. They were deemed anti-Christian. The debate would often become venomous, and it began with Tebow's first start in Miami.

Part of Fox's reason for waiting an extra week to change was that the Broncos had a bye week after the fifth game. That would give the coaches extra time to prepare Tebow and, more importantly, change the offense to suit his talent. Initially, offensive coordinator Mike McCoy had planned to play a conventional offense. During the bye week, McCoy was sipping a glass of wine one night with his wife when she asked him, "What are you going to do?"

He said with great confidence, "We're going to run our normal offense." By the time the Broncos were halfway through the game against Miami on October 16, 2011, McCoy and Broncos quarterback coach Adam Gase realized they were going to have to change to a system that took advantage of Tebow's running ability. For the first fifty-four minutes against Miami, Tebow's first start of the season looked like it was going to be the last of his career. Tebow was simply awful and sometimes comically so. He completed only four of his first fourteen passes for forty yards and was sacked five times.

That only begins to describe how rough it was. There was one pass early in the game that he threw toward the sideline. It went completely over the Denver bench. The pass also rotated end over end rather than in anything resembling a spiral. Denver was down 15–0 with fewer than six minutes remaining when Tebow completely changed. He threw the first of his two touchdown passes with 2:44 remaining. The Broncos then recovered an onside kick and scored again, and Tebow ran in a two-point conversion to tie the game and force overtime. Denver then won on a fifty-one-yard field goal. In the final six minutes, Tebow completed nine of thirteen passes for 121 yards and two touchdowns. He also rushed nine times for fifty-nine yards.

It marked the first time since the 1970 NFL merger that a team had overcome a fifteen-point deficit in the final 2:44 of a game. That type of performance was about to become a theme. After a lopsided loss to Detroit, Denver won six consecutive games and Tebow was 7–1 as a starter. The Broncos beat Oakland by two touchdowns as Tebow completed ten of twenty-one passes for 124 yards and, more importantly, rushed for 118 yards on thirteen carries. He threw for one touchdown and ran for another. Denver then won another improbable game, beating Kansas City even though Tebow completed only two of eight passes. Next, the Broncos beat the New York Jets when Tebow completed nine of twenty passes.

Tebow completed fewer than half his passes in each of his first five games, yet the Broncos were 4–1 in those games. Denver had reached 5–5 and there was growing interest in the team. At the same time, the Broncos were a long way from making a final decision about Tebow's future. That's when Fox and Elway made dueling PR mistakes even as they were trying to support Tebow. On November 22, Denver cut Orton. The Broncos knew Orton didn't have a future with them and wanted to let him catch on with another team. At that point, Fox was asked a question about whether Tebow could play in a conventional offense rather than the read-option stuff the Broncos were using.

"Tebow would be screwed," Fox said.

That was true, particularly at that point. It would have been unfair to Tebow to put him in a system he wasn't used to. Part of the art of coaching is putting players in the best position to succeed. Still, Fox had to take it back. Tebowites took Fox's statement as some type of insult. It was as if he had insulted some Hall of Fame player rather than a second-year player with a handful of career starts.

That's when it dawned on Elway and the rest of the organization that Tebow fans liked him more than they liked the Broncos. To those fans, there was no reasonable way to talk about what Tebow didn't do well or needed to improve upon. He was winning games and that was all that mattered. He could do no wrong in their eyes. Next, it was Elway's turn to endure the wrath of those fans. On a radio show that same week, Elway was asked whether he had a better feeling about the team's quarterback of the future than he had five weeks prior.

Elway said, simply, "Um, no." That was the blunt, first reaction. Elway then went on to explain that there were other factors to consider. Specifically, Tebow had to improve his third-down passing, the most critical down in Elway's view. Third down was when a quarterback made his money, in Elway's mind. To that point, Tebow had completed only six of forty-three passes on third-down. The reaction to Elway's comment was as if he had just burned the American flag at high noon in front of a Sunday school class. The *Denver Post* Broncos blog was filled with pointed criticism of Elway in the days following his remarks.

Here's a sampling:

> By the time the Broncos proclaim publicly, "Tebow's our guy,"
> Tebow, through his agent, will have already begun the process of
> requesting/working out a waiver or trade deal to another team.
> Tebow's a good guy, but he isn't stupid. He will not dedicate his
> efforts to playing for a lukewarm owner and [general manager].
> It is now perfectly clear that Tebow's NFL career DOES
> NOT live or die with the Denver Broncos. AND we all know
> the Broncos organization is light years away from functioning
> and winning at a level on par with Pittsburgh, Baltimore,

New England, Dallas, Green Bay, [New Orleans] etc. etc. etc. [Owner Pat] Bowlen, and Bowlen only, is responsible for trading off a lot of top tier talent including [Jay] Cutler, [Brandon] Marshall, [Peyton] Hillis, [Brandon] Lloyd, and others. I expect, by Elway's recommendation, Bowlen will trade one of the most unique talents that ever stepped onto a football field.

And another:

Pat Bowlen is a smart businessman and makes decisions that are going to increase the value of his business. The current Net Worth of the Denver Broncos is One Billion Dollars and their most valuable asset is Tim Tebow. He has the possibility to become the most valuable asset in the history of the NFL. You're crazy if you think he's not going to try and maximize his investment. Tim Tebow is not worth millions to Pat Bowlen, he's worth hundreds of millions to his bottom line if successful. You can guarantee that Tim Tebow will be the quarterback next year in Denver.

Then there were the inevitable comparisons of Tebow's stats in his first year as a starter to Elway's rookie year:

Elway stunk when he first started. People forget his nickname was "the comeback kid." He stunk most of the game and at the last minute in the last quarter he would finally win the game. What a double standard he has. He sure is lucky the owners at the time, didn't throw him out! Look to yourself before you judge a rookie more unfairly than YOU were judged.

At least one fan seemed to get the big picture:

So let me get this straight. The Broncos bench Orton, re-tool their offense to fit Tebow's skill, publicly state the truth—which is that no one knows how good Tebow can be yet—cut Orton,

> Fox bear hugs [Tebow] on the sideline after the Jets game with
> a smile so big it had its own zip code, and both Fox and Elway
> have stated their desire to see him succeed and be our long-term
> guy…all this, and still there are delusional people that believe
> they want him gone? Unbelievable.

The next day, Elway had to go back on the radio to clarify he hoped
Tebow "would be our guy" in the future. Elway wasn't lying. He really did
hope Tebow would become a franchise quarterback. Elway didn't want the
team to have to move on from a first-round pick, even if it wasn't his pick.
The Broncos put in an incredible amount of effort to see if Tebow could
become a legitimate starting quarterback. It only made sense. He was
under contractual control for a total of six years. When Tebow struggled
in practice, the Broncos found videotape of him from when he was in
high school, hoping to figure out the best ways to coach him.

The Broncos also worked with specialists to help with Tebow's dyslexia
and spent countless hours going over coverages and working on his
mechanics. Still, Tebow's becoming a long-term answer was a longshot,
and a couple of games at the end of the season proved it. Unable to say
anything publicly that resembled even the mildest criticism, some people
in the organization under Elway called members of the Denver media to
explain Tebow's shortcomings. They hoped the media would be able to
explain to fans that Tebow's run was more a string of luck.

Unfortunately, there was about to be a shining moment that continued
to blind the Tebowites. The Broncos eventually improved to 8–5. In the
final three games of that run, Tebow completed better than 50 percent of
his passes in each game. Two of the three games went to overtime and one
of those included a repeat of the Miami game when Denver beat Chicago.
The Bears had a 10–0 lead before Denver finally scored a touchdown with
2:15 remaining in the game. Chicago could have almost run the clock out
before running back Marion Barber mistakenly ran out of bounds to save
about thirty-five seconds for Denver. Armed with extra time, Tebow got
the Broncos into position for a game-tying fifty-nine-yard field goal by
Matt Prater.

In overtime, Prater then hit a fifty-one-yarder to win the game.

Tebow and the Broncos regressed to the norm over the next three games with losses against New England, Buffalo, and Kansas City. Essentially, each of those teams played very simplified defenses, forcing Tebow to become a passer and rendering him useless. Despite the three straight losses, Denver backed into the playoffs, and the Tebowmania was about to go to the next level.

Denver hosted the Pittsburgh Steelers in the first round of the playoffs. The Steelers were confident their blitz-oriented style would fluster Tebow and force him into one mistake after another. Ultimately, it was the Steelers who made the mistake with that game plan. Attacking Tebow played right into his style. Blitzing him did two things. First, it allowed him to use his legs to escape pressure and play to his running style. Second, it removed a defender from coverage, making it easier for him to read the defense.

An additional problem for the Steelers is that they were without safety Ryan Clark. He couldn't play in the high altitude of Denver because he was dealing with a sickle cell trait condition. Earlier in his career, Clark had played in Denver, become gravely ill, and lost both his spleen and gall bladder. Ryan Mundy, a backup who mostly played special teams, started in Clark's place. That proved to be critical in the end. Tebow led the Broncos to twenty points in the second quarter with a thirty-yard touchdown pass and an eight-yard touchdown run for a 20–6 lead at halftime. Pittsburgh rallied in the second half and the game eventually went to overtime.

For the fourth time in twelve games as a starter in the 2011 season, Tebow was going to overtime. What was about to happen was a religious experience. On the opening play of overtime, Denver had the ball at its own twenty-yard line. Tebow lined up in shotgun formation on first down with wide receiver DeMaryius Thomas on the left side. Just before the snap, Mundy charged the line of scrimmage as if he was going to blitz.

That put Mundy out of position. Tebow took the snap and found Thomas on a deep in pattern. Thomas ran through the area vacated by Mundy and went eighty yards untouched for the game-winning touchdown. With that pass, Tebow finished the game with 316 yards passing. Tebow's many religious fans took it as a sign of John 3:16 from the Bible. The moment was etched in their minds and, more importantly, their souls. This was a sign that Tebow was everything they imagined as a star. Though there was no question that Tebow played with a great sense of calm and composure in clutch situations and he was a very accurate deep thrower, he was getting by in situations that were extraordinarily improbable.

Of the eight victories he led, six were by less than a touchdown and four were in overtime, and Prater made three field goals of fifty yards or longer to tie or win games. The Denver defense had also been extraordinary during that run, holding opponents to fifteen points or less in five of the eight victories.

Then there was the matter of the style Tebow played. In basically three-quarters of a season, Tebow ran 122 times, a stunningly high total for a quarterback. That's also a pace for more than 160 carries over a full season, which would be an NFL record. By the time 2011 was done, Tebow was playing with broken ribs and was banged up everywhere. He was incredibly tough, but his style of play was simply unsustainable.

For instance, Elway, considered an excellent running quarterback, never carried more than sixty-six times in a season. Michael Vick might be the greatest running quarterback in the history of the NFL and never carried more than 123 times in a season. Vick's body took an incredible amount of punishment because of his running style. From Roger Staubach to Steve Young, there are countless stories of quarterbacks who shortened their careers by running too much.

After the Steelers' mistake, the blueprint for how to stop Tebow was finalized in the next playoff game. While New England was simply too good for Denver in the second round of the playoffs, the Patriots exposed Tebow in their 45–10 victory. The Patriots played a very simple defense during the game. Instead of blitzing Tebow, New England played coverage. New England would often rush only three players and then wait for Tebow to start running. Once he broke the pocket, then the Patriots would run toward him. It was as basic and simple a coverage as any team could play and Tebow struggled. He completed only nine of twenty-six passes for 136 yards, was sacked five times, and ran five more times for only thirteen yards. As the Patriots continued to score, they played a soft defense any competent quarterback would have at least piled up stats against.

Instead, Tebow was rendered useless. It was also a continuation of what New England, Buffalo, and Kansas City had done in the final three games of the regular season. Trying to convert Tebow to any type of normal passer was going to be difficult. First, his fans would make it impossible for him to be able to sit out long enough to change his game. Second, by Tebow's own admission, it was going to be hard for him to change. During training camp before the 2011 season, he told *Sports Illustrated* that practice wasn't the best environment to measure him.

"A lot of my game is keeping the chains moving, running for a first down, taking on a tackler, running through a hit, and inspiring my team-mates," Tebow said. "Those aren't things you do in practice. In practice you want to work on those areas where you need to get better—play-action drops, checking it down to the flats, understanding the concepts of the offense and the defense."

The problem with that approach is that coaches measure practice and try to figure out what a player is best suited to do. There's an old expression in football: quarterbacks should never miss in practice. Tebow missed a lot in practice. If you're a coach and you're trying to figure out what to call during a game, it was a giant guessing game with Tebow based on what you saw in practice. In today's NFL game, Tebow's overall accuracy of 46.5 percent during the 2011 season was unacceptable over the long haul. Orton was at better than 58 percent in 2010 and 2011, and he wasn't close to being good enough.

In other words, it was one thing for a fan to take a leap of faith with Tebow. The fan didn't have his job tied to Tebow's success. For coaches and executives like Fox and Elway, it was a completely different equation. In Elway's mind, this was about ability, not hope. Tebow was a nice enough person and legitimately a man of his faith. However, he had rubbed some people the wrong way in minor ways. When he was a backup quarterback even before Elway and Fox arrived, he didn't keep a particularly low profile. He did every interview possible and made himself available all the time. Some people in the organization believed he was upstaging Orton in the process.

One Broncos staff member described Tebow as the "most self-centered humble guy I've ever met."

Tebow turned speaking appearances into a cottage industry. He would regularly receive $50,000 for appearances, including at churches. The logic was that Tebow would draw a big crowd for fundraisers. However, when Elway's ex-wife, Janet, asked Tebow to do an appearance at a charity event, Tebow's brother asked for the $50,000. Janet declined and said her ex-husband never charged for a charity event.

When Tebow was in college, at least one prominent agent dropped out of the recruiting process because there were roughly thirty people involved in the interview process. The agent described the process as a "zoo atmosphere." At the same time, none of that would have mattered if Tebow could have played at an NFL level. Elway and the rest of the coaches and personnel people with the Broncos didn't think he could. Neither did the next three teams he played for. Still, extricating the Broncos from Tebow was going to be much harder than Elway or anyone ever imagined. The Tebowites weren't ready to accept reality.

If the Broncos were going to move on from Tebow, they were going to need an unquestionably better option. They needed an option only a zealot would disagree with. Miraculously, that option was about to reveal itself in the winter of 2012.

CHAPTER 32

PEYTON

Elway was calmly swinging a golf club as the future of the Broncos swung in the balance.

On Monday, March 19, 2012, Elway and Fox awaited a call from quarterback Peyton Manning that would decide two major questions. First, would the Broncos be able to escape from Tebowmania? Second, would they become Super Bowl contenders? Standing in Elway's office, Fox was a nervous wreck. He had spent most of the previous eleven days trying to get whatever information he could from anyone who might know anything about Manning. Fox had asked Elway days before if he should call Manning and his wife on their anniversary to wish them well. Elway told Fox repeatedly to leave Manning alone.

That was part of a pattern that had developed. Each morning, Fox came to Elway's office and asked, "Have you heard anything? Should I call Peyton?" Elway would smile and say, "No and no," each time. Each afternoon, Fox would return to ask, "Have you heard anything? Should I call Peyton?" Elway would smile and say, "No and no." Elway wanted to play this cool, sensing the whole time that the best way to deal with Manning was to leave him alone to work through his thoughts. It's not that Elway wasn't just as desperate as Fox, particularly to get his team out of an untenable quarterback situation that Tebow's fans had created. But if there's one thing Elway wasn't going to succumb to, it was the anxiety that came with the chase for Manning.

Or as Manning says, putting it simply, "John Elway doesn't beg."

So, as the Broncos waited that day, Elway took out a club and practiced his swing. It was smooth, just like his approach to Manning starting ten days before. On March 9, 2012, Manning and Elway had ended a long day of talks with a conversation that lasted for hours inside the Men's Lounge of the Cherry Hills Country Club in suburban Denver. John Lynch, whom Elway had asked to be there for reinforcement, grew so tired waiting for Manning and Elway to wrap up that he excused himself to head home to bed.

At the same time, it was probably the greatest closing conversation Elway has ever pulled in all his years in business. As other teams were tripping over themselves to get a chance with Manning, Elway was calm and, in the end, played it exactly right. As the 2011 season wrapped up with the playoffs, the Broncos were clearly at a crossroads. Tebow had done some wonderful things to lift the team to the playoffs, but it wasn't going to last in any reasonable person's estimation. Elway was set on making a change and was scouting an array of college quarterbacks, including Andrew Luck (although he was clearly going to be out of reach in the draft), Ryan Tannehill, and Russell Wilson. The team would end up taking Brock Osweiler in the second round as an insurance policy after Manning signed. But before Manning signed, everyone in the organization knew replacing Tebow with a quarterback from the draft was going to be a tough sell from a public relations standpoint.

As Tebow was creating frenzy in Denver in the 2011 season, Manning's fourteen-year run in Indianapolis was coming to an end. Injuries to his neck had forced him to miss the entire season. Worse, Manning simply couldn't throw. His arm was limp and the nerves were coming back very slowly. The Colts had gone 1–15 that season and were in line for the number one overall pick. With Luck available in the draft, the Colts were taking advantage of an opportunity to transition from an aging and injured franchise quarterback to a fresh-faced star.

Around mid-February 2012, Broncos president Joe Ellis was figuring out the budget for the upcoming season and fiscal year. Ellis walked into Elway's office one day and said the magic words.

"You know, if Peyton is available, we could do something," Ellis says he told Elway.

"That's all I needed to hear," Elway said.

Even with an injured arm, Manning was a better gamble than Tebow ever would be. More importantly, no one with common sense would argue with Elway about Manning versus Tebow. So, Elway prepared for the pursuit. On March 7, the Colts made the official announcement that they were releasing Manning. It was an emotional moment for Manning, who choked up during the press conference as the finality set in. Manning had wanted so badly to play his entire career with one team.

After the announcement, Elway called Manning's agent, Tom Condon, to see if Manning would be interested in Denver and whether the money the Broncos were offering was in line with what Manning wanted. The answer to both was yes. That conversation also put Denver at the head of the line of places Manning would visit. Yet that hardly meant Manning was going to be a Bronco. It did allow the Broncos to make serious preparations. Offensive coordinator Mike McCoy called Colts coaches Frank Reich and Clyde Christensen to pick their brains about Manning.

Fox was all over the idea of a heavy recruiting pitch. He had spent a decade earlier in his career as a recruiter in the college ranks. He came up with every idea for how to sell Manning on playing in Denver. At a certain point, part of Elway's job was keeping Fox from getting overexcited. Fox came up with one key item. He was told Manning was very concerned about weather conditions. Manning had played his entire home career indoors with Indianapolis. Fox had the Broncos staff research the average temperature of every regular season home game in team history. It was 60.1 degrees, a fact that helped ease Manning's fears about playing most games outdoors.

As the Broncos prepped, Elway theorized about the visit by picturing how he would feel in Manning's shoes.

"If I had spent my entire career with one team and now I was, essentially, out on the streets, how would I feel?" Elway says. "You put yourself in somebody else's shoes and just imagine it. I'd be upset and probably uneasy. The last thing I'd want is a hard sell from anybody."

Just as Elway imagined, Manning was still in a distracted state of shock as he landed at Denver's Centennial Airport on a clear, fifty-five-degree day. It was the first stop on an eleven-day tour that seemed to last eleven years and take 111 twists and turns. Manning said the right things, asked the right questions, and was, in theory, moving on from the Colts. But as the day played out, Elway knew Manning was a long way from a decision. After making the rounds at Denver's practice facility, asking a lot of questions about the team personnel, and meeting with the coaches, it was time for dinner. There were going to be four people dining that night: Manning, Elway, Fox, and wide receiver Brandon Stokley. Stokley had played for the Broncos from 2007 to 2009 and had spent four years earlier in his career with Manning in Indianapolis.

Stokley lived in Denver and was a trusted friend to Manning. Not only did Manning stay at Stokley's house in nearby Castle Rock during the visit, but the Broncos also re-signed Stokley for the 2012 season after Manning signed. As the foursome headed for dinner, the first trick was to lose the media. Reporters had been following Manning from the time he landed. The Broncos staff arranged for seven cars to leave the facility at the same time. All of them went to different locations and one of the TV stations supposedly following Manning ended up at a restaurant only to find out Manning, Elway, Fox, and Stokley weren't there.

Elway continued to slow-play the situation through dinner. He felt in his gut there was no way Manning was going to decide or be forced into a decision so soon. Over the coming days, there would be an endless array of reports about Manning and secret meetings and secret workouts with other teams. It was, in Elway's view, proof the NFL had become its own real-life soap opera.

Elway promised himself not to get drawn into it. In truth, the biggest concern for him was Manning's health. But even that wasn't enough to dissuade Elway. Sure, the reports about Manning's being unable to throw were troubling. At the same time, Elway knew he was talking to one of the most driven men in NFL history. Elway knew Manning would do whatever it took to get healthy. It wasn't much different than what Drew Brees had done in 2006. That off-season, Brees's arm was in a sling as

Miami and New Orleans debated whether to sign him. The Dolphins backed off and the Saints took him. People around Brees constantly said he would do whatever was necessary to play again. The rest is history.

Finally, whether Manning worked out or not, it was a way to get out from the Tebow mess. Again, no reasonable person was going to argue with the Broncos' taking Manning over Tebow, even with Manning's bad arm. After dinner, the group headed to Cherry Hills Country Club, arriving at about 8 p.m. The Men's Lounge, decorated in a Western motif befitting Denver and complete with leather couches and chairs, had a history as the backdrop of fierce sports comebacks.

On June 18, 1960, thirty-one-year-old Arnold Palmer and *Pittsburgh Post-Gazette* sportswriter Bob Drum, who had covered Palmer since he was sixteen years old, argued in that very lounge over Palmer's chances of making a comeback in the US Open. Drum said Palmer, who was seven shots back and tied for fifteenth headed into the final round, had no shot. That inspired Palmer, who was known simply as "The King," to begin one of his crowning achievements by rallying to win. On the way, he passed luminaries of the game such as Julius Boros, Sam Snead, and Ben Hogan.

More than fifty years later, Manning's equally fierce return to the top unofficially started in the same place. The only difference is Elway did a lot more listening to Manning than challenging him the way Drum did with Palmer. After sitting out a year and with many people predicting Manning would never play again, he put himself back alongside the likes of Johnny Unitas, Brady, and Elway. The first thing Elway did was spell out the next step if Manning were to join the team. He assured Manning the Broncos would trade or cut Tebow. Or as Elway told Manning, "I'm just going to tell you right now, I know it won't work with the two of you together." The distraction simply would have been overwhelming.

Lynch, who had played safety against both Elway and Manning in his career, showed up around 9 p.m. Elway told Lynch, "Dude, come help me seal the deal." Lynch and Manning had become friends over the years and had a common bond. They'd had similar neck procedures done, and

Manning had reached out to Lynch about what to expect in recovery. Still, there was no deal to seal that night—just a lot of listening and talking between two men in the very exclusive club of Super Bowl–winning quarterbacks. At the time, there were only twenty-nine men in that club. That unique bond created a sense of trust between them. Elway and Manning eventually broke away from the group and sat in front of a fireplace. There were televisions above the fireplace that showed sports. That served as an occasional distraction as the two talked. There was a view of the treetops that lined the golf course, and, as they chatted, Manning started to decompress from the previous two days. It was a perfect Denver night, so Elway didn't have to sell the city. He just listened. As his parents had told him long ago, there's a reason you're born with two ears and one mouth. Listen more and talk less.

Elway didn't need to sell Manning on the talent of young receivers DeMaryius Thomas and Eric Decker. He didn't have to sell Manning on the young talent the Broncos had collected on defense. Most importantly, Elway didn't have to prove he understood the needs of a franchise quarterback. These were two men who spoke the same language about how a team should be run and what should be expected. Both understood what it was like to play in front of 80,000 screaming people with millions more watching on television as a bunch of 300-pound men tried to chase them down with the championship of football on the line.

These were rare men even among the elite of the game. That was the logical part of the conversation. What still weighed on Manning was the fact that he was no longer with the Colts. He had developed an incredibly deep relationship with both the city and almost every member of the Colts organization. The fact that he didn't get to leave Indy on his own terms bothered him. He also had been dealing with the media for two days. After he was let go by the Colts, he flew to Miami. Helicopters followed him around town as he and his wife, Ashley, stayed at their home there. The media weren't the only ones trying to chase down Manning. After meeting with the Broncos, Manning had a meeting the next day in Denver with Shanahan, who was now the Washington coach. Except as Elway and Manning sat there that night, news broke that Washington had traded up to the number two spot in the draft to get quarterback Robert Griffin III. Elway made sure to blurt that out right away.

"Whoa, Washington just traded for the second pick. Looks like they'll get RG3," Elway said. Manning looked a little stunned and said, "What?" Manning was a hell of a poker player most of the time, but between the shock of the past couple of days and the whirlwind of finding a new team, Elway could tell right away Manning had Washington on his short list. Except now Manning was dealing with the musical chairs process of the NFL. If you don't get a seat right away, you sometimes don't get a spot. Elway and Manning continued to talk the night away. After more than two hours, Lynch called it a night.

"It was like 11:30 and I'd been there more than two hours. I could see John and Peyton were really talking about something serious by the looks on their faces. You could see they had a really strong connection because they identified with each other. It was pretty cool to watch, but I was beat. I just walked over at one point and said, 'Guys, I'm sorry, but I'm done. I'm exhausted.' I have no idea how long they stayed," Lynch says.

Manning and Stokley eventually headed to Castle Rock. Elway and Fox started the long wait for a decision. Manning worked out the next morning with Stokley and then met with the Shanahans at the coach's house in Denver even though Washington had made the trade for the number two pick. Elway couldn't resist jerking Shanahan's chain. He texted Shanahan in the middle of the meeting and told him to put in a good word for the Broncos with Manning. The other situation that worked out well for the Broncos that day was that Seattle coach Pete Carroll and general manager John Schneider flew to Denver, un-announced, called Manning, and said, "Hey, we're here, want to meet?" Anyone who knew Manning or understood what he was dealing with would never have approached Manning that way. Manning is a control freak. He doesn't like surprises.

Seattle's aggressive approach only served to make Elway and the Broncos look better. Moreover, it was only the second day of Manning's tour and both Washington and Seattle were out of the race for his services. It was still a wide-open derby with the New York Jets, Miami, Arizona,

San Francisco, and Tennessee all in the race. Elway's handicap of the situation was that it was down to Tennessee and Denver. Elway simply didn't think Manning would play for the Jets or Miami.

Being in the same city as his brother Eli didn't make much sense for Manning. The Jets realized they were out early and went out of their way to prove the point by giving quarterback Mark Sanchez a contract extension on March 12. The Dolphins were in flux, changing coaches from Tony Sparano to Joe Philbin while keeping a general manager, Jeff Ireland, who was on the outs with the fan base. Like Miami, Arizona was in too much flux for Manning, although the Cardinals were the only team on the list that played in a dome.

As for San Francisco, the 49ers made sense in every way except for one.

Elway found it hard to imagine Manning playing for Jim Harbaugh, the 49ers coach at the time. Harbaugh had quickly put together an impressive resume as a coach, but there were two problems. First, Harbaugh was very much about control and wanted to run the offense his way. Having two strong-willed people fight over control of the offense didn't seem logical. Second, Manning was the guy who replaced Harbaugh in Indianapolis in 1998. Knowing Harbaugh and how competitive he is, Elway felt there was a point where Harbaugh and Manning would clash.

That clash happened right away. A story came out a few years later about how Manning and Harbaugh were throwing together at one point during this recruiting process in 2012. Harbaugh had traveled to North Carolina to see Manning throw privately. Harbaugh, who was twelve years older than Manning and hadn't played since 2001, said to Manning's face that his passes had more "zip" than Manning's throws. Harbaugh couldn't bite his tongue on something that wasn't going to ingratiate him to Manning.

Tennessee was the wild card in the whole process for two reasons. First, there was an emotional tie to the area for Manning, who went to the University of Tennessee. Second, longtime Titans owner Bud Adams wanted Manning so badly that when the Titans didn't get him, Adams fired general manager Mike Reinfeldt following the 2012 season. Adams felt that Reinfeldt didn't do enough to get Manning. After Reinfeldt was let go, the *Tennessean* reported that it was because of the botched attempt to get Manning.

"In the days leading up to Adams going public with his interest in Manning, he repeatedly told Reinfeldt he wanted the Titans to get in the mix.... Reinfeldt was in communication with the eighty-nine-year-old Adams on a regular basis," Jim Wyatt of the *Tennessean* wrote. "Adams felt like Reinfeldt didn't take him seriously enough.... At the time, the Titans were focused on making it work with quarterbacks Jake Locker and Matt Hasselbeck."

No matter how intense the chase became, Elway wanted to slow-play it. He didn't want anyone in the organization, particularly Fox, bothering Manning. Fox still tried to work his back channel "sources" to get information. Most of what he found out was meaningless because Manning wasn't sharing any information with anyone until he was ready.

On Friday, March 16, a week after Manning first met with the Broncos, Elway and Fox flew to Raleigh, North Carolina, to see Manning throw at Duke University. Manning was working there with David Cutcliffe, who had coached him in college and who knew Manning's throwing motion better than anyone. What Elway watched was hard to put in perspective. If you took it on its own, it wasn't good. Manning's velocity wasn't great and his ability to throw deep was lacking. His accuracy was excellent, which meant he had the ability to manipulate the ball to certain spots. That was the strongest positive from a purely physical standpoint. What helped Elway understand the situation better was Cutcliffe's explaining how far Manning had come and how much further he could go. When Elway looked at a rehabbing athlete, he wasn't worried about where the athlete was in the process. Elway wanted to know where the athlete was going to get to and the chances of his getting there.

Then it was back to evaluating the person. This was Manning, so Elway wasn't concerned. After Elway had another brief discussion with Manning, he and Fox headed home to wait out the weekend. The following Monday, Elway was standing in his office, swinging away, when Manning called. Elway looked at Fox and said, "It's him." For the first time, Elway was a little nervous. He wasn't sure whether Manning was calling to give an answer or ask a question.

As Manning said he was coming to Denver and explained that Condon would be calling to negotiate the details of the deal, Elway gave Fox a thumbs-up signal. A smile of relief took over Fox's face. Other staffers were jubilant. The Broncos had to deal with Tebow right after and gave him a choice to play for Jacksonville or the New York Jets. He chose the Jets, and Elway did that even though the Jaguars offered a better deal. There was some minor drama to the deal, but there was always drama involved with Tebow.

As for Manning, his comeback was one for the history books. His velocity progressively returned, his accuracy was great, and he worked incredibly hard to improve his core strength along the way to reduce stress on his arm. But Elway saw something deeper with Manning. Elway says Manning was playing a different game than anybody else. Manning had taken all the advances in quarterback play that started in the 1980s and perfected them. The use of formations, personnel, and motion by the offense to force the defense into bad situations had become second nature to Manning. Getting to the line early in the play clock and then manipulating the defense became an art form.

"He was so far advanced in what he was doing compared to what we were doing in the 1980s," Elway says. "His greatest weapon was his ability to think through the play before the ball was snapped. When I played, we were still reading the coverage after the snap. He could see it all in advance. He was playing chess and everybody else was playing checkers."

Manning took the thinking part of the game to a new level. On top of that, he had an unbelievable memory for plays from over the years. His constant study and preparation gave him the ability to recall a situation from seven or eight years earlier. Like Elway, Manning posted better statistics at the end of his career than he did in what most people would have considered his prime. Elway did that because he was finally put next to a coach who built a system that complemented him. With Manning, he was fortunate to spend his career in pretty much the same system until his final season. Manning's greatness was basically a creation of his force of will to be great.

That was a strong force. Manning liked to control everything in his environment. For instance, he didn't like having the televisions in the player lounge and cafeteria tuned to ESPN. He didn't like it when one of his many commercials ran because he thought it put him on a pedestal and created resentment. When Manning was in Indianapolis, he asked Colts owner Jim Irsay to buy specially synchronized clocks to mount on the walls throughout the entire building instead of the typical office supply store wall clocks. Manning didn't like some of the clocks being off by a minute or two. He wanted everyone to be on time to every meeting or practice and not have any excuses.

Sometimes that controlling nature ran headlong into Elway. During his first year in Denver, Manning didn't like how the team handled the final cuts at the end of training camp. Manning said it in front of members of the organization and it got back to Elway, and the two had to have a meeting to make sure Manning understood who was in charge. Through it all, Manning turned out to be more than anything the Broncos could have imagined. The 2012 season was stunning as Manning threw thirty-seven touchdown passes. He helped get the Broncos to the playoffs and put them in position to beat Baltimore if not for critical mistakes at the end of the game.

In 2013, Manning continued his triumphant return. He put together the greatest statistical season a quarterback has ever had, including NFL records for touchdown passes (fifty-five) and yards (5,477), on the way to the Super Bowl against Seattle. Some people in the organization groused about Manning's maniacal chase of the touchdown record (nine of Manning's touchdown passes in the regular season came from either one or two yards compared to eight rushing touchdowns from that close). But it was impossible to argue with the results, including an impressive victory over New England in the AFC Championship Game. The season ended in a blowout loss to the Seahawks, but Manning had already surpassed any expectation the team had for his return. Manning and Elway had taken the Broncos from a team stuck in poor play and a cheating scandal to a title contender in only two years together.

The next two years would prove to be a roller coaster for Manning and Elway. The 2014 season was marred by more injuries for Manning and an extremely disappointing end to the season. That set the stage for a dramatic and improbable 2015 season, one that ended with a Super Bowl victory and a fair number of casualties and tension along the way. Regardless, all of it put to bed any debate about whether the team should have kept Tebow.

CHAPTER 33

FOX TROTS, MANNING DANCES

As Elway chewed on sunflower seeds, he wanted to spit nails.

Elway sat with the other Denver football executives as they watched Indianapolis dismantle the Broncos in the second round of the AFC playoffs on January 11, 2015. As Elway sat there and munched on his favorite snack, he was getting ready to take a bite out of several people, starting with coach John Fox and eventually including quarterback Peyton Manning.

In the short term, someone was going to pay with his job. Outside of a scoring drive to open the game, Denver put together a decidedly meek effort to end a season that held hope of a Super Bowl return. It was as if the team had quit on the season.

At least one significant Broncos employee had done just that before the game even started. Fox essentially told the football world he was done in Denver and was ready to take the Chicago Bears job before the playoff game started. Hours before the playoff game, FOX Sports NFL insider Jay Glazer reported that Fox might be fired if Denver lost that day. Though the news was accurate, releasing it at that moment was an obvious attempt at self-preservation by Fox. In the view of Elway and many other people within the Broncos organization, it was borderline cowardice.

Fox had to make it clear that even though he had led the Broncos to a Super Bowl appearance in the 2013 season, his job was still on the line in

2014. He wanted Bears officials to know that publicly. Chicago had hired Ryan Pace as general manager earlier in the week, and Fox wanted to get on Pace's radar. Additionally, Pace and Fox had a connection through Glazer and New Orleans head coach Sean Payton. At this point, Fox didn't care if he exposed just how bad his relationship with Elway had become after four years of working together.

Those four years produced four playoff berths and plenty of frustration because of critical mistakes by Fox. At least that was Elway's view. Now, Fox was doing the ultimate crime in Elway's view: quitting before the battle was over. To anyone who understood anything about the situation, it was obvious that Fox was in on the report. Though he may not have leaked the information to Glazer, Fox did nothing to keep it under wraps. Despite his postgame denials about being associated with the report, Fox and Glazer couldn't have been closer friends. They had known each other for almost fifteen years, since the days when Glazer was a struggling young reporter covering the New York Giants and Fox was an assistant coach.

Over the years, Glazer and Fox drank together on many occasions and discussed their friendship openly. Glazer once said in front of a group of people that he and Fox slept off a particularly late night by dozing off in Fox's office at the Broncos facility. Whenever Glazer showed up in Denver, he was allowed the run of the place by Fox. Glazer was able to walk to the middle of the field during practice to BS with Fox and the other coaches. Reporters, such as longtime Broncos beat man Mike Klis, were left to watch from the distant sidelines. When Klis and others complained to Fox about the favoritism shown to Glazer, Fox mocked them as whiners.

Elway knew all that background, knew what Fox was doing, and quietly seethed. He knew Fox could have put the kibosh on Glazer's report if Fox had wanted. Fox could have kept the distraction from percolating through the team hours before the game. Instead, he was the first man to jump ship when it became clear the Broncos' season was in trouble. In-season injuries to Manning had left him immobile and vulnerable. The struggle was obvious. Over Manning's final nine games, he threw twelve interceptions compared with only three interceptions in the first seven games. There were times at the end of the season when Manning looked almost afraid to be on the field.

Worse, Fox wasn't alone in being distracted in Elway's mind. Defensive coordinator Jack Del Rio was up for the head coach job with Oakland (he was hired by the Raiders days after the Broncos lost), and offensive coordinator Adam Gase was one of the final candidates for the San Francisco job (he didn't get it and eventually went to Chicago with Fox). So, as Elway surveyed the field from his perch high above, what he saw was his team's top three football coaches with their minds elsewhere. That gnawed at him. It was like the time he showed up at his Toyota dealership in California. One of the salesmen had recently left the dealership and then quickly returned. Elway asked why that was allowed. The manager said that's just the way things worked with salesmen. Elway said he wanted that to change. He wanted loyalty and focus.

In this playoff game, the Broncos were clearly not focused enough to handle a simple game plan by the Colts. On the second play of the game, Indianapolis defensive tackle Arthur Jones committed a personal foul by slamming Manning to the ground. In Elway's view, it was an intentional hit to get in Manning's head. As the game played out, the strategy succeeded. Manning began lobbing one deep sideline fade pass after another, knowing he could throw that route early to the outside before the pass rush could get to him. The first deep fade worked for a touchdown. The next five fell incomplete, killing one drive after another. Essentially, Manning was playing with fear. All the injuries and pain had caught up to him at that moment. It's a feeling Elway understood from his own experience as a player.

"After a while when you take that many hits, you start to feel it before they even get there," Elway says, echoing the remarks Shanahan made to him in 1995 when they reunited in Denver. "What we needed to do was find a way to help him with the running game, and we didn't."

The Broncos had done quite the opposite. In one game against St. Louis in the second half of the season, the Broncos called for fifty-six pass plays and only ten runs. Manning was harassed all game and threw two interceptions. In another game against a talented Cincinnati team, it was forty-six pass plays and nineteen runs. Manning was intercepted four times. The final interception was returned for a touchdown that sealed the game for the Bengals. Manning threw the pass off his back foot, fearing a pass rush that wasn't really that close at the time.

Denver lost both games. The playoff loss to the Colts was more of the same. The Broncos called for forty-eight passes and only twenty runs despite having an early lead. Elway watched in dismay as it unfolded. He grew increasingly dissatisfied with Fox with each passing week. It was a continuation of what had started exactly two years earlier.

After Elway took control of Broncos football operations in 2011, he hired Fox to provide a counter to the controlling, negative style of McDaniels. Fox was well-known around the NFL for his open and friendly style, whether that was with the players, the front office, or the media. That was perfect for the Broncos in 2011, as they sorted through the quarterback mess of Kyle Orton and Tim Tebow, rebuilt the defense around Von Miller, and rebuilt the team brand. The team patched enough together to make the playoffs at 8–8 and Fox was a hero in the process. The arrival of Manning in 2012 caused a seismic shift in expectations. The Broncos weren't just an interesting team headed in the right direction. They were a full-on contender. That status was amplified by Manning's resounding comeback from missing the entire 2011 season.

Denver went 13–3 in 2012 and had the number one seed in the AFC playoffs. After earning a first-round bye, Denver hosted Baltimore on January 6, 2013. It was an unusually cold, thirteen-degree day. Despite the weather, the teams traded scores throughout the game. Denver held a 35–28 lead with three minutes left and had the ball. The Broncos couldn't run out the clock. Baltimore got the ball back with 1:15 remaining and no time-outs. The Ravens started the drive at their own twenty-three-yard line. After two plays, they faced a third-and-three with the clock ticking down past the forty-second mark as the ball was snapped to quarterback Joe Flacco. The defensive call in this situation was obvious: don't worry about anything short. Just don't allow a big play. Short passes were fine because they would eat up vital time. Again, keep everything in front of you and don't get beat deep. Getting beat deep was simply unacceptable.

Then the unacceptable happened. Flacco, one of the great deep throwers in the game, stepped up and unleashed a high-arching pass that traveled fifty-five yards down the right sideline. Broncos second-year safety Rahim Moore, who was the single deep safety even though Denver was in an eight-man coverage, ran toward wide receiver Jacoby Jones. Moore badly misjudged the throw as he went to knock it away. Jones caught the ball and ran the rest of the way for a tying touchdown to force overtime.

"How does that happen to the Denver secondary?" NBC play-by-play man Greg Gumbel shouted on the broadcast as the play happened. The Ravens went on to win in overtime. Making things worse for Denver, Baltimore went on to win the Super Bowl. The throw from Flacco to Jones made Elway furious, and Baltimore's championship stoked the fire for months.

As a strong-armed quarterback himself, Elway knew better than anyone how the situation should have been defended. After the game, he met with Fox and Del Rio. The focus of the postgame had been on Moore and how badly he had misjudged the throw by Flacco. Most of the media asked about Moore's individual mistake rather than question the tactical error. As soon as Fox saw Elway, he reassured him he would deal with Moore's damaged psyche.

"He'll be all right, I'll talk to him," Fox said.

"I'm not worried about him, I want to know why the hell you played a one-deep safety on that play!" Elway said, angrily putting both coaches on the spot. While Del Rio called the defense, Fox designed it. Elway thought their lack of preparation in that situation cost Denver the game...and, later, a Super Bowl.

The following year, Fox and the Broncos made it to the Super Bowl on the strength of Manning's record-setting season. Manning threw for the fifty-five touchdowns and 5,477 yards. Still, there were moments that made Elway uneasy. In the second preseason game, Denver played at Seattle and got whipped 40–10. From the starters to the guys just trying to make the team, no one played well for the Broncos. The effort bothered Elway far more than the fact that Denver lost. In the locker room after the game, Fox was his normally upbeat self, trying not to make too much out of the loss.

Elway made it a policy not to talk to the players, but this was one time when he couldn't hold back. He wanted to make it clear such a miserable effort was not going to be rewarded. He didn't scream or yell, but he made his point in the biting fashion he had been trained in as a child.

"That's got to bother the hell out of you," Elway recalls saying in the visiting locker room at CenturyLink Field. "It bothers the hell out of me and, just so you understand, I look at my board every day. You guys are all magnets on that board. Magnets with names pasted on them. I look at the magnets and some of those magnets are going to be there and some are going to be gone. But the bottom line is, I look at the magnets and say this team can win a championship. We can put you together on that board, but you guys are the ones who have to make up your mind whether you want to be world champions or not."

Elway's primary message was obvious to the players, and it echoed things he had heard during his career from the likes of Reeves and Shanahan. His secondary concern was about Fox. Elway knew Fox didn't have the temperament to call out his players when necessary.

"Sometimes you have to be a hard-ass and Fox couldn't do it," Elway says.

Fox didn't have to during the regular season. With Manning setting records, the Broncos rolled. Denver went 13–3 and only one victory was by fewer than seven points. The Broncos rolled through the playoffs and were the favorite going up against Seattle in the Super Bowl. Elway again sensed problems during the week of preparation for the Super Bowl in New York. He thought Fox was too lackadaisical in his preparation. There was no edge to the team or to the practices. Elway fumed after Denver was drubbed, 43–8, by the Seahawks. During a postgame party at the team hotel, Elway drowned his sorrows in several cocktails of Dewar's and water and talked about all the changes he wanted to make for the following season. That wasn't necessarily unique. Elway's oldest daughter, Jessie, laid out the scenarios to her boyfriend (and future husband) before the game started.

"If we win," she recalls saying, "expect to stay up all night."

"If we lose," she then said, "expect to stay up all night."

Big games were a catharsis for Elway, overflowing with either joy or misery depending on the outcome. That night, he howled at the moon about what to do next. One of the things he thought about most was getting rid of Fox. In fact, he thought the 2013 season included proof Fox wasn't that important. Fox missed a month of the season because of emergency heart surgery. In his place, Del Rio ran the team and led the Broncos to a 3–1 record. The only loss was a dramatic overtime game in New England in which the Broncos blew a 24–0 halftime lead. In Elway's mind, Fox could be replaced by any number of coaches.

Realistically, that wasn't going to happen, and Elway knew it. Firing a coach who had just taken a team to a Super Bowl in his third season with the organization would have made no sense to the public, let alone to the players. Elway was in quite the opposite position: he was going to have to give Fox a contract extension. Fox had only one year remaining on his original four-year deal.

Not giving Fox an extension not only would have made him a lame-duck coach, it would have made it obvious Elway was angry despite the Super Bowl appearance. The story would have festered all season. So, as the off-season played out, Elway negotiated the new deal with Fox. Fox wanted a salary in line with the top coaches in the NFL. Elway resisted, making it clear to Fox he wasn't happy. Elway's willingness to draw a line made it clear to Fox that 2014 was a make-or-break season. Adding to the pressure for Fox, Elway was exceptionally aggressive in free agency that off-season. Elway followed through with the changes he envisioned in the hours after the lopsided loss to Seattle.

He signed Pro Bowl cornerback Aqib Talib to a six-year, $57 million contract and Pro Bowl safety T. J. Ward to a four-year, $23 million contract. Both signed on March 11, 2014. The next day, Elway signed seven-time Pro Bowl pass rusher DeMarcus Ware to a three-year, $30 million deal. All told, Elway committed $110 million to improving the defense. The message to Fox and everyone else was clear: the Broncos were all in on winning a Super Bowl.

On April 4, 2014, Fox agreed to the new deal that ran through the 2016 season. Glazer broke the news via Twitter. The public statements were all positive, and the deal was announced as $16.5 million for three years. The $5.5 million average was a significant jump for Fox from the $3 million per year he got on the original four-year deal in 2011. However, it was a long way removed from the more than $7 million per year threshold coaches such as Payton, Bill Belichick, Andy Reid, and Pete Carroll had already exceeded.

In the months after getting the new contract, Fox seemed to recede from the challenge instead of responding to it. Fox's deference to Manning got on Elway's nerves. Manning essentially ran the entire offense. While that was extraordinarily successful in the 2013 season, Elway saw the Super Bowl as a referendum on what the Broncos really needed to do. There needed to be more balance to the offense with an emphasis on the running game.

Just as Elway needed a running game at the end of his career, he felt that Manning needed the same thing. In addition, Elway thought Denver should have been playing to the strength of its improving defense. With Fox's giving Manning carte blanche to run the offense, the overall approach wasn't going to change. That led to flare-ups during the 2014 season. Elway started to criticize Fox more openly around the Broncos facility. At one point, Del Rio got wind of it and criticized Elway during a team meeting. When that got back to Elway, the two men had a loud disagreement some people thought might end in a fistfight.

"I was just defending my boss," Del Rio says, diplomatically referring to Fox. "I think some things were said that didn't need to be said and I'll just leave it at that."

The tension got worse after Manning got hurt. By the end of the 2014 season, the Broncos offense was in trouble and everyone knew it. When Chicago fired coach Marc Trestman and general manager Phil Emery and hired Pace to replace Emery, Fox saw the situation as a golden parachute out of the Mile High City.

As the team readied for the playoff game against Indianapolis, other reporters were getting wind of the full rift between Elway and Fox. Klis was asking questions about Fox's future on the Friday before the game. Glazer confirmed the story and put it out on the pregame show early Sunday. Denver's flaccid effort against Indianapolis meant that three consecutive seasons under Fox had ended in vast disappointment in Elway's view. Worse, Elway had seen this show in the first ten years of his career. What the Broncos needed was a bold overhaul of the entire coaching staff, in his view.

By the next day, Fox and the Broncos announced they had agreed to a "mutual parting," a polite way of saying the team had fired Fox and he was content to leave. That's when Elway went back to his roots. Though he wasn't going to hire Shanahan, he was going to get the next best thing: Shanahan's longtime lieutenant and Elway's longtime friend Kubiak. Kubiak had spent eight years with middling results in Houston and had spent the 2014 season as the offensive coordinator with Baltimore.

What Elway wanted was a disciplined approach to the entire operation. He wanted someone who would stand up to Manning and put in the running game Manning needed.

First, however, there was going to be a meeting of the minds between Elway and Manning and a bitter pill for Manning to swallow. Shortly after the season ended and Kubiak was hired, Elway and Manning met in Elway's office. Elway described to Manning his disappointment with how the season ended. Manning expressed that he was disappointed Fox had been let go and that he believed the team could still have won a title under Fox. At one point in the conversation, Elway referred to how he believed Fox, Del Rio, and Gase were distracted during the playoff loss.

Then Elway asked Manning a rather loaded question.

"Why didn't you do something about it?"

That was the beginning of an uneasy off-season between them. Manning was already concerned about the transition in offensive systems. Kubiak's offense required much more work from under center rather than in shotgun formation. It also required more lateral movement from the quarterback. That was important for the running game and the use of more play-action fakes in the passing game. Then there was the matter of money. Manning was due to make $19 million in the 2015 season, and that contract would become fully guaranteed on March 9. As Elway and Manning concluded their meeting, Elway said he needed to know before March 9 if Manning wanted to play and whether he would take a pay cut.

Elway indicated to Manning's representatives that he wanted to reduce Manning's base pay to $9 million with the chance to make back the other $10 million with incentives. To Elway, it was important for Manning to take a cut because the Broncos needed the cap space. Additionally, it was important to Elway to make a statement to the rest of the team that there were no sacred cows. If the team didn't perform to expectations, there were going to be changes, whether that was head coach or franchise quarterback.

That request was met with anger from the Manning camp. Manning had always prided himself on being among the top-paid quarterbacks and players, period. That was partly because he believed it was his duty to make sure the pay rate for quarterbacks was as high as possible. Secondarily, the whole situation seemed like part of a power play between the two men, a continuation of the move to dump Fox in favor of Kubiak. At first, Elway was adamantly pushing the severe pay cut and said he was willing to let Manning walk. Likewise, Manning's agent, Tom Condon, checked with other teams to see whether any would sign him if he refused the pay cut. There was interest, but not from any teams where Manning felt there was a chance to both win and be productive.

Still, there was tension as Manning pondered the pay cut and Elway pondered a future without Manning. By February 12, Broncos chief executive officer Joe Ellis got involved in the process as peacemaker. Ellis flew to New Orleans in a private jet to pick up Manning and bring him to Denver for a meeting with Elway. Ellis also told Elway the idea of cutting Manning wasn't wise for the immediate future of the team. Elway relented from his demand for a large cut and the sides continued to talk. By the beginning of March, Manning agreed to a reduction to $15 million with a chance to make $2 million if the Broncos reached the Super Bowl and another $2 million if they won the Super Bowl.

Manning eventually made all the money back, but this was an ugly start to what would become one of the strangest championship seasons in NFL history. It also was the swan song to Manning's great career and Elway's shining moment as an executive.

CHAPTER 34

MIRACLE ON 13655 BRONCOS PARKWAY

Manning was able to walk away from the NFL as a champion.

But it was a painful journey aided by the defense Elway built and operated by defensive coordinator Wade Phillips, who returned to Denver with head coach Gary Kubiak.

The 2015 Broncos season is one of the most improbable championship seasons in NFL history. It was filled with doubt and tension and results that defied all sensibilities about the modern offensive game. The Broncos became the first championship team since the 1980 Oakland Raiders to throw more interceptions than touchdown passes during the regular season. Individually, Manning finished the regular season tied for the worst touchdown-to-interception ratio (nine touchdowns and seventeen interceptions) for a Super Bowl–winning quarterback ever, matching the stats of Bart Starr in 1967.

Though that may sound like trivia, it made for some nearly impossible situations. Game plans essentially became running gags as coaches looked at one another and said, "What absurd way are we going to win this week?" As the season wore into the holidays, the coaching staff came up with a name for what was unfolding. The name didn't exactly roll off the tongue, but it did ring true.

"We called it the *Miracle on 13655 Broncos Parkway*," says Broncos special teams coach Joe DeCamillis, referring to the address of the team facility. It was a riff on *Miracle on 34th Street*, but with just a few too many syllables to really work. Yet Denver's championship run topped the Christmas movie classic in one significant way.

The Broncos season was a reality. It was a chaotic and crazy reality. In some ways, the season reflected Elway's never-say-die mentality. It was also a direct reflection of his vision and expertise as a personnel man. By the time the Broncos won the Super Bowl against Carolina, they had become exactly what Elway envisioned in the aftermath of the team's Super Bowl loss to Seattle two years earlier. They had a great defense that was augmented by an offense that did just enough.

Some would say barely enough, and that would be fair.

Through the first five years of his tenure, Elway's strength as an evaluator was picking defensive players. When he was first trying to break into personnel in the early 2000s, he was asked to evaluate college cornerbacks. His breakdowns were exceptionally strong, largely because he had studied so many of them from his days as a quarterback.

"If a guy turned his back a lot in college, I would say that's the type of guy I would go after as a quarterback," Elway says by way of example. "He doesn't trust his ability to react and make up ground."

Elway would make other evaluations on defensive players that the scouts agreed with and found useful. He put an emphasis on finding pass rushers. His first pick in 2011 was Von Miller. While some have dismissed that as an obvious pick, there were plenty of people who believed the Broncos should have taken defensive tackle Marcell Dareus or cornerback Patrick Peterson. Elway identified Miller's unique ability to combine his explosive speed and strength with a unique ability to contort his body around blockers. Miller had at least ten sacks in seven of his first eight seasons (missing the mark in 2013 because he was limited to nine games). Miller had ninety-eight sacks in his first eight seasons and won the Super Bowl Most Valuable Player Award at the end of the 2015 season, putting him on a strong path to the Pro Football Hall of Fame.

Miller's run with the Broncos wasn't without hiccups. In 2013, he was suspended for six games because of a failed test for a recreational drug and for trying to circumvent the NFL's testing program. He eventually returned and played two months before tearing the anterior cruciate ligament in his right knee at the end of that season and missing the Super Bowl against Seattle. Though Miller became a concern for the Broncos on both the drug and injury fronts, he eventually erased that concern. He had fourteen sacks in 2014 and followed that up with eleven in the 2015 regular season to go with the spectacular run in the playoffs. He also became a leader in the locker room with his play and sense of humor.

With Miller as the centerpiece, Elway built the rest of the defense. The Broncos signed cornerback Chris Harris as an undrafted free agent in 2011. Denver drafted defensive linemen Derek Wolfe and Malik Jackson and linebacker Danny Trevathan in 2012. In 2013, the team signed linebacker Brandon Marshall to the practice squad and drafted defensive lineman Sylvester Williams. Those seven players, along with 2014 first-round pick Bradley Roby as the number three cornerback, became the core of the defense. The Broncos augmented that group with linebacker DeMarcus Ware, cornerback Aqib Talib, and safeties Darian Stewart and T. J. Ward in free agency.

Still, with an inconsistent offense, trying to devise a plan each week was difficult.

"It was an amazing challenge," DeCamillis says. "We'd work on the game plan and just say, 'We're going to have to find a way.' Our offense... I mean, there's really no way to describe it other than to say it was a miracle what we pieced together from week to week that season."

Kubiak was brought in to give the Broncos the type of discipline and offensive system Denver had when Elway was playing under Shanahan. Only half of that statement ended up happening. The Broncos were disciplined. To his credit, Manning tried to make it work. The fact is his thirty-nine-year-old body was continuing to break down.

By the beginning of training camp that season, Manning's discontent with Elway had faded and his focus on winning returned. Manning went along with the idea of changing offenses in his eighteenth season. It wasn't easy and required a tremendous dedication. Kubiak's offense required more movement by the quarterback than Manning had been used to in the second half of his career. During the previous three seasons, Manning had operated almost exclusively in shotgun formation.

The shotgun reduced how much Manning had to drop back and gave him a better look at the field. It also restricted the running game, giving the running back less ability to get started in one direction or the other or even get much momentum going toward the line. Now, Kubiak was asking Manning to play far more from under center, hoping to allow for more movement in the running game.

Manning was physically ready in training camp. He moved effectively and even looked better on rollout passes than twenty-four-year-old backup Brock Osweiler. Despite dealing with leg injuries at the end of the 2014 season, Manning worked hard to comply with what Kubiak wanted. Manning privately worried about how the increased movement would wear on his body. Kubiak just worried about keeping pressure off Manning.

Manning's fears were realized in training camp when he developed plantar fasciitis in his left foot. The condition is, essentially, a progressive soreness in the thick tissue at the bottom of the foot. It's an injury that tends to mend faster if the tissue tears. If it just remains sore, it can take weeks and sometimes months to heal. As Manning tried to play through the injury, it predictably got worse and made it harder for him to move and run the offense Kubiak had installed.

That led to one progressively uglier game after another. At the same time, the Broncos kept winning with defense, most of which Elway and his staff had assembled. The opener was an indicator. Denver beat Baltimore 19–13. Manning completed twenty-four of forty passes, but for only 175 yards. He was also sacked four times. The Denver defense won the game as Talib returned an interception fifty-one yards for a touchdown, Roby knocked away a possible touchdown pass, and Stewart intercepted another pass in the end zone with twenty-eight seconds remaining to seal the win.

Manning was better in the second week with three touchdowns to rally the Broncos in Kansas City. Kubiak relented in the second half and allowed Manning to play out of the shotgun during the comeback. Still, it was the defense that pulled out the win in the end. Roby returned a fumble for a touchdown with twenty-seven seconds remaining and a 31–24 victory. The Broncos continued to play a high-wire act all the way to a 7–0 start. They got by Minnesota with a field goal in the final two minutes. They beat Oakland 16–10 when Harris returned an interception seventy-four yards for a score. They survived against Cleveland on a field goal in overtime. They beat Detroit by forcing three turnovers and then pulled off the most impressive feat to that point by limiting quarterback Aaron Rodgers to only seventy-seven yards in a lopsided win over Green Bay.

The truth was Manning was being carried through the first half of the season and everyone knew it. His reputation kept most believing a turnaround was about to happen. Quite the opposite was true in the short term. Manning threw two interceptions in a loss at Indianapolis in which the Colts essentially dared him to throw. The Colts put extra defenders close to the line to throttle the Denver running game, but Manning was unable to take advantage. He then bottomed out in a loss to the Chiefs in Denver. Manning was aching from head to toe with a bad right shoulder, aching ribs, and the sore foot. He completed only five of twenty passes for thirty-five yards. He was also sacked twice and intercepted four times. He exited the game with a 0.0 quarterback rating, which is almost statistically impossible.

Manning admitted afterward he shouldn't have played. Kubiak said he never should have allowed Manning to play when he saw how much pain the quarterback was in before the game. The Broncos were 7–2, but Manning looked like a shell of himself. His seventeen interceptions in nine games were part of a trend dating to the 2014 season. He had twelve interceptions over his final ten games that season, meaning he now had twenty-nine over a nineteen-game stretch. That was the worst stretch since his rookie season carried into his second year. Some people made the excuse that the new offense didn't fit his style. While true, there was no question his body was essentially shot.

That week, the Broncos said Manning was going to be out for an extended time. That put Osweiler in position to play and prove whether Elway's faith in him was deserved. Osweiler had been a second-round pick by Denver in 2012. He was an insurance policy in case Manning didn't work out as a free agent. Until 2015, the Broncos had never had to cash in on the policy. In his first three seasons, Osweiler had thrown only thirty passes. He had one touchdown pass, and there was no telling whether he was a good player.

Elway had selected Osweiler partly because he knew the player better than most. Osweiler had gone to Arizona State with Elway's son Jack and the two played together briefly. At six-foot-seven, Osweiler was both big and athletic. He had been recruited to play major college basketball before deciding to focus on football. He became a full-time starter in his junior season and decided to forego his senior year to turn pro. In a draft featuring Luck, Robert Griffin III, Ryan Tannehill, and Brandon Weeden in the first round, Elway took Osweiler at the end of the second round. Other quarterbacks to go later were Russell Wilson and Nick Foles in the third, Kirk Cousins in the fourth, and Case Keenum as an undrafted player.

Osweiler's first three seasons were personally frustrating on two levels. Though he and Manning had a cordial and professional relationship, they weren't exactly close. Manning wasn't willing to give an inch in terms of playing time if he could avoid it. Like other greats such as Favre and Marino, Manning's obsessive, controlling, and competitive style didn't make him the greatest mentor for someone trying to take his job. This was his job and he was going to keep it until somebody pried it from his hands.

That's one of the reasons Osweiler resisted several attempts by Elway and the Broncos to sign him to a contract extension before the 2015 season. Elway talked with agent Jimmy Sexton about a deal, but Sexton never entertained serious talks. Osweiler wanted a chance to play and knew it wasn't going to happen if Manning was around. Sexton also knew the free agent market for quarterbacks after the 2015 season was sparse and there was a great chance Osweiler would be free. Because the Broncos hadn't signed Miller to a contract extension, Denver was going to have to put the franchise tag on Miller and let Osweiler hit the market. Sexton figured it would be easy to get a better deal than the $5 million a year (not including incentives) the Broncos were offering on an extension. While Elway was annoyed Osweiler wouldn't take the deal, he wasn't going to budge and, in some ways, liked how things were playing out as the season unfolded.

"We'll see how he reacts to the opportunity," Elway said at the time with a casual shrug and a grin. "You don't really know how someone is going to react until they get into the situation."

Would Osweiler be ready to step up and become a star or melt under the pressure? The answer would tell Elway a lot about what he wanted to do going forward. The early returns for Osweiler were good. He led the Broncos to a tight win at Chicago to improve Denver to 8–2. Then came a critical game at home against 10–0 New England that set the stage for the rest of the season. The Patriots jumped out to a 14–0 lead in the first half and a 21–7 lead after the first play of the fourth quarter, a sixty-three-yard touchdown pass from quarterback Tom Brady to running back Brandon Bolden. That score looked to be a knockout blow for Denver.

With a thin blanket of snow collecting on the field, the Broncos looked done. Osweiler threw three straight incomplete passes as Denver was forced to punt. But when the Patriots fumbled the punt and Denver recovered, the Broncos had renewed hope. On a critical third-and-six, Osweiler beat a blitz and hit Emmanuel Sanders for a first down. The Broncos then scored on the next play to make it 21–14. Denver scored a field goal on its next drive to make it 21–17 with 6:08 remaining in the game.

The teams traded punts over the next three possessions until Denver took over at its own seventeen-yard line with 2:31 remaining. On first down, Osweiler hit wide receiver Demaryius Thomas down the right sideline for a thirty-six-yard gain to put the Broncos at the New England forty-seven. Two plays later, Osweiler uncorked another big throw, this time down the left sideline for thirty-nine yards to Sanders. After a penalty, Denver had a first-and-goal at the four. Osweiler hit wide receiver Andre Caldwell on a fade pattern to the left corner of the end zone to give Denver a 24–21 lead with 1:09 remaining. New England had enough time to drive for a field goal and forced overtime. The Broncos pulled out the victory when running back C. J. Anderson broke a forty-eight-yard touchdown run in the extra period.

Osweiler had just slayed the defending champions with a series of four critical throws in the fourth quarter, erasing a fourteen-point deficit in the process. That game, by itself, was probably worth the second-round pick Elway spent on Osweiler when you consider the results of the season. Moreover, Osweiler showed the arm strength Manning simply didn't have anymore. The following week, Osweiler helped Denver win at San Diego to improve to 3–0 under him and 10–2 overall. Among the coaches and front office, there was a feeling Osweiler might give the Broncos a strong enough offense to carry the team through the playoffs. Both locally and nationally, there was talk about what the Broncos should do with Manning. Kubiak maintained that Manning was still in the mix to start if he got healthy. Manning wasn't healthy yet, and Denver was taking it slowly with Osweiler playing well.

While Elway and Kubiak talked on a regular basis, Elway was clear: Kubiak had the call on the quarterback position. Despite speculation to the contrary, Elway didn't get involved in making decisions. He'd offer his opinion, if asked. However, he considered his job to evaluate the big picture, not micromanage. He had hired Kubiak because he trusted his former teammate, coach, and friend. He wasn't going to second-guess him now. At the same time, Elway felt that the team was rallying around Osweiler.

But the team was careful not to overplay the situation. It was reported by *Bleacher Report* that Osweiler would remain the starter unless he played poorly. Elway and the Broncos responded by saying no decisions had been made. The team was walking on eggshells around the situation with Manning. The careful moves were wise because Osweiler began to crack.

The Broncos lost to Oakland 15–12 in a home game during which Oakland star pass rusher Khalil Mack sacked Osweiler five times. The next week at Pittsburgh, Denver built a 27–13 lead at halftime behind Osweiler. In the second half, however, he completed only six of twenty-five throws and the Steelers rallied to win. The Broncos were 10–4 with two games to go, trailing New England (12–2) and Cincinnati (11–3) for one of the top two seeds in the AFC playoffs. That week, Cincinnati came to Denver. The Broncos needed to win their final two games and have

New England lose its final two to get the number one seed. That's exactly what happened. Getting to that point wasn't simple. On a Monday night in Denver, the Bengals took a 14–0 lead in the first half before Osweiler again rallied the Broncos in the second half to tie the game at seventeen and force overtime. The Broncos won in overtime after their defense came up with a fumble recovery to set up a field goal.

As the Broncos got ready for the season finale at home against San Diego, Manning was finally healthy enough to play. He had been working out away from the eye of the media as Kubiak kept tabs on his progress. At the same time, the Broncos were 4–2 with Osweiler as a starter. The offense wasn't great, but it was better than it had been with Manning. The growing concern about Osweiler was deeper than simply stats and efficiency. Kubiak felt that Osweiler wasn't demanding enough in games, particularly in the early going. The victories over New England and Cincinnati were great, but there was going to come a point when trying to overcome an early deficit was going to be problematic.

Additionally, Denver was loaded with a lot of powerful personalities on defense who could become problems at any time. Talib and Ward were incredibly vocal and opinionated to the point of occasionally being out of control and very negative. During the frustrating loss to the Colts earlier in the season, Talib poked Indianapolis tight end Dwayne Allen in the eye, resulting in a one-game suspension that cost Talib the Kansas City game. If Denver started to veer off course because of a lack of leadership, Talib and Ward might have sent them careening.

"Aqib and T. J. could have easily become the alpha males of that locker room in a negative way. [Miller] was the best player and Peyton was the general, but Von is just kind of a goof. He just wants to have fun. And Peyton was hurt and playing crappy. You can't lead when you're not playing *and* you're not playing good. Aqib and T. J. would have led us right into a ditch if they got control of the locker room," says one of the assistant coaches. "We needed the quarterback to lead. Whether it was Brock or Peyton, it didn't matter. But one of them had to step up....I'm not sure Brock knew how to do that. He didn't then and he didn't later on."

Finally, there was the issue of home-field advantage. If the Broncos had any hope in the playoffs, playing home games was going to be critical. Being one of the top two seeds in the AFC was a must. Kubiak went over all the options with the coaching staff, including whether to start Manning against the Chargers. For the time being, Kubiak was going to stay with Osweiler. But the leash wasn't going to be long.

It turned out to be roughly half the game. As the final Sunday of the regular season played out, opportunity opened. New England played an inexplicably uninspired game at Miami and lost 20–10. Suddenly, if Denver won, the Broncos would be the number one seed. With a goal in sight, the Broncos opened the game with a flourish. On the second play from scrimmage, Osweiler hit Thomas for a seventy-two-yard touchdown. The Chargers responded with a field goal, but Denver was ready to roll on its next drive. Osweiler hit Sanders on a forty-six-yard deep pass and Sanders appeared ready to score before fumbling.

That play began a run of sloppiness Kubiak couldn't accept. Over a span of seven drives including the opening drive of the second half, the Broncos turned the ball over five times and punted twice. While Osweiler made only one of those turnovers and Denver led the game 7–6, Kubiak didn't like how his quarterback approached the situation. Osweiler didn't command the team. He didn't demand that his teammates play sharp enough in what was, in Kubiak's view, a playoff game. With those thoughts flowing through his head, Kubiak called on Manning to return to the lineup on the second drive of the second half. It was a prototypical movie moment where the general returns to address the troops and lead them to victory. The Broncos immediately took notice of both Manning's presence and the message Kubiak was trying to send.

"It was like, 'Oh crap, daddy's back, better pay attention,'" Sanders says.

"No disrespect to Brock, but it's a whole different deal when Peyton is in the huddle," Thomas says. "It's like, you better be on your game or you're not going to see the ball for a long time. Peyton just has that kind of control. He's as smart as any coach you'll ever meet. It's like, 'Man, you better not mess up.'...Kubs was basically saying, 'Get your act together right now.' It had to happen and it had to happen right then."

That is exactly how the situation played out. Denver scored on four of the next five drives to take a 27–20 victory. The win gave the Broncos the number one seed in the AFC playoffs, which meant not only a bye week, but also control of their path to the Super Bowl. Elway and some of the other executives were a little surprised Kubiak made the move to Manning, but none of them were against the idea. This was a team living on a narrow margin. Over the course of the season, the Broncos had won five games with second-half comebacks and had gone 3–0 in overtimes.

"Kubs was gutsy. As I told everybody, it was always his call. He's the one who had the feel for the team and I'll never get in the way of that, whatever the decision is," Elway says.

In the bye week, Pittsburgh beat Cincinnati to earn a trip to Denver for the second round of the playoffs. The Steelers had defeated the Broncos only a month earlier. Pittsburgh quarterback Ben Roethlisberger and wide receiver Antonio Brown had combined to put on a show. Roethlisberger had completed forty of fifty-five passes for 380 yards and three touchdown passes. Brown caught sixteen passes for 189 yards and two touchdowns. In the playoffs, however, Brown was out with a concussion. That allowed Denver's pass defense to have slightly better control of the game. Not full control, but better control. Roethlisberger completed twenty-four of thirty-seven passes for 339 yards this time, not far off his totals the first game. That is with one big exception: Roethlisberger didn't throw a touchdown pass.

The defense was spectacular in shutting down the Steelers whenever they got close to scoring. Pittsburgh made seven trips into Denver territory, including three inside the Denver twenty-yard line, and scored only one touchdown and three field goals. Phillips baffled Roethlisberger with a combination of blitzes and zone defenses.

Not that the Broncos offense and Manning were much better. Over the first three quarters, Denver settled for four field goals and trailed 13–12 going into the fourth quarter. In the fourth quarter, Pittsburgh appeared on the way to a score by getting to the Denver thirty-five. That's when the Denver defense came up with the only turnover of the game, a fumble recovery. In response, Manning came up with Denver's only touchdown drive of the game and the biggest throw of the game. After nearly getting picked off by William Gay, Manning hit a thirty-one-yard pass over the middle to Bennie Fowler on a third-and-twelve play. The next ten plays by Denver covered only thirty-six yards, including Anderson's going over for a one-yard score. Coupled with a two-point conversion, the Broncos took a 20–13 lead on the way to a 23–16 victory.

Manning's stats were a reasonable twenty-one of thirty-seven for 222 yards and no touchdowns. The bigger accomplishment was Manning continually kept the Broncos out of trouble. If the Broncos lined up in the wrong play, Manning would fix it right away. It didn't lead to great stats, but it played to the strength of the defense. It was also a great example of Manning's putting his ego aside. The same man who only two years earlier had chased all sorts of records was now putting himself in a supporting role. Manning was masterful in how he managed both the offense and himself. Elway watched with quiet approval from his luxury box.

The AFC Championship Game on January 24, 2016, featured a little more Manning and just as much of the Denver defense. New England returned to Denver for a second engagement of the rivalry for the season and the seventeenth time Brady had gone up against Manning in their own storied rivalry. It would be the last time they would meet and, appropriately, with the Super Bowl on the line for the fourth time. Brady ended up winning eleven of the seventeen games, but Manning won three of the four AFC Championship Games.

Kubiak and Manning took a clever chance on Denver's first drive. With the Patriots loaded up to stop the run, Manning threw on the first three plays and seven of the first twelve overall. The final pass of the eighty-three-yard drive was a beautifully placed twenty-one-yard throw to the back of the end zone to tight end Owen Daniels. In the second quarter, Manning took advantage of an interception of Brady by Miller at the New England sixteen-yard line. Manning hit Daniels for a twelve-yard score this time.

Denver led 14–6 at that point and the game became cat-and-mouse from there on. Denver scored only two more field goals and took advantage of the fact that New England got too desperate, too early. Brady looked rattled throughout much of the game because of the Broncos' pass rush (he completed twenty-seven of fifty-six for 310 yards and was sacked four times), and Denver had a 20–12 lead with 10:02 remaining in the game. New England got to the Denver sixteen-yard line and went for it on fourth down instead of kicking a field goal with more than six minutes remaining.

As Denver struggled to run out the clock, New England got the ball back. The Patriots quickly marched to the Broncos' fourteen and faced a fourth down. Again, the Patriots went for it and failed. Denver again couldn't get a first down as it refused to take chances with Manning, who completed seventeen of thirty-two for only 176 yards. New England got the ball back one last time with 1:52 remaining at the fifty-yard line.

Again, the Denver defense harassed Brady into three straight incompletions, putting New England in a fourth-and-ten situation. Brady then summoned upon his greatness to hit tight end Rob Gronkowski for a forty-yard pass to the Denver ten. The drama only continued to peak as the Broncos forced a fourth-and-goal situation from the four. This time Brady hit Gronkowski for a four-yard touchdown to make the score 20–18 with twelve seconds remaining.

On the two-point conversion attempt, Sports Authority Field shook with anticipation. Brady held the ball as long as he could. As Miller approached, he threw toward wide receiver Julian Edelman, but Talib knocked the pass away. The Broncos defense thwarted New England one final time, but the Patriots had made life harder on themselves by not taking a field goal earlier in the quarter. New England attempted an onside kick, but Denver recovered, and Manning took a knee to run out the clock on the final play.

It was both exhilarating and excruciating for everyone, but particularly Elway. Getting back to the Super Bowl after the frustration of the 2014 season and doing it behind the defense he had helped build was proof he was on the right track. The Denver defense had just contained Roethlisberger and Brady in the playoffs after also beating Brady in a key regular season game. At the time, those two quarterbacks had combined for six Super Bowl victories. There was still one big challenge left for the Super Bowl against Carolina quarterback Cam Newton, the NFL Most Valuable Player that season and the self-proclaimed Superman of quarterbacks.

Yet as everyone reveled in returning to the Super Bowl, this was a moment for Elway to savor. The wins over Pittsburgh and New England were confirmation to Elway that his drastic move to push out Fox was the correct call. At the same time, leaving the control up to others was difficult.

Not that he let it show.

"It's amazing because it's so tense when we're sitting there and watching," says Denver director of player personnel Matt Russell. "You live and die with calls and your stomach churns. Some guys will pound tables or yell. John doesn't do any of that. He just sits there calmly, taking it all in, thinking about the whole picture of what he sees."

That's because Elway knows the feeling from the field all too well.

"It's a completely different feeling because you do your job and you hand it over to someone else," Elway says. "I wouldn't call it helpless, but it's not anything like being in control, being on the field and making the decisions."

That's exactly what Manning was being asked to do. His primary duty in the playoffs was to get the Broncos in the right plays consistently and avoid mistakes. After throwing seventeen interceptions in the regular season, Manning had zero turnovers in three games dating to the season finale against San Diego. In the Pittsburgh game, he had only one big throw to make. Against New England, his two touchdown passes were the only critical plays he had to come up with. The greater part of his job was to keep the Broncos out of trouble, and he did it brilliantly. Elway's off-season instruction to Manning to let the defense do the work for him and protect the ball was working.

It was about to send Manning out as a champion.

CHAPTER 35

SUPER BOWL 50

The biggest accomplishment of Super Bowl 50 went unnoticed.

It was drowned out by the obvious story lines. There was Manning's swan song, Miller's brilliance, and Newton's meltdown. Manning continued to be the quietly efficient self he'd been against Pittsburgh and New England. Meanwhile, Von Miller was the one creating havoc. Miller's two and a half sacks led a dominant defensive performance by the Broncos that both carried Manning and crushed Newton. Finally, there was Newton's losing his composure after the game and walking out on an interview.

What few took note of, including Elway himself, is the mountain Elway climbed in the process of helping guide the Broncos to a 24–10 victory over Carolina and the Panthers' offensive juggernaut. This wasn't just Elway executing the plan he came up with after the devastating loss to Seattle in Super Bowl 48. This wasn't just Elway doing his part to help Manning even though the two men were at odds along the way. This was Elway arriving at rare ground few people even try to reach.

Elway stepped into a unique and exclusive category of competitors. He became only the second man in NFL history to win a championship, make the Hall of Fame as a player, and then come back to win a championship as a head coach or top executive. The only other person to do that was Mike Ditka. The only other men to even try were Bart

Starr, Mike Singletary, Willie Wood, Raymond Berry, Sammy Baugh, Tom Fears, Otto Graham, Forrest Gregg, Art Shell, Norm Van Brocklin, and Mike McCormack. McCormack might be the most notable because his chase was enduring. He was the head coach of three teams and the general manager of two. There were also a host of men, such as Elroy Hirsch, Steve Owen, and Blood McNally, who won championships in the pre–Hall of Fame days and came back to coach.

Though the list of names is mostly trivia, the effort is anything but trivial. Football, like almost all sports, is a place where young gladiators go to compete. Once they reach the top, trying to get back is a brutal journey. It's not only taxing on one's inner desire, but it also exposes people to external ridicule. After years of training, practicing, and playing, most great football players have no desire to chase that dream through the long hours of coaching or scouting. They have enough money, more than enough fame, and plenty of other opportunities.

Most of all, the passion has usually been drained from them. Elway became one of the rarest of men in NFL history because he chased his desire to compete from the field to the front office. He dealt with the questions and the ridicule. He waited patiently to sign Manning and then moved quickly to get men like Ware, Ward, and Talib. He then watched on February 7, 2016, from his luxury box at Levi's Stadium, again helpless to impact how the game played out.

The lead-up to Super Bowl 50 was perfect in Elway's eyes. The media was focused on Manning's likely retirement and Newton's leading the high-powered Carolina Panthers over Denver's defense. Disregarded and disrespected in that process was the Broncos defense. As the week played out, they stewed in all the attention paid to the quarterbacks.

"It's all about Peyton and Cam or Cam and Peyton," Denver cornerback Chris Harris said that week. "Like we don't really exist."

Harris smiled. As an undrafted player, he was used to being overlooked. It reminded him of the struggle it took to break into the NFL. It was the grain of sand that made him a pearl in the football world. Furthermore, he knew how it would play with the minds of his teammates. Dismiss or disrespect a group of athletes like Miller, Ware, and Talib and see how that plays out for you. The Broncos had just stopped the likes of Roethlisberger and Brady on the way to the Super Bowl. They weren't about to bow down to Newton just out of hand or even if the betting public expected it.

Carolina had gone 15–1 that season, including a 14–0 start to the season. The offense had been overwhelming at times. The Panthers scored thirty-three points or more in eight of their nine games heading into the Super Bowl, including forty-nine against Arizona in the NFC Championship Game. They had been held to fewer than twenty points only once all season. Carolina was a juggernaut and Newton was at the top of his talented game. He had thrown a career-high thirty-five touchdown passes, rushed for ten more scores, and thrown only ten interceptions. The Carolina defense had a league-leading twenty-four interceptions and allowed 308 points, the sixth-lowest total in the league.

On the Denver side of the ledger, there was a great defense and a heartwarming comeback/farewell story at quarterback. Put it together and Carolina entered the game as a five-and-a-half-point favorite. Elway, the rest of the front office, and the coaching staff loved it because they saw how it was playing out in the minds of men such as Miller, Ware, Talib, and Harris. Elway and the others also believed it would create a false sense of confidence in Newton, who spent much of the week complaining about all the media responsibilities he had to deal with. To Elway, this was just like his last two Super Bowl appearances as a player. He either was facing a cocky opponent (Green Bay) or had become a secondary character in a bigger drama (Reeves ruffling Shanahan's ego).

The game played out perfectly from Denver's perspective. As they had against New England, the Broncos opened the game throwing and Manning completed three of four throws for forty-six yards to lead a field goal drive. The Broncos got inside Newton's head early with a frenetic pass rush that overwhelmed the Carolina offensive line all game long. In a matchup of the number two and number one picks of the 2011 draft, Miller sacked Newton and stripped him of the ball in the first quarter. That led to a defensive touchdown for the Broncos that built a 10–0 lead. The Panthers responded with a touchdown in the second quarter but ended the first half with eight drives in which only one went longer than thirty-one yards.

The second half started more promising for Carolina with drives of fifty-four and fifty-two yards. But those ended with a missed field goal and an interception. Carolina had six more possessions in the game, getting one field goal. Five of the six drives were seven yards or fewer. The Panthers, who were held to a season low in points, hadn't been stopped like this in any game that season, and it got to Newton. He completed only eighteen of forty-one for 265 yards, was sacked six times, and finished with the interception and two lost fumbles. On the last fumble, Newton shied away from contact as offensive and defensive linemen dove for it. By not diving for the ball, Newton had stepped into a horrible mess he would have to answer for.

Not that he was in the mood for much talking. Newton walked out of the postgame interview. The Broncos officially owned real estate in his head. Manning didn't play substantially better, committing two turnovers himself and completing thirteen of twenty-three passes for only 141 yards. After throwing for forty-seven yards in the first drive of the game, Manning threw for ninety-four over the final thirteen possessions. Again, Manning's greatest accomplishment was to keep the Broncos out of trouble as much as possible. Neither of his interceptions put the Panthers in position to score, meaning he was essentially brilliant throughout the playoffs at being anonymous.

Manning's playoffs could be summarized by three critical throws (the completion to Bennie Fowler against Pittsburgh and the two touchdowns to Daniels against New England) and avoiding any costly error. Manning did what he needed to do.

In the process, the Broncos became only the fifth team in Super Bowl history to win a title after having more interceptions than touchdown passes during the season and only the second in more than four decades. Manning joined Elway as one of only twelve quarterbacks to win two Super Bowl titles. Manning held his son in his arms on the field after the game and politely talked to as many media people as he could. In the locker room after the game, Manning took it all in. He hugged and high-fived teammates. He shook hands with reporters, some of whom told him what a privilege it had been to watch him play through his great career.

As that played out, Elway circulated through the locker room to congratulate his players and talk to the media as well. The unusually warm weather that day added to the steamy atmosphere of the locker room as players shouted with excitement, danced in joy, hugged one another repeatedly, and recorded the moment on their camera phones. This was the definition of jubilation, grown men acting as if they were twelve-year-olds all over again and celebrating a big team win for the first time. It was a moment the players, coaches, and staff members would remember for the rest of their lives.

Despite the heat and the outpouring of energy from the players, Elway was a vision of *GQ* cool, dressed in his blue blazer and orange-and-blue striped tie. He also wore a satisfied grin. No one there would have guessed Elway was the man in that room who burned the hottest with competitive passion.

Between handshakes, he took questions from a series of reporters who stopped him for impromptu press conferences. The queries generally revolved around two people. There was Miller, who had won the game's MVP award with his dominating performance. Miller, who was the first player Elway drafted after taking over the team, not only was the hero but he was the hero with great timing. He was about to hit free agency in a little more than a month and the payoff was going to be rich.

Reporters wanted to know how the negotiations would play out. Elway couldn't have cared less at that moment and politely talked about what a great accomplishment the season had been and what a fabulous job the players had done. Then there were the questions about Manning, which were far more serious. Would he retire? If he didn't, would the Broncos even want to bring him back? Was it possible Elway could cut a fellow legendary quarterback after a Super Bowl victory?

As Elway answered some questions and deftly avoided talking about the near future of Miller or Manning, he focused completely on the greatness of the team's accomplishment. In the process, people missed his accomplishment. That was OK by Elway as he enjoyed the moment.

"It's not the time to talk about something personal," Elway says. "It's time to enjoy it for the whole team. We're going to have to think about getting back here soon enough."

CHAPTER 36

THE NEXT CHALLENGE

Surely, Elway knew the secret.

Of all the people who have ever dared to pick players in the NFL, you'd have to believe Elway, above all people, understood the characteristics that went into being a Super Bowl–winning quarterback. Not just the arm strength, accuracy, and other measurable qualities, but the psychological makeup that seems so incredibly elusive.

There's only one problem with that assumption: there really isn't a secret. It's like trying to cross a diamond with a pearl and the result usually being charcoal. For every Peyton Manning, there are many more quarterbacks who end up being a lot more like Ryan Leaf, Art Schlichter, or Todd Marinovich. It's roughly as easy to find true love on Tinder as it is to find a great quarterback. There's a lot of swiping left and not a lot of commitment. Elway was about to go from the challenge of helping maneuver a team to a Super Bowl victory to the even harder task of finding a great quarterback to win another one.

The process looks something like this from a numerical perspective: in the fifty-two seasons since the NFL and AFL agreed to do a joint draft in 1967 on their way to a full merger in 1970, there have been 712 quarterbacks drafted. That doesn't include hundreds of other quarterbacks who were signed as undrafted free agents, including Kurt Warner, the only undrafted quarterback to ever lead his team to a Super Bowl win.

Of the 712, only 25 so far have gone on to win a Super Bowl. Only eleven have gone on to make the Pro Football Hall of Fame, although that number is likely to grow as the likes of Tom Brady, Peyton Manning, Aaron Rodgers, Drew Brees, Russell Wilson, Ben Roethlisberger, Philip Rivers, and Eli Manning eventually come up for selection.

Regardless of how you want to measure greatness among quarterbacks, the odds of finding one are small. Incredibly small. Between 2.5 and 3.5 percent of all quarterbacks reach some tangible level of greatness, be that winning a Super Bowl, going to the Hall of Fame, or both. That's approximately one of every twenty-nine to forty quarterbacks drafted. For general managers and other personnel executives whose careers hang on finding a great quarterback, those odds aren't good. Those executives have tried to devise countless ways to study and measure quarterbacks to extrapolate which ones will become champions. Even coaches who took over teams with quarterbacks considered destined for greatness have seen those plans come up short.

No coach/executive proves that point more than Bill Belichick, arguably the greatest coach in NFL history and the top decision maker over personnel since taking over the New England Patriots. Yet before Belichick formed the stunning collaboration with Brady, he was the same coach who went through six years of struggle despite having three former number one overall picks as his quarterbacks. Belichick took over in Cleveland in 1991 in part because Bernie Kosar (the number one pick of the 1985 supplemental draft) was a cerebral quarterback Belichick thought he could work with. That changed by their second season together, and Belichick eventually moved on to Vinny Testaverde, the number one overall pick in 1987. When Belichick took over in New England in 2000, former 1993 number one overall pick Drew Bledsoe was the starter and had already led the Patriots to a Super Bowl appearance. Their relationship changed by the second year when Bledsoe got hurt and Brady took over.

Brady was a sixth-round pick and the 199th overall pick, yet he far outproduced three quarterbacks who were considered surefire franchise passers taken at the top of the draft while working with the same coach. How did that happen? How could a quarterback passed over 198 times become the greatest quarterback of the Super Bowl era? Years after Brady had established his legacy, Belichick was able to identify two characteristics that jumped off the page in what makes up a great quarterback.

"You better have accuracy and decision making," Belichick says. "If you don't have that, nothing else matters."

Though it's fair to say those are absolute prerequisites, the bigger issue is more complicated. What exactly is accuracy? What is decision making? If you don't have enough arm strength to deliver the ball, even the most accurate throwers have problems, as the likes of Chad Pennington and Alex Smith proved over the years. If you don't have a personality that will get teammates to rally around you, it's tough to be a leader. Or as Elway himself said, "It's hard to be a quarterback if you have zero personality."

Executives have tried forever to figure out the puzzle. Arizona Cardinals general manager Steve Keim started to work his way up the personnel ladder in 1999 as a scout. Keim was an offensive lineman during his brief NFL career and spent plenty of time around quarterbacks. As a scout, he tried to figure out some way to measure their performance. He would keep copious notes and stats on everything from passer accuracy to velocity to winning percentage to height and weight. He watched arm angles, studied the quickness of drop backs, and timed the release of the ball. He looked at Wonderlic scores and birthdays. If it could be timed, counted, or broken down in some mathematical way, Keim had it. After years of poring over the data, Keim gathered up his notes in a big pile of papers.

"And I threw it all out," Keim says.

> I couldn't figure out anything. I couldn't find one thing that correlated to another. The best I could come up with is that a guy better have requisite talent. He has to be able to throw a good out pattern. He has to have enough velocity and arm strength. Not the most velocity and arm strength, but enough. Yeah, Belichick is right, he has to be accurate and throw to the right guy. And then he better be off the charts in terms of his personality to be able to handle everything that's thrown at him. I mean everything. The fans, the coaches, teammates,

management, the media, and, most importantly, what the opposition is trying to do to him.

Others, such as Super Bowl–winning quarterback and former first-round pick Trent Dilfer, have called the collection of characteristics the "dude factor." Can a quarterback comfortably toggle back and forth between his role as an extension of management and being a teammate? Can he both command respect and be the face of the franchise, the guy everyone stares at in the critical moment, the hardest worker, and the voice of reason in a tense moment, all while still being one of the guys? It's a delicate balance that even great players often come up short on. It is, in the simplest terms, some secret personality trait that is nearly impossible for even the smartest people in football to recognize. Including Elway, who as a quarterback was probably the ultimate "dude," in Dilfer's parlance. Shouldn't "The Dude" be able to recognize a dude?

If only it were that easy.

In essence, Elway was about to take his mountain climbing to a new level. After winning a combined three Super Bowls as a player and executive, he was about to attempt to scale the El Capitan of football challenges: find a great quarterback.

Before Elway and the Broncos could even get to the process of finding another quarterback in 2016, there was the matter of a breakup to be handled. For roughly a month after Denver defeated Carolina, the Broncos and Manning went through a very quiet psychological dance. Manning vacillated on whether he should play again or retire. His friends and family politely told him it was time to stop playing and privately feared that he would get more seriously hurt. But it was one thing to gently nudge a man as committed to his craft and the art of competing as Manning. It was quite another to tell him what you really thought.

"Nobody was going to tell Peyton, 'You're done.' He had to come to that conclusion on his own...if you saw everything he did to come back, you'd understand there was no way to tell him to stop," said one of Manning's closest confidantes. Elway and the Broncos stayed silent on the matter, but the message was clear to Manning's camp. There was no way the team was bringing him back, let alone for the $19 million he was scheduled to make in 2016. Not after what they had seen over the previous season and a half. Not even Denver executive Joe Ellis was going to intercede this season.

Yet Manning still struggled to decide whether to give up what he loved so much. That's why Elway stayed silent. He understood the angst Manning was dealing with. Elway had been there and done it himself, walking away from everything he loved from the time he was a child. On March 7, 2016, Manning informed the Broncos that he was going to retire, keeping the team from having to cut him once the NFL's fiscal year started a few days later. Manning held a press conference on March 8 to make the decision official. That put in motion a difficult immediate set of issues for Elway. The Broncos had a long list of significant free agents to deal with, starting with Super Bowl Most Valuable Player Von Miller and including the likes of defensive lineman Malik Jackson and linebacker Danny Trevathan.

While the Miller negotiations ended up dominating the off-season, the biggest issue was still about who would be the next starting quarterback. Elway's hope was that backup Brock Osweiler would step into the job. Osweiler was on that list of free agents Elway wanted to re-sign. But as agent Jimmy Sexton, who represented Osweiler, had figured prior to the 2015 season, there was a market for his client. Not a huge one, but an expensive one. The Houston Texans, desperate to finally get a quarterback, went after Osweiler. Texans owner Bob McNair and general manager Rick Smith were so hell-bent on getting Osweiler that they didn't even consult head coach Bill O'Brien during the talks. Prior to Osweiler's signing, he and O'Brien never met. On top of that, Osweiler was upset with the Broncos. His ego was still stung from having been pulled in the final game against San Diego when other people were also making mistakes.

In return, there were plenty of concerns within the Broncos organization about Osweiler's mental toughness. Even evaluators from other teams had reservations. Osweiler was a good kid and athletically gifted. He had also come through in critical games against New England and Cincinnati while the Broncos were trying to keep their playoff hopes alive.

Still, Osweiler didn't exude leadership and tenacity. He wasn't demanding or pushy enough at the right time. Armed with that evaluation, Elway was only willing to commit so much. He drew a line at three years and $45 million. That was nowhere close to where the Texans ended up (four years, $72 million, and $37 million guaranteed). The decision was a no-brainer for both Elway and Osweiler. As it turned out, Elway was right to draw a line.

Osweiler lasted only one season in Houston. By the end of the year, he was at odds with O'Brien. The two got into multiple screaming matches during the season, and O'Brien got into it with management about the failure to consult with him before signing Osweiler. A year after signing Osweiler, Houston shipped him to Cleveland. The Texans thought so little of Osweiler they basically gave up a second-round pick to the Browns to get Osweiler off their roster.

Still, the loss of Osweiler in March 2016 created a massive hole for the Broncos, who had only number three quarterback Trevor Siemian on the roster. Siemian had been drafted in the seventh round in 2015 out of Northwestern. He projected much more as a backup quarterback in the mode of what head coach Gary Kubiak had been to Elway during their careers together. Siemian had dutifully watched Manning and Osweiler throughout his rookie season, trying to take in as much as he could. But he also didn't throw a single pass all year and was active for only one game.

His presence didn't scream starter on a defending championship team. Shortly after Osweiler signed with Houston, Denver traded a conditional draft pick to Philadelphia for the rights to former first-round draft pick Mark Sanchez to give the team some depth.

In early April 2016, Elway turned his attention to a far more gifted quarterback who would end up becoming one of the dominant figures in sports and culture, but not for his playing ability. The San Francisco 49ers were trying to trade quarterback Colin Kaepernick, and Elway was intrigued. This was four months before Kaepernick started his protest of the national anthem by kneeling on the field. His protest set off fireworks around the country.

Prior to that, Kaepernick's talent on the field had been far more attention-grabbing. San Francisco had drafted him in the second round in 2011 from Nevada. The Broncos and Elway had strongly considered taking him as well, but passed on the chance, trading the pick that ultimately became Kaepernick to the 49ers. In 2012, Kaepernick took over as the 49ers' starting quarterback when incumbent starter Alex Smith was injured. Kaepernick's combination of a strong arm and explosive running ability took the NFL by storm. San Francisco used him in a modified formation called the "Pistol" offense that put an emphasis on the combination of his running ability and a power running attack. The NFL had problems adjusting to what the 49ers were doing in the short run, and the team made it all the way to the Super Bowl before losing to Baltimore.

In three subsequent seasons, the NFL caught on to Kaepernick, and the 49ers' talented roster, including a rugged defense, declined substantially. In addition, coach Jim Harbaugh had his issues with San Francisco management and left for Michigan after the 2014 season. By 2015, Kaepernick was beset by injuries and lack of surrounding talent. He played in only eight games and had to have surgery on his left shoulder after the season. In addition, the 49ers changed coaches again after the season, hiring Chip Kelly.

The upshot is that the 49ers were rebuilding and looking to get out from underneath Kaepernick's contract, which included a fully guaranteed $11.9 million base salary for the 2016 season. Again, this was months before Kaepernick set off angst around the country with his protests. From a pure talent standpoint, Kaepernick was better than anything the Broncos were going to find with the number thirty-two overall pick in the draft. Elway knew that talented quarterbacks Jared Goff and Carson Wentz were going to be drafted at number one and number two, overall. There was no way for him to get in range for one of them.

That made Kaepernick so appealing that Elway met with him twice. The second of those meetings was at Elway's home in Denver as the two discussed football and philosophy. Elway liked Kaepernick from a competitive standpoint. Kaepernick, as he proved with his public statements, didn't back down from anything. He believed strongly in his own talent. The problem with getting a deal done was that Elway wanted Kaepernick to join the Broncos on Elway's terms. Elway wanted him to take a significant pay cut from the $11.9 million he was guaranteed to approximately $4 million. Kaepernick could make up the rest and more in incentives.

That was a non-starter for Kaepernick. The idea was broached that the 49ers could possibly pay some of the difference (the harbinger of what Houston would do a year later with Osweiler). The 49ers were unwilling to do that. Kaepernick returned for the 2016 season, created controversy, played reasonably well on a 49ers team that cratered to 2–14, and has been in free agency limbo ever since after alienating the league. The season was a disaster all the way around for the 49ers, who also fired Kelly after only one season.

Though the failure to lure Kaepernick allowed the Broncos to avoid dealing with the political fallout that might have been created by his presence, it didn't solve the immediate problem. With no other prominent quarterbacks available in free agency and none available in trade, Elway was left to find a quarterback in the draft.

In Elway's first five years of drafting and running free agency, the Broncos had turned out strong results, particularly in building the defense. Beyond Miller, he had selected defensive linemen Derek Wolfe, Malik Jackson, and Sylvester Williams, linebacker Danny Trevathan, and cornerback Bradley Roby. He had also signed cornerback Chris Harris as an undrafted free agent. Six of those players started in the Super Bowl, and Roby played more than half the game as a nickel cornerback. Of the other five starters (linebackers DeMarcus Ware and Brandon Marshall, cornerback Aqib Talib, and safeties T. J. Ward and Darian Stewart), all of them had been signed as free agents under Elway. On offense, three starters (center Matt Paradis, offensive tackle Michael Schofield, and running back C. J. Anderson) were all drafted or signed as undrafted players during Elway's time. Another seven players had been signed as free agents, including offensive tackle Ryan Harris, who had been with Denver in 2010.

All told, only two of the twenty-two men who started for Denver in the Super Bowl had been starters or even on the Broncos roster prior to Elway's arrival. Obviously, Manning was the biggest name in that group and had played a vital role in transforming the Broncos into a contender. At the same time, Manning would likely never have signed with Denver if not for the presence of Elway and his understanding of what it took to win. Though the men hadn't always seen eye-to-eye, their four-year partnership produced two Super Bowl appearances and one title. In addition, it allowed the Broncos to seamlessly escape the Tim Tebow experiment, which threatened to drag the organization down for another year or two, minimum.

Having built that resume, Elway now had to venture into the market to replace Manning. With Osweiler gone and only Siemian on the roster, Elway set his sights on the 2016 draft. Again, he knew he had no shot at Goff or Wentz, but the rest of the draft was filled with interesting prospects. There was Paxton Lynch, another tall (six-foot-seven) passer who was a former basketball player like Osweiler. Beyond Lynch, Christian Hackenberg out of Penn State, Jacoby Brissett from North Carolina State, Cody Kessler from Southern Cal, Connor Cook from Michigan State, Dak Prescott from Mississippi State, and Cardale Jones from Ohio State were all selected by the end of the fourth round. Of those seven, only Prescott lasted more than two seasons with his original team.

Lynch had been a three-year starter at Memphis after redshirting his freshman year and then declaring for the draft a year early. He had improved his accuracy and touchdown-to-interception ratio each year. Considering his unusual ability to move at his size, he seemed fully capable of operating Kubiak's offense, which put a premium on the quarterback's ability to move to help trigger the running game with outside handoffs.

Denver wasn't the only team that liked Lynch. Dallas was looking for a young quarterback to groom as a successor to Tony Romo and made inquiries about moving up from the early part of the second round of the draft to just in front of the Broncos at the later end of the first round. Word about the Cowboys' interest got back to Elway, and now it was a battle to see who could jockey up the board. Eventually, Elway gave up Denver's first-round pick and a third-round pick to move up five spots to get Lynch. Dallas didn't take Prescott until the fourth round.

That situation proved yet again how difficult it is to judge quarterbacks. The Broncos released Lynch after only two seasons while Prescott became a starter immediately for Dallas because of an injury to Romo, who also retired after the 2016 season.

Lynch struggled from the start to learn the playbook as he made a transition from a spread offensive at the University of Memphis to the pro game. Lynch's biggest deficiency was his lack of presence in the pocket, particularly when it started to break down. He regularly dropped his eyes as defenders got close to him, making it impossible for him to find open receivers in the most critical moments. The Broncos coaching staff recognized the problem quickly and hoped Lynch would overcome it. Sadly, he never did. In the meantime, the coaches went with Siemian to start the season.

Siemian was a reasonable backup. He was also tough and eventually took his lumps as the full-time starter over the 2016 and 2017 seasons. His problem was that he had limited upside typical of a seventh-round pick. When defenses took away the first and second read, he would improvise and take chances his arm strength just couldn't handle. Still, the 2016 season opened with promise, including a dramatic win over Carolina in the season opener. The Broncos rode that momentum to a 4–0 start and a 7–3 record before having a bye week in November.

There were warning signs during that 7–3 start. In week five, coach Gary Kubiak missed a game with extreme fatigue and flu-like symptoms. Members of the coaching staff said Kubiak was running himself ragged. In addition, Lynch was forced to start in week five because of an injury to Siemian. The results were ugly. Lynch was sacked six times as the worst fears of the coaching staff were realized.

After the bye week, Denver split a pair of games to move to 8–4 before hitting an offensive tailspin. Over a three-week stretch, the Broncos were held to ten or fewer points in each game as opposing teams figured out Siemian's limited skills. As defensive coordinators figured out ways to stifle him, he was forced to throw short passes that did little damage. The result was a three-game losing streak that caused the Broncos to finish 9–7 overall and out of the playoffs a season after winning the title.

As the season fell apart, there was increasing pressure on Kubiak, who was realizing how much of a toll the stress took on him. Elway was discussing changes to the coaching staff while Kubiak was considering bigger changes to his life. Kubiak retired at the end of the year, and Elway had to go on a coaching search.

Elway quietly considered hiring former coach Mike Shanahan. Some acquaintances wanted him to consider Shanahan's son Kyle, who had just helped Atlanta get to the Super Bowl against New England. Kyle had been the offensive coordinator, and the Falcons had a brilliant offensive season. Atlanta quarterback Matt Ryan set an array of statistical bests and was named the NFL's Most Valuable Player. Kyle was hailed as a genius around the league and was in serious demand (San Francisco eventually hired him along with general manager John Lynch, Elway's longtime friend). Elway resisted the temptation to go back to his roots and the results were disastrous. Elway hired Vance Joseph, who had been the defensive coordinator in Miami and became the first black head coach in Broncos history. Elway liked Joseph's disciplined approach and defensive background. Elway was trying to maximize the depth of talent the team had on defense to make another run at the Super Bowl.

Except the quarterback position continued to be a problem, and Joseph compounded the issue by being overwhelmed by the job. He was short on game management skills. The team went 5–11 in 2017 as it went through three quarterbacks, including a return of Osweiler in the second half of the season after Houston had traded him to Cleveland and then Cleveland cut him. The Broncos started 3–1 before losing eight straight games in which only one game was decided by less than a touchdown. The Broncos were simply uncompetitive. Joseph fired offensive coordinator Mike McCoy after eleven games, but that did little to solve the problem. By the end of the season, Elway was ready to fire Joseph, but reconsidered when his friends told him he was getting a reputation around the NFL as a coach killer. Between his clash with Fox, the stress on Kubiak, and the impatience with Joseph, many around the NFL were wondering whether Elway was a good person to work for.

The truth is Elway didn't interfere with game plans or strategy. He was, in many ways, hands-off in terms of personnel decisions in games. But if asked, Elway wasn't afraid to state his opinion.

"After this much time, I think I have an idea about how things should be done," Elway told one confidant at the end of the 2017 season as he pondered the Joseph decision. "If you ask me what I think, I'm going to tell you."

The greater issue for Elway was the criticism he was starting to receive for not solving the quarterback situation. By the end of the 2017 season, the depth chart at quarterback represented Elway's efforts to replace Manning. He had Osweiler, Siemian, and Lynch, who was already a bust. Elway then cleared the deck. He released Lynch and didn't re-sign Osweiler and Siemian in the 2018 off-season. Instead, Elway signed free agent Case Keenum, who had been successful in his one season as the starter in Minnesota but had otherwise been a journeyman. The Broncos were the fourth team Keenum had played for in his seven-year career and third in three years. The Vikings cast him aside when they decided to pursue Kirk Cousins, even though Keenum had led Minnesota to the NFC Championship Game that season (a playoff run that included a dramatically improbable Hail Mary pass to beat New Orleans).

Elway told associates he was as confident in signing Keenum to a two-year, $36 million deal as he would have been signing Cousins to the three-year, $84 million, fully guaranteed deal the Vikings handed out. In truth, neither worked in the short run. The Vikings failed to return to the playoffs in 2018 and the Broncos didn't get any better. Keenum proved to be little better than the combination of quarterbacks the Broncos fielded in 2017. Over a four-year stretch after the Super Bowl title, Denver had gone 9–7 in 2016, 5–11 in 2017, 6–10 in 2018, and 7–9 in 2019. Along the way, the Broncos also went through two head coaches and four offensive coordinators. All the quarterbacks, head coaches, and offensive coordinators were eventually fired and replaced by coach Vic Fangio in early 2019, who then pushed for quarterback Joe Flacco in trade from Baltimore. The trade for Flacco was mocked roundly and Elway took the brunt of the criticism. At the same time, Elway put together what most analysts believed was a strong draft in 2019, including the selection of Missouri quarterback Drew Lock in the second round. Most analysts believed the Broncos were going to take Lock in the first round at number ten overall. Instead, Elway traded back to get more picks and ended up with Lock anyway. As a rookie, Lock showed promise. He eventually displaced Flacco as the starter by the end of the season, and the Broncos went 4–1 with Lock at quarterback.

Still, whether the signing of Flacco or the drafting of Lock would make a difference would take time to play out. Flacco, after all, had already beaten the odds by becoming one of the twenty-five quarterbacks drafted since 1967 to lead a team to a Super Bowl title. Lock was just one of the 712 draft picks since 1967 to take his shot at NFL glory.

The point is that the parade of subpar performances from 2016 to 2018 was at times as dizzying as it was disappointing to an organization so conditioned to being competitive. The back-to-back sub-.500 seasons marked the first time Denver had done that since the 1971 and 1972 seasons. The team hadn't had back-to-back seasons with ten losses in more than fifty years.

Almost half of that five-decade stretch had featured Elway as part of the organization. He and Bowlen were the dominating faces of that run. Bowlen received his recognition for that in February 2019 when he was voted into the Pro Football Hall of Fame, joining Elway. What Bowlen didn't get to share with Elway was any of the blame for what was going wrong.

Elway's critics dismissed the five-year, two–Super Bowl appearance, one-championship run as more of a creation of Manning's excellence than of Elway's shrewd personnel insight. Never mind that the Broncos won a title only because their defense was so dominant in 2015, the critics said— this was the Manning Era in the eyes of so many. The critics flooded the airwaves on radio and were unrelenting on Twitter. Elway's success in the draft and free agency was nitpicked to death. The fact that he was the key to signing Manning was ignored.

The failure to find another quarterback was consistently the theme. Again, it was one thing for Elway to go through coaches. Coaches are disposable in the minds of most fans. Quarterbacks are different. Elway's true expertise was supposed to come out in this situation. He was supposed to beat the long odds when it came to selecting a quarterback. This is, after all, the man who had spent a lifetime beating the odds. First down at your two-yard line on the road in the AFC Championship Game? No problem. Too old and too much of an underdog to beat the defending Super Bowl champions at the end of your playing career? Did that, even if he had to spin like a helicopter. Too distracted by a retired life of leisure to seriously run a team as an executive? Elway answered that with five playoff appearances and a Super Bowl title.

The trolls of the world took their shots at Elway yet again. The easy take from fans was that Manning had done everything to cover for Elway's faults. For instance, there was this gem:

> *Stop begging #elway. Manning saved his ass over the years. Elway is horrendous.*
> *@de_bono2018 on ProFootballTalk.com*

Then there was this remark on Twitter shortly after Elway and the Broncos took tight end Noah Fant with the number twenty pick in the first round of the 2019 NFL Draft, a pick that was considered a good first step in a strategically sound overall draft:

> *#FireElway This is quite possibly the worst possible move that John Elway has ever done. What a waste of a pick! I cant believe how dumb Elway is.*
> *@BcCarmin*

Some people did seem to have a sense that there was dogpiling going on:

> *How much you wanna bet that even if John **Elway** drafted Kyler Murray, pundits would be like "Oh here we go again. Another swing. If this doesn't work out, is **Elway** on the hot seat?" It doesn't matter what QB is drafted or where, they'll bash **Elway** because it's popular to do so.*
> *@BMiller4164 on Twitter*

Elway took most of it in stride.

"Lots of people have opinions, but only one person is ultimately responsible for the decision. You get that responsibility and everything that goes with it, good and bad," he says.

Elway wasn't being flip or dismissive, just factual and driven. As much as the criticism and, more importantly, the failure of the team bothered him, it wasn't as bad as the alternative. He couldn't just walk away the way some other stars such as Magic Johnson or Dan Marino did when the job got to be too much. He couldn't flash his three Super Bowl rings and simply walk away knowing he had accomplished more than millions of others who had ever tried.

No, deeply ingrained in Elway's soul was the endless desire to compete— a passion fired by joy and love for the battle, not simply by some need for fame or money. It was instilled there and nurtured by a father he loved and respected. In fact, that desire and competitiveness bubbled to the surface again in the early days of 2017, just as Elway was beginning to deal with the struggles of the team.

In January 2017, buddy John Lynch called Elway for advice. Lynch got an earful. Lynch was weighing whether to take the job as 49ers general manager and work with Kyle Shanahan. At the time, Lynch had a good life as an NFL analyst with FOX. He had been on television for nine years and had become one of the best at his craft. At forty-six, Lynch had a great resume. He had won a Super Bowl with Tampa Bay, made the Pro Bowl nine times, been inducted to the ring of honor of both the Buccaneers and the Denver Broncos, and been a finalist three times for the Pro Football Hall of Fame.

Lynch had also been a second-round draft pick in baseball out of Stanford, playing briefly in the minors for the Florida Marlins. He was married, was a father of four children, and had dabbled with classes at the Stanford Business School. When Lynch called Elway, he was expecting a deep, thoughtful conversation about the pros and cons of jumping straight into management of an NFL team. Perhaps Elway could give him a primer, especially considering the years Elway had spent honing his craft in the Arena Football League—something, anything that would give him a sense of what he should do. After all, Elway sort of owed him for being part of the reinforcements at that famous meeting with Manning back in 2012.

Elway answered the call and listened to Lynch explain the situation. Lynch said he was leaning heavily toward taking the job and asked for Elway's guidance.

What he got was the voice of Jack Elway coming back at him.

"It's about time you do something with your f—ing life," John Elway said. Lynch laughed. Elway chuckled. There wasn't some secret ingredient inside of Elway that made him want to compete. It was everything about his existence and how he was raised. It coursed through his body like blood.

Or, as Lynch said simply, "That's John."

ACKNOWLEDGMENTS

This project has been years in the making and has been steered along the way by the likes of my agent David Black and his staff, along with the excellent editing and guidance of Brant Rumble and the staff at Hachette Book Group. There was also the patience of my wife Alana, who put up with more than a few nights of editing and provided her thoughts along the way.

There were more than 200 people who were interviewed or provided other assistance along the way. They include, but are not limited to, Mike Aldrete, Craig Andrisen, Steve Antonopulos, Jim Armstrong, Steve Atwater, David Baker, Dave Baldwin, John Beake, Tom Beckett, Bob Beers, Paul Bergman, Tim Birtsas, Keith Bishop, Tom Brady, Gil Brandt, Joby Branion, Joe Browne, Bubby Brister, Earnest Byner, Harry Carson, Michael Chernoff, Steve Clarkson, Jim Clymer, Jackie Neumeier Cohen, Joe Collier, Joel Collier, Tom Condon, Mark Cooper, Jim Corsi, Mike Dailey, Terrell Davis, Eddie DeBartolo Jr., Joe DeCamillis, Eric Decker, Jack Del Rio, Marvin Demoff, Rick Dennison, Jim Deshaies, Orestes Destrade, David Diaz-Infante, Trent Dilfer, Mike Dotterer, Rod Dowhower, John Dutton, Ace Eason, Joe Ellis, Jack Elway, Jan Elway, Janet Elway, Jessica Elway, Jordan Elway, Juliana Elway, Paige Elway, Dennis Engel, Dennis Erickson, Jim Fassel, Rashad Floyd, Dan Fouts, John Fox, Terry Frei, Pierce Gagnet, Adam Gase, Wally Gaskins, George

Genovese, Alan George, Alex Gibbs, Claude Gilbert, Jim Ginnetti, Jay Glazer, Darrien Gordon, Otto Graham, Jacob Green, Harvey Greene, Brian Griese, Brian Habib, Jeff Haile, Eric Hardgrave, Chris Harris, Matt Hasselbeck, Dee Hawkes, Jerry Heathcote, Jud Heathcote, Calvin Hill, Brian Holloway, Mike Holmgren, John Hopkins, Paul Howard, Gary Hughes, Wayne Huizenga, Brooks Hurst, Jim Irsay, Mark Jackson, Keith Kartz, Steve Keim, Jim Kelly, Cortez Kennedy, Donald Kennedy, Paul Kirk, Mike Klis, Bernie Kosar, Gary Kubiak, Babe Laufenberg, James Lofton, Don Lonsinger, Ronnie Lott, Sonny Lubick, John Lynch, Peyton Manning, Kenny Margerum, Dan Marino, Mark Marquess, Scott Marshall, Ed McCaffrey, Mike McCoy, Von Miller, Warren Moon, Rob Moore, Bill Moos, Mike Munchak, Tom Nalen, Chuck Narikiyo, Darrin Nelson, Ozzie Newsome, Mike Ornstein, Steve Ortmayer, Ken Orvick, Brock Osweiler, Ryan Pace, Woody Paige, Matt Paradis, Sean Payton, Chad Pennington, Wade Phillips, Jake Plummer, Bill Polian, Dana Potter, Hein Poulus, Mike Price, Dan Reeves, Rick Reilly, Mike Reinfeldt, Ron Rivera, Eugene Robinson, Greg Robinson, Bill Romanowski, Matt Russell, Jim Saccomano, Vince "V-Sak" Sakowski, Mark Sanchez, Al Saunders, Paul Scheper, Mark Schlereth, Tim Schmidt, Turk Schonert, Marty Schottenheimer, Al Sever, Steve Sewell, Mike Shanahan, Shannon Sharpe, Trevor Siemian, Mike Silver, T. J. Simers, Phil Simms, Neil Smith, Rick Smith, Rod Smith, Patrick Smyth, Michael Sokolove, Chuck Solberg, Eric Sondheimer, Jeff Sperbeck, Roger Staubach, Jan Steele, Brandon Stokley, Dean Stotz, Darryl Strawberry, Daryl Stroh, Dave Studdard, Michael Sullivan, Chris Sutton, Harry Swayne, Aqib Talib, Rick Telander, DeMaryius Thomas, Billy Thompson, Yoshiko Toyosaki, Marc Trestman, Gary Tyrrell, Rebecca Villanueva, DeMarcus Ware, Steve Watson, Paul Wiggin, Gerald Willhite, Alfred Williams, Brian Williams, Doug Williams, Kellen Winslow, Derek Wolfe, Dave Wyman, Michael Young, and Gary Zimmerman.

Finally, to John Elway, thank you for being a fascinating subject.

INDEX